Policy Studies Institute
(The European Centre for Political Studies)

COALITION GOVERNMENT
IN WESTERN EUROPE

List of Contributors

Klaus von Beyme is Professor of Political Science at the University of Heidelberg.

Vernon Bogdanor has been a Fellow of Brasenose College, Oxford, since 1966.

Brian Farrell is Acting Head, Department of Ethics and Politics, University College, Dublin.

Ken Gladdish is Senior Lecturer in Politics at the University of Reading.

Colin Mellors is Lecturer in Politics and Deputy Chairman of the School of European Studies, Bradford University.

Jan de Meyer is Professor of Constitutional Law at the University of Louvain, where he was President of the Instute for Political and Social Sciences from 1964 to 1967 and Dean of the Law School from 1971 to 1974.

Pertti Pesonen was Professor of Political Science and Dean at the University of Tampere (1965–71) and the University of Helsinki (1972–79).

Geoffrey Pridham is Reader in European Politics at Bristol University.

Bo Särlvik is Professor of Political Science at the University of Göteborg.

Manfred G. Schmidt received his doctorate at the University of Tübingen in 1975. He is at present at Konstanz University.

Alastair H. Thomas is Head of the Division of Political Science at Preston Polytechnic.

Jan Vis is Professor of Constitutional Law at Groningen University, Holland.

Policy Studies Institute
(The European Centre for Political Studies)

Coalition Government in Western Europe

Edited by
Vernon Bogdanor
Fellow of Brasenose College, Oxford

 Heinemann Educational Books

Heinemann Educational Books Ltd
22 Bedford Square, London WC1B 3HH
LONDON   EDINBURGH   MELBOURNE   AUCKLAND
HONG KONG   SINGAPORE   KUALA LUMPUR   NEW DELHI
IBADAN   NAIROBI   JOHANNESBURG
EXETER (NH)   KINGSTON   PORT OF SPAIN

ISBN 0 435 83104 6

Phototypeset by Inforum Ld, Portsmouth
Printed in Great Britain by Biddles Ltd, Guildford, Surrey

Contents

Preface

As Vernon Bogdanor remarks in his introductory chapter, this book was designed to fill a striking gap in the comparative study of European politics: although most European countries are normally ruled by coalition governments, and the rest of them may sooner or later be in the same position, there has so far been no systematic comparison of the various forms that coalition government may take, or of its many implications for different national systems.

The European Centre for Political Studies at PSI, which was set up to carry out research on the problems of democratic political life in Europe, was fortunate in enlisting the cooperation of Vernon Bogdanor as the main designer of the two-day seminar held at PSI in October 1982, and as editor of the book containing revised versions of the papers presented there. The Centre's thanks are also due to Dr David Butler, Fellow of Nuffield College, Oxford, for his vigorous and constructive chairmanship of the proceedings; to the participating academics, politicians, officials and journalists for their contributions (particularly to members of the London embassies of several of the countries under discussion); to the Nuffield Foundation and the Parliamentary Democracy Trust for financial support; to Margaret Cornell for editing the text; and to Avis Lewallen, Sandra Jeddy and Amanda Trafford for ensuring the smooth running of the whole enterprise. With this book the European Centre for Political Studies makes, I believe, an important contribution to an important debate.

Roger Morgan.

1 Introduction
Vernon Bogdanor

In Anglo-Saxon countries, coalition government is regarded as an aberration. On the Continent of Europe, it is the norm. By the middle of 1983 only three European democracies – Britain, Spain and Greece – enjoyed single-party majority government. The rest were ruled either by minority governments or by coalitions.

Little excuse is needed, therefore, for this study of coalition government in Western Europe. It is hardly possible to understand European political systems without taking into account the working of coalitions. Accepted generalisations about Cabinet government, the role of legislatures and political parties all demand a fresh appraisal in the light of the exigencies of coalition politics. The processes of government formation and dissolution, the role of the head of state and the working of the cabinet are all likely to be affected by coalitions, and the conventions regulating these processes may well differ from those operative in countries enjoying single-party government. In addition, the strategies of political parties are likely to be affected by the knowledge that they will be unlikely to win power on their own but will have to share power with like-minded allies. The dynamics of a multi-party system in which coalition is the norm will, therefore, inevitably prove more complex than those in a system of the Westminster type with its presumption of two parties alternating in office, each in turn enjoying the full plenitude of power and patronage.

The study of coalition government can, however, do more than illuminate the working of particular political systems. It can also cast light on wider questions – to what extent is the substance of policy affected by coalition government? Does the process of bargaining which coalition necessitates lead to *immobilisme* or does it, on the contrary, allow the coalition partners to overcome the ideological constraints which can prevent single-party governments from being effective? Do coalitions promote stability and consensus; or do they rather weaken accountability and so make it more difficult for the electorate to attribute responsibility for the acts of government? All of these questions are important ones for the democratic theorist as well as for the student of comparative government, but they tend to be ignored by those who equate 'majority rule' with single-party government. Indeed, since it is rare in modern democracies for one party to win over

50 per cent of the vote in a general election, majority rule in effect means coalition government. So the study of coalitions is at the same time a study of the preconditions and consequences of majority rule as it operates in practice in modern democratic regimes.

In Britain, such questions have come to seem of more than theoretical interest in recent years. Britain, to paraphrase Disraeli, may not love coalitions, but, since 1974, it has been compelled to face the increasing likelihood of future general elections producing indecisive results. This is a consequence not only of the greater strength of third parties – Liberals, Scottish Nationalists and the Northern Ireland parties – but also of trends in electoral behaviour over the past thirty years. These trends, as John Curtice and Michael Steed have demonstrated,[1] make it less likely that the 'first past the post' electoral system can continue to fulfil its function of producing single-party government in Britain. For, since 1955, the two major parties have each become more solidly entrenched in their areas of existing electoral strength, Labour in the North and the industrial conurbations, the Conservatives in the South and in rural England. The consequence is that there are more safe seats than there were thirty years ago, and so a given swing will lead to a smaller number of constituencies changing hands. For a general election to produce a decisive result, therefore, swings will have to be considerably larger than they have been for most of the post-war period.

The Curtice/Steed analysis was conceived before the formation of the Liberal/SDP Alliance, and, since the SDP had not fought in a general election by the time the analysis was published, it does not take account of the effects of the Alliance upon the electoral situation. Yet, clearly, the Alliance will add strength to the third-party challenge in Britain. The formation of the Alliance therefore strengthens the conclusion of the Curtice/Steed analysis that single-party majority government in Britain will become less likely in the future than it was in the past, and that minority or coalition government could become a very real possibility for Britain in the years ahead.

Moreover, were the Liberal/SDP Alliance to succeed in its aim of securing reform of the electoral system, this would make single-party majority government a thing of the past except on those very rare occasions when one party succeeded in gaining around 50 per cent of the vote. Thus the debate about proportional representation, which was reopened in Britain in the 1970s, is also a debate about the relative merits of coalition and single-party government. For to support proportional representation is, in effect, to support coalition also. The essays in *Coalition Government in Western Europe* are highly relevant, therefore, to the argument about Britain's constitutional future, an argument likely to increase in intensity in the years to come.

It was for these reasons that the European Centre for Political Studies decided to sponsor a conference in October 1982 on coalition government in Western Europe at which most of the chapters in this volume were first discussed. The countries chosen for analysis were those which, since the war, have become accustomed to coalitions: the German Federal Republic, where every government since the founding of the state in 1949 has been a coalition; the Scandinavian countries, where coalition government has proved compatible with political stability and economic progress; Belgium and the Netherlands, where the actual processes of forming coalition governments seem to be vital factors in securing national unity; Italy, where the complexities of coalition-building are intensified by the rivalry between the different factions (*correnti*) of the ruling Christian Democrat Party; and Ireland where hitherto a coalition between the fairly conservative Fine Gael party and Labour has been the only method by which the dominant Fianna Fail party can be ousted from government. All of these countries elect their legislatures by some method of proportional represent-ation, the Continental countries by one of the list systems, and Ireland by the single transferable vote (STV). France was excluded for the obvious reason that it has a presidential system of government.

The Irish Republic is the only example in Western Europe of a political system based on the assumptions of the Westminster Model having to accommodate itself to coalition government. It is of particular relevance, therefore, in evaluating how far the advent of coalition might alter the conventions of the British Constitution. In Britain, coalitions have been the product of war or economic crisis rather than parliament-ary arithmetic, so that attention has been given to the question of what changes would be needed in constitutional conventions to accommodate the practice of regular coalition government. But one area of British life where coalitions are common – far more than is generally realised – is local government. Colin Mellors' chapter on coalitions in local government is, therefore, not only of importance in illustrating how British parties cope with situations where no party can win a majority; it is also, to the best of my knowledge, the first analytical study of this peculiarly fascinating topic.

Types of coalition
'Coalition', far from designating the name of a single category of government, covers a variety, or rather a spectrum, of different types. For coalition implies co-operation between political parties, and this co-operation can take place at one (or more) of three different levels – *governmental*, *parliamentary* and *electoral*. The various possibilities are schematised in Figure 1.1.

The mode in which coalitional relationships are expressed will

Fig. 1.1 Types of coalitions

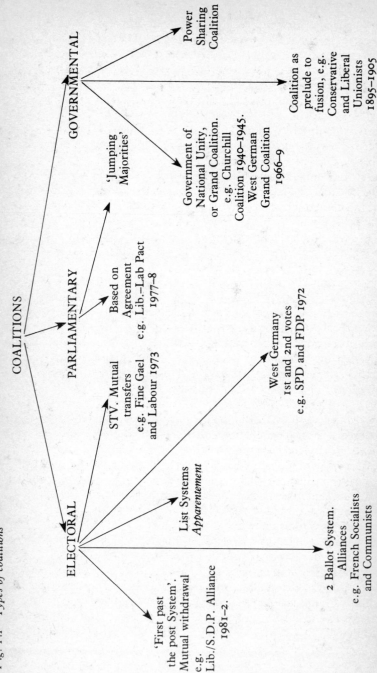

depend upon a country's constitutional framework and its electoral system. *Parliamentary* coalitions occur when, in a situation in which no single party enjoys an overall majority, the party asked to form a government prefers to rule as a minority government relying upon an arrangement with another party or parties to secure its survival. Such an arrangement may be of a long-term kind or for a limited period with a definite date of termination, as with the Lib-Lab pact in Britain in 1977–8; or alternatively, a government may seek support from different parties for different items of legislation – a method much used in Denmark where it is known as government by 'jumping majorities'. Finally, a minority government might survive without outside support on a basis of toleration by the opposition parties which for tactical reasons are unwilling to defeat it. That was in general the situation of the three Labour minority governments in Britain in 1924, 1929–1931, and 1974.

In Belgium, the Netherlands and West Germany, majority coalition rather than minority government is the invariable rule. But in Denmark, and, to a lesser extent in the other Scandinavian countries, as Pesonen and Thomas show, minority government can sometimes be the outcome of the process of government formation. In Italy, also, single-party (*monocolore*) governments have been formed, and rely on external support to survive. Nevertheless in both Scandinavia and Italy majority coalition is almost always the preferred alternative to minority government. In Britain, by contrast, on those occasions in the twentieth century when one party has failed to gain an overall majority – the two general elections of 1910, the elections of 1923, 1929 and February 1974 – the result has always been minority government. In local government also, as Colin Mellors shows, single-issue or episodic coalitions have generally been preferred to power-sharing arrangements. In Ireland, coalition has been the instrument by which the parties opposed to Fianna Fáil have sought to constitute an alternative government. Fianna Fáil as the dominant party has refused to consider coalition; and when it has lacked an overall majority, as in 1932–3, 1937–8, 1943–4, 1951–4, 1961–5 and 1982, it has ruled as a single-party minority government. In 1933, 1938 and 1944, De Valera called snap elections to gain an overall majority; in 1951 and 1961, De Valera and Lemass respectively governed with the support of Independents. In 1982, Haughey attempted to do the same, but his administration was defeated in the Dail after nine months. In Ireland, therefore, if no party wins an overall majority, Fianna Fáil will govern alone if it is near to a majority; if it is not, the opposition parties will form a majority coalition.

Where minority governments are formed, their survival can be aided by constitutional rules. Denmark is the country whose constitution affords the greatest encouragement to minority government, since there is no requirement for a new administration to secure a vote of confidence at its investiture. Instead the government survives until a positive decision is made by the other parties in the Folketing to defeat it: in other words, the government survives unless there is a majority *against* it. Thus the Hartling government was able to survive from 1973 to 1975 although commanding only 22 out of the 175 seats in the Folketing. In Sweden, the 1974 Instrument of Government, which is, in effect, the constitution, provides that a Prime Minister, nominated by the Speaker, is confirmed in office unless there is an absolute majority of the Riksdag against him. When in 1978 Ola Ullsten, the leader of the Liberal Party, was proposed by the Speaker as Prime Minister, he received only the 39 votes of the Liberal Party, and was opposed by the 72 votes of the Conservative and Communist parties. The other parties abstained. As the votes against him did not amount to an absolute majority of the 349 votes in the Riksdag, Ullsten was confirmed as Prime Minister even though he commanded the positive support of less than 10 per cent of the legislature.

The vote in Sweden to confirm the Prime Minister, although it makes minority government possible, affects the operation of minority government in a manner subtly different from that in Denmark. For in Sweden the vote carries the implication of a declaration by the parties of their attitude to the new government. In 1978, for example, the Social Democrats, although unwilling to support the Ullsten Government, had made it clear that they would not do anything to overturn it. This means that a Swedish government, unlike a government in Denmark, relies upon the support of particular parties, and will not be inclined to depend upon 'jumping majorities', a different majority for each item of legislation, which is a more common method in Denmark. The absence of a vote on the formation of a Danish government makes possible the method of 'jumping majorities'. The vote of confirmation in Sweden makes this method very difficult if not impossible.

The rules relating to the dissolution of the legislature will also affect the possibility of minority government. Broadly, the easier it is for the Prime Minister of a minority government to secure a dissolution, the easier it will be for his government to survive. For the Prime Minister will be able to threaten his opponents with a dissolution if he is defeated in the legislature. He will be under no pressure to negotiate with other parties to secure a coalition agreement if he believes that he has a dissolution 'in his pocket'. Here, too, Denmark is the country whose constitutional conventions offer the greatest encouragement to minority government since the monarch cannot refuse a dissolution to a government even if it is in a minority in the Folketing.

In Britain, the question of whether the Sovereign can refuse a dissolution to a minority government if she believes that an alternative government is available is one that cannot be answered definitively. But Prime Ministers have generally assumed that they will be able to secure a dissolution at a time of their own choosing. That was certainly how Ramsay MacDonald in 1924, and Harold Wilson in 1974, understood their constitutional position.

Where a government can dissolve at its discretion, it can gain a partisan advantage which can be used as a deterrent to other parties, preventing them from overthrowing it. Where, on the other hand, parliament cannot be dissolved before its term is complete, as in Norway, or dissolution is only possible in exceptional circumstances as in West Germany, Italy and Finland, minority government is likely to prove unsatisfactory since the parties opposing the government will know that they can defeat it without being required to face the electorate. Indeed, opposition parties may feel that they themselves enjoy a good chance of acquiring power in the reshuffle which will follow the defeat of the government.

Thus the constitutional procedures governing the formation and dissolution of parliament play a vital role in determining the acceptability of different patterns of government. In Britain, party attitudes and preconceptions have also played their part and they have done so by predisposing parties against coalition. For the last fifty years, the Labour Party has attempted to exorcise the ghost of Ramsay MacDonald, and part of the process of exorcism has been to reject coalition even in circumstances wholly different from those of 1931. Thus in 1974 Harold Wilson preferred to seek a tactical dissolution rather than co-operation with other parties. Even the Liberal Party refused until 1974 to face the implications of the fact that it was unlikely to be able to influence government without taking part in a coalition. It had its own folk memories of past coalitions with the Conservatives in which breakaway Liberal groups – Liberal Unionists, Lloyd George Liberals, and Liberal Nationals – had found themselves either swallowed by Conservatives (the Liberal Unionists and Liberal Nationals, later called National Liberals, were absorbed in 1912 and 1966 respectively) or extruded, as were the Lloyd George Liberals in 1922, when they had served their purpose.

The existence and nature of *electoral* coalitions will depend upon the electoral system. Under the 'first past the post' system used in Britain, two (or more) parties seeking to co-operate can do so only by reaching an agreement providing for the mutual withdrawal of candidates so as to avoid splitting the vote. That is always difficult to achieve where the parties have strong local organisations unwilling to surrender their right to put up a candidate. Yet, in 1886, Home Rule could only be defeated in the general election because Conservative candidates were willing not to oppose those Liberal members – Liberal Unionists – who rejected Home Rule. When, at the beginning of the century, the newly formed Labour Party seemed about to threaten Liberal seats and split the left-wing vote, the (secret) Gladstone-MacDonald pact was negotiated in 1903 so that the two parties could complement rather than fight each other. In 1918, the coalition leaders, Lloyd George and Bonar Law, issued a 'coupon' in an attempt to prevent Liberal and Conservative supporters from running against each other; while in 1931, the leaders of the three parties forming the National Government – Ramsay MacDonald, Stanley Baldwin and Sir Herbert Samuel – agreed on arrangements whose purpose was to ensure that only one anti-Labour candidate stood in each constituency. More recently, the two parties comprising the Alliance – the Liberals and the SDP – have, after some difficulty, completed arrangements by which the constituencies of Great Britain (the Alliance is not proposing to fight seats in Northern Ireland) will be divided between the two parties so that candidates for the two wings of the Alliance do not oppose each other. But for both sides the process has been an agonising one.[2]

Other electoral systems allow electoral coalitions to be formed in different ways. The two-ballot system used in France offers a premium to a party which can attract the votes of allies in the second ballot, and a corresponding handicap to a party such as the Communists which cannot. List systems of proportional representation which allow electoral alliances – *apparentement* – offer a premium to parties too small to win seats on their own but able to secure a seat through combining their lists.

The West German electoral system with its provision for two votes – one for a constituency candidate, the other for a party list – allows a coalition government to appeal explicitly for endorsement as a coalition. In 1972, for example, the leaders of the SPD/FDP coalition, Willy Brandt and Walter Scheel, asked voters to support the coalition by giving their constituency votes to the SPD but their list votes to the FDP. Constituency votes for the FDP, which has not won a constituency seat since 1957, would be wasted; while if the FDP did not secure a sufficient number of list votes to surmount the 5 per cent threshold, it would not secure representation in the Bundestag, and the SPD might then be ousted by the CDU/CSU. In fact the general election of 1972 has proved to be the only one in the history of the Federal Republic in which the SPD succeeded in gaining more votes than the CDU/CSU.

The percentages of constituency and list votes of the three main West German parties in 1972 were as shown in Table 1.1.

It is clear that a sufficient number of SPD voters followed their party's advice to split their vote so enabling the FDP to surmount the 5

Table 1.1   Constituency and list votes of the main German parties, 1972

	Constituency votes %	List votes %
SPD	48.6	45.9
CDU/CSU	45.2	44.8
FDP	4.8	8.4

The constituency votes of list FDP voters were as follows: SPD 52.9 per cent; CDU/CSU 7.9 per cent; FDP 32.8 per cent; others/invalid votes 1.0 per cent

per cent threshold and secure representation in the Bundestag. The pattern of voting constituted a clear mandate for a continuation of the SPD-FDP coalition.

The single transferable vote system allows the electorate the widest opportunity to endorse or reject a governmental coalition. For under this system no coalition arrangement agreed by the political parties can be effective unless it is endorsed by the voter transferring his vote from one of the coalition partners to the other. In general, the Irish political parties have hesitated to offer explicit indications to voters as to how they should use their transfers, but in 1973 Fine Gael and Labour formed a 'National Coalition', issuing a joint programme and appealing for transfers on this basis. The Coalition's victory in the ensuing general election was due to the solidity of the pattern of transfers between the two parties, rather than to any accretion of support, since the total percentage of first preference votes of the two parties was smaller in 1973 than in the previous election of 1969 when, fighting separately, they had been unable to dislodge Fianna Fáil from government. The voting was as shown in Table 1.2.

Table 1.2   The Irish General Elections of 1969 and 1973

	% First preference votes	% Seats
1969		
Fianna Fáil	45.7	51.7
Fine Gael	34.1	35.0
Labour	17.0	12.6
Total Fine Gael and Labour	51.1	47.6
1973		
Fianna Fáil	46.2	47.6
Fine Gael	35.1	37.8
Labour	13.7	13.3
Total Fine Gael and Labour	48.8	51.1

Under STV, there need be no mutual withdrawal of candidates, the parties can fight separate campaigns, and voters remain free to endorse or to reject a coalition arrangement proposed by the party of their first choice. By contrast to Continental countries, therefore, parties can be allies in the constituencies as well as in government, rather than allies only in government but enemies in the constituencies. This is found to have profound effects on the working of coalition government.

Coalition *governments* can be of three main types. The first – the type to which Britain is most accustomed – is the Government of National Unity, whereby most, if not all, of the main parties join together to meet a national emergency, whether war or economic crisis. Four coalitions in Britain during the twentieth century fall into this category – the Asquith coalition which lasted from May 1915 to December 1916, the Lloyd George wartime coalition formed in December 1916, the National Government under Ramsay MacDonald formed in August 1931, and the Churchill coalition which governed from May 1940 to May 1945. (Table 1.3 lists the various coalitions and electoral pacts in Britain.)

This type of government is rare in normal peacetime conditions both in Britain and on the Continent. The most notable example since the war is the 'Grand Coalition' in West Germany between 1966 and 1969 which had the effect of bringing the SPD back into government after an interval of thirty-six years. This coalition, since it united the two main streams of opinion in Germany, leaving only the third party, the FDP, to constitute an opposition, seems to have given a stimulus to extremism; both the New Left and the neo-Nazi NPD gained in strength, and in the elections of 1969, the NPD nearly succeeded in surmounting the 5 per cent threshold to gain representation in the Bundestag. A similar consequence had attended the last parliamentary coalition of the Weimar Republic, the grand coalition led by Hermann Müller which ruled Germany between 1928 and 1930, when voters reacting against the government's handling of the depression found themselves, in the absence of moderate opposition, driven to support the extremes of Communism and Nazism. This type of coalition, therefore, can only operate effectively when the whole nation is agreed upon some fundamental aim such as victory in war. In peacetime, it is likely to encourage an extremist revolt against parliamentary government so that if a grand coalition needs to be formed in a period of economic emergency, it should be established only for a very limited period and dissolved as soon as the immediate crisis is over.

The second type of coalition is that which is a prelude to the fusion of parties. This too is familiar in twentieth-century British politics. Indeed, two of the three coalitions which were not Governments of National Unity fall into this category – the coalition between Liberal

Table 1.3 Coalitions and electoral pacts in Britain since 1895

Coalition governments

Dates of Formation and Dissolution	Prime Minister	Parties Comprising Coalition	Type of Coalition
June 1895– December 1905	Lord Salisbury, 1895–1902 A.J. Balfour, 1902–1905	Conservatives and Liberal Unionist	Prelude to fusion, achieved in 1912
May 1915– December 1916	H.H. Asquith	Liberals, Conservatives and Labour	Wartime government of national unity
December 1916– November 1918	David Lloyd George	Lloyd George Liberals, Conservatives and Labour	Wartime government of national unity
November 1918– October 1922	David Lloyd George	Lloyd George Liberals, and Conservatives	Attempted fusion, but dissolved by Conservatives, 1922
August 1931– May 1940	J. Ramsay MacDonald, 1931–1935; Stanley Baldwin 1935–1937; Neville Chamberlain 1937–1940	National Labour, Conservatives, Liberal Nationals, and until September 1932, Liberals	Attempted government of national unity. Prelude to fusion of National Labour and Liberal Nationals with Conservatives (1945 and 1966 respectively)
May 1940–May 1945	Winston Churchill	Conservatives, Labour and Liberals	Wartime government of national unity

Electoral pacts without coalition	Component Parties
1903: Gladstone–MacDonald pact	Liberals, and Labour Representation Committee (later Labour Party)
1981–1983	Liberals and Social Democratic Party (SDP): Alliance

Unionists and Conservatives which ruled Britain from 1895 to 1905, and the National Government after September 1932 when the independent Liberals resigned from it, leaving only the small National Labour and Liberal National parties as partners of the Conservatives. The Lloyd George peacetime coalition, formed by the Lloyd George

Liberals and Conservatives after Labour decided to leave the government in 1918, was originally intended by some of its protagonists to lead to fusion, but in the event the Conservatives decided to break with Lloyd George and his Liberal supporters in 1922. Coalitions of this second type have played a valuable role in securing party realignment, thus enabling the parties to become more responsive to contemporary issues rather than to those which agitated a previous generation. It could be argued, indeed, that the absence of any similar realignment in the years since 1945 has prevented the parties from modernising themselves, and has led to the ossification of the British political system.

It is, however, with a third type of governmental coalition that *Coalition Government in Western Europe* is primarily concerned, a type entirely familiar to Continental countries, but comparatively unknown in Britain. This third type may be called a *power-sharing* coalition. It occurs when two or more parties, none of which is able to gain an overall majority on its own, combine to form a majority government. Power-sharing coalitions differ from Governments of National Unity since they do not embrace – or indeed attempt to embrace – all of the parties in the political spectrum in order to implement a 'national' programme. On the contrary, they seek to implement a programme agreed between the coalition partners but probably opposed by those parties which do not belong to the coalition. This type of coalition realigns the parliamentary opposition, but does not eliminate it. Power-sharing coalitions also differ from coalitions of the second type – those which are a prelude to fusion – since there is no intention on the part of the coalition partners to surrender their separate identity. The parties comprising the coalition do not join together in an electoral pact, but continue to compete electorally with their coalition partners. This form of co-operation is encouraged by systems of proportional representation which prevent one party gaining a majority on its own: and by constitutional traditions requiring the search for a majority coalition to precede the formation of a single-party minority government. Constitutional rules on the Continent generally *require* the negotiation of a power-sharing coalition, and only when no such arrangement is possible will a single-party government be nominated. In Britain, on the other hand, the electoral system has made single-party majority the norm, while, on the rare occasions when no party has gained an overall majority, constitutional conventions have made for minority government and not coalition, such minority governments being regarded as temporary deviations from the norm. No coalition in twentieth-century Britain owes its formation to a hung parliament after a general election. Not only is effective coalition government a phenomenon of Continental political systems but the very understanding of coalition on the

Continent remains alien to British experience. (The impact of the brief power-sharing experiment of 1974 in Northern Ireland upon British political thinking has been quite minimal.) It is hardly surprising therefore that so much of the Continental literature on coalitions seems remote to British concerns. One of the purposes of *Coalition Government in Western Europe* is to open up what until now has too often resembled a dialogue of the deaf.

Political science and coalition government

Until recently, political scientists devoted little attention to the analysis of coalitions, but contented themselves with the well-worn generalities of classical writers such as Lowell and Bryce[3] who insisted that coalition government was weak government, and that it led to unsatisfactory compromises and political instability. The constitutionalist approach characteristic of traditional political science tended to emphasise conflict between executive and legislature and between the political parties, rather than the comparative mechanics of coalition. Since constitutions draw no distinction between the different types of procedures to be followed in the case of single-party and coalition governments, nor did political scientists. Indeed, the very categories which political scientists used – 'executives', 'cabinets', 'legislatures' – tended to assume away the question of whether the *modus operandi* of single-party governments and coalitions was fundamentally different.

More recently, there has been a flood of writing on coalitions, influenced by the conclusions of political scientists such as Eckstein, Lijphart, Rokkan and Sartori[4] that multi-party coalitional systems are *not* necessarily unstable and ineffective. Indeed political scientists have long realised that the dichotomy between 'two-party' and 'multi-party' systems is far too crude to do justice to the complexities of political life in modern democracies. Much of the work on multi-party systems, however, has focused less upon their implications for government than upon the relationships between social cleavages and different types of party systems, and the social preconditions of political stability. For this reason the relationship between party systems and the functioning of government has remained a comparatively neglected area of research.

Much of the writing on coalitions has been deeply influenced by the application of quantitative methods to the social sciences and especially by the work of von Neumann and Morgenstern on the theory of games.[5] Indeed, formal coalition theory has become one of the growth areas of political science. Yet the achievements of formal theory have been very limited. For political scientists have become accustomed to concentrate upon questions which can be answered in quantitative terms, questions such as 'Which coalitions will be formed in typical multi-party situations, assuming that party leaders behave as rational economic actors?' and 'How will different coalitions apportion ministerial portfolios and other pay-offs amongst themselves?'[6]

The quantitative approach is by no means wholly sufficient for understanding coalition government, however. The main focus of *Coalition Government in Western Europe* is directed at issues generally left undiscussed in quantitative and other more formal analyses. The essays analyse the problems of coalition by means of three different yet converging approaches. The first approach is the *constitutional* one and deals with the place of coalition in the basic framework of a country's political life. Thus the chapters by Klaus von Beyme, Pertti Pesonen and Alastair Thomas, Jan Vis and Jan de Meyer seek to answer the questions: How are coalitions formed, what are the particular characteristics of the government formation process in the coalitional systems of West Germany, Scandinavia, Belgium and the Netherlands? What is the role of the head of state in the process? To what extent does the process enhance or detract from democratic accountability?

The second aspect of coalition government discussed in this book is the *governmental* and the *political*: what are the effects of coalition upon the traditional institutions of government, upon the role of the cabinet, upon the legislature, and upon the political parties? These are the questions considered in the chapters by Klaus von Beyme, Bo Särlvik, Geoffrey Pridham and Brian Farrell, which seek to explain the workings of coalition government in four very different political systems. systems.

Finally, the chapters by Manfred Schmidt, Bo Särlvik and Ken Gladdish discuss the *policy consequences* of coalitions. In what respects are the policy outputs of coalitions likely to differ from those of single-party governments? Have they led in West Germany, Scandinavia and the Netherlands to social and economic progress or to *immobilisme*? These questions are given added point by the onset of recession and the quest for a philosophy of government with which to combat it. To what extent is the method of power-sharing as exemplified in coalition government likely to prove a positive response to the recession? Or is coalition unworkable in such a climate, since politics becomes a zero-sum game, the benefits accruing to one of the coalition partners implying losses for the others? The answers to such questions are, of course, relevant not only to the countries of the Continent but also to the internal debate in Britain on the merits of proportional representation and coalition government. It is hoped, therefore, that the essays in *Coalition Government in Western Europe* offer a contribution to this internal debate as well as to a better understanding of the political systems of Western Europe. For in the study of government as in many areas of public policy, Britain and the Continent find themselves converging, as the English Channel comes to be seen as a purely geographical rather than an intellectual or political frontier.

Notes

1. John Curtice and Michael Steed, 'Electoral Choice and the Production of Government: The Changing Operation of the Electoral System in the United Kingdom since 1955', *British Journal of Political Science*, Vol. 12, 1982.
2. John Curtice and Michael Steed, 'Turning Dreams into Reality: The Division of Constituencies Between the Liberals and the Social Democrats,' *Parliamentary Affairs*, Vol. 36, 1983.
3. See, for example, James Bryce: *Modern Democracies* (London, Macmillan, 1921), Vol. I. pp. 121–2.
4. Harry Eckstein: 'A Theory of Stable Democracy' in *Division and Cohesion in Democracy: A Study of Norway* (Princeton NJ, Princeton University Press, 1966); Arend Lijphart: *The Politics of Accommodation: Pluralism and Democracy in the Netherlands* (Rev. edn. Berkeley, University of California Press, 1976); Arend Lijphart: *Democracy in Plural Societies* (New Haven, Yale University Press 1977); Stein Rokkan: *Citizens, Elections, Parties* (Oslo, Universitetsforlaget, 1970); Giovanni Sartori: *Parties and Party Systems: A Framework for Analysis* (Cambridge, Cambridge University Press, 1976), especially Chapters 5 and 6.
5. John von Neumann and Oskar Morgenstern: *Theory of Games and Economic Behaviour* (3rd edn. Princeton NJ, Princeton University Press, 1953).
6. Compare the preface by Anatol Rapoport to Abram De Swaan: *Coalition Theories and Cabinet Formations: A Study of Formal Theories of Coalition Formation Applied to Nine European Parliaments After 1918*: (Amsterdam/New York/London, Elsevier, 1973).

2 Coalition Government in Western Germany
Klaus von Beyme

Constitutional aspects

Coalition government was a traumatic experience for the founding fathers of the Federal Republic of Germany. The Weimar coalitions had been increasingly manipulated by the popularly elected Reich President who had acquired growing influence, and coalition government was considered to be one of the reasons for the breakdown of democracy. The development of polarised pluralism, with the growing strength of anti-system parties and semi-loyal oppositions, made coalition politics increasingly impossible.[1]

The future of the West German party system was only indirectly open to influence by the decision-makers, who were able to outlaw disloyal oppositions and thus sustain a wide range of coalition alternatives, and to provide for a five per cent clause limiting the number of parties in the legislature.

On the one hand, the creation of a president with next to no discretionary power in the process of government formation precluded certain possible abuses of presidential power (after all, Hitler was legally called into power by President Hindenburg). The need for stability, however, impelled the founding fathers to look for a stabilising element. It was found in the strong position of the head of government, the Federal Chancellor. For the first time in German history the Chancellor was to be formally elected by parliament and not nominated by the head of state, with (Weimar) or without (Second Empire) the obligation to guarantee a supporting parliamentary majority for all important acts of government.

The alternative was to create a presidential system on the American model and thus avoid coalition government entirely, but this was advocated only by minor groups in the CSU and among the Liberals.[2] Germany remained conscious of the fact that her traditional political culture was fragmented, and that in streamlining the constitutional framework she had only a limited choice between the extremes of the Anglo-Saxon models of alternating governments without coalition in the West and involuntary block-systems under the guidance of leftist parties in the East.[3]

The compromise envisaged a Chancellor as coalition leader with wide discretionary powers in selecting his cabinet. This could be toppled not by shifting coalitions, but only by a constructive vote of no-confidence. His 'Richtlinienkompetenz', power to lay down policy guidelines, was a kind of constitutional safegard against the 'horse trading' (*Kuhhandel*) of the Weimar parties. It was intended to secure stable government even after wearisome periods of coalition formation, the possibility of which was not excluded by the formal election of the Chancellor. On coalition-building itself the constitution was silent; no detailed instrumental or auxiliary procedures were envisaged, as were later provided for in certain other national constitutions, such as in Sweden (1971, Chapter 5, para 2), Portugal (1976, Art. 190) and Spain (1978, Art. 99.2).

The constructive vote of no-confidence, in combination with the provisions for government formation, made it clear that it was not the breakdown of coalitions, as in Weimar, but the democratic principle of the designation of the leading party and its candidate for the Chancellor's office via elections which was envisaged by the founding fathers as the normal procedure of government formation. There have been fourteen governments of the Federal Republic since 1949 (see Table 2.1) – not counting certain cabinet reshuffles, as is sometimes done,[4] and of the governments up to 1980, eight have worked according to the founding fathers' intention.

Resignation after elections became the dominant form of government dissolution, and only two government changes – if we include the resignation of Adenauer in 1963 which was only formally voluntary – were caused by a break-up of the coalition. The only case where this was without previous planning was Erhard's resignation in 1966. In the Weimar Republic, by contrast, out of eighteen cabinets up to Brüning I in 1930 which still functioned in the normal way, eleven toppled through the disintegration of a coalition and only three as a consequence of elections.[5] The fall of Erhard proved, however, that the ingenious invention of the constructive vote of no-confidence had rather destructive consequences from the psychological point of view, since Erhard's Liberal (Freidemokratische Partei FDP) coalition partner and sections of his own party were forced to enter into negotiations for a new coalition behind the back of the acting Chancellor. Stubbornly clinging to office, Erhard proved unusually tough in ignoring the disintegrating forces in his coalition and his own party.

In contrast to other multi-party systems with moderate pluralism and without major polarisation, such as the Benelux states, coalition bargaining in Germany can best be studied in cabinet formation after elections. Unlike 'partitocrazia' systems where party élites dominate the coalition-making process, the FDP broke the old élitist pattern of

Table 2.1   Governments of the Federal Republic of Germany

	Chancellor	Parties in government	Reason for resignation
20. 9.1949	Adenauer (CDU)	CDU–CSU/FDP/DP	Elections
20.10.1953	Adenauer II	CDU–CSU/FDP/DP/BHE	Elections
24.10.1957	Adenauer III	CDU–CSU/DP	Elections
14.11.1961	Adenauer IV	CDU–CSU/FDP	Voluntary resignation
17.10.1963	Erhard (CDU)	CDU–CSU/FDP	Elections
26.10.1965	Erhard II	CDU–CSU/FDP	Coalition disintegration
1.12.1966	Kiesinger (CDU)	CDU–CSU/SPD	Elections
21.10.1969	Brandt (SPD)	SPD/FDP	Question of trust. Refused dissolution of parliament. Elections
15.12.1972	Brandt II	SPD/FDP	Voluntary resignation
16. 5.1974	Schmidt (SDP)	SPD/FDP	Elections
15.12.1976	Schmidt II	SPD/FDP	Elections
5.11.1980	Schmidt III	SPD/FDP	Vote of no-confidence
1.10.1982	Kohl (CDU)	CDU–CSU/FDP	Elections
6. 3.1983	Kohl II	CDU–CSU/FDP	

open alternatives before elections. In order to rid themselves of the image of a 'commuters' party' and of the effects of the drop in their vote since the 1970s, the FDP clearly indicated the conditions under which they would form a coalition and the partner they envisaged before the elections – even in the case of a 'renversement des alliances', such as occurred in the Saar in 1977, the first coalition of the FDP with the Christian Democrats (CDU) at the *Land* level since 1969. So the old proposition of research on electoral law, that proportional representation creates parties which normally bargain only after knowing the election results, was proved wrong in the German case.[6]

Unexpectedly after the Weimar experience, alternating coalitions developed fairly early in the Federal Republic. The precarious status of the West German rump state might easily have led to all-party coalitions or at least grand coalitions between the two major parties, as existed at the *Land* level in some cases. But when the SPD (Sozialdemokratische Partei Deutschlands) proposals for an SPD economic director and power-sharing with the Christlich-Demokratische Union

– Christliche Soziale Union (CDU-CSU) were rejected by the Economic Council (Germany's main decision-making body) in July 1947, the Social Democrats went into opposition.[7] They maintained this status throughout the constitution-making process in 1948/9 in the premature hope that they would win the first Federal elections. This was a miscalculation and it led to certain hasty concessions in the process of the elaboration of the Basic Law which the party later had cause to regret.

After the first elections in 1949 there was again discussion in both major parties about the feasibility of a grand coalition. The left wing of the *Sozialausschüsse* (the CDU's trade union committees) and the CDU of the Soviet Occupation Zone were considering a 'grand coalition' against the wishes of Adenauer and Erhard.[8] SPD sources frequently blamed Adenauer for the non-realisation of a grand coalition, since he had declared before the negotiations began that the voters had decided between a 'market society' and 'socialism'. On the other hand, Adenauer's counterpart, the SPD leader Schumacher, was not interested in becoming a junior partner and he deliberately asked for conditions which were unacceptable to the CDU.[9] The antagonism of the two party leaders reinforced the tendency towards polarisation, and opened the road to alternating coalition instead of the 'éternel marais du centrisme' existing in the Weimar system up to 1930.

The concentration of the German party system between 1949 and 1961 – only indirectly a result of the restrictions which the electoral law imposed on minor parties – made the coalitions of the Adenauer period untypical. After 1961 coalition formation was predominantly a bargaining process among the three parties in the Bundestag. New parties even at the *Land* level, where they managed to get into the legislature, (such as the Neofascist Nationaldemokratische Partei Deutschlands (NPD) and recently the ecologists) were not considered eligible for coalition (*'Koalitions-fähig'*). Only recently has passive toleration of a *Land* government by the 'Green Movement' (Hamburg 1982 Hesse 1982/1983) become a possibility.

Coalitions and political institutions

The German two-and-a-half party system makes it unusually difficult to test the propositions of the formal coalition theories which are so popular in the United States, though the 'two-against-one' constellation can be considered the ideal study ground for coalition behaviour.[10] The frequent existence of minority governments (such as disturb the calculations in Scandinavia) has been no problem so far in the Federal Republic, except for the last period of Erhard's second government, when the FDP ministers resigned because of conflicts over the budget. The fewer parties there are, the easier it seems to be to measure the ideological distance between parties, a necessary pre-condition for formal coalition theories.[11]

The problem is, however, to keep ideological distance constant over time. The main explanation in the German case for the move of the FDP into coalition with the Social Democrats was hardly a greater share of power, but rather a wearisome shift of ideological preferences within the Liberal party. The FDP moved from the position of an 'anti-socialist bourgeois block' to a social-liberal position, but not without fierce internal conflicts and the loss of certain elements which were once predominant in the party. Formal coalition theories tend to overlook singular factors in the party systems which made the German case unique:

- Political culture and tradition determines coalition behaviour, in the German case the above-mentioned traumatic experiences with the first German Republic.[12]
- The geopolitical situation of a divided country, the raison d'être of which was anticommunism, influenced the behaviour of the Liberals and caused them to persist in the attitude of an anti-socialist bourgeois block, even when they became increasingly dissatisfied with Adenauer in the late 1950s.
- The federal system with a variety of coalition governments at the *Land* level, develops a dynamic of its own. Dissenting wings can experiment with new coalitions at *Land* level even when this new coalition pattern is not yet acceptable to the majority of the party. The most important case was the revolt of liberal 'young Turks' (Weyer, Doering, Scheel) against CDU Prime Minister Arnold in the biggest *Land*, North-Rhine-Westphalia, in February 1956, and the formation of a coalition with the SPD under Steinhoff. Even among the majority of Liberal party members this was considered an emergency act against arbitrary CDU politics. The conflict was caused by the introduction of a bill envisaging a new electoral law which might have eliminated the FDP, and not because it was a 'natural coalition'.[13] It was not by chance that 16 Liberal deputies, including 4 Federal ministers, left the parliamentary group in opposition to this revolt.

With some exceptions (Hamburg 1957–66 and Bremen up to 1971) the FDP increasingly coordinated its efforts in the *Länder* with the exigencies of coalition-building in Bonn. After 1969 the polarisation was even stronger in the *Länder* than in Bonn, and *Land* elections more and more became reflections of the federal situation. The divergence of patterns of political behaviour at federal and *Land* level led to many frictions in the system.[14]

The *'correntocrazia'* in the CDU–CSU government party – less unique than other factors, since it also exists in Christian Democratic parties in other parliamentary systems – slowed down the change in liberal attitudes in matters of coalition. Chancellor Erhard, the successor to Adenauer and previously Minister of Economic Affairs, minimised the ideological divergencies between the Christian Democrats and the Liberals as regards economic policies. He was more market-oriented than a good many Christian Democrats after the war. In social policies, such as in the Law on the Constitution of Enterprises (*Betriebsverfas-sungsgesetz*) the CDU still bowed to FDP conditions, but in the case of th bill on worker participation in the coal and iron industries, the Christian Democrats passed the law with the support of the opposition Social Democrats against the FDP. The predominance of anti-socialist feelings in the CDU – which quickly abandoned certain Socialist elements of the CDU programme of Ahlen in the British Zone – made a coalition with the Liberals possible, though in matters concerning nationalism, policies between the two German states, and neutralism versus integration into the Western camp, there sometimes seemed to be more traits in common between the Social Democrats and the Liberals than between the CDU and the FDP.

All these factors make a quantification of the bargains at stake accord-ing to the rules of formal coalition theory scarcely rewarding in the German case. Against the logical intentions of a system which forms governments by formal election of a parliamentary majority, the principle of government formation has changed during the existence of the Federal Republic. In a democracy, it may be argued, the plurality principle should apply to government formation, i.e. the largest party should normally have the possibility of forming the government. Though after Erhard's resignation in 1966 a coalition of SPD and FDP seemed numerically feasible, the SPD (Schmidt and Wehner against Brandt) did not seriously consider trying to outdo the Christian Demo-crats by concluding an agreement with the Liberals on the basis of their slim majority of six seats. By 1969, however, views on what majority was necessary had become more modest. When Genscher was asked how many seats he thought necessary for the formation of a coalition with the SPD, he said that six would suffice.[15]

In 1966, apparently, the SPD had even more respect for the plurality principle than in 1969, when its share of power made it more cour-ageous. The underlying principle for this kind of coalition-building by the second largest party was a kind of trend principle (which party had increased most) or gravitational principle (which party was most likely to bring about a stable coalition). But even in 1969 there were quite a few SPD leaders – such as Schmidt – who favoured the continuation of the grand coalition. President Heinemann (SPD), whose election in 1969 with the votes of the Liberals was the first step to the *Machtwechsel* (change of power), had to encourage the wavering candidate Brandt: 'Willy, get on with it' (*Willy, ran, mach's*).[16] Only in 1972 was the SPD the strongest party. In 1969, 1974, 1976 and 1980 it formed govern-ments as the second largest party, thus excluding the biggest party from power via coalition. By international standards this has happened as frequently only in Australia and Ireland.[17]

The CDU lamented this a good deal at the national level, but used the same practices at the *Land* level in order to keep the Social Democrats out of power. The last occasion this happened was in May 1980 in the Saar, when the CDU was accused of falsifying the voters' will (*Wahlverfälschung*).[18]

In the late 1970s the Liberals saw the danger that they might become a kind of permanent coalition partner to the SPD, as they were considered to be for the CDU up to 1966 (only interrupted by the period of absolute majority rule of the CDU in 1957–61 when the FDP remained in opposition). The FDP started experimenting with a reorientation beginning in 1977 in the Saar. In 1982 the Hesse FDP voted for coalition with the CDU after the *Landtag* elections. In Berlin the FDP threatened to exclude even those who voted for the CDU Prime Minister von Weizsäcker after a party convention had decided not to support the CDU. The parliamentary group leader, Vetter, and three of his colleagues, were sentenced by a party court for violating party discipline and deciding on support for the CDU on an individual basis via a 'coalition-like relationship'.[19]

But in the long run it proved impossible to prevent a reorientation of the party by such disciplinary measures. On 1 October 1982 the majority of the FDP for the first time participated in a successful constructive vote of no-confidence against Schmidt.

The survival of the centre: FDP dilemma

The FDP in the 1970s strengthened its anti-hegemonic image. It made it clear that it would not support any of the major parties which won an absolute majority, thus discouraging oversize coalitions of the type of the Adenauer era. This prevented it from entering a coalition with the CDU after the 1979 election in Rhineland-Palatinate. By these principles the FDP avoided the image of a mere satellite party, like the Country Party in Australia.

The 'wavering party' image (*Wackelpartei*) was, however, strengthened again in 1982 by further discussion among the FDP élite on the necessity for a change of coalition partners. Federal President Scheel (FDP), who in 1969 was one of the promoters of the first *Machtwechsel*, tacitly favoured a change of partners for his party while in office. This would have guaranteed him a second term with a comfortable majority. After he stepped down – having no chance of re-election – he favoured the switch of the FDP to the CDU more openly.[20]

Some observers date the beginning of the erosion of the SPD-FDP coalition back to 1973.[21] The mandate for the *Ostpolitik* by the majority of the electorate was taken by the SPD as a mandate for far-reaching internal reforms which increasingly led to conflicts with the more conservative wing of the FDP. It was not the break-up of the coalition but the wearisome procedure which was unusual. For the FDP, the hesitation was caused by the danger of an internal split in the party. The SDP was cautious because of the trauma of leaving power on account of a minor quarrel over the budget, as happened in 1930 when the last SPD chancellor in the Weimar Republic, Müller, resigned. These trauma made both sides prepared for a long time for concessions which did not really represent their political convictions. A double 'betrayal syndrome' bewildered both coalition partners. The FDP was increasingly vexed by the approaches SPD leader Brandt and others made to the ecological movement, and the SPD was more and more irritated by the knowledge of secret negotiations between the FDP and the CDU. In September 1982 the FDP ministers finally resigned, thus anticipating Schmidt's decision to dismiss them.

The coalition drama has been frequently analysed in terms of the old Teutonic sagas of traitors and heroes, which showed the propensity of many Germans for '*Nibelungentreue*'. It was hardly caused by the individual characteristics of party leaders, such as Genscher.[22] And it was not caused but rather reinforced by certain institutions of the West German system which were the fruit of an excessive concern with stability on the part of the founding fathers. Since Erhard's resignation it has been this author's stubborn belief that the German parliamentary system was not so ingenious as many commentators believed it to be, for three reasons:

- The constructive vote of no-confidence has highly destructive results in psychological terms. The coalition partner in 1982 and elements in the Chancellor's own party in the last days of Erhard 1965/66 had to conspire behind the scenes to secure the vote of no-confidence.
- The question of confidence has been perverted into a manipulative instrument for forcing a dissolution of parliament. This is not in consonance with what the founding fathers had in mind. It is not justified to blame the new Chancellor, Helmut Kohl, for planning, while still commanding a comfortable majority, to use the question of no-confidence to secure a dissolution by asking some of his followers to vote 'no' or to abstain. Schmidt in his last days had similar plans, and Brandt has frankly admitted that he did the same in 1972. The constitutional court only grudgingly accepted Kohl's procedure in 1983.
- The procedure of dissolution is so clumsy and restricted that the normal functioning of countervailing powers does not work in the Federal Republic. Dissolution on the basis of a two-thirds majority vote – as in Israel and in some German *Länder* – could be an alternative. It was recommended by the Committee on Constitutional Reform in 1976, and is widely debated now, but its implementation on an *ad hoc* basis is hardly feasible.

The FDP fell victim to these deadlocks in the system, and this reinforced the impression on the part of many voters that 'treason' was involved. This led to a severe punishment in the first two elections after the ousting of Schmidt, in the *Land* elections in Hesse and Bavaria. In both cases the FDP secured less than five per cent of the vote and failed to get into the legislature. In the federal elections in March 1983, in spite of unfavourable survey results the FDP won 6.9% of the list votes and entere~ a new coalition government under Kohl. The anti-Strauss effect had ed its life.

Other factors based on the changing attitudes of the electorate rather than on the institutions, have put the FDP in a dilemma. (i) Increasingly conflicts arise between the democratic principle of the majority's will exerted during elections and the parliamentary principle of allowing governments to be formed and dissolved between elections. The FDP has contributed to strengthening the first principle by indicating ahead of time since 1972 which was its favourite coalition partner, and by renouncing *'partitocrazia'* and post-electoral bargaining in more than minor details of cabinet formation. (ii) The return of ideology on issues such as *Ostpolitik* or liberalisation of citizens' rights has given the impression that the SPD-FDP coalition was more than a pragmatic alliance. (iii) The very fact that coalition orientations change only over a very long period of time (1949–1966, 1969–1982) makes it difficult, in the perception of many voters, for the FDP to shift from one partner to the other.

The FDP was fighting for survival. A change in coalition is a deadly risk which can lead to a change in membership and voting support ranging from one-third to two-thirds of a constituency party. Surveys show that the German electorate normally favours the coalition in office. The grand coalition, which was unpopular among the intellectuals and almost identified with an authoritarian one-party state by the rebellious students in 1968, proved to be the most popular of all the possible models among the majority of the electorate.[23] This pattern was repeated in the 1982 coalition crisis. A survey before Schmidt's downfall showed that about 60 per cent of the middle level of the FDP leadership were against a change and only 20 per cent favoured a coalition with the CDU, while the remaining 20 per cent would at least not resist a change of coalition partner. In the meantime, we have another proof that politicians should not confound demoscopy and democracy: 58 per cent of the FDP voters in a recent survey welcomed the shift to the new coalition.[24]

The consequences for the internal structure of the FDP are not yet apparent. On the road to the first change of coalition partners, the FDP lost a good many of its members from 1956 onwards. After 1969 the membership went down from 58,750 to 53,302 in 1971, and only since 1973 has a new upward trend shown that new members have been won to replace the lost national-liberal wing.[25] The change of partner in 1969 seemed to be daring, since the party polled only slightly above 5 per cent (5.8 per cent). In 1982 the situation appeared easier. The FDP had its second-best result during the 1980 elections, but the party leadership was cautious enough not to overrate the anti-Strauss aspect of this kind of casual following. The downward trend in the elections for the *Länder* parliaments (Berlin 1981, Hamburg 1982, Hesse and Bavaria, 1982) showed that the situation was even more dangerous: the FDP lost its representation in some *Länder* parliaments as the ecological movement jumped the five per cent hurdle. (Hamburg, Lower Saxony, North-Rhine Westphalia, and Hesse – only in Bavaria did the green lists not hit the 5 per cent mark.)

FDP voters have normally shown a higher inclination than the voters for the two large parties to participate in citizens' action groups. This also makes the small party organisation of the FDP – lacking the huge conveyor organisation of big interest groups which the two bigger parties (formerly based on subcultures) have as an auxiliary potential – more vulnerable to losses as more voters move to support the green movement than ever before. The process of quick social change within the party also makes it open to huge ups and downs in the trend of party identification.[26]

The dangers for the FDP in the long run, however, have been overrated. Among the elites – with the exception of the military and the trade unions – the FDP is rather over-represented, and even if temporarily voters are lost it is likely that these liberal elites will re-create the equivalent of the old party.[27] The FDP elites are more government-oriented than the SPD – parts of which have never lost the old nostalgia for opposition. It is an old German tradition for the more national rather than radical heritage of liberalism to shy away from opposition,[28] and to maximise participation in government. This trend has been strengthened by the dangers to the very existence of the FDP. The traumatic experience of grand coalitions, which makes former coalition partners consider the elimination of the third party, does not recommend a new experiment in opposition. German liberals were recently quite glad when the FDP in Rhineland-Palatinate looked for a way out of its pledge not to coalesce with the CDU which had the absolute majority, and seemed willing to adopt from their Luxembourg colleagues across the border the liberal slogan: 'Opposition is stupid'.[29]

Actors, pay-offs and procedures

Since William Riker, the *minimum size principle* for the winning coalition has been one of the standard assumptions of coalition theory.[30] Comparative studies later discovered exceptions to this: oversized cabinets are said to be formed in parliaments 'characterized by high *a priori* willingness to bargain combined with low information certainty'.[31] This would seem to apply more to highly fragmented multi-party systems with low party discipline and constantly changing coalitions of roughly the same parties, such as in Belgium or the Netherlands.

Germany has had occasional *oversized coalitions* (1953–7 and 1966–9) which were justified by the need to pass constitutional amendments; the federal constitution requires two-thirds of the Bundestag to agree to amendments. The oversized coalition between the CDU and the Deutsche Partei (DP), 1957–61, when Adenauer won an absolute majority, can be explained in terms of the client relationship between the two parties. There was a common parliamentary group from 1951 to 1959, and the junior partner, the DP, was able to conserve its status as a party above the 5 per cent level only via a 'system of riding on the back' (*Huckepacksystem*), i.e. the CDU had to give up running in certain constituencies to give the DP a chance.[32] This oversized coalition was also a prudent move on Adenauer's part. He did not count on a permanent absolute majority, and it proved to be a shrewd move to save a certain number of votes by offering the DP a coalition. This cushioned his dominant position for the future. In 1953 the oversized coalition included besides the DP and the FDP the refugees' party Bund der Heimatvertriebenen und Entrechteten (BHE), which was needed to carry through Adenauer's policy, although there were a good many divergences between the CDU and the BHE in social policy.[33]

The ideological or policy distance between the coalition partners is another concern of formal coalition theories.[34] In Germany this was overshadowed by the special situation of a divided country. In social matters the BHE might have had more affinity to the SPD, but its anti-communism and basic acceptance of Adenauer's policy of integration with the West led it reluctantly into an Adenauer coalition. The FDP had certain points in common with the SPD in legal and educational policies and in foreign policy, and over the problem of the two Germanies. On the other hand, it was a typical liberal or radical party, with, according to Herriot's *bon mot*, 'Coeur à gauche – portefeuille à droite'. The divergences in economic and social policies counted for more until the protest movement made 'coeur' more important than 'portefeuille'. Policy distance in this case is hard to measure, since the relative weight of certain policies changed over time. The *Ostpolitik* acquired an importance after 1966 which it never had before, but by 1982 it was no longer important. In view of the global deterioration of East-West relations, the *Ostpolitik* has not been as successful as had been hoped, though on the whole relations between the two German states have remained better than relations between the superpowers.

The coalition bargaining process has proved to be relatively easy and quick, compared to more fragmented party systems, such as those in Belgium or the Netherlands. According to the ideas of the founding fathers, the incoming Chancellor should be the coalition-builder. But his position in many governments has proved much weaker than expected, for two reasons:

- Most Federal Chancellors were not the undisputed leaders of their party at the time of access to office.
- Election of the Chancellor normally took place somewhere in the middle of the bargaining process, but usually before the bargaining between the parties over details came to an end. The parliamentary group leaders might have an interest in settling all questions before the Chancellor is elected, but apparently they continue to have strong influence even after the election of the Chancellor.[35]

During the formal elections no Chancellor gets all the votes of the coalition partner. Adenauer failed to get 3 votes in 1949, 19 in 1953, 7 in 1957 and 8 in 1961; Erhard lost 25 votes in 1963 and 19 in 1965. Kiesinger with his large majority lost as many as 92 votes. Brandt lost 19 in 1969. In 1972 after an abortive attempt to topple Brandt by a constructive vote of no-confidence in favour of Barzel, there was a unique result: 289 voted for Brandt, though there were only 242 SPD and 42 FDP members. Schmidt came to power in 1974 with 267 votes in his favour out of 284 deputies.[36]

In 1949 Adenauer was not yet the accepted party leader, though there was hardly any serious competitor. In his Memoirs he played down his leading role too much: 'I was surprised when someone interrupted me and proposed me as Federal Chancellor. I looked into the faces and answered: If all those present share this opinion, I accept.'[37] As regards Erhard, it was sometimes even doubted whether he was a member of the party, and he became party leader reluctantly when Adenauer finally gave up his last position of power. But even then Erhard continued to build on the image of the 'people's Chancellor' rather than prime minister of the party. Kiesinger was never an efficient party leader. Brandt cherished the image of statesman as Mayor of Berlin rather than as opposition leader. But he came somewhat close to Adenauer's position of a coincidence of the two offices of Chancellor and party leader, whereas Schmidt again left the party leadership to Brandt. The differentiation of top party offices – in the case of the SPD the triumvirate included the important figure of the parliamentary group leader, Wehner – did not strengthen the Chancellor's position, though it is an exaggeration to call his position weak in coalition-building and to argue that ministers are largely imposed on him.[38]

Parliamentary groups are normally strengthened by the necessity for coalition governments. Germany, however, does not belong to those systems which are a *partitocrazia* par excellence with a predominance of party elites at all levels.[39] The party leader's position is usually too strong for a mere *'particratie'*. Under Adenauer the parliamentary group as a whole was hardly consulted in the coalition formations of 1953 and 1957.[40] The bargaining process which led to the grand coalition *in* 1966 strengthened the situation of the parliamentary group, but the parliamentary group leader was, after all, one of the candidates for the highest office. Thus the CDU never fitted completely into Duverger's type of a committee party with the parliamentary group predominant. Parliamentary groups are an autonomous locus of power[41], but their impact varies greatly according to the situation (post-election or in a mid-term coalition crisis), the strength of the Chancellor or the candidate for Chancellor, and the political issues at stake.

According to old typologies since Duverger, Socialist parties tend to give priority to the party outside parliament. The SPD, however, under the weak leadership of Ollenhauer up to 1963 and the leadership of Brandt, who while Mayor of Berlin was frequently absent, developed increasingly towards a situation where the parliamentary group became almost as important as in the case of the bourgeois parties.[42] During the grand coalition this trend continued, though Brandt as party leader was permanently present on the political stage in Bonn. An increasing share of delegates to the party convention were parliamentarians (about 20 per cent) and so were nine out of eleven members of the presidium. The newly created office of a 'Bundesgeschäftsführer' (federal manager) was to improve the contacts between party organisation and parliamentary group.[43] The parliamentary group thus became more important in coalition formation than it was supposed to be according to the ideological principles of a Socialist party. This trend began in 1962 when the FDP left Adenauer's cabinet because of the '*Spiegel* affair'. Ollenhauer, Wehner and Erler started negotiating with the CDU for a 'grand coalition', but the parliamentary group did not follow its leaders.[44] When a sudden change in the highest governmental office occurred for the first time with Brandt's resignation in 1974, the parliamentary group as a whole was hardly involved. The parliamentary group leader Herbert Wehner was one of the most active figures, however, more so than Schmidt, who was to succeed Brandt. Even FDP leader Scheel asked for at least a kind of suspensive veto, when he wrote to Brandt saying that he should not resign before the FDP leadership and the coalition partners had had a chance to deliberate. When Brandt finally stepped down, the party presidium took the first step. It nominated Schmidt and the coalition partners made the choice. A special nominating party convention was not even considered.[45]

In the coalition crisis of the summer of 1982, the CDU – especially Helmut Kohl's rivals – did not exclude the possibility that an extraordinary party convention should decide on the candidate for the Chancellor's office if Schmidt's government disintegrated before the normal elections in 1984. Kohl, however, preferred to leave the decision to the parliamentary group.[46] The CSU did not – as in 1980 – try to boycott any majority decision against its candidate Franz Josef Strauss, since Strauss was unlikely to be nominated again.

The CDU has usually elected the candidate for the Chancellorship in the parliamentary group. In 1963 Erhard was the only candidate; in 1966 Kiesinger needed three ballots to win over his rivals Schröder and Barzel. Since Adenauer opposed Erhard as his successor, a kind of intra-party *'informateur'* was necessary; Brentano filled the function as *'Kanzlersucher'*.[47] In 1966 Erhard was toppled. The parliamentary group leader, Barzel, however, was not in a strong position, since he was himself a candidate competing with others for the highest office.

Traditionally the position of the parliamentary group has been strongest in the FDP. Since there was never any question of putting up a candidate for the highest office, the party leader was under less pressure than in the two bigger parties. But there were situations where the party leader was also not completely in control of his parliamentary group, as in 1961. FDP party leader, Mende, when he joined a coalition with Adenauer – despite the party having fought the electoral campaign under the slogan 'Together with the CDU but without Adenauer' – had to promise Adenauer that he would first test opinion in his parliamentary group by holding a tentative secret ballot. Only when the group voted 48 to 12 for Adenauer did he dare to commit it to the procedure provided by the constitution of electing Adenauer for a fourth – limited – term.[48]

Among the stakes in coalition building usually the ministries are mentioned first. Since the grand coalition of 1966 an increasing number of parliamentary secretaries have been added. In 1949 Adenauer deliberately brought the office of the Federal President and of the Speaker of the House into the bargaining.[49] The president's office occasionally played a role later also. In 1968 SPD member Heinemann was elected and he coined the much resented term 'a bit of a change of power' (*'ein Stück Machtwechsel'*). The election of Carstens (CDU) in 1978 was, however, also considered as a new first step to a *'Machtwechsel'* the other way round.[50]

The parties' policy preferences are normally translated into preferences for certain portfolios during the bargaining for a coalition. When the refugee party BHE entered the coalition in 1953, it was obvious that they would get the refugee ministry. Adenauer actually went a long way in making concessions to the appointee, as became clear when Oberländer later came under attack for his Nazi past. Adenauer was warned by close collaborators, but he pretended to be under pressure from a powerful interest group: 'I have asked the refugee groups several times to offer me another man, they insist on Oberländer.'[51] Even Adenauer's collaborators were astonished at how many concessions he made for his oversize coalition; this was justified on the ground of foreign policy needs and rearmament.[52] A similar logic seemed to dictate that the conservative regionalist Deutsche Partei (DP) should normally get the Ministry of Bundesrat Affairs.

But a party is hardly able to insist on its 'own' portfolios when it changes partners. In coalition with the CDU the FDP used to get the Ministries of Justice and Economic Co-operation. These were taken over by the SPD in 1969, but the FDP got more important offices, like Foreign Affairs and the Interior. In 1972 the FDP obtained the important portfolio of Economics, since they complained of not being represented in economic affairs (except for the Ministry of Agriculture). The FDP has provided evidence that parties are indeed looking for redistributive pay-offs to improve their position in forthcoming elections.[53] The smaller partners usually have over-representation in the cabinet. The number of ministries available in West Germany is comparatively small for a middle-sized country – generally not more than 16 – and it leaves little room for manoeuvre. Nevertheless the opposition used to criticise the increasing number of offices during the parliamentary debates on the government address[54].

In 1953 the creation of ministers without portfolio did not please Adenauer's collaborators,[55] and he confessed in his memoirs that the number of ministries was considered too big by himself as well as by the court of auditors (*Bundesrechnungshof*).[56] Most frequently the FDP was blamed for having pressed too hard for a large share of offices. But it cannot really be proved that it was only the desire for the maximum number of offices which motivated the Liberals in their final decision to accept a coalition offer. When Kiesinger, after a fairly good electoral result, perceived that he was not the 'natural coalition builder' he thought himself to be on election night, the victory was celebrated without the anticipation that a new coalition could annihilate the fruits of the election campaign. He made much higher offers to the FDP than Brandt had done: half a dozen ministries (instead of four), and even some help in the formation of coalition governments at the *Land* level is reported to have been offered. Scheel, however, decided differently.[57] But it was not to be expected that the Liberals would behave according to the rules of formal coalition theories, coolly calculating the material pay-offs in a period when the 'end of ideology' had become a self-destroying prophecy and the FDP had adapted to the new trend to the left.

Bargaining for portfolios is not only a matter of coalition parties. The various currents in the CDU under Adenauer gave rise to demands by particular sections of the party and their supporting interest groups. Examples are the left wing of the 'social committees', which usually got the Labour Ministry, or the Farmers' Associations which pressed for certain individuals as Minister of Agriculture, or sometimes tried to veto others (Lübke, for example, who later became Federal President).[58] Status groups with no countervailing organised interest proved to be more open to penetration by the parliamentary groups and the legislative committees, and this normally also brought a good deal of influence in coalition building. After 1969 some leading trade unionists entered the cabinet: Leber, Arendt, Gscheidle, Rohde. All of them left in the late 1970s. When Ehrenberg was nominated Minister of Labour in 1977, the trade union congress, Deutsche Gewerkschafts-bund (DGB), complained of not having been consulted. After strong criticism of the unions for encroaching on the '*Richtlinienkompetenz*' of the Chancellor, DGB president Vetter admitted: 'We don't have a right of codetermination for the nomination of Federal ministers.' On the whole, the influence of interest groups has declined under Brandt and Schmidt as compared with Adenauer or Erhard. The discipline of German interest groups has made it impossible for them to use strikes and other instruments to influence coalition-making, as has sometimes happened in Denmark (1978), Finland or Italy.[59] When Brandt was confronted with a constructive vote of no-confidence in 1972 and some groups of workers organised strikes and rallies in favour of the Chancellor, he had to play down public indignation by hinting at the fact that the parliamentary mechanisms of confidence were a legal instrument.[60] This showed, however, that the Germans had deeply internalised the consensus that government formation should occur after elections. A change in the highest governmental office by decision of the parliamentary majority was legal but unpopular. As we said earlier, the strange rules of confidence as laid down in the Basic Law have contributed to this. When the CDU failed to topple Brandt in 1972 the Chancellor considered recourse to the electorate. He could only do this via a question of confidence in parliament. The psychological consequences are as negative as in the case of the constructive vote of no-confidence if a Chancellor poses the question of confidence in order to be able to dissolve the federal parliament only to get a negative answer.[61]

Coalition bargaining on the whole has always been concluded 'within a reasonably short time span',[62] normally slightly more than one month. The time span is, however, not simply a function of the difficulties of the coalition-building process. On the only occasion when a coalition was not necessary, in 1957, when the Christian Democrats won an absolute majority, Adenauer deliberately took an unusually long time to form his cabinet.[63] But what has been a good record, as compared to the Benelux countries or Italy, has not prevented the German opposition from criticising very severely the time span and the horse trading, or from ridiculing the outcome as a weak government. Schumacher did this with his usual irony: 'If all the gentlemen who were promised a ministry and did not get one were integrated into a parliamentary group it would not be the smallest group of the Bundestag'.[64]

Brandt put it more smoothly in 1961: 'It would be easy to shed light on the disgusting horse trading during the government formation. It is really difficult not to write a satirical sketch. But this topic is dealt with by the cabarets in the country.'[65] The CDU took its revenge in 1976 and 1980, not altogether without good reason.[66]

This comparatively good performance in forming coalitions is again partly due to institutional factors: no formal approval of the cabinet list by the whole party caucus is needed, nor does the whole cabinet need the confidence of parliament. The founding fathers deliberately excluded the possibility, which existed in the Weimar Republic, of individual unpopular figures in the cabinet being removed by votes of no-confidence or disapproval.

Steering the coalitions

A last question is how coalitions, once they are formed, are steered in order to maximise homogeneity of decisions and how they are justified in public.

In the first years of its existence the CDU was able to bind its junior partners more or less by what Adenauer said. The more he strengthened his position and the more authoritarian his style of leadership appeared, the more formally were the coalition agreements laid down. The most extreme case was in 1961, when Adenauer got the FDP to enter his coalition only on condition that he would promise to resign before the next election. Adenauer's victory was almost a Pyrrhic one, and it showed the erosion of the grand old man's power. At this moment German constitutional lawyers began to suspect that the coalition agreement was tending to become a subsidiary part of the constitution itself.[67] Adenauer had to defend himself in the parliamentary debate on his government programme, and he argued that an agreement on a programme by a coalition could not be more unconstitutional than the right of every single party to agree on a government platform.[68] During the grand coalition the second party, the SPD, was unusually successful in getting the main issues of an 8-item programme, which they had already sketched before the elections, into the coalition agreement.[69]

The FDP under the Brandt and Schmidt governments continued its old predilection for coalition agreements. They became more detailed, the more divergences appeared between the two partners after the honeymoon between Brandt and Scheel was over. This was particularly true of the agreement of 1980 which resulted from 60 hours of coalition bargaining.[70] The work on the paper, however, was not as important as some of the agreements on principles, which were not included in the text. The paper was not published either in 1980 or in 1983.

Coalition agreements are one thing, their implementation is another. Coalition government seems to imply steering bodies to maintain a common course of government policy. This is most likely in a grand coalition under almost equal partners. But the ominous example of the Austrian grand coalition up to 1966 prevented the two German parties from creating a formal coalition steering committee.[71] In 1967 when the first conflicts in the grand coalition arose, Chancellor Kiesinger invited leading politicians to a resort on Lake Constance, Kressbronn. The 'Kressbronn circle' was later institutionalised. Its main purpose was to integrate the two leaders of the parliamentary groups, Barzel and Schmidt, who were critical of the coalition, into the decision-making process, but this was not always successful. Both left the circle on one occasion because the talk was too barren. It had no legal competence.[72] It could not even increase parliamentary group discipline, since the two parliamentary group leaders developed into a secret sub-government. When someone remarked in the cabinet that the two parliamentary group leaders were 'capable men', Kiesinger yelled back 'capable of anything' ('*fähig zu allem*')[73]. But the 'sub-government' was not a two-man team. There was a kind of parliamentary roundtable every Tuesday which included Alex Möller (SPD) and Richard Stücklen (CSU). This was considered more effective than the Kressbronn circle, which had aroused so much attention and suspicion from the media.[74]

Under the SPD-FDP government the friction between the Chancellor and the parliamentary group leaders was less open. Wehner, who never thought that Brandt was capable of governing, was however loyal before the resignation crisis in 1974, and resisted Helmut Schmidt's ambitions. But the parliamentary group leader seems to have acted very brutally in ousting Brandt, when the scandals concerning the GDR agent, Guilleaume, and the private affairs of the Chancellor became known.[75] In the early stages of the coalition crisis of 1982, Helmut Schmidt was saved largely by the loyalty of the FDP group leader, Mischnick, who clung to the SPD-FDP coalition even when ministers seemed ready to desert it. Formal steering bodies were no longer necessary.

A final concern of coalition theory is the durability of coalitions. The truism venerated since Bryce and Lowell that coalition governments tend to be less stable than single-party governments is still correct on an international comparison, but it is hardly telling in the German case. There have been only three premature resignations: Erhard (1966), Brandt (1974), and Schmidt (1982). The erosion of Erhard's power was accompanied by a coalition crisis with the FDP, but the basic problem was that Erhard was no longer in command of his own party. During Brandt's resignation crisis, his coalition partner, Scheel (FDP), was one of the staunchest supporters of his staying in office. This was the opposite of a coalition crisis, and Brandt was toppled owing to internal fights between the leading politicians in the SPD.

In spite of these internal crises Germany can match non-coalition systems in the Anglo-Saxon countries in governmental stability. Indeed, Germany's stability is rather too high than too low, since alternation is so difficult, though considering the number of parties and the constitutional system the pre-conditions for alternative governments are good.

Conclusion

Hardly any other parliamentary system has done so much indirectly in the Constitution and the electoral law to streamline the coalition-building process as West Germany (strong position of the Chancellor, constructive vote of no-confidence, the regulation of the parties in the constitution, the possibility of outlawing disloyal opposition, the five per cent clause). This was a result of the traumatic experience of the Weimer Republic.

The coalition-building process has been influenced, however, by factors which the founding fathers could not entirely foresee such as the political culture, the geopolitical situation of the Federal Republic, the functioning of federalism, and the development of large catch-all parties.

Since the concentration of the party system up to 1961, coalition-making has mostly been a matter of winning over the FDP. To get rid of its 'commuter party' image the FDP became increasingly reluctant to change coalition partners. Twice the party was endangered by the rise of a fourth party (1969 by the NPD, and 1982 by the ecological movement). The question of survival makes rational coalition politics even more difficult for the FDP, and the party is forced to resort to strategic thinking.

An analysis of the pay-offs of coalition-building shows some results which deviate from the normal propositions of coalition theory: over-sized coalitions were necessary because of the clumsy amendment procedure in the federal system. The principle of coalitions which are closest in policy affinity was not easy to test, since the FDP had many things in common with the SPD, but until 1969 was still most deeply influenced by its anti-Socialist trend. Policy preferences are not fixed data in the game; they have proved to be subject to quick changes in the perceptions both of the elites and the masses of the electorate.

The coalition-making process does not have the typical '*partitocrazia*' traits of more highly fragmented multi-party systems. The position of the Chancellor and the few decision-makers around him is fairly strong. Interest-group influence proved stronger during the predominance of the Christian Democrats than in the era of the SPD-FDP coalition. The number of portfolios proved to be of less relevance than the policy-orientation of the office and its projected value for showing pay-offs to a party's clientele in the electorate. The process of coalition-making in spite of all the criticism proved to be fairly efficient and was done in a reasonable time span.

Coalition agreements are widely used, but their implementation is not very institutionalised, since coalition steering is highly informal. Parliamentary group leaders have developed a decisive role. Government stability is high, almost too high. Alternating governments are not easy because of the special legitimacy problems of the FDP. New parties, such as the Neofascists and the Green Movement from time to time endanger the coalition game of a cartel between three parties, but so far they have not upset the established balance.

Notes

1. cf. Juan J. Linz, *Crisis, Breakdown and Reequilibration*. Vol. 1 of Juan J. Linz/Alfred Stepan (eds), *The Breakdown of Democratic Regimes* (Baltimore, Johns Hopkins University Press, 1978), pp. 25ff.
2. Klaus von Beyme, *Das präsidentielle Regierungssystem der Vereinigten Staaten in der Lehre der Herrschaftsformen* (Karlsruhe, C.F. Müller, 1967), pp. 75ff.
3. cf. Dolf Sternberger, 'Bildung und Formen der Koalitionsregierung' in Dolf Sternberger (ed.), *Lebende Verfassung* (Meisenheim, Hain, 1956), p. 124.
4. cf. Helmut Norpoth, 'The German Federal Republic: Coalition Government at the Brink of Majority Rule' in Eric C. Browne and John Dreijmanis (eds), *Government Coalitions in Western Democracies* (London, Longman, 1982), p. 12.
5. cf. Klaus von Beyme, *Die parlamentarischen Regierungssysteme in Europa* (Munich, Piper, 1973 2nd edition), p. 912.
6. cf. A.J. Milnor, *Elections and Political Stability* (Boston, Little Brown, 1969), p. 188.
7. Peter H. Merkl, 'Coalition Politics in West Germany' in Sven Groennings, E.W. Kelly, Michael Leiserson (eds), *The Study of Coalition Behavior* (New York, Holt, Rinehart and Winston, 1970), p. 19.
8. Franz Alt, *Der Prozeß der ersten Regierungsbildung unter Konrad Adenauer* (Bonn, Politische Akademie Eichholz, 1970), p. 76.
9. Klaus Schütz, 'Der Beginn der Opposition' in Max Gustav Lange *et al.*, *Parteien in der Bundesrepublik* (Stuttgart, Ring Verlag, 1955), p. 237; Lewis Edinger, *Kurt Schumacher. Persönlichkeit und politisches Verhalten* (Cologne/Opladen, Westdeutscher Verlag, 1967), p. 298.
10. Theodore Caplow, *Two Against One. Coalitions in Triads* (Englewood Cliffs, Prentice Hall, 1968).
11. Michael A. Leiserson, *Factions and Coalitions in One-Party Japan* (APSR, 1968); Robert Axelrod, *Conflict of Interest. A Theory of Divergent Goals with Applications to Politics* (Chicago, Markham, 1970).
12. cf. Heinz Rausch, 'Ein neuer "Phoenix" aus der Asche?' Bemerkungen zur formalisierten Koalitionstheorie', *Civitas*, 1976, p. 97.
13. Heino Kaack, *Die F.D.P. Grundriß und Materialien zur Geschichte, Struktur und Programmatik* (Meisenheim, Hain, 1978, 2nd edition), p. 20.
14. cf. Gerhard Lehmbruch, *Parteienwettbewerb und Bundesstaat* (Stuttgart, Kohlhammer, 1976), p. 31.
15. Reinhard Appel, 'Bonner Machtwechsel' in Roderich Klett and Wolfgang Pohl (eds), *Stationen einer Republik* (Stuttgart, DVA, 1979), p. 162.
16. Quoted from Arnulf Baring, *Machtwechsel. Die Ära Brandt-Scheel* (Stuttgart, DVA, 1982), pp. 176, 174.

17. Klaus von Beyme, *Parteien in westlichen Demokratien* (Munich, Piper, 1982), p. 387.
18. For background, see Klaus Bohnsack, 'Bildung von Regierungskoalitionen, dargestellt am Beispiel der Koalisionsentscheidung der F.D.P. von 1969', *Zeitschrift für Parlamentsfragen*, 1976, pp. 400–425.
19. Hans Haibach, 'Nach dem Schiedsspruch sind Partei und Fraktion zerstrittener denn je,' *Frankfurter Allgemeine Zeitung*, 5 March 1982, p. 3.
20. 'FDP auf dem Podest,' *Der Spiegel*, No. 28, 1982, p. 25.
21. Arnulf Baring, 'Die Wende kam schon vor acht Jahren', *Die Zeit*, No. 41, 1982, pp. 4ff.
22. Members of the Schmidt administration are, however, inclined to look for certain individual 'traitors'. For details see 'Da war ein richtiger großer Schmerz. Klaus Böllings Tagebuch über die letzten 30 Tage des Kanzlers Helmut Schmidt,' *Der Spiegel*, No. 41, 1982, pp. 61–126.
23. Helmut Norpoth, 'Choosing a Coalition Partner. Mass Preferences and Elite Decisions in West Germany', *Comparative Political Studies*, 1980, p. 447; Udo Bermbach, 'Situationen der Regierungsbildung 1969', *Zeitschrift für Parlamentsfragen* 1970, No. 1, p. 5.
24. Oskar Niedermayer, 'Möglichkeiten des Koalitionswechsel. Zur parteiinternen Verankerung der bestehenden Koalitionsstruktur im Parteiensystem der Bundesrepublik Deutschland', *Zeitschrift für Parlamentsfragen*, 1982, p. 107; and a recent survey, 'Stirbt die FDP, überlebt Kohl: Spiegel-Umfrage über die politische Situation nach dem Regierungswechsel in Bonn', *Der Spiegel*, No. 41, 1982, pp. 33–9.
25. Kaack, *op. cit.*, p. 68.
26. Klaus von Beyme, *The Political System of the Federal Republic of Germany*, Aldershot, Gower, 1983, pp. 52ff.
27. Ursula Hoffmann-Lange, 'Sozialliberale und konservative Vorstellung in der FDP' in Lothar Albertin (ed), *Politischer Liberalismus in der Bundesrepublik* (Göttingen, Vandenhoeck & Ruprecht, 1980), p. 173.
28. Lothar Albertin, 'Die koalitionspolitische Umorientierung der FDP 1966–1969. Fall oder Modell?' in Albertin, *op. cit.*, p. 211.
29. Eckhart Kauntz, 'Opposition ist dumm. Die rheinlandpfälzische FDP sucht einen Weg zur Koalitionsaussage für die CDU', *Frankfurter Allgemeine Zeitung*, 26 July 1982, p. 8.
30. William H. Riker, *The Theory of Political Coalitions* (New Haven, Yale University Press, 1962).
31. Lawrence C. Dodd, *Coalitions in Parliamentary Government* (Princeton, Princeton University Press, 1976), p. 208.
32. Hermann Meyn, *Die Deutsche Partei. Entwicklung und Programmatik einer national konservativen Rechtspartei nach 1945* (Düsseldorf, Droste, 1965), p. 146.
33. Franz Neumann, *Der Block der Heimatvertriebenen und Entrechteten 1950–1960* (Meisenheim, Hain, 1968), pp. 105.
34. Abram de Swaan, *Coalition Theories and Cabinet Formations* (Amsterdam/London/New York, Elsevier, 1973), p. 80.
35. Gerhard Loewenberg, *Parliament in the German Political System* (Ithaca, Cornell University Press, 1967), Chap. 5.
36. Deutscher Bundestag, *Chronik, Debatten, Gesetze, Kommentare*. Vols. 1–8. (Bonn, Presse-und Informationsamt des Deutschen Bundestages).
37. Konrad Adenauer, *Erinnerungen 1945–1953* (Stuttgart, DVA, 1965), p. 228.
38. Wolfgang Kralewski, 'Bundesregierung und Bundestag' in Carl-Joachim Friedrich and Benno Reifenberg (eds), *Sprache und Politik. Festgabe für Dolf Sternberger zum 60. Geburtstag* (Heidelberg, Schneider, 1968), pp. 424, 426.
39. For this type see Wilfried Dewachter, 'De partijenstaat in den Westeuropese polyarchie: en proeve tot meting,' *Res Publica*, 1981, pp. 115–123.
40. Jürgen Domes, *Mehrheitsfraktion und Bundesregierung Aspekte des Verhältnisses der Fraktion der CDU/CSU im Zweiten und Dritten deutschen Bundestag zum Kabinett Adenauer*. Westdeutsche Verlag, Cologne Opladen, 1964, p. 76.

41. cf. Gerhard Lehmbruch, 'The Ambiguous Coalition in West Germany' in Mattei Dogan and Richard Rose (eds), *European Politics. A Reader* (London, Macmillan, 1971), p. 557. For a descriptive account of the bargaining process, see Wolfgang F. Dexheimer, *Koalitionsverhandlungen in Bonn 1961, 1965, 1969* (Bonn, Eichholz Verlag, 1973).

42. For this general typology see Klaus von Beyme, *Parteien in westlichen Demokratien*, *op. cit.*

43. Heribert Knorr, *Der parlamentarische Entscheidungsprozeß während der Großen Koalition 1966 bis 1969. Struktur und Einfluß der Koalitionsfraktionen und ihr Verhältnis zur Regierung der Großen Koalition* (Meisenheim, Hain, 1975), p. 48.

44. Kurt Klotzbach, *Der Weg zur Staatspartei* (Berlin/Bonn, Dietz, 1982).

45. Baring, *Machtwechsel, op. cit.*, p. 755; Ulrich Lohmar, *Das hohe Haus. Der Bundestag und die Verfassungswirklichkeit* (Stuttgart, DVA, 1975), p. 140.

46. 'Kohl erhebt öffentlich Anspruch auf die Kanzlerkandidatur', *Frankfurter Allgemeine Zeitung*, 31 July 1982, p. 1.

47. Klaus Günther, *Der Kanzlerwechsel in der Bundesrepublik. Adenauer – Erhard – Kiesinger* (Hannover, Verlag für Literatur und Zeitgeschehen, 1970), p. 54.

48. Erich Mende, 'Die schwierige Regierungsbildung 1961' in Dieter Blumenwitz *et al.*, *Konrad Adenauer und seine Zeit* (Stuttgart, DVA, 1972, Vol. I), p. 325.

49. Adenauer, *op. cit.* Vol. I, p. 228; cf. also Alt, *op. cit.*, p. 74.

50. Appel, *op. cit.*, p. 150.

51. Felix von Eckhardt, *Ein unordentliches Leben. Lebenserinnerungen* (Düsseldorf, Econ, 1967), p. 274.

52. *ibid.*, p. 276. See also Neumann, *op. cit.*, p. 108.

53. Bruce Bueno de Mesquita, 'Coalition Payoffs and Electoral Performance in European Democracies', *Comparative Political Studies*, Vol. XII, No. 1, 1979, p. 78.

54. For details see Klaus von Beyme (ed.), *Die großen Regierungserklärungen der deutschen Bundeskanzler von Adenauer bis Schmidt* (Munich, Hanser, 1979), p. 42.

55. von Eckhardt, *op. cit.*, p. 273.

56. Adenauer, *Erinnerungen*, Vol. I, *op. cit.*, p. 236.

57. Willy Brandt, *Begegnungen und Einsichten. Die Jahre 1960–1975* (Hamburg, Hoffmann & Campe, 1976), p. 295.

58. See Klaus von Beyme, *Die politische Elite in der Bundesrepublik Deutschland* (Munich, Piper, 1974, 2nd edition), p. 49.

59. See Klaus von Beyme, *Die parlamentarischen Regierungssysteme in Europa* (Munich, Piper, 1973, 2nd edition), p. 828.

60. Baring, *Machtwechsel, op. cit.*, p. 569.

61. Brandt, *op. cit.*, p. 571 'My question of confidence . . . was answered negatively according to my wishes', which seems to be a contradiction in terms.

62. Norpoth, 'The German Federal Republic: Coalition Government at the Brink', *op. cit.*, p. 22.

63. von Eckhardt, *op. cit.*, p. 521.

64. *Verhandlungen des Deutschen Bundestages*. (henceforth quoted as Sten. Ber. = Stenographischer Bericht) Vol. I, 21 September 1949, p. 33B.

65. Sten. Ber. Vol. 50, 6 December 1961, p. 533.

66. Sten. Ber. Vol. 100, 17 December 1976, p. 56C.

67. Adolf Schüle, *Koalitionsvereinbarungen im Lichte des Verfassungsrechts* (Tübingen, Mohr, 1964), p. 101.

68. von Beyme, *Die großen Regierungserklärungen*, *op.cit.*, p. 126.

69. Brandt, *op. cit.*, p. 178.

70. Text in Udo Bermbach, 'Stationen der Regierungs – und Oppositionsbildung 1980'. *Zeitschrift für Parlamentsfragen*, 1981, p. 76.

71. Knorr, *op. cit.*, p. 223.

72. Ernst Benda, 'Verfassungsprobleme der Großen Koalition' in Benda (ed.) *Die große Koalition. 1966–1969* (Freudenstadt, 1969), p. 165.

73. Quoted in Brandt, *op. cit.*, p. 182.

74. Alex Möller, *Genosse Generaldirektor* (Munich, Knaur, 1980), p. 379.

75. Baring, *Machtwechsel, op. cit.*, p. 713.

3 Two Logics of Coalition Policy: The West German Case
Manfred G. Schmidt

Introduction

The literature on coalition governments has been dominated by studies which focus on the formation, patterns of stability and instability, and the internal mode of operation of coalitions.[1] Another topic which has been frequently addressed in the literature is policy pay-offs in the form of cabinet seats.[2] However, topics such as the relationship between coalitions and the substance of policy have until recently been a rather underdeveloped research area. Moreover, second-and-third-order consequences of these policies have rarely been examined.

This chapter addresses some of these policy topics. One of the questions which will be investigated concerns the extent to which the policies of coalition governments have differed from those pursued by single governing parties. I also propose to study in more detail to what extent the differential political composition of coalition governments has had a measurable impact on policy. My focus will be on the West German coalition governments in Bonn and in the *Länder* from the early 1950s up to the breakdown of the Sozialdemokratische Partei Deutschlands – Freidemokratische Partei (SPD-FDP) coalition in September 1982.

The argument will proceed as follows. An overview of the coalitional status and the political composition of the governments in Bonn and on the level of the *Länder* will be presented in the first part of the chapter. It will be shown that a wide variety of coalitions characterise government in West German politics, although there has been a trend at *Land* level away from all-inclusive coalition towards oversized and minimum-winning coalitions of bourgeois-liberal or, alternatively, of social democratic-liberal complexion, and then towards single governing parties in the 1970s. In contrast to this, the political situation in Bonn has been characterised almost exclusively by coalitions. Among the smaller coalition parties, the FDP has commanded a strategic role. Its ideological goals, its social composition and its position as regards policy within the party system must therefore be discussed.

In the second part of the chapter, the major studies and data on the policies pursued by the various governments will be summarised. It will become apparent that the policies of Christlich-Demokratische Union/Christliche Soziale Union (CDU/CSU) and SPD-dominated governments have many characteristics in common. However, it will also be shown that measurable policy differences do exist which are broadly in accordance with the parties' ideologies and the interests of their social constituencies. For example, CDU/CSU-dominated governments have pursued policies which were guided by the model of 'social capitalism', whereas SPD-dominated governments tended to base their policies on the model of the 'Keynesian welfare state'. In each case, the impact of the coalition with the FDP is also more or less clearly measurable.

In the third part of the chapter, the focus is on two hypotheses which have been frequently advanced: the policy-immobilisme hypothesis, according to which coalition governments tend towards an 'under-production' of policy, and the policy-overproduction hypothesis, according to which coalitions tend to produce a surplus of policy. I shall argue that the policy outcome of coalition governments depend cru-cially on two additional variables. Coalitions in periods of economic prosperity and coalition governments, whose political complexion is more or less in harmony with the power relationships in the party system and in industrial relations, will typically 'overproduce' policies. In contrast to this, periods of economic crisis and a large discrepancy between the political composition of governments and the power relationships in the political substructure are likely to generate a pattern of policy-immobilisme on the part of the coalition government, with the SPD-FDP coalition in the second half of the 1970s being one of the major examples of this. The analysis suggests that a distinction between 'two logics of coalition policy' is fruitful. Finally, some of the problems which will confront a government dominated by the CDU/CSU will be discussed.

Political composition and coalitional status

Coalitions have been the typical form of government in West German politics. In this respect, politics in the Federal Republic deviate from the pattern of alternating single governing parties which characterises the majority of Anglo-American democracies. However, the West German coalition pattern is also at variance with that of many other industrial democracies. Governments in West Germany have been characterised by a wide variety of types of coalition. All-inclusive coalitions were prevalent in the immediate post-war period. There were three main reasons for this. One was the post-totalitarian, anti-fascist consensus among politicians and parties. A second reason seems to have been a latent pattern of opposition to the Occupation forces, and a third appears to have been the attempt to share responsibilities and pay-offs equitably in a period of utter scarcity.[3] However, as soon as the Cold War began, all-party coalitions were replaced by coalitions which excluded the Communist Party and, later on, by minimum-winning coalitions of various political compositions. Although a clear trend towards minimum-winning coalitions had emerged in the 1950s, grand coalitions between the CDU and the SPD had already been a familiar phenomenon in the *Länder* and, from 1966 to 1969, also in Bonn. At the level of the *Land* government, it was not until the late 1960s that the Christian Democrats and the SPD formed single-party governments, whereas at federal level different coalition patterns have prevailed (see Tables 3.1 and 3.2).

The FDP's strategic role

The frequency of coalition governments demonstrates that neither of the major parties in the Federal Republic has yet succeeded in mobilising a majority, although the proportion of the vote gained by the smaller parties has declined. As far as the federal government and the majority of the *Land* governments are concerned, the FDP has commanded a strategic position. To an increasing extent, minimum-winning coalitions could be formed only if the cooperation of the FDP was won. Although the FDP vote has been moderate in size – it ranges from some 5 per cent to some 12 per cent – its participation in government has been quite disproportionately strong. Thus the Liberals have disposed of an important role in the policy formation process.

As regards policy, the FDP is asymmetrically located between the CDU/CSU and the SPD. Its economic and political liberal ideology reflects the interests of a social constituency which is characterised by a middle-class ideology, a low degree of religious affiliation, belief in a competitive economic market and a preference order, according to which 'self-reliance' in the market is more important than social protection organised by the welfare state and/or the trade unions. Thus, the Free Democrats' position in the cleavage structure of the Federal Republic stands in marked contrast to the positions taken by its larger coalition partners.

The FDP experienced a major change in the 1960s and early 1970s. Broadly speaking, it was a change from a party dominated by its national-liberal wing to a party in which the relative weight of the left-wing has strongly increased.[4] Nevertheless, some of the major characteristics have been left unchanged: in contrast to both the SPD and the CDU/CSU, the FDP is not a party which is ideologically affiliated to the trade unions; in contrast to the CDU/CSU, it is strongly secular in character; and finally, and again in contrast to both the CDU/CSU and the SPD, it is only marginally linked to the interests of the welfare state bureaucracy and the interests of the 'transfer classes'[5]

Two Logics of Coalition Policy 41

Table 3.1 Political composition and coalition status of federal governments (1949–82)

9/1949– 9/1953a)	CDU/CSU, FDP, DP	Bourgeois minimum-winning coalition
9/1953–10/1956a)	CDU/CSU, FDP, DP, GB/BHE	Oversized bourgeois coalition
10/1956– 9/1957	CDU/CSU, DP (FVP)	Bourgeois minimum-winning coalition
10/1957– 9/1961a)	CDU/CSU, DP	Bourgeois minimum-winning coalition
10/1961– 9/1965a)	CDU/CSU, FDP	Bourgeois minimum-winning coalition
9/1965–11/1966a)	CDU/CSU, FDP	Bourgeois minimum-winning coalition
12/1966– 9/1969	CDU/CSU, SPD	Oversized great coalition
10/1969– 9/1972a)	SPD, FDP	Social-Democratic minimum-winning coalition
10/1972– 9/1976a)	SPD, FDP	Social-Democratic minimum-winning coalition
10/1976– 9/1980a)	SPD, FDP	Social-Democratic minimum-winning coalition
10/1980– 9/1982a)	SPD, FDP	Social-Democratic minimum-winning coalition
9/1982–10/1982	SPD	Social-Democratic minority government
10/1982– 3/1983a)	CDU/CSU, FDP	Bourgeois minimum-winning coalition

a) National election

Table 3.2   Political composition of land governments 1949–82 (month/year)

		All-party-government		
Baden-Wuerttemberg	SPD+DVP/FDP 4/52–9/53 CDU+SPD 12/66–4/72	All-party-government 10/53–6/60 CDU 4/72–12/82	CDU+FDP+BHE 6/60–6/64	CDU+FDP 6/64–12/66
Bavaria	SPD+BVP 5/45–9/45 CSU+FDP+BHE 10/57–12/62	SPD+CSU+KPD 10/45–12/46 CSU+BP 12/62–12/66	CSU+SPD 12/46–12/54 CSU 12/66–12/82	SPD+BP+FDP+BHE 12/54–10/57
Berlin West	SPD+FDP+CDU 1/49–9/53 SPD 4/71–4/75	CDU+FDP 9/53–1/55 SPD+FDP 4/75–6/81	SPD+CDU 1/55–3/63 CDU 6/81–12/82	SPD+FDP 3/63–4/71
Bremen	SPD+BDV+KPD 6/45–1/48 SPD 12/71–12/82	SPD+BDV 1/48–11/51	SPD+FDP+CDU 12/51–12/59	SPD+FDP 12/59–12/71
Hamburg	CDU+SPD+FDP 8/45–9/46 SPD+FDP 12/57–4/66	SPD+FDP 11/46–2/50 SPD 4/66–4/70	SPD 2/50–12/53 SPD+FDP 4/70–6/78	CDU+FDP+DP 12/53–11/57 SPD 6/78–12/82
Hesse	SPD+CDU+KPD 10/45–12/46 SPD+GB/BHE 1/63–1/67	SPD+CDU 1/47–1/51 SPD 1/67–11/70	SPD 1/51–1/55 SPD+FDP 12/70–10/82	SPD+GDB 1/55–12/62 SPD 10/82–12/82

Lower Saxony	SPD+CDU+NLP+KPD 11/46–4/47 CDU+DP+FDP+BHE 5/55–11/57 SPD+CDU 5/65–7/70 CDU 5/78–12/82	SPD+CDU+NLP+Z 6/47–3/48 SPD+CDU+DP 11/57–5/59 SPD 7/70–6/74	SPD+CDU+Z 6/48–6/51 SPD+FDP+BHE 5/59–6/63 SPD+FDP 6/74–12/75	SPD+BHE+Z 6/51–5/55 SPD/FDP 6/63–5/65 CDU+FDP 1/76–5/78
North Rhine Westphalia	SPD+FDP+Z+KPD 8/46–12/46 CDU+FDP 7/54–2/56 SPD+FDP 12/66–6/80	CDU+SPD+FDP+Z 12/46–4/47 SPD+FDP+Z 2/56–3/58 SPD 6/80–12/82	CDU+SPD+KPD+Z 6/47–7/50 CDU 7/58–7/62	CDU+Z 7/50–7/54 CDU+FDP 7/62–12/66
Rhineland–Palatine	CDU+SPD+KPD 12/46–6/47 CDU 5/71–12/82	CDU 6/47–7/47	CDU+SPD+KPD 7/47–6/51	CDU+FDP 6/51–5/71
Saar	CDU+DPS+SPD 1/56–1/59 CDU+FDP 7/65–7/70	CDU+SPD+CVP 2/59–4/59 CDU 12/70–4/77	CDU+SPD+CVP/CSU 4/59–1/61 CDU+FDP 4/77–12/82	CDU+FDP/DPS 1/61–7/65
Schleswig-Holstein	CDU+SPD+KPD 9/46–11/46 CDU+FDP 6/51–7/51	CDU+SPD 11/46–4/47 CDU+FDP+BHE 7/51–1/63	SPD 4/47–4/50 CDU+FDP 1/63–5/71	CDU+BHE+FDP+DP 9/50–6/51 CDU 5/71–12/82

which have been created by the welfare state.

Table 3.3 indicates in more detail the different parties' positions on a number of simple left-right policy scales. It also shows the relative distance between the parties. For example, in the case of an SPD-FDP coalition one would expect in some issue areas, such as foreign policy, measures intended to increase equal opportunity, and citizens' rights, a high degree of ideological affinity between the parties. By contrast, however, SPD-FDP coalitions tend to be overloaded with economic issues and pro-labour and pro-welfare state measures. In these areas the FDP is ideologically much closer to the CDU/CSU. On the other hand, Christian Democratic-Liberal coalitions tend to be put under strong pressure by religious and citizens' rights issues and by conflicts about law and order.

Whenever the FDP has participated in government, it has always been well endowed with cabinet posts. Relative to the number of parliamentary seats it has held, it has always managed to get a disproportion of cabinet seats (mostly the Department of Justice or the Department of the Interior, the Ministry of Finance or the Department of Economic Affairs, the Department of Foreign Affairs or the Department of Development Aid, and – from 1969 onwards – the Department of Agriculture).

Table 3.4 demonstrates clearly the exorbitant pay-offs exacted by the smaller pivotal coalition partners, especially the Deutsche Partei (DP), the CSU in the 1950s and the FDP in the 1970s.

To what extent has the command of cabinet seats affected the substance of policy? That is the question which the next section of this chapter attempts to answer.

From CDU/CSU social capitalism to SPD welfare capitalism

Considering the predominance of coalitions in the Federal Republic, it is not surprising that there are many similarities in the policies pursued by governments of quite different political composition. One could plausibly argue that the bargaining process within coalitions tends to exclude extreme policy stances and issues which are highly controversial between the partners, and therefore that conditions are conducive to the diminution of policy differences.

This view finds some confirmation in the evidence. The CDU/CSU Governments, the grand coalition and the governments dominated by the SPD have basically operated with similar policy instruments and within a set of broadly similar constraints, with the capitalist economy, the democratic political order and the 'tax state'[6] being some of the major constraints on and imperatives of policy-making.[7] For example, CDU- and SPD-dominated governments have invested a great deal of effort in supporting the private economy. Both have also softened the

Table 3.3 Party position on issues

Issue	Rank order on left–right scale[a]		
1) Nationalisation and control of means of production	1) SPD	2) CDU/CSU and FDP	
2) Government role in economic planning	1) SPD	2) CDU/CSU and FDP	
3) Public debt	1) SPD	2) CDU/CSU and FDP	
4) Distribution of wealth	1) SPD	2) CDU/CSU	3) FDP
5) Collective provision of social welfare	1) SPD	2) CDU/CSU	3) FDP
6) Protection and support of trade unions	1) SPD	2) CDU/CSU	3) FDP
7) Extension of non-class political participation	1) SPD and FDP	2) CDU/CSU	
8) Centralisation/decentralisation of state	1) SPD	2) FDP	3) CDU/CSU
9) Equal opportunity	1) SPD	2) FDP	3) CDU/CSU
10) Protection of environment	1) SPD and FDP	2) CDU/CSU	
11) Strict law and order policy	1) SPD and FDP	2) CDU/CSU	
12) Degree of political tolerance towards new political movements	1) SPD and FDP	2) CDU/CSU	
13) Secularisation of society	1) FDP	2) SPD	3) CDU/CSU
14) Foreign policy: cooperation with Eastern countries	1) SPD	2) FDP	3) CDU/CSU
15) Development Aid	1) SPD	2) FDP	3) CDU/CSU

a) The rank order is based on a summary of data from the 1960s and 1970s. John Clayton Thomas, *The Decline of Ideology in Western Political Parties: A Comparative Analysis of Changing Policy Orientations* (Sage Professional Papers, Contemporary Political Sociology Series, 1975) and Lawrence C. Dodd, *op. cit.* and common sense on the part of good journalists were particularly helpful in constructing this table. The entries have also been successfully checked with data on the preferences and attitudes of elites in the FRG in the late 1970s (Rudolph Wildemann, *Linkage Problems: Positional Elites and Party System in the FRG*, IPSA World Congress, Rio de Janeiro, 1982)

practice of capitalism by means of regulations and welfare provisions. Moreover, the foreign policies chosen by the various governments have basically been geared to economic, military and political integration into the Western world. Finally, the CDU- and SPD-dominated governments have not hesitated to undertake repressive measures against radical political movements (mostly of left-wing complexion).

In order to explain the wide range of policy similarities, one must

Table 3.4   Coalition pay-offs: ratio of cabinet posts and Bundestag seats 1949–82

Year	Ratio of cabinet posts and Bundestag seats held by coalition parties[a]					
	CDU	CSU	FDP	DP	BHE	SPD
1949	0.78	1.84	0.86	1.79	—	—
1953	0.78	0.96	1.40	2.20	1.25	—
1956[b]	1.28	1.01	—	2.30	—	—
1957	0.88	1.20	—	1.90	—	—
1961	0.88	1.23	1.15	—	—	—
1963[b]	0.99	0.89	1.09	—	—	—
1965	0.90	1.23	1.08	—	—	—
1966[b]	0.93	1.29	—	—	—	0.99
1969	—	—	1.58	—	—	0.92
1972	—	—	1.74	—	—	0.82
1974[b]	—	—	1.65	—	—	0.88
1976	—	—	1.62	—	—	0.89
1980	—	—	1.20	—	—	0.95
1982[c]	—	—	—	—	—	1.00
1982[b][d]	0.80	1.33	1.36	—	—	—

a) Scores larger than unity indicate pay-offs of disproportionate size. Scores are computed as follows: Party A's ratio of cabinet posts divided by party A's proportion of sum of Bundestag seats held by coalition parties.
b) Reshuffle within a legislative period.
c) SPD minority government in September 1982.
d) October 1982.

Source: The data up to 1966 were taken from Peter Merkl, *op. cit.* The data from 1969 to 1982 were computed from *Keesings Archiv der Gegenwart.*

go beyond the coalition-bargaining hypothesis and the concept of a democratic 'capitalist state'.[8] Over and above politico-economic constraints, the strong degree of continuity in policy-making is derived from two characteristics of West German politics: a high degree of interaction between the state, the law and society (*Verrechtlichung*) and an extraordinarily high degree of interlocking in the federal political structure (*Politikverflechtung*) reduce the directive capacity of party competition and thus strongly confine the room for manoeuvre available to governments.[9]

Institutional arrangements and politico-economic structures act both as constraints and imperatives for government activities, but they do not determine the content of the policy-making process. However limited the degree of freedom may be, politics does make a difference in policy outputs and outcomes. Comparing the performance of West German governments, one can clearly observe measurable and politically important differences as well as a solid base of commonly shared ideologies and policies. The ideologies of the governing parties did have a measurable impact, with the 'social capitalism' model of the CDU/CSU[10] and the SPD model of a 'Keynesian welfare capitalism' being without doubt more important than the ideologies held by the smaller liberal coalition partner.

CDU/CSU-dominated coalitions in Bonn

The CDU/CSU-dominated coalitions in Bonn established the 'social capitalism' model. Policies were generally geared to the reconstruction and growth of a capitalist market economy. Although a number of fairly comprehensive social security measures were enacted, the politically important traditional middle class, the economically strong property-owners and the higher-income employees were in a privileged position. The free enterprise approach and the welfare provisions advocated by the CDU/CSU coincided with a strict anti-Socialist and anti-Communist policy stance in domestic and foreign policy-making. The dominant mode of policy-making in the 1950s and early 1960s was pluralist, distributive and process-oriented in character.[11] It was characterised by a lack of co-ordination, medium- and long-term planning, redistribution or anticipatory demand management.

This mode of policy-making proved to be insufficiently equipped to deal with the challenges generated by the increasingly complex nature of the economy in the 1960s and the increase in demands for redistributive reforms in domestic and foreign policy.

The grand coalition (1966–9)

Probably the major achievement of the grand coalition between the CDU/CSU and the SPD in Bonn from 1966 to 1969 lies in one of these areas. Though some critics have rightly pointed to the government's limited capacity for structural reform,[12] it is apparent that the coalition partners had pushed each other towards a major innovation in the field of economic and budgetary policy, with the Keynesian law on growth and stability (*Stabilitätsgesetz*), the reform of the fiscal constitution (*Finanzverfassung*) and the introduction of budgetary planning instruments being some of the major examples. The foundations of the Keynesian welfare state of the SPD-FDP coalition governments in the 1970s were thus clearly laid during the grand coalition era.[13] It would seem plausible to argue that these reforms were, at least to some extent, the price for the SPD's consent to two other projects of the government: the ratification of the *Notstandsverfassung* (emergency law) and the maintenance of the *status quo* in foreign policy vis à vis the Socialist countries.

SPD-FDP coalitions in Bonn 1969–76

The second push towards the modernisation of West German policy-making began with the SPD-FDP coalition in 1969. The new *Ostpolitik of cooperation* with the Socialist countries and policies of domestic reform feature prominently on the coalition's agenda. Conservative critics have frequently argued that the new *Ostpolitik* 'sold out' West German interests. They also argued that the politics of domestic reform introduced a transition to socialism. These views are not compatible with the evidence. More balanced accounts of SPD-FDP policy-making do indicate important policy changes towards the SPD model of a Keynesian welfare capitalism which is characterised by a wider range of state intervention, policies more in the interest of organised labour, and comprehensive welfare provisions.[14] But though these changes were important, they did not fundamentally change the social, political and economic fabric of West German society.

The expansion of the welfare state and the pro-trade union measures were, of course, strongly supported by the SPD, whereas the liberal coalition partner tolerated the expansion of the welfare state with an attitude of critical neutrality. However, there was one noteworthy exception from this pattern: the introduction of a generous social security system for farmers and the self-employed middle class was actively supported by the FDP. The reasons for this are basically political in character, for these latter measures coincided strongly with electoral interests on the part of the FDP.

There were other policy areas where the impact of the FDP's ideology was important such as reform of the divorce and abortion laws. In policy areas where the coalition partners' ideology differed widely – the codetermination issue, the reforms of industrial training and the revision of the law on works councils (*Betriebsverfassungsgesetz*), for example – the ultimate compromise clearly indicated an unwillingness on the part of the FDP to endorse far-reaching pro-labour controls of the private economy.

SPD-FDP coalitions in a period of economic crisis (1975/6-82)

The expansion of the welfare state and the commitment to full employment under SPD-FDP rule in the first half of the 1970s generated some unintended side-effects. Revenues collected by the state increased both in absolute terms and relative to GDP to such an extent that the government became increasingly confronted with symptoms of tax-welfare backlash. Moreover, the considerable increase in social security contributions tended to move non-wage labour costs beyond a critical level. Finally, a government committed to social reform tended to strengthen the expectations of its supporters and also to provoke protest on the part of those who perceived themselves to be on the losing side. It would thus seem plausible to argue that the maturing of the Keynesian welfare state under SPD-FDP rule has contributed to the slow-down in economic growth and the rise in unemployment since the mid-1970s, because the employers, who had always been critical of a SPD government, now subscribed more rapidly and intensively to labour-saving technologies, capital export measures, and alternative investment opportunities on the money market than would otherwise have been the case.[15]

The economic crisis, mass unemployment and growing budget deficits tended to undermine the room for manoeuvre needed to continue the pattern of a reform-oriented Keynesian welfare state. The SPD-FDP initially attempted to manage the crisis without touching the previously implemented reforms. However, expenditure cuts and cuts in welfare provisions soon proved to be an indispensable way out of the policy stalemate which had been generated within the coalition. The FDP had successfully wrested from the SPD the policy of a firm limitation on deficit spending. The Liberals also resisted an increase in the tax revenue of the state, and successfully bargained tax reductions for labour market programmes. In conjunction with the consistently high level of unemployment and the strict control of inflationary pressure, this policy clearly forced the government to adopt a more restrictive fiscal policy stance than the majority of the SPD and the trade unions would have preferred.

The social constituency of the SPD was hit much harder by high levels of unemployment and cuts in state expenditures than was that of the FDP. The SPD was not unrealistic in assuming that the impact of the crisis would weaken the support it had mobilised over the previous decade. Moreover, it was the SPD which tended to be the main loser on another domestic front: the moderate pro-atomic-energy policy pursued by the government, the overreaction to the terrorist activities in the autumn of 1977, the '*Berufsverbot*' issue and the government's participation in the NATO decision to counter the deployment of Soviet SS-20 missiles by a stepped-up armament policy in 1983 (*Nachrüstungsbeschluß*) tended to estrange many young and better educated voters from the SPD.

Within the SPD-FDP coalition, the capacity and willingness to build a consensus declined dramatically after the 1980 election. Both partners increasingly brought their original policy goals to the fore. Within the FDP, the right wing and centre activated its liberal economic programme. According to this programme a restrictive fiscal policy was required to overcome the crisis, with a reduction of the public debt, cuts in direct taxes and an increase in indirect taxes, generous support for private investment by means of tax reforms and deregulation, redistribution between public consumption and public investment expenditures, the dismantling of labour protection laws and the law on the protection of tenants, and cuts in public income maintenance programmes being among the major measures needed.

In contrast to this, the SPD tended to favour a policy which was meant to make a strategy of supply-oriented modernisation of the economy compatible with the maintenance of a strong welfare state. It is obvious that this policy would, at least in the short run, have required a greater increase in tax revenues, or alternatively higher levels of deficit spending than were acceptable to the Free Democrats. The final breakdown of the coalition was thus structurally programmed by the incompatibility of a strong welfare state and a market-economy-oriented policy approach.

Policies of the Land governments

As far as the relationship between governments and policy in the *Länder* is concerned, one can, broadly speaking, identify a pattern similar to the one we have observed at the level of the federal government. In those policy areas where the *Länder* still dispose of a relatively high degree of autonomy (education, law and order, labour market policy in the public sector and to some extent welfare provisions) a more or less consistent party difference is observable. Controlling for levels of economic wealth and availability of fiscal resources, the typical pattern is as follows. SPD-dominated coalitions and single SPD governments have produced policies which are moderately different from those of CDU- or CSU- dominated governments or single Christian Democratic governments.[16] Under Christian Democratic rule, governments have tended to spend somewhat less on education and social affairs than SPD governments. They have also hesitated to secularise and reform the educational system. Moreover, the Christian Democrats have been less active in expanding the public economy and the level of public employment and less active than their SPD counterparts in transferring resources into the maintenance of law and order. While the greater propensity to spend on law and order under Social Democratic rule is partly explained by the different socio-economic structures of SPD- and CDU-dominated Länder (the latter are on average somewhat less urbanised and less rich), it would also seem to indicate a conscious choice on the part of the SPD leadership: the party attempts to demonstrate its ability to rule and to win the critical neutrality or the active support of the police and of those parts of the electorate which are in favour of a 'strong state'.

On the other hand, party differences do not spill over into every policy area. For example, no systematic differences exist in areas such as economic policy and industrial infrastructure. It should further be pointed out that although the *'Berufsverbot'* issue has been highly controversial, no clear-cut policy differences in terms of the political composition of governments have been observable. Restrictive and repressive practices have been undertaken by many CDU- and SPD-governed *Länder*, though the latter have ultimately been more inclined to change and to liberalise their previously implemented rules.

Overall, the policies pursued by governments in the *Länder* indicate that the parties' policies are, at least in some areas, in accordance with their respective ideologies. The SPD tends to build a society which is regulated by a state with strong political, economic, social and coercive capacities, whereas the Christian Democrats' model is based on a strong market sector, a somewhat lower degree of state intervention, and less equality.

Policy immobilisme

The political performance of coalition governments has often been the subject of controversy. For example, it has been argued that coalitions tend to generate a policy immobilisme. According to another view, coalitions tend to overproduce policy. It can be argued that both hypotheses shed some light on the dynamics of coalition in West Germany, if they are put into the context of a broader model of the policy-making process.

Viewed from a theoretical perspective, both hypotheses seem plausible. Moreover, evidence does seem to exist for each of them. According to the policy-immobilisme hypothesis, the dynamics of consensus-building within coalitions tends to exclude all those issues and activities which are characterised by a zero-sum game for the coalition partners. According to this view, a filter system would operate in the process of agenda-building which excluded issues that were incompatible with the least common ideological denominator. It could be further argued that this common dominator is smaller, the greater the ideological, social and political heterogeneity within the coalition. Hence, one would expect that coalitions tend to 'underproduce' policy, in the sense that they do less than is required or would be the case under a single governing party. According to another version of the policy-immobilisme hypothesis, coalitions can politically well afford a policy immobilisme, since their expected joint vote is likely to be sufficient to maintain a majority position or, alternatively, at least sufficient to gain a majority by means of marginally increasing the number of coalition partners.

Empirically, there is indeed evidence which supports the immobilisme hypothesis. For example, the all-party government and the mechanisms inherent in the referendum system in Switzerland seem to account for much of the underproduction of reforms and the policy immobilisme. It is also a well-established fact that the bourgeois

coalitions in Sweden between 1976 and 1982 and the bourgeois-Social
Democratic coalitions in Belgium in the 1970s and early 1980s have had
enormous difficulties in reaching a compromise on redistributive
issues, such as the linguistic, regional and economic conflicts in
Belgium and the welfare-versus-taxation issue and the atomic energy
issue in the Swedish case. An increasing inability to compromise and a
tendency towards policy stalemate between coalition partners is also a
well-known feature of West German politics, with the CDU/CSU-FDP
government in Bonn in 1966 and the SPD-FDP government in the
early 1980s offering major illustrations.

On the other hand, there is evidence which is clearly incompatible
with the policy-immobilisme prediction. According to an alternative
hypothesis, coalitions can manage to overcome constraints which are
set up by broad exclusion principles and unanimity requirements. It is
argued that the mechanism which broadens the room for manoeuvre is
basically a bargaining process offering sufficient pay-offs to each participant to make concessions possible. According to this view, the
consequence would be an overproduction of policy; and indeed there is
also evidence for this view. Some of the West German coalitions are
good cases in point.

– For example, the federal governments in the 1950s and early 1960s produced
  remarkably high levels and rates of expansion of welfare provisions. In fact,
  the CDU/CSU-dominated coalition governments produced a 'too high
  degree of state intervention' and 'too much collective welfare' – relative to
  their ideology and the performance of other OECD nations with a similar or
  even more left-wing biased complexion of governments.[17]
– We could also argue that a similar process of policy overproduction occurred
  under the grand coalitions between the CDU/CSU and the SPD. The overproduction of new economic policy instruments between 1966 and 1969
  strongly deviated from the 'politics of non-planning'[18] which had characterised the previous governments' approach. There was also the extraordinary
  expansion of educational expenditure under the new CDU-SPD coalition in
  Baden-Wuerttemberg at the end of the 1960s.
– Moreover, the strong increase in welfare state efforts and in transfer classes[19]
  under SPD-FDP rule in the 1970s has also been higher than one would expect
  on the basis of ideological preferences held by the FDP.
– Finally, the most comprehensive evidence in support of the overproduction
  hypothesis has been put forward in recent comparative policy studies. For
  example, studying state expenditures in twelve OECD nations, Jürgen Kohl
  has advanced the hypothesis that 'centre governments' (mostly conservative-
  socialist coalitions) and 'centre-right coalitions' have the greatest propensity
  to increase social transfer expenditures and total state expenditures, followed
  by 'centre-left governments'. In contrast to this, purely conservative governments have the least propensity to expand the public economy. Jürgen
  Kohl's findings suggest[20] that the dynamics of coalition governments override left and right differences . . . The necessity to build coalitions in order to
  gain or to preserve executive power requires compromises, and the attempt to

reconcile competing political priorities by allotting resources to each of them may even accelerate the growth of expenditures.

A recent study conducted by Jens Alber on social security expenditures in thirteen Western nations from 1950 to 1977 has broadly been in accordance with the overproduction hypothesis. According to Alber's study, the left-centre coalitions have expanded the welfare state at a faster pace than have single party Socialist governments, and centre-right coalitions have also promoted social security expenditures in a more pronounced way than cabinets formed by a single governing bourgeois party.[21]

Although the policy overproduction hypothesis is thus supported by evidence from various countries, its major shortcoming is a theoretical underspecification. At least two important background variables which seem ultimately to account for the emergence of policy immobilisme or, alternatively, of policy overproduction, have been left out of the prediction; first, the economic environment (economic prosperity versus economic crisis), and secondly the degree of disharmony between the political complexion of government and the power relationships in the party system and industrial arenas.

This criticism can be supported by a brief discussion of a few cases which contradict the overproduction hypothesis. For example, the conflict between the FDP and the CDU/CSU and the ultimate breakdown of the coalition in Bonn in 1966 are clearly cases which deviate from the overproduction hypothesis. The FDP had opposed the CDU/CSU's budgetary policies. The Christian Democrats had planned to finance a large deficit (which had largely been the result of generous electoral policy gifts) primarily by means of an increase in taxes, both indirect and direct. In contrast to this, the FDP had been in favour of cuts in welfare provisions, defence spending and development aid. Both parties were ultimately unable to compromise. The coalition broke down in 1966 and gave way to the grand coalition.

The most recent period and the breakdown of the SPD-FDP coalition in September 1982 is another case in point. We have already pointed out how the incompatibility between the strong welfare state favoured by the SPD and the market economy approach favoured by the FDP had increasingly generated a policy stalemate. In comparison with other OECD nations with governments dominated by Social-Democratic parties in the 1970s (Sweden until 1976, Norway until 1981 and Austria), the policy performance of the West German SPD-FDP coalition was remarkably 'centre' or even 'centre-right' in character.[22] Inflation control, modernisation of the economy and the maintenance of welfare state provisions were the main priorities. The price to be paid was a consistently high rate of unemployment. By international comparisons, the labour market crisis in the Federal Republic has been one of the worst in the OECD area (the rate of unemployment only partially indicates the steep fall in the number of employed people), whereas the increase in social security expenditure and also in public debt has been rather moderate and close to the average score for OECD nations.

Taking the various pieces of evidence together, one seems to be justified in concluding that coalition governments do not necessarily overproduce policies. The crucial point is that the overproduction hypothesis would seem to be broadly applicable in periods of economic prosperity, whereas periods of economic crisis tend to be characterised by a different logic of policy-making. In periods of economic prosperity, large ideological differences between coalition partners can be easily overcome by means of bargains and the mode of distributing increments. In such times, the FDP could easily tolerate its respective partners' endeavours to expand the welfare state, although its ideology has been far from outspokenly pro-welfare state. In contrast to this, the environment of policy-making in periods of economic crisis is quite different in character. The room for manoeuvre on the part of the government and of the coalition partners becomes narrower, economic conflicts tend to become more intense, and if large-scale deficit spending is excluded, it is no longer possible to distribute increments. In contrast to this, redistribution and policies of *de*crement are now required. If these conditions are fulfilled, the coalition partners will for political reasons have to activate their core ideological goals and will become less able to compromise.

One can thus observe a strong asymmetry in the policy capabilities of coalitions. In periods of economic prosperity it is easy to give a great deal to a great many people. Hence the ideological and social heterogeneity of the coalition is not a crucial obstacle. Things change completely in periods of economic crisis: the social and ideological heterogeneity is a crucial problem, because redistributive issues and zero-sum games are now on the agenda.

Having pointed out that policy immobilisme or, alternatively, the overproduction of policy are dependent upon economic circumstances, it is also necessary to mention another independent variable. The SPD-FDP coalition will again serve as an illustrative case. The policy immobilisme which characterised the last period of the coalition has to some extent also been the result of what one might call the gap between the political composition of the government and the power relationship in the party system and in industrial relations.[23] The SPD-FDP coalition was a government which had been, so to speak, 'too left-wing' in its political complexion, in comparison with the dominance of the bourgeois tendency in the economy, in the party system, and in the parliamentary second chamber (*Bundesrat*). The discrepancy between the 'political mechanics' at the level of the federal government and the 'political mechanics' at the level of the 'political substructure', as well as the impact of the economic crisis, also seems basically to account for the limited room for manoeuvre on the part of the government, and for the strength and success with which the bourgeois tendency opposed it.

Conclusion: two logics of coalition policy

One is thus inclined to argue that the case of the West German coalition governments indicates a pattern which seems to be of more general applicability. A policy immobilisme tends to be the typical outcome of a coalition which operates under difficult conditions: an economic crisis, or a strong discrepancy between the 'political mechanics' at the government level and at the level of the party system and the economy.

In contrast to this, policy overproduction tends to be the most likely result of a coalition if its environment is characterised by economic prosperity and a high degree of harmony between the political composition of the government and the power relationships in the arenas of the 'political sub-structure'. It would consequently seem fruitful to distinguish two logics of coalition policy (for a summary of the characteristics of each type see Table 3.5).

Table 3.5   Two logics of coalition policy

	Policy overproduction	Policy immobilisme
Typically generated by . . .	Economic prosperity and low degree of disharmony between political composition of government and power relationships in political substructure	Economic crisis and high degree of disharmony between political composition of government and power relationships in political substructure
Dominant mode of policy	Distribution of increments	Distribution or redistribution of decrements
Nature of the game	Non-zero-sum game	Zero-sum game
Degree of exclusion of issues	Moderately low	High
Capability of meeting demands of social constituencies	High	Low
Consensus-building	Easy	Difficult
Likelihood of breakdown of coalition	Low	High

At the time of writing (January 1983) it is still too early fully to evaluate the policy-making of the CDU/CSU-FDP coalition which has been in power since October 1982. The new government claims to be the agent of a fundamental change in West German economic and social policy-making, promising to bring market forces to the fore and to cut down the size of the public debt. In contrast to the dramatic changes in the sphere of rhetoric, the content of the policies pursued by the new government did not really differ from those of the SPD-FDP government. Admittedly, public income maintenance expenditure plans were cut. The government was also very quick to remove regulations concerning the media and it did not hesitate partially to dismantle the law on the protection of tenants. However, these measures are broadly in line with the policy stance and the plans adopted by the former coalition government. Moreover, and in contrast to its original plans, the new government did not adopt a strongly restrictive fiscal policy. On the contrary, it actively contributed to pushing the public debt up to the highest level ever known in West Germany. The CDU/CSU-FDP coalition is nevertheless in a privileged position: it has strong support from private investors, the banks and the conservative wing in the mass media, although its policy substance is not very different from that of its predecessors.

However it is highly questionable whether support from the entrepreneurs and the government's support both active and symbolic of private investment will really result in increased employment. Given the availability of new labour-saving techniques, the decoupling of growth and changes in the level of employment and the demand gap on the domestic and world markets, it is far more likely that such a policy will at best boost the rate of productivity, but will not solve labour market problems. The Christian Democrats seem to hope that the Golden Days of the social market economy of the 1950s and 1960s will return, while the SPD opposition increasingly tends to adopt active labour market programmes. Whilst the former party tends to underestimate the economic and technological nature of the labour market crisis, the SPD tends to underestimate the strength of political opposition on the part of private investors *vis-à-vis* state-financed battles against unemployment. Both strategies might soon prove to be dead ends. On economic and political grounds, it would seem as if a Christian-Democratic Social-Democratic policy mix is required to handle the current economic and labour market crisis effectively. However, that kind of explicit or quasi-grand coalition behaviour is very unlikely to occur. Whilst a CDU/CSU-SPD coalition would in theory be possible, the underlying value orientations in both political tendencies are far more distant from each other than are the means and goals of policy.

Notes

1. See, for example, Sven Groennings, E.W. Kelly and Michael Leiserson (eds), *The Study of Coalition Behavior* (New York, Holt, Rinehart and Winston, 1970); Abram de Swaan, *Coalition Theories and Cabinet Formations* (Amsterdam/London/New York, Elsevier, 1973); Lawrence C. Dodd, *Coalitions in Parliamentary Government* (Princeton, Princeton University Press, 1976); Ian Budge and V. Herman, 'Coalitions and Government Formation; An Empirically Relevant Theory', *British Journal of Political Science*, No. 4, 1978.
2. See, for example, B. Bueno de Mesquita, 'Coalition Payoffs and Electoral Performance in European Democracies', *Comparative Political Studies*, Vol. XII, No. 1, 1979.
3. Peter Merkl, 'Coalition Politics in West Germany' in Sven Groennings *et al.*, *op. cit.*, p. 15.
4. Heino Kaack, *Zur Geschichte und Programmatik der Freien Demokratischen Partei* (Meisenheim, Hain, 1976).
5. Rainer M. Lepsius, 'Soziale Ungleichheit und Klassenstrukturen in der Bundesrepublik Deutschland' in Hans-Ulrich Wehler (ed.), *Klassen in der Europäischen Sozialgeschichte* (Göttingen, Vandenhoek und Ruprecht, 1979).
6. Joseph A. Schumpeter, 'Die Krise des Steuerstaats' in Rudolf Hickel (ed.), Rudolf Goldscheid/Joseph Schumpeter, *Die Finanzkrise des Steuerstaats* (Frankfurt, Suhrkamp, 1976, originally published 1918).
7. Claus Offe, *Berufsbildungsreform* (Frankfurt, Suhrkamp, 1975).
8. *ibid.*
9. Fritz W. Scharpf, Bernd Reissert, Fritz Schnabel, *Politikverflechtung* (Kronberg, Scriptor, 1976); Gerhard Lehmbruch, *Parteienwettbewerb und Bundesstaat* (Stuttgart, Kohlhammer, 1976).
10. Hans-Hermann Hartwich, 'Sozialstaatspostulat und gesellschaftlicher Status quo', *Politische Vierteljahresschrift*, Sonderheft No.8, 1977.
11. Frieder Naschold, 'Gesellschaftreform und politische Planung', *Österreichische Zeitschrift für Politikwissenschaft* I, No. 1, 1972.
12. Gerhard Lehmbruch, 'The Ambiguous Coalition in West Germany', *Government and Opposition*, Vol. III, No. 2, 1968.
13. See also Peter Nahamowitz, *Gesetzgebung in den kritischen Systemjahren* (Frankfurt/New York, Campus, 1978) and Hartwich, *op. cit.*
14. Hartwich, *op. cit.*; Manfred G. Schmidt, 'The Politics of Domestic Reform in the Federal Republic of Germany', *Politics and Society*, VIII, No. 2, 1978; Erich Standfest, *Sozialpolitik als Reformpolitik.* (Köln, Bund Verlag, 1978).
15. For an earlier version of this argument see Michael Kalecki, 'Political Aspects of Full Employment', *Political Quarterly* XIV, No. 3, 1943.
16. Alf Mintzel, *Geschichte der CSU* (Opladen, Westdeutscher Verlag, 1977); Manfred G. Schmidt, *CDU und SPD an der Regierung. Ein Vergleich ihrer Politik in den Ländern.* (Frankfurt/New York, Campus, 1980).
17. See OECD, *Public Expenditure Trends* (Paris, OECD, 1978) and *Long-Term Trends in Tax Revenues of OECD Member Countries, 1955–1980* (Paris, OECD, 1981).
18. Hans-Joachim Arndt, *West Germany: The Politics of Non-Planning* (Syracuse: Syracuse University Press, 1969).
19. Jens Alber, 'Some Causes and Consequences of Social Security Expenditure Development in Western Europe, 1949–1977' (IPSA World Congress, Rio de Janeiro, 1982) and 'The Emergence of Welfare Classes in West Germany: Theoretical Perspectives and Empirical Findings' (World Congress of Sociology, Mexico City, 1982).
20. Jürgen Kohl, 'Trends and Problems in Postwar Public Expenditure Development in Western Europe and North America' in Peter Flora and Arnold J. Heidenheimer (eds), *The Development of Welfare States in Europe and America* (New Brunswick/London, Translation Books, 1981) p. 327.
21. Alber, 'Some Causes and Consequences', *op. cit.*, table 9.

22. Manfred G. Schmidt, 'The Role of Parties in Shaping Macroeconomic Policy' in Francis G. Castles (ed.) *The Impact of Parties, Politics and Policies in Democratic Capitalist States*. (London/Beverly Hills, Sage Publications, 1982); Manfred G. Schmidt, *Wohlfahrtsstaatliche Politik unter bürgerlichen und sozialdemokratischen Regierungen. Ein internationaler Vergleich* (Frankfurt/New York, Campus, 1982); Manfred G. Schmidt, 'The Welfare State and the Economy in Periods of Economic Crisis: A comparative analysis of 23 OECD nations': *European Journal of Political Research*, XI, No. 1.

23. See for the original sketch of the argument Otto Kirchheimer, 'Weimar und was dann? – Analyse einer Verfassung' in Kirchheimer, *Politik und Verfassung* (Frankfurt, Suhrkamp, 1981, originally published 1930) pp. 42–4.

4 Coalition Formation in Scandinavia
Pertti Pesonen and
Alastair H. Thomas[1]

Introduction

The countries of Scandinavia have lived with a multi-party system throughout the twentieth century and their politicians fully understand (what is not often understood in Britain) the distinction between an election to choose members of an assembly and the quite distinct process of forming a government. All the Nordic countries have recent or current experience of coalition governments and have evolved procedures for their formation which operate with certainty and without undue delay, while still leaving most if not all of the significant decisions in the hands of the leading politicians. Finland's President has political powers akin to those of the President of the Fifth French Republic. But Denmark, Norway and Sweden are constitutional monarchies in which the role of the monarch has, within the past century, become strictly non-partisan, as is that of the President of Iceland. Only in Sweden, however, does the monarch have no role at all to play in the government-formation process. In Denmark, Finland, Iceland and Norway the head of state plays a significant part as arbiter in the orderly transition from one government to the next, and therefore (at least potentially) as guardian of the very strong tradition of parliamentary democracy which thrives throughout the region.

In Sweden recent constitutional changes have transferred this function of arbiter to the Speaker of the Riksdag, and have substantially codified the conditions under which governments are formed and dissolved. In the other countries of Scandinavia, however, procedures are governed largely or entirely by conventions and patterns of behaviour which allow time for the sometimes confusing or self-contradictory implications of election results to be considered and for a variety of possibilities of governmental co-operation between parties to be discussed. Scandinavian experience therefore has much to offer British politicians as they contemplate the prospects and possibilities offered by multi-party politics.

The four party systems

Proportional representation has obviously been a major reason why all

Scandinavian countries have a firmly institutionalised multi-party system. The basic pattern is a five-party one with its closest approximation in Sweden. Indeed the *Swedish* pattern represents the least complicated case, consisting of a strong Social Democratic party and a weak Communist group on the left, plus the Conservatives, the Liberals, and an Agrarian Party to the right of the socialist/non-socialist cleavage. The earlier *Finnish* pattern was the same, with two exceptions: the greater strength of the Communist movement and the existence of an ethnic party, the Swedish People's Party. Splinter movements added new parties; first an opposition group broke off from the Social Democrats and then the opposition group of the Agrarian Union/Centre Party grew as the Rural Party. The Christian League also gradually gained parliamentary representation.

In *Norway* the pattern has been rather similar to the Swedish one. However, the left Socialists have been more durable than their Finnish counterparts, while the Communists had lost parliamentary representation by 1961. In addition, the Christian People's Party has occupied a well-established place in the Norwegian party system. The *Danish* party system has many elements similar to those of the other three countries. It has political parties left of the biggest one, the Social Democrats, and it has its conservative, agrarian, and liberal components. However, the non-socialist parties are more numerous in Denmark and have changed more than those in the other countries while liberalism is represented by two parties – the Liberals and the Radical Liberals. There is also a splinter party from the Social Democrats called the Centre Democrats. Of particular interest is the Danish Progress Party formed in 1973, a 'populist' party which has shared certain similarities with the Finnish Rural Party.

One can find several dimensions and cleavages in the Scandinavian party systems. However, the most important dimension is quite obvious. It is the left-right dimension, also represented by the socialist/non-socialist party cleavage. Characteristic of Finland and Denmark has been a non-socialist parliamentary majority, whereas the Swedish and the Norwegian electorates have in most elections returned a socialist majority to their parliaments.

The net turnover of parliamentary seats across this dividing line has generally remained rather small. The biggest net changes moved 16 out of 200 seats in Finland in 1966, 12 out of 349 seats in Sweden in 1982, 14 seats out of 175 in Denmark in 1973, and four seats out of 150 in Norway. The turnover has been greater inside the bourgeois group of parties, and it has also occasionally shaken leftist representation, for example in Norway and also in Denmark in 1973 and in the recent election of 1981.

The importance of the left-right dimension has been evident in the

voting behaviour of the electorates, as well as in the legislative behaviour of the members of the assemblies. Furthermore, it has provided the basic guideline for coalition formation when the composition
of cabinets has been negotiated and decided upon.

Among the electorates, the socialist/non-socialist party cleavage in
the Scandinavian countries is firmly rooted in the social structure,[2]
although more so in relation to the people's subjective than objective
class position,[3] and it seems to be becoming less firmly rooted.[4] But
there are other important cleavages in the party systems. Norway has
sharp regional and cultural contrasts and in the 1970s attitudes towards
the European Communities became one more salient dimension.[5]
Organised ethnic minorities include the now much diminished German
minority in Denmark and, more significantly, the Swedish minority in
Finland. The rural/urban cleavage has been significant in all the
Scandinavian countries and remains most important in Finland, where
the Communist/non-Communist cleavage is significantly superimposed upon the socialist/non-socialist divide.[6]

Tables 4.1–4.4 present the results of the parliamentary elections in
Denmark, Finland, Norway and Sweden since 1945. Norway with a
fixed election term of four years has held ten elections during this time.
In Finland the term was extended from three to four years in 1954, and
a couple of dissolutions shortened the life-time of the parliaments in the
1970s; the number of elections from 1945 to 1983 has been twelve.
Sweden switched from four to three years in 1970 and there were some
early dissolutions during the 1960s; there have been thirteen elections.
In Denmark the election period is also four years, but dissolutions of
the Folketing have been so frequent that the country experienced
sixteen elections between 1945 and 1981. Because all the Scandinavian
countries use some form of proportional representation, the distribution of seats among the political parties gives a fairly accurate picture
of the distribution of popular votes in the respective elections.

Tables 4.5–4.8 list the cabinets of the four countries during the same
period. Since 1945, when Norway and Denmark were freed from
German occupation, there have been thirteen cabinets and nine prime
ministers in Norway, 18 cabinets and ten prime ministers in Denmark,
34 cabinets and 18 different prime ministers in Finland, but only ten
cabinets and five prime ministers in Sweden.

Despite the pattern of divisions revealed by electoral support for
relatively complex multi-party systems, both Sweden and Norway are
good examples of a uni-dimensional base for *coalition formation*. In
Sweden, six out of ten cabinets have been formed by one single party
(Table 4.8). The Social Democratic cabinets have either controlled a
majority on their own, or have governed with the support of the
extreme left. Therefore, the four per cent threshold which Swedish

Table 4.1   Party distribution of seats in the Danish Folketing 1945–81

Party	1945	1947	1950	1953a	1953b	1957	1960	1964	1966	1968	1971	1973	1975	1977	1979	1981
Communist	18	9	7	7	8	6	—	—	—	—	—	6	7	7	—	—
Left Soc.	—	—	—	—	—	—	—	—	—	4	—	—	4	5	6	5
Socialist PP	—	—	—	—	—	—	11	10	20	11	17	11	9	7	11	21
Social Dem.	48	57	59	61	74	70	76	76	69	62	70	46	53	65	68	59
Radical Liberals	11	10	12	13	14	14	11	10	13	27	27	20	13	6	10	9
Justice Party	3	6	12	9	6	9	—	—	4	—	—	5	—	6	5	—
Lib. Centre	—	—	—	—	—	—	—	—	—	—	—	—	—	—	—	—
German min.	—	—	—	—	1	1	1	—	—	—	—	—	—	—	—	—
Centre.Dem.	—	—	—	—	—	—	—	—	—	—	—	14	4	11	6	15
Danish Unity	4	—	—	—	—	—	—	—	—	—	—	—	—	—	—	—
Christian PP	—	—	—	—	—	—	—	—	—	—	—	7	9	6	5	4
Agr. Liberal	38	49	32	33	42	45	38	38	35	34	30	22	42	21	22	20
Independent Party	—	—	—	—	—	—	6	5	—	—	—	—	—	—	—	—
Progress Party	—	—	—	—	—	—	—	—	—	—	—	28	24	26	20	16
Conservative	26	17	27	26	30	30	32	36	34	37	31	16	10	15	22	26
Socialist	66	66	66	68	82	76	87	86	89	77	87	63	73	84	85	85
Non-Soc.	82	82	83	81	93	99	88	89	86	98	88	112	102	91	90	90
TOTALa)	149	150	151	151	179	179	179	179	179	179	179	179	179	179	179	179

a) Including the representatives from Faroe Islands and Greenland

Table 4.2   Party distribution of seats in the Finnish Eduskunta 1945–83

Party	1945	1948	1951	1954	1958	1962	1966	1970	1972	1975	1979	1983
FPDU (Comm.)	49	38	43	43	50	47	41	36	37	40	35	27
Socialist WP	.	.	.	.	3	2	7	—	—	—	—	—
SDP	50	54	53	54	48	38	55	52	55	54	52	57
Agr./Centre	49	56	51	53	48	53	49	36	35	39	36	38
Rural Party	—	—	—	—	—	—	1	18	18	2	7	17
Unity Party	.	.	.	.	.	.	.	.	.	1	—	—
Swedish PP	14	14	15	13	14	14	12	12	10	10	10	11
Liberal PP	9	5	10	13	8	13	9	8	7	9	4	—
Christian U	.	.	.	.	—	—	—	1	4	9	9	3
Conservative	28	33	28	24	29	32	26	37	34	35	47	44
Constit. PP	.	.	.	.	.	.	.	.	.	1	—	1
Others	1	—	—	—	1	—	—	—	—	—	—	2
Socialist	99	92	96	97	101	87	103	88	92	94	87	84
Non-Soc.	101	108	104	103	99	113	97	112	108	106	113	114
TOTAL	200	200	200	200	200	200	200	200	200	200	200	198

Note: The two Green representatives cannot be grouped as either Socialist or non-Socialist.

Table 4.3   Party distribution of seats in the Norwegian Storting 1945–81

Party	1945	1949	1953	1957	1961	1965	1969	1973	1977	1981
Communist	11	—	3	1	—	—	—	—	—	—
Socialist PP	—	—	—	—	2	2	—	16	2	4
Labour	76	85	77	78	74	68	74	62	76	66
Liberal	20	21	15	15	14	18	13	2	2	2
New People P.	—	—	—	—	—	—	—	1	—	—
Christian PP	8	9	14	12	15	13	14	20	22	15
Agr./Centre	10	12	14	15	16	18	20	21	12	10
Conservative	25	23	27	29	29	31	29	29	41	54
Progressive	—	—	—	—	—	—	—	4	—	4
Socialist	87	85	80	79	76	70	74	78	78	70
Non-Soc.	63	65	70	71	74	80	76	77	77	85
TOTAL	150	150	150	150	150	150	150	155	155	155

Table 4.4   Party distribution of seats in the Swedish Riksdag 1945–82 (Lower and Upper Chamber 1945–69, Single Chamber 1970–82)

Party	1945	1949	1953	1957	1959	1961	1965	1969	1970	1973	1976	1979	1982
Communist	17	11	9	9	7	7	10	4	17	19	17	20	20
Soc. Dem.	198	196	189	185	190	191	191	204	163	156	152	154	166
Liberal	40	75	80	88	70	73	69	61	58	34	39	38	21
Agr./Centre	56	51	51	44	54	54	54	60	71	90	86	64	56
Conservative	69	47	51	55	61	58	59	55	41	51	55	73	86
Others	—	—	—	—	—	—	1	—	—	—	—	—	—
Socialist	215	207	198	194	197	198	201	208	180	175	169	174	186
Non-Soc.	165	173	182	187	185	185	183	176	170	175	180	175	163
TOTAL	380	380	380	381	382	383	384	384	350	350	349	349	349

parties need to surmount in order to gain representation has in some elections endangered the parliamentary representation of the Communists and thereby also the rule of the Social Democrats. In 1973 the socialist and non-socialist blocs were evenly balanced with 175 votes each, so that some issues had to be decided by lot – although of course on important matters the Social Democratic government sought out additional non-socialist support beforehand. In consequence, it was deemed wise to reduce the number of Riksdag seats to an uneven number (see Table 4.4). Subsequently, the three non-socialist parties proved capable of co-operation in 1976, and in 1981 it was the party furthest to the right – the Conservatives – which walked out of the cabinet coalition. The one small exception to the uni-dimensional model in Sweden was Tage Erlander's cabinet in 1951–7, because then the Social Democrats co-operated in a Red-Green alliance with the Agrarian Party rather than with the Communist left.

The *Norwegian* Labour Party had a majority in the Storting until 1961, but then became dependent on the support of the new Socialist People's Party. One significant withdrawal of that support caused the temporary fall of the Labour cabinet. In 1963, when the Labour Party had been in power for a period of 28 years, it was voted out for a period of 28 days. Not for any longer, because as Stein Rokkan put it,[7]

the four-party opposition to the right had again been reminded of a stubborn fact of Norwegian political life: the numerical majority of the mobilised citizens has been to the left in all elections since the war and a crisis such as the one of the summer of 1963 could only have been brought about through dissidence and splinter movements within this majority.

Table 4.5   The political composition of Cabinets in Denmark 1945–82

Year	Prime Ministers	Parties
1945	Knud Kristensen (Agr. Lib.)	Agr. Lib.
1947	Hans Hedtoft (Soc. Dem.)	Soc. Dem.
1950	Erik Eriksen (Agr. Lib.)	Cons., Agr. Lib.
1953	Hans Hedtoft II (Soc. Dem.)	Soc. Dem.
1955	H.C. Hansen (Soc. Dem.)	Soc. Dem.
1957	H.C. Hansen II (Soc. Dem.)	Rad. Lib., Soc. Dem., Justice P
1960	Viggo Kampmann (Soc. Dem.)	Rad. Lib., Soc. Dem., (Justice P to Sept. 1960)
1962	J.O. Krag (Soc. Dem.)	Rad. Lib., Soc. Dem.
1964	J.O. Krag II (Soc. Dem.)	Soc. Dem.
1968	Hilmar Baunsgaard (Rad. Lib.)	Cons., Agr. Lib., Rad. Lib.
1971	J.O. Krag III (Soc. Dem.)	Soc. Dem.
1972	Anker Jørgensen (Soc. Dem.)	Soc. Dem.
1973	Poul Hartling (Agr. Lib.)	Agr. Lib.
1975	Anker Jørgensen II (Soc. Dem.)	Soc. Dem.
1978	Anker Jørgensen III (Soc. Dem.)	Soc. Dem. Agr. Lib.
1979	Anker Jørgensen IV (Soc. Dem.)	Soc. Dem.
1981	Anker Jørgensen V (Soc. Dem.)	Soc. Dem.
1982	Poul Schlüter (Cons.)	Cons., Agr. Lib., Cent. Dem., Christ. PP

But before the above-quoted chapter by Stein Rokkan was published, he needed to add a postscript in September 1965: 'the four co-operating parties of what we have termed the "established opposition" were finally confronted with the task of forming a regular majority cabinet.'

There has been no case in Norway since 1945 in which Labour has formed a coalition with any bourgeois partner. But there have been cabinet coalitions of the four bourgeois parties. There have also been two non-socialist minority cabinets which have enjoyed the indirect support of the other non-socialists in the legislature. However, the most recent election in 1981

resulted in a marked swing to the right, a trend which has been evident since the middle of the 1970s . . . After an unsuccessful attempt to form a coalition government between the leading bourgeois parties, the Conservative party, the Agrarian Centre Party and the Christian People's Party, the Conservatives formed a minority government with parliamentary support from the two other parties.[8]

Table 4.6   The Presidents and Governments of Finland 1943–83

The President and Prime Minister (Indep.)	Party affiliation of Cabinet Members						
	Cons.	Lib.	SwPP	Cent.	SDP	FPDU	+Opp.
Risto Ryti							
Edwin Linkomies 5.3.1943–	3	1	2	4	5	·	1
C.G. Mannerheim							
Antti Hackzell 8.8.1944–	2	1	1	4	5	·	2
U.J. Castrén 21.9.1944–	1[a]	1	1	4	6	—	3
J.K. Paasikivi II 17.11.1944–	—	1	2	4	4	4	3
J.K. Paasikivi III 17.4.1945–	—	1	1	4	4	5	2
J.K. Paasikivi							
Mauno Pekkala 26.3.1946–	—	—	1	5	5	6	1
K.A. Fagerholm I 29.7.1948–	—	—	—	—	15	—	1
J.K. Paasikivi							
Urho Kekkonen I 17.3.1950–	—	2	3	10	—	—	—
Urho Kekkonen II 17.1.1951–	—	1	2	7	7	—	—
Urho Kekkonen III 20.9.1951–	—	—	2	7	7	—	1
Urho Kekkonen IV 9.7.1953–	—	—	3	8	—	—	3
Sakari Tuomioja 17.11.1953–	4[a]	3[a]	2[a]	—	—	—	6
Rolf Törngren 5.5.1954–	—	—	1	6	6	—	1
Urho Kekkonen V 20.10.1954–	—	—	—	6	7	—	1
Urho Kekkonen							
K.A. Fagerholm II 3.3.1956–	—	1	1	6	6	—	1
V.J. Sukselainen I 27.5.1957–	—	3	3	6	—	—	1
V.J. Sukselainen I 2.7.1957–	—	4	—	9	—	—	1
V.J. Sukselainen I 2.9.1957–	—	2	—	6	5[a]	—	2
Rainer von Fieandt 29.11.1957–	—	—	—	4[a]	—	—	10
Reino Kuuskoski 26.4.1958–	—	1[a]	—	5[a]	4[a]	—	4
K.A. Fagerholm III 29.8.1958–	3	1	1	5	5	—	—
V.J. Sukselainen II 13.1.1959–	—	—	1[a]	14	—	—	—
Martti Miettunen I 14.7.1961–	—	—	—	14	—	—	—
Urho Kekkonen							
Ahti Karjalainen I 13.4.1962–	3	2	2	5	—	—	3
Reino Lehto 18.12.1963–	—	—	—	—	1[a]	—	14
J. Virolainen 12.9.1964–	3	3	2	7	—	—	—
Rafael Paasio 27.5.1966–	—	—	—	5	7	3	—
Urho Kekkonen							
Mauno Koivisto I 22.3.1968–	—	—	1	5	7	3	—
Teuvo Aura 14.5.1970–	1[a]	1[a]	1[a]	3[a]	4[a]	—	3
Ahti Karjalainen II 15.7.1970–	—	2	2	5	5	3	—
Ahti Karjalainen II 26.3.1971–	—	2	2	5	8	—	—
Teuvo Aura II 29.10.1971–	1[a]	1[a]	1[a]	4[a]	3[a]	—	5
Rafael Paasio II 23.2.1972–	—	—	—	—	17	—	—
Kalevi Sorsa I 4.9.1972–	—	1	2	5	7	—	1

Table 4.6 (cont.)

The President and Prime Minister Indep.	Party affiliation of Cabinet Members Cons.	Lib.	SwPP	Cent.	SDP	FPDU	+Opp.
Keijo Liinamaa 13.6.1975–	Ia	Ia	Ia	3a	5a	—	6
Martti Miettunen II 30.11.1975–	—	1	2	4	5	4	2
Martti Miettunen III 29.9.1976–	—	3	3	9	—	—	1
Kalevi Sorsa II 15.5.1977–	—	1	1	5	4	3	1
Urho Kekkonen							
Sorsa II cont. 2.3.1978–	—	2	—	5	4	3	1
Mauno Koivisto II 25.5.1979–	—	—	2	6	5	3	1
Mauno Koivisto							
Kalevi Sorsa III 19.2.1982–	—	—	2	6	5	3	1
Kalevi Sorsa IV 30.12.1982–	—	1	2	6	8	—	—
Kalevi Sorsa V 6.5.1983–	—	—	2	5	8	—	2b

a Without explicit backing of own party.

Table 4.7   The political composition of Cabinets in Norway 1945–82

Year	Prime Minister	Parties
1945	Einar Gerhardsen (Lab.)	Coalition
1945	Einar Gerhardsen II (Lab.)	Lab.
1951	Oscar Torp (Lab.)	Lab.
1955	Einar Gerhardsen III (Lab.)	Lab.
1963	John Lyng (Cons.)	Cons., Lib., Chr. PP, Centre
1963	Einar Gerhardsen IV (Lab.)	Lab.
1965	Per Borten (Centre)	Cons., Lib., Chr. PP, Centre
1971	Trygve Bratteli (Lab.)	Lab.
1972	Lars Korvald (Chr. PP)	Lib., Chr. PP, Centre
1973	Trygve Bratteli II (Lab.)	Lab.
1976	Odvar Nordli (Lab.)	Lab.
1981	Gro Harlem Brundtland (Lab.)	Lab.
1981	Kåre Willoch (Cons.)	Cons.

'In *Sweden* the Social Democratic Party has been in power almost without interruption since 1932', wrote Nils Stjernqvist in 1963, characterising the situation as either 'stability' or 'a stable deadlock'. This did not differ much from what Rokkan had seen in Norway. Stjernqvist also quoted Gunnar Heckscher, a fellow political scientist and the leader of the Conservatives:[9]

Table 4.8   The political composition of Cabinets in Sweden 1945–82

Year	Prime Ministers	Parties
1945	Per Albin Hansson (Soc. Dem.)	Soc. Dem.
1946	Tage Erlander (Soc. Dem.)	Soc. Dem.
1951	Tage Erlander II (Soc. Dem.)	Agr., Soc. Dem.
1957	Tage Erlander III (Soc. Dem.)	Soc. Dem.
1969	Olof Palme (Soc. Dem.)	Soc. Dem.
1976	Thorbjörn Fälldin I (Centre)	Cons., Lib., Centre
1978	Ola Ullsten (Lib.)	Lib.
1979	Thorbjörn Fälldin II (Centre)	Centre, Lib., Cons.
1981	Thorbjörn Fälldin II (Centre)	Centre, Lib.
1982	Olaf Palme II (Soc. Dem.)	Soc. Dem.

In fact the concentration of power in the government and in the governing party is the most characteristic feature of Swedish politics just now . . . The Social Democratic government is more and more impatiently dictatorial, and the Social Democratic Party is concentrating on an unceasing and indisputable possession of power.

The 44 years of 'unceasing' Social Democratic power finally came to an end in 1976 (see Tables 4.4 and 4.8), and Sweden's 'established opposition' took over governmental responsibility for two electoral periods. But that has now come to an end. While the political wind in Norway blew strongly to the right, the popularity of Sweden's ruling coalition of two centrist parties declined and the leftists, in opposition for six years, scored in turn a convincing victory in the elections to the Riksdag on 19 September 1982.

While the predominance of the Norwegian Labour Party and the Swedish Social Democrats for long went effectively unchallenged, the Danish Social Democrats never attained a parliamentary majority. From 1905 the *Danish* party system was a largely stable constellation of Conservatives, Liberals, Radical Liberals and Social Democrats (the 'four old parties' with origins at or before the turn of the century), plus the Socialist People's Party dating from 1959. At the 1973 general election the new Progress Party, led by Mogens Glistrup, entered on the right, attracting a broad spread of voters to its populist anti-tax policies. The Centre Democrats had precipitated the election by breaking away from the right wing of the Social Democrats on the issue of housing policy, while the recently formed Christian People's Party opposed easier abortion and other issues raised by 'permissive society' legislation. In addition, the single-tax Justice Party and the Communists both regained parliamentary representation after periods of absence, producing an unprecedentedly fragmented chamber which, in turn, reflected a high level of electoral volatility. The non-socialist parties in the Folketing have not yet worked out a stable internal rank-order along the left-right dimension.[10] In 1929–40 and again in 1957–64 the Social Democrats governed in coalition with the Radical Liberals (in 1957–60 with the addition of the Justice Party). Since then cabinet coalition formation has been in line with the uni-dimensional left-right model, except in the case of the Social Democratic-Liberal coalition of 1978–9 (see Chapter 5, Table 5.2, p. 119 below). But it has to be remembered that the prevalent pattern of minority government in Denmark has accustomed the parties to parliamentary alliances, which may vary from issue to issue but generally embrace a broad range of the political spectrum. Until the 1982 Schlüter Government was formed, only 'the four old parties' were regarded as *ministrable*. The inclusion of the Centre Democrats and the Christian People's Party in the government significantly extends the range of possible coalition partners therefore, although not so far as to include the Progress Party, which thus remains an obstacle to the formation of a *majority* non-socialist government.

Poul Schlüter, the first Danish Conservative Prime Minister for 80 years, saved his position very narrowly in October 1982 when his cabinet's tight economic policies were brought to a vote in the Folketing. The precariousness of the government was further emphasised when it avoided defeat by abstaining on, and therefore by implication accepting, a motion by the Social Democrats to suspend until further notice future Danish appropriations intended for the infrastructure necessary to support NATO's programme of intermediate nuclear missiles, while leaving unchanged the country's other defence, security and disarmament activities within NATO and the United Nations. In effect, this meant that in future specific support from parties outside the government (most probably Social Democratic and/or Progress Party votes) would be needed for any such appropriation.

A third illustration of the limitations facing the Schlüter Government was its inability to obtain the support of a majority in the Folketing Market Committee for the agreement to which it had assented in Brussels on fisheries policy. It was this which gave Kent Kirk, MEP, the opportunity for his well-publicised fishing excursion in January 1983.

The dominant pattern in Denmark since 1964 has been one of Social Democratic minority governments, only once strengthened by a bourgeois partner and twice interrupted by bourgeois rule (see Tables 4.5 and 4.9). The Schlüter Government appointed on 8 September 1982 is a non-socialist coalition of four parties but is, nevertheless, a minority government enjoying the direct support of only 66 of the 179 members of the Folketing.

Over the years, the Finnish party system has deviated most from the basic Scandinavian five-party model. The constitutional position of the Finnish Prime Minister and his cabinet also differs from that of their Scandinavian counterparts (except Iceland) in one important respect: Sweden, Norway and Denmark are monarchies, while Finland's head of state is an elected president with strong powers of his own. Thus the three other countries are purely parliamentary, while Finland since 1919 has had a dualistic Constitution not unlike the French Constitution of 1958. In addition, the relationship of the cabinet to the parliament has some unique aspects in all the Scandinavian countries. For example, the Norwegian Storting cannot be dissolved during its four years and in Sweden the government can call new elections only for the remainder of the three-year election term. In Denmark and Finland, dissolutions of parliament are more effective tools which the government (or the President) can use when attempting to solve a political crisis.

Indirectly, Sweden's 1982 election result triggered a minor cabinet crisis in *Finland*. The very day, 8 October, when Olof Palme's Social Democratic cabinet formally came to power, the Swedish Krona was devalued. The Finnish Mark followed suit two days later, but the two Communist ministers present at that Sunday's cabinet meeting voted against the devaluation. Finland's Social Democratic Prime Minister was upset by this dissent, but after subsequent negotiations and considerable wheeling and dealing with and among the Communist ranks, the dispute was settled and the four-party cabinet coalition seemed destined to rule until the parliamentary election of March 1983. But in December 1982 the Communists were dismissed from the government because they could not accept the proposed defence budget. This illustrates one stubbornly persistent fact of Finnish political life. During President Urho Kekkonen's second term (1962–8) the three socialist parties won a majority in the Eduskunta and the Communists were taken into the cabinet in 1966. The 'popular front' coalition of Centre party, Social Democrats and Communists controlled the political scene until late 1982. The Communist party has suffered a loss of internal cohesion and a decline in its popular support, but the Communists generally prefer the fruits of power, while the other parties like to see them share some responsibility. Nor was the coalition pattern of 1966 altered by the change of President in 1982. It remains to be seen how much more the Conservative opposition parliamentary group needs to grow before an alternative coalition pattern again breaks in.

In what follows, we shall take a more detailed look at the experience of government formation in each of the Scandinavian countries.

Patterns of government formation in Denmark

While the Social Democratic Party in Sweden and the Labour Party in Norway have held parliamentary majorities for much of the period during and since the 1930s, this goal has always eluded the Danish Social Democrats: in 1935 they succeeded in obtaining 45.9 per cent of the seats in the Folketing, but have never again obtained more than 43.4 per cent. Despite this lack of a parliamentary majority, they have been the dominant party in Danish politics. Since 1924 they have always been the largest party, and for much of that time they have been in government, sometimes in coalition and often, especially since 1971, as a single-party minority government.

From 1929 to 1940 the Social Democratic coalition with the Radical Liberals enacted extensive social reforms, introduced the Danish welfare state, and successfully applied Keynesian principles to mitigate the effects of world economic depression. During the second World War there was a national coalition which excluded only the Communists (outlawed by the German occupying power) and lasted, except for the breakdown of political government in 1943–5, until the first post-war election. A series of minority governments followed until the Social Democratic-Radical Liberal combination was revived in 1957–64, this time with the Justice Party as a make-weight up to 1960 and then with a Greenland representative performing a similar function.

The problem for the other parties, as in Norway, was to bury their differences sufficiently to form a coalition capable of counteracting this Social Democratic predominance. The first move was made in 1950–3, when the Liberal leader Erik Eriksen constructed a coalition with the Conservatives, ending the suspicion which had prevailed between their two parties since the bitter contest for franchise extension and cabinet responsibility to parliament which had been achieved in 1901. The two parties controlled only 39.6 per cent of the parliamentary vote, but Eriksen skilfully used the issue of constitutional reform to preserve his government from defeat: the strongest advocates of reform were the Radicals and the Social Democrats, but the Radicals opposed Danish membership of NATO, a policy which all three other parties supported. The Eriksen Government could not continue once the reform of the constitution was successfully and amicably concluded, and an attempt to revive the combination in 1957 was pre-empted by the Social Democratic-Radical Liberal-Justice Party coalition.

The only majority non-socialist coalition government to be formed in Denmark since 1929 was that of 1968–71. This owed its formation to the willingness of the Liberal leader, Poul Hartling, to look to wider working relationships than Eriksen's with the Conservatives; to the Conservatives' willingness to forego leadership of the coalition; and to the success of the Radical Liberal leader, Hilmar Baunsgaard, in attracting votes to his party, so that the three parties emerged from the 1968 election with almost 56 per cent of the Folketing seats. The possible party combination had been discussed extensively during the election campaign and the three parties had already anticipated some of its implications. Its achievements lay mainly in the passage of permissive social legislation, but it was not successful in significantly changing patterns of public expenditure or levels of taxation. The 1971 election deprived it of its parliamentary majority.

The next period of non-socialist government was for fourteen months in 1973–5 when the Liberals, as the established party least damaged by the electoral earthquake of 1973, formed a single-party minority government under Poul Hartling which had the direct backing of only 22 MPs, about one eighth of the total. The Prime Minister called an election early in 1975, doubling his party's parliamentary strength as a result. But his attempts to form a more broadly based non-socialist government came to nothing at the very last moment before its members took office: the tacit support of the Progress Party, which Hartling thought he had obtained, was withdrawn by Mogens Glistrup, its leader. The Social Democrats, as the largest single party, then stepped in with the first of a series of minority governments.

This incident revealed the difficulties of government or majority formation in the fragmented party system which has been characteristic of Denmark since 1973. While the socialist parties have been in a clear minority throughout, the non-socialist parties have lacked the cohesion necessary to use their numerical majority constructively: the Social Democratic origins of the Centre Democrats initially made them suspect; the Radicals, with their earlier history of working with the Social Democrats, would have preferred a coalition 'across the centre' (i.e. spanning both Social Democrats and Liberals, with themselves in the middle); the policies of the Justice Party and the Christian People's Party did not clearly locate them in the non-socialist bloc on economic issues; but, most significantly, the uncompromising opposition of the Progress Party to most of what the established parties stood for meant that an important part of the political spectrum, on the far right, was 'uncoalitionable'.

Nevertheless, the abortive effort to form a non-socialist coalition in 1975 laid the foundation for closer relations between the Conservatives, Liberals, Christian People's Party and Centre Democrats. This resulted initially in more cohesive opposition to several Social Democratic proposals, and ultimately to the formation in 1982 of the first Conservative-led Danish Government for over 80 years – albeit a minority coalition which could count on the support of only 65 members of the Folketing (37 per cent of the total) and which, as we have seen above, soon discovered the limits of its authority.

The Danish experience of various types of government in the period 1945–82 is summarised in Table 4.9, which also illustrates the prevalence of single-party minority governments and the predominance of the Social Democrats. Indeed, the Social Democrats have been in office for almost three-quarters of the post-war period, providing continuity in what might otherwise seem a fragmented pattern. This continuity is all the greater if allowance is made for the death in office of Prime Ministers Hedtoft and Hansen and the retirement because of ill-health of Prime Minister Kampmann. There was, in fact a period of continuous Social Democratic rule during 1953–68, with substantially the same ministerial team in majority coalition during 1957–64. More recently, the Social Democrats have been in office throughout the 1970s except for the interlude of the Hartling Government. For most of this period they ruled as a single-party minority government with parliamentary support from the small parties of the centre-right. Their minority coalition with the Liberals in 1978–9 was only just short of a majority, however, and it fell because of internal disagreement over economic policy and trade union pressures on the Social Democrats rather than as a direct result of parliamentary defeat. While the crude average duration of each government is 22.6 months, the average period of office of Prime Ministers during 1945–82 is 32.3 months, and Anker Jørgensen held office continuously for seven years eight months during the 1970s.

Despite the profusion of parties in Denmark, governments have been formed almost entirely from the 'four old parties' whose origins go back to or before the beginning of the century: Social Democrats alone, or in coalition with the Radicals, or in 1978–9, with the Liberals: Liberals alone (1973–5), in minority coalition with the Conservatives (1950–3), or extending this coalition to include the Radicals (1968–71). Inclusion of the Justice Party in 1957–60 was an expedient which brought that party electoral oblivion for thirteen years. Attempts by the Social Democrats to build on a socialist numerical majority in 1966–8 precipitated a split in their Socialist People's Party allies, and when the opportunity of a socialist majority recurred in 1971–3 (with two of the Faroes and Greenland representatives promising support) the minority SD government was preoccupied with European Community negotiations, for which it had ample support from the Liberals and Conservatives. The Schlüter Government formed in 1982 is therefore breaking new ground in giving Centre Democrats and the leader of the Christian People's Party ministerial experience. Of the parties represented in the Folketing in 1981/3, the two on the radical left and the Progress Party were *non-ministrable*.

Table 4.9   Denmark: types, numbers and duration of governments, May 1945 to December 1982

Type of government	No.	No. of P.M.s	Aggregate duration Years	Months	% duration
Single-party minority	11	6	21	7½	58
Minority coalition	3	3	4	3½	11
Majority coalition	5	4	11	1	29
All-party coalition	1	1		6	1
Totals	20	14	37	8	99

Denmark: duration of party participation in government (months), May 1945 to December 1982, by type of government

Type of government	Party						
	SD	RV	RF	CD	KrF	V	C
Single party minority	223½					38	
Minority coalition	14			2½	2½	51½	37½
Majority coalition	87½	133	41½			45½	45½
All-party coalition	6	6				6	6
Total (months)	331	139	41½	2½	2½	141	89
Percentage of period 1945–82	73%	31%	9%	1%	1%	32%	20%

Parties
SD: Social Democrats
RV: Radical Liberals
RF: Justice (or Single-
    Tax) Party
CD: Centre Democrats
KrF:Christian People's Party
V: (Agrarian) Liberals (*Venstre*)
C: Conservatives

Patterns of government coalition in Finland

Finland became an independent country in December 1917. Between that date and the outbreak of the second World War there were 22 cabinets. During the war Finland had three other grand coalitions before the cabinet of Edwin Linkomies, which is the first one mentioned in Table 4.6. Thus the first post-war cabinet of J. K. Paasikivi (1944–5) was the twenty-ninth since independence, and the third cabinet of Kalevi Sorsa (1982-) is the sixty-second during Finland's 65 years of independence.

Ever since 1937 the backbone of Finnish government coalitions has consisted of co-operation between the Agrarian Union, now the Centre Party, and the Social Democratic Party. It ended the long era of left opposition in Finland, broken only once by a homogeneous SDP minority cabinet in 1926–7. During Finland's war effort (1939–44) this was extended to the grand coalition of all the major parties. A distinctly new period began in 1944 when the Communists (outlawed from 1930 to 1944) re-entered the political scene. At the same time, the Communists participated in the governments of seven other capitalist countries, including France. In Finland this type of government – Agrarians, Social Democrats and Communists – has been called the 'popular front coalition'. The first two coalitions of this type were headed by the former conservative leader, J. K. Paasikivi. The period ended in 1948 when the Communist Minister of the Interior was given a vote of no confidence in the Eduskunta, and the Communists also suffered an electoral defeat.

Between 1948 and 1966 the Social Democratic Party and the Agrarian Union (since 1965 the Centre Party) fought for the role of leading government party. There was considerable instability in the government coalitions, but for a long time after the election of President Urho Kekkonen in 1956 the Agrarian Union was clearly the dominant party. During one election period, 1962–6, the coalition was rather unusually based on the pre-1937 pattern of co-operation between the Agrarian Union and the conservative Coalition Party.

In 1966 the socialist parties gained a majority in the Eduskunta, and the Social Democratic Party took a step to the left. There was also some internal dissatisfaction within the Centre Party ranks concerning the experience of co-operation with the conservatives. The popular front model was re-established and it has remained the core of subsequent governments, which have sometimes also included the Swedish and Liberal People's Parties, but never the conservative Coalition Party except for brief caretaker periods and without the explicit backing of their party.

Because the basic coalition pattern has shown little dynamism, the duration of governments has also increased and the function of the Eduskunta elections has become less important. Political competition and campaign methods have calmed down and one can speak of a broad general consensus. During the 1983 election campaign the conservative Coalition Party registered the support of over 25 per cent of the electorate and raised speculation about their possible inclusion in a future government. But the outcome on election day gave them only marginally greater popular support, and three fewer seats in the Eduskunta. Their hopes of a part in the new government were dashed.

Only 32 out of Finland's 62 cabinets were directly supported by a majority in the Eduskunta. We can group the cabinets according to the type of their political base as follows:

	1917–44	1944–82	Total
Grand coalitions	6	2	8
Majority coalitions	7	17	24
Minority coalitions	9	4	13
Single-party cabinets	4	4	8
Semi-partisan and non-party cabinets	2	7	9
	28	34	62

The parties of the left have never formed a coalition between themselves. Since the war the SDP has formed two minority cabinets on its own (1948, 1972), whereas Communist participation has always been of the 'popular front' majority type (the Paasikivi cabinets in 1944 and 1945 were listed above as grand coalitions). The other typical majority coalition has been based on the 'red earth' SDP/Agrarian co-operation which began in 1937 (1951, 1954, 1956, 1971, 1972, 1983), and which has often involved some minor parties and also included the conservatives in 1958. Since the war, non-socialist majority coalitions have been formed only in 1962 and 1964.

The four minority coalitions since the war have involved the Agrarian Union/Centre Party with the Swedish People's Party or the Liberals or both. In the autumn of 1976 the conservatives made it quite clear that they also supported this type of minority coalition, because it represented for them a welcome break in the pattern of 'popular front' coalitions. Several cabinet crises have been solved by the temporary 'caretaker' solution of non-partisan civil servant cabinets (1957, 1963) or cabinets in which most ministers have had a known political label but, nevertheless, have served in their capacity as experts, without the explicit political support and responsibility of their party's parliamentary group (1953, 1958, 1970, 1971, 1975).

Caretaker governments occur frequently in Finland, where they may be appointed to cover the period preceding or immediately following an election, either to take a decision for which the politicians do not wish to take responsibility, or in other ways to allow time for one or more of the coalition partners to distance themselves from coalition policy positions as the election approaches. Elsewhere in Scandinavia the term caretaker government applies only during the period between one government's resignation and the appointment of its successor, when the outgoing ministers continue in office but, in the words of the 1953 Danish Constitution (paragraph 15(2)), they may 'do only what is necessary for the purpose of the uninterrupted conduct of official business'. The time taken to form the succeeding government may then vary from two or three days to two or three weeks, depending on the complexity of the political situation, during which time attention can be given to its policies and composition, while the country is assured that routine matters are still receiving ministerial attention.

Between 1944 and the end of 1982 in Finland the ten Social Democratic Prime Ministers (four different persons) have held office for a total of 16 and a half years, while the 13 Agrarian/Centre Party Prime Ministers (five persons) have been in office for a total of close to 13 and a half years. Only one Prime Minister (Mauno Pekkala, 1946–8) belonged to the FPDU (the Finnish People's Democratic Union, the alliance of the radical left which includes the Communist Party), and the conservative J. K. Paasikivi was Prime Minister twice. Once a prime minister from the Swedish People's Party (Ralf Törngren, 1954) held the balance in an otherwise two-party Agrarian/SDP coalition. Six different people have served as Prime Ministers in the seven non-party cabinets.

The Centre (formerly Agrarian) Party enjoys the most favourable tactical position in the party system: it has been represented in 25 cabinets, or in every partisan cabinet except the two homogeneous SDP minority cabinets. Although its support has declined, it has been capable of adding the parliamentary strength of the bourgeois opposition to its own weight in the coalitions. At times, the SDP was equally capable of making use of the combined parliamentary strength of the left. The SDP has been a partner in only 19 cabinets, because it was not quite *ministrable* between 1957 and 1966, a period of tension in Finnish-Soviet relations which reached its height with the Note Crisis of 1961. But it has captured quite a central role in the more recent Finnish cabinets: most Prime Ministers since 1972 have been Social Democrats, although there has been a non-socialist majority in the Eduskunta.

Obviously it is in the interest of the SDP to include the Communists in the coalition, because that may weaken Communist propaganda, especially in the work-place. However, the majority of the FPDU have also preferred participation in cabinet to the role of a less influential outsider. And international Communist meetings have recommended the co-operation of the Communists with 'leftist, progressive and democratic forces'. But the minority wing of the Finnish Communist Party has often found it difficult to swallow broadly based government policies which conflict with its own party programme. This is a key reason why the party has been for a long time in serious internal trouble.

The role of the two small People's Parties is no longer very significant, but the Swedish People's Party has nevertheless found itself in no less than 20 cabinet coalitions. The Liberals were in 15, until they decided in 1979 to stay out in their last attempt to create a distinct party profile of their own. In June 1982, however, they finally decided to merge with the Centre Party.

The conservative Coalition Party grew since 1966 from fourth-ranking party with 26 seats to second largest with 47 seats in 1979. But the doors to government have remained closed. According to a Gallup survey in 1981, 15 per cent of Finns considered it essential and 47 per cent necessary that the conservatives should become a government party.[11] A survey in October 1982 showed that the 'popular front' coalition was liked by only 34 per cent, while 49 per cent wanted to include the conservatives in the coalition, leaving 17 per cent 'don't knows'.[12] The composition of Finland's next cabinet emerged as a major issue in the Eduskunta election of March 1983.

But the election created a new puzzle from the point of view of coalition formation. The result brought additional support for the reduced version of the Sorsa government and, at the same time, weakened the power base of the larger original version of the same government. Does this justify keeping the second largest party, the conservatives, who both gained votes and lost seats out of the coalition? What was the use of the non-socialist majority of 114 seats if the three truly *ministrable* non-socialist parties comprise only 92 of the 200 seats in the parliament while the fourth one, with 17 seats, had the image of being an unreliable co-operating partner? What is now clear is the stronger position of the Social Democratic party in the process of cabinet formation. An easy way out might have been to carry on with the red–green coalition, although 106 seats does not constitute a very large majority if there is hostile opposition from both left and right.

That seemed to be the solution, because the Social Democrats again refused to co-operate with the Conservatives. Furthermore, the Social Democrats demanded a majority in the Cabinet, phrasing their demand as 'proportional distribution of portfolios'. They did offer the Centre Party the option of bringing in the Rural Party, thinking that this was impossible. But it was not impossible after all. Surprisingly, the leaders of the two arch-enemies announced their agreement to co-operate. The Rural Party, the parliamentary 'bad boys' of the 1970s, became a freshly polished coalition partner, so safeguarding the cabinet's non-socialist majority.

Patterns of government formation in Norway

The Labour Party came to power in Norway in 1935 and for the following 30 years formed single-party governments continuously except during and in the immediate aftermath of the second World War and for the four-week bourgeois government of 1963, to which we have already alluded. The central problem for the non-socialist parties was to find ways of co-operating with each other so as to provide the only viable alternative to Labour government. As Sven Groennings has shown,[13] this was initially a matter of tactical electoral alliances, in circumstances in which party loyalty was strong and party shares of the vote were extraordinarily stable, so that realistic predictions of the results could be made. The three centre parties, Liberals, Centre Party (until 1959, Agrarians) and Christian People's Party, had been moving steadily closer to each other since 1947, and during 1958–61 they became involved in a persistent and partially successful effort to work together at electoral and parliamentary level so as to offer a governmental alternative. They did not have a joint majority, but hoped to obtain Labour support on some issues and Conservative support on others. But the Conservative wish to share in the pay-off soon brought them into the proposed coalition, for which the brief 1963 government was a rehearsal. It proved to be a turning-point in Norwegian coalition politics, persuading the Liberals to abandon their tradition of not governing with the Conservatives and showing the Labour Party that the non-socialist parties could, after all, agree on a government and a programme. The country had moved from Labour dominance to real prospects of alternation in power. At the same time, the long preliminary stage had resolved many of the questions of composition and policy which hung over such a possible development. The four coalition parties emerged from the 1965 election with 80 of the 150 Storting seats. Whereas the premiership had been allocated to the Conservative leader, John Lyng, in 1963 in recognition of his role as broker during the months leading up to formation of the government, in 1965 the three centre parties agreed that this time one of their own leaders should become Prime Minister, with Per Borten, the leader of the Centre Party, proving to be the most widely acceptable.

The non-socialists retained their majority at the 1969 election, but the coalition fell in 1971 and Labour took office as a minority government, relying on non-socialist support to get its policies through the Storting: the non-socialist parties were divided by the European Communities issue, so that the four-party alternative to Labour could no longer be maintained. Prime Minister Borten's handling of a press leak about the state of Norway's EC negotiations precipitated the government's fall, and brought accusations of disloyalty and calls for resignation from his Conservative, Christian and Liberal ministerial colleagues[14] – a situation which decreased the chances of restructuring the coalition. The Labour Party and the Conservatives supported EC entry but, once freed of their coalition commitments, most of the Centre Party opposed it, and the negative result of the referendum led Labour Prime Minister Trygve Bratteli to hold to his threat of resignation.

In a very confused political situation, formation of the next government after the referendum was difficult. None of the parties which had supported EC membership relished undertaking negotiations for the free trade agreement which would now be necessary, and the leaders of the Labour, Conservative and Liberal parties therefore refused to join a government. The Centre Party was unwilling to govern alone but was ready to join a coalition. The Christian People's Party initially wished to see all the members of the divided Liberal Party included, but once the pro-market Liberals broke away to form the New People's Party, they dropped this condition. The CPP chairman, Lars Korvald, became Prime Minister and the government comprised three other members of his party and six Centre Party and four Liberal ministers, with the backing of only 38 of the 150 members of the Storting.[15] It remained in power to negotiate the free-trade agreement which had been the main purpose of its formation, and in due course the Conservatives and the New People's Party voted for the agreement, both as a logical consequence of their promise to respect the result of the referendum campaign and as an economic necessity for the country.

The Labour Party continued to suffer the effects of its internal divisions. The reverberations of the EC decision continued into the September 1973 election, in which Labour lost a large share of its vote, as did both the Liberals and the New People's Party. The main gainers were the Socialist Electoral Alliance, a grouping similar in composition to the Finnish People's Democratic Union. Their 16 seats were sufficient to give the socialist parties a bare majority. It was on the strength of this, and because it was still the largest party, that Labour formed the next government. The possibility of a coalition between Labour and one of the other parties, whether of the left or the centre, was ruled out by both: the Labour Party has never shared cabinet power but has always governed alone. The government's weakness was that, as in 1963, it could be outvoted in the Storting, but its strength was that such a parliamentary majority could not be turned into an alternative government.

The 1977 election left the relative strengths of the socialist and non-socialist blocs unchanged, though Labour regained all its lost ground. The real change of fortunes came in 1981 when the non-socialist parties, and especially the Conservatives, made substantial electoral gains. The electoral campaign was conducted mainly between the Labour and Conservative leaders, but the possibility of a Conservative-Christian-Centre coalition, led by the Conservative Kåre Willoch was also debated during the campaign. Although this grouping gained a Storting majority, a 'pure' Conservative government was formed, for reasons detailed by Bo Särlvik in the following chapter (p. 123).

Norway had a long period of single-party *majority* government by the

Labour party from 1945 TO 1961, differing from Denmark in this respect, as is clear from Table 4.10. The 1965–71 government was the only majority *coalition*; there were brief periods of minority coalition in 1963 and 1972–3, but for the remainder of the post-war period (apart from a brief initial all-party coalition) the country has been governed by single-party minorities. The Labour Party has been in office for 79 per cent of this period, while the Centre, Christian People's Party and Conservatives have each been in power for about 20 per cent of the time. The only exclusions from participation in government have been on the extremes of the political spectrum. On the left, this omission was significant only in 1963 and 1973–7, as we have seen. The Progress Party, and its predecessor Anders Lange's party, has never been in a position to exert significant leverage from its position on the right wing.

Table 4.10 Norway: types, numbers and durations of governments, 1945–82

Type of government	No.	No. of P.M.s	Aggregate duration Years	Per cent duration
Minority single-party	7	5	14	37
Minority coalition	2	2	1	3
Majority coalition	1	1	6	16
Majority single-party	3	2	16	43
All-party coalition	1	1	$\frac{1}{2}$	1
Totals	14	11	$37\frac{1}{2}$	100

Norway: duration of party participation in government (years), 1945–82 by type of government

Type of government	Labour	Centre	Party Chr. P.P	Liberal	Cons.
Minority single-party	13				$1\frac{1}{4}$
Minority coalition		1	1	$\frac{1}{12}$	$\frac{1}{12}$
Majority coalition		6	6	6	6
Majority single-party	16				
All-party coalition	$\frac{1}{2}$	$\frac{1}{2}$	$\frac{1}{2}$	$\frac{1}{2}$	$\frac{1}{2}$
Totals	$29\frac{1}{2}$	$7\frac{1}{2}$	$7\frac{1}{2}$	$6\frac{7}{12}$	$7\frac{10}{12}$
Percentage of period 1945–82	79	20	20	18	21

Patterns of government formation in Sweden

The classic case of Social Democratic party dominance is that of Sweden, where the party has been in government continuously since 1936 except for an interlude during 1976–82. This dominance rested on electoral support rather than on the ability to find willing parliamentary allies. The party's electoral strength relied in turn on a close relationship with the trade unions and on the pursuit of welfare policies. As Särlvik shows in the following chapter, (pp. 123ff.) this pattern started to break up at the beginning of the 1970s, just as the new constitutional arrangements began to take effect. The reader is therefore referred to Särlvik's account of the relationships between the parties in Sweden, and we turn now to a consideration of the constitutional laws and conventions which regulate the formation of governments in the Nordic countries.

Rules and conventions of government formation

We may usefully begin by drawing on the analysis of the stages of coalition bargaining developed by Olafur Grimsson in the Icelandic context,[16] a model which can also be applied more widely. Grimsson perceives five stages: presidential, exploratory, policy, portfolio and acceptance. In the first, the head of state chooses a party leader to try to form a government. This is followed by an exploratory stage in which the chosen leader conducts informal discussions with the leaders of other parties, especially those most suitable as partners by reason of (a) parliamentary and (b) policy affinity. This stage culminates either in failure, in which case the head of state chooses another bargaining leader, or in success. There then follows the policy stage, in which a small committee of senior members of the participating parties discuss salient policy areas and compile a programme for the prospective government. Once policy agreement is complete, or so nearly complete that no major problems are anticipated, portfolios are allocated. At this stage the main limitations are: the customary size of the cabinet, which is unlikely to be exceeded unless there are pressing policy demands to be accommodated; the choice of a prime minister – usually, but not invariably, this is the person chosen by the head of state to conduct the coalition bargaining. Party ideology, policy emphases, and clientele relationships will also influence the allocation of portfolios, and there may also be some over-representation in the cabinet of the smaller coalition parties, by comparison with their proportion of parliamentary seats. The final stage involves acceptance of the government's programme and the number and distribution of portfolios by the parliamentary groups, and sometimes also the central committees, of the participating parties. Only then is the new government formally appointed by the head of state. The success or failure of the negotiations is likely to be determined at the exploratory and policy stages, rather than when portfolios are allocated.

It will be useful to bear this generalised description in mind as we review the constitutional laws and conventions which apply to the process of forming governments in Denmark, Finland, Norway and Sweden in the following sections.

The parliamentary principle in Danish practice

Although extensively revised in 1953, the Danish Constitution has little to say on government formation procedures, but its Article 14 (reprinted with the rest of the constitution by K. E. Miller,[17]) states that:-

> The King shall appoint and dismiss the Prime Minister and the other Ministers. He shall decide upon the number of Ministers and upon the distribution of the duties of government among them.

While it is useful to be reminded of this formal position, which is broadly similar to that in Britain, we shall see that most of the practical decisions are taken politically, before this formal stage is reached.

The parliamentary principle is clearly incorporated in Article 15 of the Constitution, but it is in a negative form which requires that:

(1) A Minister shall not remain in office after the Folketing has passed a vote of no confidence in him.

(2) Where the Folketing passes a vote of no confidence in the Prime Minister, he shall ask for the dismissal of the Ministry unless writs are to be issued for a general election. Where a vote of censure has been passed on a Ministry, or it has asked for its dismissal, it shall continue in office until a new Ministry has been appointed . . .

The negative formulation, which contrasts with the Swedish practice discussed below, has permitted the relatively frequent minority governments which Denmark has experienced, often as the only feasible solution to a fragmented political system, and allows governments to seek their support from different quarters for different issues. The non-party caretaker governments of Finland are not resorted to: although not excluded by the Constitution, precedents from 1919 and 1940 indicate that the appointment of a ministry outside the Folketing would probably be in conflict with the Constitution.[18]

The main emphasis in the Constitution is on the consequences of the loss of a no-confidence vote. Usually, however, the prime minister is able to retain the initiative sufficiently to determine the timing of his resignation, not least in the aftermath of a Folketing election. In such circumstances he may retain full powers until submitting his resignation, and caretaker powers until the new administration is appointed. This was borne in on Prime Minister H. C. Hansen by his subsequent Radical Liberal coalition partners in 1957, when they were able to prevent an expected Liberal-Conservative government, and instead established a majority three-party coalition by including the Justice Party.[19] This is a useful addition to a prime minister's power to choose the timing of a general election, within the four-year overall time limit, which has been exercised every second year during the 1970s, coinciding with the two-year cycle of wage bargaining.

The well-established procedure of government formation, as outlined by Sørensen,[20] begins, normally on the prime minister's advice, when the monarch seeks the views of the leaders of each of the parties represented in the Folketing. If representatives of parties which together have a majority in parliament advise that a specified individual should be commissioned to form a government, the monarch need only follow that advice. It makes no difference, in this respect, whether the government is a minority government with indications of parliamentary support from other parties or a coalition including members of several parties.

If the party leaders' advice does not at first indicate a clear governing majority, the monarch may invite them to negotiate among themselves to clarify the situation. The monarch can also invite an individual politician, whether the outgoing and still acting prime minister or someone else, to lead negotiations whose purpose is the formation of a government with majority support. This may well happen when party leaders representing a majority have advocated this course of action to the monarch, but the possibility also exists in other circumstances.

If negotiations between the parties do not produce a possible government, the monarch may as a last resort give the task of forming a government to the leader of a minority group. The choice must then be between various possibilities, the decisive factor being which possible government has the best prospect of surviving a confrontation with the Folketing. In such circumstances, the monarch's personal evaluation of the situation may have significant influence on the government which is formed, whether the choice is of an individual to conduct negotiations between the parties, or the designation of the next prime minister. It is personal in that it is unlike any of the monarch's other governmental actions, which are exercised on the (political) responsibility of a minister. But the monarch's constitutional function is primarily to ensure that parliamentary rule functions in conformity with the constitutional system. It can well be argued that it is part of this function to surmount the difficulties which follow from the party divisions characteristic of a modern society.

Sørensen's summary in 1969 of the 'rules of the parliamentary game' has withstood well the subsequent turbulent years of Danish experience. Queen Margrethe II succeeded King Frederik IX in 1972 and was faced the following year with an election result which doubled the number of parties represented in the Folketing to ten and in which all the parties with governmental experience lost heavily. She could draw on the experience of the cabinet secretary, a civil servant who acts as an important link between monarch and politicians, as adviser, in addition to the advice of the politicians themselves. On the next occasion of government formation, in 1975, the Queen commissioned the Folketing Speaker to negotiate a broadly-based majority government, but the extended discussions[21] proved unsuccessful. This was the only occasion in recent times when such negotiations have been entrusted to someone who was not himself a contender for office as prime minister, and it seems that this precedent, which is reminiscent of standard practice in Belgium and the Netherlands, is unlikely to be followed in Denmark.

We can see the conventions in operation by following the events leading up to the formation of the Conservative-led four-party minority coalition government in 1982, following its Social Democratic predecessor's inability to obtain a majority for a comprehensive set of economic measures to meet the country's difficulties and the resignation of Prime Minister Anker Jørgensen on 3 September. The Conservatives, the Progress Party and the Radical Liberals indicated that Poul Schlüter, as leader of the largest non-socialist party, the Conservatives, should try to form a government. The advice to the monarch from the Liberals, the Centre Democrats and the Christian People's Party, on the other hand, was that the former Foreign Minister and leader of the Liberals, Henning Christophersen, should be asked. The Schlüter proposal was backed by 51 votes in the Folketing, as against 40 for the Christophersen proposal, so Schlüter was preferred. He tried to form a majority government, initially including the Social Democrats in the discussions, and when that failed he tried for a coalition of all six non-socialist parties, but this was rejected by both the Progress Party and the Radical Liberals. This left the four which had already worked together in opposition: the Conservatives, the Liberals, the Centre Democrats and the Christian People's Party. Who should be prime minister was still in dispute, but this was resolved on 6 September after a meeting between the Conservative and Liberal negotiating delegations which lasted almost five hours. They eventually agreed on Schlüter, and the other two coalition parties accepted the decision. The Conservatives and Liberals were allocated eight portfolios each, with four for the Centre Democrats and one for the leader of the Christian People's Party. This compares to their parliamentary strengths which were in the ratio 26:21:15:4 respectively. The Radicals promised a responsible and loyal attitude to the new government's economic policy, but they had not been part of the four-party opposition alliance, having instead given limited support to the previous Social Democrat government, and therefore remained outside the Schlüter government coalition. The coalition could, however, expect support from both the Radicals and the Progress Party on most issues. When forthcoming, this support would give the government 91 of the 179 Folketing mandates, an adequate majority.

The working of Finnish parliamentarianism

According to the Constitution of 1919, the President appoints the ministers, who 'have to enjoy the confidence of the Eduskunta'. But confidence is defined in a negative way only: it exists, until the Eduskunta expresses a lack of confidence. In addition to the President, the electorate and the parliamentary parties, one needs to remember the role which the leaders of the party organisations, the government *formateur* and often the trade unions play in the process of forming a cabinet coalition.

When a cabinet resigns, the President takes the initiative. He negotiates with the Speaker of the Eduskunta and with the representatives of each parliamentary group, in an attempt to form an opinion on how to solve the cabinet crisis. The aim is to form a majority government, although this does not always succeed. After the first round of negotiations the President determines fairly independently who should form the cabinet; the prime minister-to-be either does or does not succeed in putting together a coalition with the parties in question. The President's personal role has become more and more important, but so has the role of the party organisations: Mauno Pekkala in 1946 is reputed to be the last prime minister who actually chose the ministers for his cabinet. Now the choice of persons – when the formula has been agreed upon – is virtually an internal matter in each participating party.

The exclusion of the Conservatives as well as the periods when the Communists have been excluded from the Finnish cabinets would seem to support the 'minimal range theory' of coalition formation.[22] On the other hand, the Finnish experience has given very little support to the 'minimal winning theory'[23] or the 'coalition of minimal size'.[24] On the contrary, the 'popular front' majorities have been indications of an attempt to broaden the coalition and to create a consensus climate of mutual co-operation, somehow in accordance with the 'policy distance theory' of coalitions.[25]

During cabinet negotiations agreement is reached on the policy goals of the new government. The government does not present its programme to the Eduskunta for approval, but the programme is included by the prime minister in the minutes of the new cabinet and it gets a great deal of publicity. More detailed agreements may also be made during the negotiations, giving concrete information about the government's political aims. Compromises are necessary at this stage, and the increasing consensus mentality has somehow brought together not only the partners in the cabinet coalition but also the labour market organisations and sometimes even the political opposition. This 'social contract system' combines presidential, parliamentary and corporatist power and also includes top civil servants and interest groups. The more complicated the political problems have become, the more consensus there seems to be in the decision-making system. Careful foreign policy, the stagnation of the international economy, and the joint effort to reduce unemployment, may be quoted as reasons why consensus has been broadening. One of the structural results, on the other hand, has been the tendency to concentrate decision-making in a smallish 'elite cartel' of leading individuals from different power centres.

Stability and concentration of power may have led to a concentration of spoils also. Public subsidies for party activity have this character, and so have partisan appointments to permanent civil service positions. Card-carrying party members, especially Social Democrats and Centre Party members, have competed for public jobs under very favourable conditions during the 1970s. Once appointed, many have made use of their office hours to write memoranda to their parties rather than to their ministries. The increased party politicisation of society has been an additional but related development that in part accounts for the increased alienation of the people from the political parties in Finland. And the percentage of people favourable toward the bureaucracy declined from 53 per cent in 1977 to only 24 per cent in 1979 (as reported in *Helsingin Sanomat*, 5/6 January 1980).

Thus the position of the majority coalition has grown very strong since 1966. It dominates the drafting of new legislation as well as the passage of bills in parliament, and it also dominates the mass media. Elections have not caused many worries for the parties in power, because there have been no realistic alternative coalitions in sight.

Nevertheless, the parties in the governing coalition have attempted to limit further the role of the parties in opposition. For example, attempts have been made to amend the qualified majority enabling parliamentary minorities to prevent constitutional amendments and to leave bills pending until the next general election. Often the government negotiates with interest groups, such as the employers' union, rather than with the Conservative MPs. In very recent years, when some Conservatives have also been accepted into the 'cartels', the new small parties have remained as the special target of the government parties.

Because the opposition parties have little 'instrumental' power in the Eduskunta, they have often relied on more 'expressive' legislative behaviour. For example, in 1979 the Rural Party introduced no less than 369 amendments to the government's budget bill for 1980, knowing very well that none of its proposals had any hope of being accepted. Membership organisations also seem a more important tool for the opposition than for the governing parties. But the most peculiar type of opposition in Finland has been the internal minority of the Communist party, which has often voted against bills proposed by the cabinet in which its own party is a coalition partner.

A similar situation arose in Iceland in 1980, when the Prime Minister, Gunnar Thoroddsen of the Independence Party, formed a coalition with the centrist Progressive Party and the leftist People's Alliance, while most of his own party remained in opposition. This government held together until after the April 1983 election, when it was succeeded by a coalition under Mr Hermannsson with four Progressive Party and six Independence Party ministers.

Political parties obviously view their participation in coalitions with two different goals in mind: the strategy goal concerned with power and influence, and the policy-oriented goal concerned with the issues and contents of policy. In this process the importance of the parties, and especially of their membership organisations, has gained sufficiently in significance actually to move the focus of power from parliament as an institution to the parties and their leaders. In order to influence policies the government parties may need to be ready to ease their ideological rigidity and to accept compromise deals and joint 'packages'. But those, in turn, may not always be easily acceptable to their members and supporters.

And every cabinet comes to an end. Only four out of 62 resignations have been caused by the interpellation procedure leading to a vote of no confidence in the Eduskunta; eight times parliamentary rejection of government proposals has been considered as a sign of no confidence. In 15 cases the cabinet resigned due to Eduskunta elections, and ten times also after the president was elected. But many a cabinet has collapsed due to internal problems, after the links that held the coalition together were eroded from within.

Constitutional laws and conventions in Norway

The Norwegian Constitution dates from 1814 and envisages (in Article 12) that:

The King himself chooses a Council of Norwegian citizens, who must not be under thirty years of age. The Council shall consist of a Prime Minister and at least seven other members,

It also provides that:

The King shall apportion the business among the members of the Council of State as he deems suitable.

But the decisive change in the prime minister's status which was a consequence of the introduction of the parliamentary form of government in 1884 has received no constitutional recognition, except that implied by Article 31:

All decisions made by the King shall, in order to become valid, be countersigned . . . by the Prime Minister or, if he has not been present, by the next highest ranking member of the Council of State present.

Otherwise the position, rights and duties of the prime minister and the manner of his and the cabinet's appointment are left to convention, and practice does not diverge far from the pattern suggested as a general model by Grimsson above. Certainly it is clear from Groennings' account of the way the 1965 coalition was negotiated that the King played no more than a formal role.[26] All the details were settled between the parties, many of them well in advance of the election which gave the coalition its majority. This included the choice of prime minister, an issue which was settled for two of the parties concerned by a vote in their parliamentary groups for one of the leaders of the other two coalition parties.

Swedish constitution and conventions

Swedish constitutional legislation of 1809 contained no rules on government formation, and the process was governed only by convention until 1975, when constitutional changes came into force. In contrast, the 1974 Instrument of Government (IG) defines the government as consisting of the prime minister and other cabinet ministers (*statsråd*), at least five constituting a quorum, but no upper limit is imposed on size.

Perhaps the most striking change made in 1975 was that the king is now no longer involved in the formation of the government. Instead, it is the duty of the Speaker to propose a new prime minister. Before doing so, he must confer with the representatives of the parties represented in the Riksdag and with the Deputy Speakers. The proposal of the Speaker is then submitted to the Riksdag for a vote. If not more than half the total number of members of the Riksdag vote against the proposal, it is approved. In any other event, it is rejected (IG 6:2). Consequently there is no obligation on the majority of the Riksdag to express themselves in favour of the new prime minister and his programme. The programme should evidently be known by the time of the voting; it should also be known whether parties other than the one led by the proposed prime minister will form part of the government. The purpose of the vote is to find out whether more than half of the total number of members of the Riksdag lack confidence in the proposed cabinet. Thus the procedure is the same as in the case of a vote on a motion for a declaration of no confidence.

If the Speaker's proposal is rejected, it is his duty to start the procedure all over again and present a new proposal. Nothing prevents him from reiterating his earlier proposal after having gone through the prescribed consultations. In order to prevent the procedure from becoming too prolonged or deadlocked, it is prescribed in IG 6:3 that if the Riksdag rejects the Speaker's proposal four times, the process is discontinued until new elections for the Riksdag have been held. In that case, extra elections must be held within three months unless ordinary elections are to be held within the same period. It has been assumed that the threat of extra elections will force the parties to reach agreement on the formation of a government, at any rate before the fourth vote takes place.

If Riksdag elections have led to the government's resignation, it is up to the Speaker of the newly-elected Riksdag to lead the deliberations and to propose a new prime minister. But according to statements made during the preparatory stages for the new Instrument of Government, the Speaker of the former Riksdag should not be prevented from taking an active part at an initial stage, *inter alia* by receiving and considering a resignation. While the Speaker acts impartially by convention and would normally continue in office despite government changes, it is possible that difficulties might arise in the event of his death or incapacity, or if the election of a new Speaker brought his impartiality in the government formation process into question.

It is the prime minister who appoints the other ministers (IG 6:1) and it is his duty to report his appointments as soon as possible to the Riksdag (IG 6:4). However, no vote concerning the appointed ministers takes place. A cabinet minister is discharged in the following cases:

i) If the Riksdag has declared that the minister does not enjoy its confidence, the Speaker is responsible for discharging him. The effect of the declaration of no confidence ceases if the government issues an order for extra elections within one week (IG 6:5).

ii) If the minister in question so requests. The prime minister is discharged by the Speaker, and any other minister by the prime minister (IG 6:6).

iii) If the prime minister decides to discharge a minister (IG 6:6).

iv) If the prime minister is discharged or dies, the Speaker then discharges the other ministers (IG 6:7). A government which has resigned functions as a caretaker government until a new government has taken office.

The process of negotiating the formation of governments in Sweden before 1975 can be described in the following terms. The starting point was when the government in office decided to resign or was forced to do so and handed in its resignation to the head of state. The head of state then invited representatives of the parliamentary parties to give their views on the composition of the next government. Of course it was possible for the parties to confer with each other and in fact they did so. Nevertheless, it was the head of state who assessed the recommendations made by the parliamentary parties. It was then up to him to decide who was to be given the task of forming a government. If the task was accepted by the person concerned and was successfully carried through, the head of state accepted the resignation handed in by the government in office. After this the new cabinet was appointed.

The first occasion on which a coalition government was formed after the 1975 constitutional law came into force was in 1976, following the electoral defeat of Olof Palme's minority Social Democratic Government. As a result of the 1976 election the three non-socialist parties controlled 180 seats, against 169 for the Social Democrats and Communists. Compared to the election results in 1973, the change was very small, but it had produced a non-socialist majority. On the day after the election, Olof Palme presented his resignation to the Speaker, Henry Allard. It was accepted, but the Palme Government stayed in office, as the new constitution prescribed, until a new government was appointed.

On the same day the three non-socialist parties met to discuss the situation and begin their negotiations. Their initial positions were as follows. The Conservative Party wanted negotiations to start at once, with the three parties treated equally and with portfolios allocated in proportion to each party's electoral support, i.e. nine for the Centre Party, six for the Conservatives, and four for the Liberals. The priorities of the Liberal Party were that the negotiations should be led by themselves together with the Centre Party; that a government declaration should be elaborated in detail by these two parties; that the Liberal Party should have one more member in the government than the Conservative Party; and, fourthly, that it should obtain the ministerial posts which allowed it to give due emphasis to its own specific policies. In its turn, the Centre Party wanted to base the essential negotiations on the views shared by the Centre Party and the Liberal Party; after that the organisation of ministries should be discussed and finally the selection of ministers. Moreover, the Centre Party wanted a more open approach to the Conservatives, although the basis of the negotiations with them should be the common views shared by the Liberal Party and the Centre Party. It was quite clear to all three parties from the very beginning that the leader of the Centre Party, Thorbjörn Fälldin, should head the new government.

During the next few days delegations of the Liberal Party and the Centre Party met for preliminary talks. There were two especially contentious issues: energy supply and whether or not nuclear power should be used; and policies of equality for women and the provision of day-care for children. From the start it was agreed that special committees should work on these.

After the first joint meeting between the three non-socialist party leaders on 22 September, representatives of the Centre and Liberal Parties met to discuss a common inventory of political issues. This inventory was later presented to representatives of the Conservative Party and negotiations on the most important questions began. At this stage, the three parties were well aware of what issues divided two of the parties from the third. On the use of nuclear energy and the ongoing reform of higher education, a compromise was possible between the Liberals and the Conservatives against the Centre Party. On taxation, housing and the use of land, common views were held by the Centre Party and the Liberal Party which differed from those of the Conservative Party. Finally, on the social policies mentioned above, common views were shared by the Conservative Party and the Centre Party; on these questions the Liberal Party was closer to the Social Democrats.

Negotiations among the party representatives on the conflicting issues and on other minor questions were increasingly linked to the distribution of ministries between the parties and to prospective candidates. The Liberal and Centre parties managed to prevent the Conservative candidate from obtaining the post of Minister of Justice. The solution was to nominate someone not affiliated to any particular party. On 5 October a compromise was reached on the use of nuclear power. In this case, as in the other main conflicting issues, agreement was made possible by mutual compromise. The distribution of portfolios was also agreed: the Centre Party got eight ministries, the Conservative Party six and the Liberal Party five, and there was one non-party minister. On 8 October the new Prime Minister, Thorbjörn Fälldin, announced the list of ministers and the declaration of the new government to the Riksdag.

We conclude our discussion of the coalition bargaining in 1976 with some comments on the relations between the parties and the strategies used during the negotiations. To begin with, the Centre Party acted as mediator between the Conservatives and the Liberals. Compromises were reached on the basis of the mutual interest in forming a new coalition government. But threats were also used, especially over the use of nuclear power and perhaps to a lesser extent over the distribution of portfolios between the parties. Finally, at an early stage a time limit was agreed, that political agreement should be reached and the new government formed by the time of the opening of the newly elected Riksdag. This was, of course, to encourage the willingness to make compromises.

Before the 1979 election the non-socialist parties had made it clear that a non-socialist majority in the Riksdag should form a non-socialist government. The results of the election gave the non-socialist parties a majority of one. The Conservative Party had a substantial success and the Centre Party suffered a comparable loss. Among the Conservatives it was thought that, at least in principle, the Prime Minister should be from the largest party. Although this was advocated by representatives of the Conservative Party and by conservative newspapers, it was not long before it became clear that a Conservative prime minister was not acceptable to the Centre and Liberal Parties. As in 1976, the parties then agreed upon the leader of the Centre Party as Prime Minister.

The second stage, the distribution of portfolios, caused the main problem during these negotiations. The Conservative Party firmly advocated a proportional distribution. But politics and mathematics are not the same thing. The Conservative Party succeeded at least to the extent that they were able to reduce their under-representation as compared with 1976. The negotiations were carried through early in October and a new non-socialist government was appointed on 12 October.

Despite the constitutional role allocated to the Speaker in Sweden, the main actors in the government-forming process are the political parties, and especially their leaders. During the negotiations the party leaders inform and consult the parliamentary groups formally, and are in frequent informal contact with their closest advisers. While the negotiations in 1976 were mainly about the distribution of portfolios rather than the choice of individuals, there was general concern to increase the proportion of women in the government.

The governments formed in 1976 and 1979 were both three-party non-socialist coalitions, supported initially by majorities in the Riksdag of, respectively, eleven and one. In both cases they ceased to function due to internal divisions. In 1978 the cause was the use of nuclear power plants and in 1981 it was taxation reform. In 1978, after negotiations between the parties and contacts with the Speaker, it became possible to let the Liberal Party form a government. The interesting thing was how the Riksdag would react to the Speaker's proposal that the Liberal leader should be given the task of forming the new government. As stated before, the vote on such a proposal was intended to ensure that the proposed prime minister and government were not opposed by a majority in the Riksdag. In this case the Conservatives and the Communists opposed, with the Social Democrats abstaining and the Liberals and Centre Party in support. Thus there was no majority against and – as the Constitution requires – the proposal was approved. Much depends on what a vote of confidence, a vote of no-confidence, and an abstention really stand for. In the Royal Commission that prepared the new Constitution the intention was that the vote should be a check by the Riksdag to ensure that a new prime minister and his government were not opposed by a majority. Explicit support was not prescribed because the new Constitution was not intended to hinder the formation of a minority government. When the Riksdag finally passed the new IG, it was said that the vote for the Prime Minister also implied a vote on the policy of the future government. It can thus be concluded that there is in practice an element of a vote of confidence. Whether this element will be strengthened in future is hard to say but it is implicit in the wording of the Constitution.

When the three-party government was transformed into a Centre-Liberal minority coalition in 1981, the Conservatives abstained in the Riksdag vote on the Speaker's proposal, while the Social Democrats and the Communists voted against. The result was 174 against and 102 in favour, with 73 abstentions. Thus not more than half the total number of members of the Riksdag had voted against, and the proposal was therefore approved. When the new government took office it was able to obtain Liberal, Centre and Social Democratic support for a measure of taxation reform, passed with a comfortable vote of 256 against the Conservative opposition. With a general election due to be held within the year, there was little support for an extra election in 1981. When it came, the 1982 election brought a socialist majority. Olof Palme returned to power with a minority Social Democratic government which relied on the Communist Left to make up its majority.

Conclusions

The four Nordic countries which have been the main subject of review here (although some reference has also been made to Iceland) differ considerably in their experience of coalition and minority governments: in Finland and Iceland coalitions are the rule and changes are frequent; in Denmark minority governments are frequent and are sometimes minority coalitions, while majority coalitions have been in power for only three-tenths of the post-war period. By contrast, both Norway and Sweden have had long periods of single-party government, with a majority assured either from its own party or from an ideologically compatible party which was generally unable to offer a serious threat to the ruling party. For politicians it is clear from Norwegian experience in 1965 and Danish experience in 1982 that co-operative tactics in opposition may bring their later reward of governmental power.

Constitutionally, the Norwegian and Danish monarchies are probably closest in practice to that of the United Kingdom, with procedures in the Icelandic Republic not very different from theirs. The role of the President of Finland in government formation has its nearest parallel in

France rather than Britain, while Swedish experience in handing over this function to the Speaker and requiring a specific vote of confidence for an incoming government has both the attractions and possibly also the pitfalls of novelty.

The main constitutional lesson for Britain may perhaps be the formalised rounds of advice offered to the Danish monarch and to other heads of state by the leaders of all the parliamentary parties interspersed with opportunities for negotiations between them. As a result, possibilities of co-operation between parties, whether at cabinet or parliamentary level, can be explored and clarified. This, in turn, goes a long way towards reducing the danger of compromising the head of state's role as impartial guardian of the parliamentary principle.

Notes

1. The authors would like to thank Professor Henrik Hermerén of the University of Lund for his help with the section on the Swedish Constitution and the conventions of government formation.
2. Richard Rose (ed.), *Electoral Behaviour: A Comparative Handbook* (London, Collier Macmillan, 1974), p. 17.
3. Pertti Pesonen and Risto Sänkiaho, *Kansalaiset ja Kansanvalta* (Porvoo, WSOY, 1979), pp. 125–30 and 135–140.
4. Henry Valen, *Valg og Politikk*. (Oslo, NKS – Forlaget, 1981), p. 131.
5. *ibid*. pp. 225–33.
6. Sten Berglund and Pertti Pesonen, 'Political Party Systems' in *Nordic Democracy* (Copenhagen, Det Danske Selskab, 1981), pp. 83–5.
7. Stein Rokkan, 'Norway: Numerical Democracy and Corporate Pluralism' in Robert A. Dahl (ed.), *Political Oppositions in Western Democracies* (New Haven/London, Yale University Press, 1966), p. 73.
8. Henry Valen, 'Norway: the 1981 Election Confirms Trend to the Right', *Electoral Studies* I, No. 2, August 1982, p. 243.
9. Nils Stjernqvist, 'Sweden: Stability or Deadlock?', in Dahl, *op. cit.*, pp. 116, 146.
10. Berglund and Pesonen, *op. cit.*, p. 100. See also Ole Borre, 'The Danish Parliamentary Election of 1981', *Electoral Studies*, I, No. 2 August 1982, pp. 250–54, and Hans Jørgen Nielsen, 'The Danish Election of 1981', *West European Politics*, V, No. 3, July 1982, pp. 305–7.
11. Onni Rantala, *Suomen puolueiden muuttuminen* (Helsinki, Gaudeamus, 1982), p. 207.
12. *Uusi Suomi* No. 287, 24.10.1982, p. 5. 'Include the conservatives' was the opinion of 92% of Conservatives, 52% of Centre Party, 62% of other bourgeois party, 32% of SDP and 15% of FPDU supporters.
13. Sven Groennings, 'Patterns, Strategies and Payoffs in Norwegian Coalition Formation' in Sven Groennings, E.W. Kelly, and Michael Leiserson (eds), *The Study of Coalition Behavior: Theoretical Perspectives and Cases from Four Continents* (New York, Holt, Rinehart and Winston, 1970).
14. Hilary Allen, *Norway and Europe in the 1970s* (Oslo, Universitetsforlaget, 1979), p. 110.
15. *ibid.*, pp. 170–1.
16. Olafur R. Grimsson, 'Iceland: a multi-level coalition system', in Eric C. Browne and John Dreijmanis (eds), *Government Coalitions in Western Democracies* (New York/London, Longman, 1982), pp. 158–62.
17. K.E. Miller, *Government and Politics in Denmark* (Boston, Houghton Mifflin Co., 1968).

18. Max Sørenson, *Statsforfatningsret* (Copenhagen, Juristforbundets Forlag, 1969), p. 118.
19. See Alastair H. Thomas, 'Denmark: coalitions and minority governments' in Browne and Dreijmanis, *op. cit.*, pp. 123–7.
20. Sørenson, *op. cit.*
21. Thomas, *op. cit.*, pp. 131–3.
22. Michael Leiserson, 'Factions and coalitions in one-party Japan: an interpretation based on the theory of games', *American Political Science Review* 62, 1968; Robert Axelrod, *Conflict of Interest: A Theory of Divergent Goals with Applications to Politics* (Chicago, Markham, 1970).
23. John von Neumann and Oskar Morgenstern, *Theory of Games and Economic Behaviour* (New York, Wiley, 1967).
24. William H. Riker, *The Theory of Political Coalitions* (New Haven, Yale University Press, 1962) and William Gamson, 'A Theory of coalition formation', *American Sociological Review*, 26 June 1961.
25. Abram de Swaan, *Coalition Theories and Cabinet Formations: A Study of Formal Theories of Coalition Formation Applied to Nine European Parliaments after 1918*. (Amsterdam/New York/London, Elsevier, 1973).
26. Groennings, *op. cit.*, pp. 74–9.

5 Coalition Politics and Policy Output in Scandinavia: Sweden, Denmark and Norway
Bo Särlvik

Introduction

When in the 1930s and during the first post-war decades the Nordic region acquired a reputation as a haven of political stability and progressive social change, this had much to do with the standing of the Social Democrats as the dominant parties in Sweden and Norway and – to a lesser extent – in Denmark. Among the Nordic countries Finland was, of course, always a deviant case but it could nevertheless be seen as a political system striving to practise the Nordic style of politics under adversary circumstances. Indeed, it may be that its affinity to the common Nordic political culture enabled Finland to overcome more traumatically intense internal and external strains on the political system than the other countries of the Nordic region have experienced.[1]

In the last decade the picture of stability changed in some significant respects.[2] The era of uninterrupted Social Democratic hegemony came to an end in Sweden and Norway. All three countries with which we shall be concerned here – Sweden, Denmark and Norway – experienced a change in the political climate. The balance of political forces in the electorate was affected by a new mood of disenchantment with at least some aspects of the performance of the social democratic welfare state as well as by 'post-industrial' doubts about the economic growth philosophy of the preceding decades. The strains caused by the stagnation of the world economy during the 1970s exerted a powerful influence – but the signals of change were there well before the shockwaves from the international oil crisis reached the Nordic economies. On social and economic issues, the Social Democrats were weakened both by a shift towards the right in public opinion and – as a complementary sign of disenchantment with the social democratic style of government – by losses of voting support to parties on their left flank. Moreover, old cleavage patterns were complicated by the emergence of new issues: the question of membership of the European Communities in Denmark and Norway; the early 'green wave' of the 1960s, followed by the intense controversy over the future of nuclear power in Sweden. Increasing electoral volatility (a phenomenon observed across Western

Europe) was one of the concomitants of this change; another was new instability in the party systems that had been presumed frozen for so long. The challenges to the established parties were particularly forceful in Denmark, but they were felt also in the form of a further fragmentation of the centre and a strengthening of the far left in Norway, whereas in Sweden the main effect was to broaden the electoral appeal of the old Agrarian Party, now transformed into the Centre Party.

It would be tempting to conclude from the developments in the late 1960s and 1970s that the Scandinavian multi-party systems are simply reverting to type. The life-expectancy of governments has become shorter. Minority governments reflect the inability of parties, from time to time, to form cohesive majority coalitions. Changes in government occur not only as a result of elections but also between them. These were characteristic features of parliamentary government in all these countries in the 1920s. Yet, the political reality is more complex. The Scandinavian party systems have never really fitted the ideal model of a system with parties arrayed from left to right and a centre in a pivotal position that allows either left-centre or right-centre coalitions to be formed. Or, more precisely, the single-dimension model fits as long as we are referring only to the presence of left, centre and right in the party system and to social and economic issues. But it fails to take into account, firstly, that the centre of the party systems in Norway and Sweden has been divided by additional cleavages (rural versus urban and religious/moral values versus secularisation) and, secondly, that the centre has also been split – albeit on a different pattern – in Denmark.

Moreover, the parties that occupy a centre position on an ideological left-right dimension – in the sense of being placed between the Social Democrats and the Conservatives – need not therefore be in a position to play the role of a pivotal centre in the way required by the ideal model of multi-party politics that we have just referred to. As we shall see, the presence of a dividing line between socialist and non-socialist parties – the tendency to a two-bloc formation – can impose constraints on what coalitions the parties between the Social Democrats and the Conservatives are willing to join; such constraints may then have their grounds in actual policy disagreements or electoral considerations, or both. Finally, in Norway and Sweden – and for a short time in Denmark – the socialist parties' combined electoral strength was sufficient to allow the Social Democrats to govern on their own. Indeed, it may well be argued that it was this ability of the Social Democrats to govern alone, as much as the ideological divide, that made for the emergence of two-bloc politics.

In this chapter we shall explore how the changing patterns of parliamentary politics in Denmark, Norway and Sweden have affected government formation and policy output. We shall thus attempt to gauge the policy consequences of periods of minority government, two-bloc politics and coalition government during different political eras. In the latter part of the chapter we shall return to the consequences of the Social Democratic decline in the late 1960s and 1970s. One effect was virtually unavoidable: the politics of government coalitions took on a new significance. What was not unavoidable, however, was the return to minority-government parliamentarism: that had to do with the difficulties of the non-socialist parties in forming durable, cohesive coalition governments.

Before our review of parliamentary politics, however, a brief discussion of the concept of coalition is required. We shall also address ourselves briefly to the question of the relevance of party politics for the policies that countries pursue.

Varieties of coalition politics
In multi-party systems, policy-making will often be determined by the outcomes of coalition politics, by agreements and compromises arrived at within coalition governments. But as becomes abundantly clear when one studies the working of the parliamentary system of government in Scandinavia, coalition politics does not only take the form of coalition governments. Minority governments can be sustained in office either by pacts or agreements comprising a range of policies with one or more supporting parties, or they can survive by forging together *ad hoc* coalitions on specific policy decisions. Even when a single party commands a parliamentary majority, as we shall see, it may seek to strengthen its parliamentary base through co-operation with one or more parties outside that base. And the forming of policy-coalitions among opposition parties – though they are bound to be losing coalitions – also has an impact on the overall political situation: it can freeze into two-bloc politics if the opposition consistently presents a cohesive alternative, or there may be room for a more fluid pattern of inter-party pacts and agreements.

The type of coalition politics that is being pursued will depend on the structure of the party system: the number of parties, the nature of their electoral bases, and the competition between them. The distribution of strength among the parties will decide, firstly, whether a coalition is needed and, secondly, if no party commands a majority, what combinations of parties could form a winning coalition. In the latter case, the ideological distances between the parties as well as policy disagreements on other grounds will impose constraints on what combinations are considered feasible. Finally, the shaping of coalition politics will depend on the constitutional framework as well as on conventions pertaining to government formation that have evolved within a given party system.[3] The following survey of parliamentary politics and government formations in Scandinavia will illuminate the interactions between these factors and their joint effects on the policy-output of these countries.

Does party politics matter?

It is not our intention to argue in this chapter that the policy output of a political system is all determined by party politics or by the characteristics of party systems. The last decade has certainly brought it home, if it needed to be, that national policy-making occurs in the context of a world economy confronting countries at a similar stage of industrial development with similar problems – and often leaves them little choice but to respond with the same kinds of policies, irrespective of the party complexion of the government of the day.[4]

There is no doubt, either, that in a longer time perspective we can observe a degree of convergence in policy-making among countries that are similar in respect of social and economic structure – again, irrespective of whether left, centre or right occupies the commanding heights in parliamentary politics.[5] Yet, we need only look back at an earlier decade – the 1930s – to find evidence that different political systems can respond very differently to the same worldwide economic crisis. Moreover, with regard to the post-war period, empirical research on the connections between politics and policies in industrially developed liberal democracies has provided evidence that it does indeed matter – at least in some areas of economic and social policy-making – whether countries are governed by the right or the left. Over time, party politics does make some difference to measurable policy output.[6]

The 1920s: Four-party format and minority government parliamentarism

In the beginning there was Left and Right. That is, in the late nineteenth century when modern party systems emerged, a Conservative Right supported by big landowners, bureaucracy and the new industrialists stood against a Liberal Left which had its strongest base among the farmers and smallholders, although it also included an urban faction.

In the ensuing struggle for constitutional reform – extension of the suffrage and the firm establishment of a parliamentary system of government – the new social democratic parties were at first mainly support parties to the Liberal Left. In the early 1920s – when that process had been completed and proportional representation had been introduced – the setting of the party system had also changed. The Conservative party was still there as the major force on the right, although its share of the vote was reduced as a result of the enlargement of the electorate to include the industrial workers; with increasing industrialisation its social centre of gravity had also become more urban-industrial. But the old Left had become a centre, with a large socialist force forming the left of the party system. In Denmark and Sweden the Socialist parties had become the dominant working-class parties with small Communist parties on the far left. The Norwegian development was, at first, more turbulent, but by the end of the decade the division of the working-class vote had settled to a pattern not unlike that of the two other countries, although the Norwegian Labour Party maintained a more radical profile well into the 1930s. In the centre of the party system, the urban-rural cleavage now also came to the surface in Norway and Sweden, providing the basis for Agrarian parties with a somewhat ambiguous ideological position on the centre-right but draining off a substantial portion of the old Left's rural voting support. Born half as protest movements and half as political appendages to the farmers' economic interest organisations, the Agrarian parties were certainly anti-socialist, but primarily pressure groups for farmers' interests organised as parties. Denmark followed a somewhat different path: the old Left had already split in 1905 into a moderate liberal Left comprising the large majority of the farmers (wealthier than in Norway and Sweden) and a radical Left that gained the support of the small-holders as well as a significant centre-left urban support. (In the tables, later on, we refer to these parties as the Agrarian Liberals and the Radicals; their party names in Danish still include the old labels: in literal translation the Left and the Radical Left, respectively). Yet, as in Norway and Sweden, the centre was split. The four/five party format that was to appear 'frozen' for so long had been formed in all the three countries.[7]

Neither the new left, nor the centre or right, could achieve a majority of their own in this new situation. The scene seemed to be set for coalition formation with the parties in the centre joining with either side to form a governmental majority. Instead, in all three countries, the 1920s became a period of minority governments: the rules of parliamentarianism were re-interpreted – a government could be formed if it had a reasonable expectation of being *tolerated* by, rather than supported by, a majority in the parliament. Depending on elec-toral fortunes, this allowed short-lived governments by the right and the centre as well as the left to be formed, although the Social Demo-crats' experiments with governments were more short-lived than those of the centre and the right. There were several reasons why this situation arose. The alliance between left-centre Liberals and Social Democrats broke up as soon as their common goal of constitutional reform had been achieved; the Liberals supported the Social Democrats on the eight-hour working day, but they were not prepared to go much beyond that. In particular, their economic liberalism led them to side with the employers in the industrial disputes of the decade: it also prevented a political understanding with the Social Democrats. On the other hand, the divide between the right and the parties with their roots in the old left was still deep enough to make them unwilling to form lasting coalitions of all the non-socialist parties.

The centre undoubtedly held a pivotal position in parliamentary legislation, and its passive tolerance was required when Conservative or Social Democrat minority governments were formed – but at the same time it blocked the road to government by majority coalitions. The working of this system was facilitated by the absence of rigid constitutional rules for government formation: the monarch would confer with party leaders and give the task of forming a government to the party that seemed to have the best chance of being tolerated for some time by parliament. What counted was not only the parliamentary strength of parties – some minority governments had an extremely narrow base – but also the tendencies displayed in the most recent election result. Increasingly, parties' *unwillingness* to govern became almost as important a factor as their ambition to gain office: a party that had just suffered an electoral setback after a frustrating spell in office could well be eager to shift the burden of governing to someone else.

Perhaps this mode of parliamentary government saved the Scandinavian countries from a political polarisation that could have been more dangerous than governmental instability. Yet, the 1920s could hardly qualify as a time of consensus politics. It was rather a time when important social and economic questions were left unresolved, and a decade of large-scale and bitter confrontations in the labour market.

In some respects, however, the experiences of the 1920s had a lasting impact on the Scandinavian version of the parliamentary system of government: the distinction between, on the one hand, a government's party composition and its potential 'law-making' support in parliament, on the other, was clearly recognised; it was also recognised that the latter could shift from one issue to the other – this was why minority governments of the centre could show remarkable durability; and, finally, the system learned to live with the subtle parliamentary rules of the game required to sustain minority governments in office. It is interesting to note how easily the conventions thus established were invoked when they were again required in the 1970s and early 1980s.

The Social Democratic ascendancy: a socialist bloc with an annex
The root cause of the minority-government parliamentarism of the 1920s was an unsettled relationship between left, centre and right in all three countries. The centre could play a pivotal role in the making of

parliamentary majorities for legislative purposes – but it was not prepared to take part in government coalition formation with either side. At every turn, it appeared that the distance between centre and right was too great on some issues (for example, defence), whilst at the same time disagreement with the left was equally discouraging on other issues (for example, labour market policy). When that stalemate came to an end, the main reason was the electoral growth of the Social Democrat parties in the 1930s. But the electoral surge towards the Social Democrats does not of itself provide a sufficient explanation for the change. In fact, the Social Democrats established themselves as dominant parties as well as natural parties of government in the 1930s without achieving parliamentary majorities of their own (together with the left-socialists/communists the Swedish Social Democrats could indeed muster a majority in the Lower House from 1936, but they still had to contend with a bourgeois majority in the Upper House). In all three countries, the change was made possible when the Social Democrats succeeded in prising off a party in the centre and persuading it to join in a stable coalition or pact.

The change came first in Denmark, in 1929, when the left-centre Radical Liberals finally joined a coalition with the Social Democrats. In fact, the coalition government succeeded in creating an even broader parliamentary base for important parts of its legislative programme by also reaching an agreement with the Agrarian Liberals. The government remained of minimum size, however, including only the two parties required to form a majority in the Lower House and it was made feasible through the split between the left-centre and the right-centre. The coalition government's understanding with the Agrarian left did of course frequently result in an oversized 'law-making majority'. That was necessary for the coalition government to carry out its policy, because only agreements with the Agrarian Liberals could give it a majority in the Upper House.

The crucial factor from the outset was the split between centre-right and centre-left and the crucial actor was the Radical Liberal party. In fact, the Radicals never really had the two-sided choice of coalition partners that normally is associated with the role of a pivotal party in the centre of a left-right array of parties. They could hardly have maintained their profile as a left-centre party if they had joined forces with not only the Agrarian Liberals but also the Conservatives in a bourgeois majority coalition. Yet, the Radical party was clearly in a position to extract concessions from the Social Democrats as the price for taking the risk of co-operating with a party on the other side of the bourgeois-socialist divide; it did so, and the compromise was facilitated by the Social Democrats' increasingly pragmatic, non-ideological strategy.

The formation of a majority parliamentary base for Social Democratic government in Sweden, and somewhat later in Norway, followed a different path. There was no traditional ideological division between centre-left and centre-right which the Social Democrats could exploit. Instead, they formed an alliance with the Agrarians, a party whose position in the centre was determined more by the logic of the situation than by its ideological stance; no bridge could be built with what remained of the old Liberal Left. Whilst seeking support in the centre, the Swedish and Norwegian Social Democrats also exploited a second dimension in the party system – the urban/rural cleavage – when they found their support party. The alliance was made possible by a compatibility between the policies which the Social Democrats and the Agrarians wanted to pursue to overcome the economic depression. The difference between the social bases of the two parties also meant that they avoided a dilemma that parties clearly adjacent on a single ideological dimension often experience: competition for the same votes. The Agrarians and the Social Democrats could continue mobilising the support of farmers and manual workers, respectively, without trespassing too much on each other's ground.

However, the difference between the Swedish-Norwegian route and the Danish case should not be exaggerated. In all three countries compromises between farmers' interests and those of the industrial workers were at the heart of the political consensus that allowed the Social Democratic party to take the lead in a large-scale social policy programme. Although Denmark did not have an agrarian party of quite the same type as Sweden and Norway, the Radical Liberals' voting support included a significant base among the smallholders. The similarity becomes even more clear if one takes into account that the Social Democrat-Radical coalition reached a détente – if not a pact – with the Agrarian Liberals which shared one important characteristic with the Swedish horse-trading: the recognition that at a time of economic depression there could be a common denominator for workers' and farmers' interests in a programme of economic policies that differed from those of previously orthodox economic theory.

The era of Social Democratic ascendancy in the 1930s – especially in Sweden – has rightly been characterised as one in which an historical compromise between capital and labour was reached after the bitter confrontations of the preceding decade.[8] It is all the more noteworthy that this compromise was contingent upon a compromise, in the political arena, between industrial workers and farmers. (It was perhaps this similarity to the New Deal coalition that led left-of-centre American observers to look so favourably upon the Scandinavian mode of 'middle-way' politics.)

In the situation that was then created the scene was also set for a reconciliation in the labour market. On the one hand, the employers' organisations were faced with the fact that the political balance of power had shifted in favour of the Social Democrats and the trade unions; a continued policy of confrontation could lead to nothing but economic disruption, and thus a reasonably amicable accommodation came to be recognised as a far more preferable alternative. On the other hand, the trade unions could move speedily towards a more conciliatory posture when they had the backing of a friendly, rather than a hostile, administration.

In the political arena, a new basis for consensus emerged. The adoption of a new economic policy strategy was certainly controversial but it also meant that the Social Democrats moved away from dogmatic socialism and that made compromises with the non-socialist parties possible. Moreover, their far less controversial social policy programme was given priority on the agenda. So the Social Democrats moved towards a middle-ground consensus. At least as important, however, was the fact that the middle ground, where compromises could be reached, had moved towards the left. Much of the social welfare programme was supported also by non-socialist opposition parties. The pragmatism of the politicians who represented the agricultural sector certainly helped. But perhaps it also had to do with the sagacious observation of the leading Swedish Social Democrat, Ernst Wigforss: social reformism in the centre is a sensitive plant – it can flower only in the shadow of a large socialist party.

Two-bloc politics in the post-war era

Two-bloc politics require that a multi-party system functions as if it were a two-party system, if not in elections at least when it comes to government formation. In contrast to the more fleeting relations among parties in a system with a changeable centre, the voter knows when he casts his vote that he is supporting one or other of two governmental alternatives. The bloc that achieves a parliamentary majority will also be the bloc that takes office, as a coalition. Since no third basis of government formation is available, no party really occupies a pivotal position in the sense of coalition theory.

With the Norwegian Labour Party holding a majority of its own and with the Swedish Social Democrats mostly commanding a parliamentary majority with the support of the Communists, the two-bloc model appeared for a time to offer a plausible scenario for the working of the parliamentary system of government in both countries.[9] The social democratic parties might form the government of the day, but once the bourgeois parties had achieved a majority they would naturally be expected to take office as a cohesive coalition. It is true that the Swedish Agrarians temporarily broke ranks and joined the Social Democrats in a coalition, 1951–7, but the electoral fortunes of both parties suffered, and the need for the three bourgeois parties to offer a credible joint alternative appeared if anything even more compelling. Denmark was a different case, as we shall see, despite the fact that the Social Democrats continued to be seen as a natural party of government.

That the Swedish Social Democrats wanted to embrace the Agrarians in a government coalition had much to do with the fact that their parliamentary base was more fragile than that of the Norwegian Labour party. The Swedish Social Democrats could always count on the Communists in their parliamentary base for the mere purpose of government formation: no bourgeois government could be formed when the socialist parties had a majority in the Lower House (as well as in the Upper House, and in joint votes). But the Communists were not necessarily a reliable partner in policy-making, and to be seen relying exclusively on Communist support did anyhow involve considerable political risks at the height of the Cold War. Again, it was a compatibility of policy preferences that allowed the Agrarians and the Social Democrats to join forces. The Social Democrats' policy of economic growth required stable and low interest rates and, in turn, this required the use of fiscal and regulatory measures to cope with inflationary pressures. Low interest rates were deemed to benefit the farmers, and on that issue the Agrarians differed from Liberals and Conservatives who wanted to pursue a more liberal monetary policy. In return, the Social Democrats were more prepared to use state intervention to sustain the standard of living of the farmers in a difficult transition period. As time went on much of this commonality of interest petered out, however. When the Agrarians broke from the coalition, they were, moreover, set to broaden their electoral base under the new Centre party label, partly at the expense of the Social Democrats.

The 1960s was perhaps the time when Swedish parliamentarism came closest to the two-bloc model. The Social Democrats' plan to introduce a new income-related pension system including all wage earners had already in 1957 resulted in a clear divide between socialist and non-socialist parties. The non-socialist parties did not really form a cohesive bloc, it must be added, but they were united in their rejection of the Social Democrat proposal. Only shortly after the pensions issue had been decided in their favour (after a referendum and a dissolution of the Lower House), the Social Democrats forced through the introduction of a general sales tax against the united opposition of the bourgeois parties.[10] On that issue, the Communists refused to support the Social Democrats. But almost as in a two-party situation, the government forced the dissenters to acquiesce by effectively making the decision a vote of confidence. The Communists dared not be seen to have brought down a socialist government and abstained in the crucial vote. The prestige of the Social Democrats was considerably enhanced by their success on the pensions issue, and the sales tax provided the financial basis for a rapid expansion of public services during the 1960s. Towards the end of the decade, the Social Democrats embarked upon an ambitious programme of regional policy and a strengthening of state controls over industrial investment and the credit market, all of which combined to widen the gap between them and all three bourgeois parties. It became a generally recognised fact that no coalition bridging the bloc-divide was feasible: the alternative was a three-party bourgeois coalition. The only flaw in an almost ideal-type two-bloc situation was the Conservative party's tendency to move rather more to the right than the parties in the centre could condone. In response, the People's party and the Centre party established a kind of pact of the centre, but the purpose was rather to enhance their combined political weight in a prospective three-party coalition than to exclude the Conservatives from a prospective government.

In Norway, Social Democrat dominance in post-war politics was even more decisive than in Sweden: but it ended earlier. Indeed, during the first economic reconstruction period after the war, the Social Democrats could rely on near consensus for an economic programme that involved determined economic planning as well as the establishment of state-owned industries, especially in the devastated north of the country. Two-bloc politics appeared to be the obvious way of effecting alternation in government – when it came. It came perhaps sooner than many had expected: after the election of 1961, the Labour Government was able to hold on to office only with the support of a small left-socialist party. When the left-socialists temporarily withdrew their support in 1963, the result was the formation of a coalition government comprising all the non-socialist parties. The experiment lasted only for a few weeks, but its political impact was more significant than that. It showed that – somewhat to the surprise even of the non-socialist parties – they were able to offer a governmental alternative. The opportunity came in 1965, when Labour lost its majority. With a Centre party politician as Prime Minister, the four non-socialist parties proved quite capable of playing their role in a system of two-bloc parliamentarism – that is, they did so until they fell victim to an entirely new issue: the question of membership of the European Communities. This will be discussed later.

Denmark, as we have already said, was a different case. The Social Democrats emerged from the war much weaker than their sister parties in Norway and Sweden. Even when they had recaptured ground lost to the Communists in the first post-war election, their electoral strength hovered around 40 per cent of the vote, some 6 per cent less than the Social Democratic parties in the two other countries could normally achieve until the late 1960s. Moreover, the Social Democrats found that the Radical Liberals were now prepared to exploit their pivotal position in the centre to shift the balance in favour of either a minority government of the left or one of the right; it was not until the late 1950s that the Social Democrats could persuade the Radicals to join a coalition government (and then in company with the small Justice Party). Rather than the marked two-bloc tendency in Norway and Sweden, the characteristic feature of the Danish parliamentary situation was the existence of two poles – the Social Democrats on the one side and the Agrarian Liberals in a fairly stable partnership with the Conservatives on the other – both lacking a majority of their own, and both attempting to attract the Radicals in the centre.

Ironically, perhaps, the arrival of two-bloc politics in the Danish parliamentary arena coincided with an electoral setback for the Social Democrats in the 1966 election. The new, left-wing Socialist People's Party scored a remarkable success but, as was bound to happen, largely at the Social Democrats' expense. Nevertheless, for the first time in Denmark's post-war history, the country had a socialist majority both in the electorate and in the Folketing. What followed had as much to do with the dynamics of party competition and parties' expectations of influencing policy-making as with formal coalition theory. As coalition theory would lead us to expect, the Radicals would not become a member of an oversized coalition of the left: for one thing, they did not want to be locked into a government in which the Social Democrats with the support of the Socialist People's Party could push through more radical policies than they were willing to go along with. The Social Democrats, on the other hand, had to take into account, of course, the apparent shift to the left in the electorate's mood. It was also in their interest to harness the challenge from the left by making the Socialist People's Party share some responsibility for the policies of a government of the left. At the same time, however, there was almost certainly still a need to call upon at least occasional support from the centre for the government's legislative programme, and for a moderate social democratic party there was danger in being seen to shift too far to the left. The situation was resolved by the Social Democrats forming a minority government with the Socialist People's party as an acknowledged support party outside the government and with an unprecedented liaison committee (the 'red cabinet') for consultations between government and support party.

The dynamics of two-bloc politics began to operate: when the Social Democrats lost office in 1968, a three-party non-socialist government took over. The price demanded by the Radicals for committing themselves so firmly to the bourgeois bloc was high, however: they got the premiership. When the Social Democrats came back into office, 1971–3, it was again in a one-party government. The parliamentary base was precarious, including the uncertain support of the Socialist People's Party and a split-off left-socialist party as well as leftist representatives for the Faroe Islands and Greenland. Two-bloc politics was not to materialise again in the 1970s or the early 1980s in the shape of a formal government coalition of all the non-socialist parties. But the divide between the two blocs had also deepened enough to prevent the Radicals from joining a formal government coalition with the Social Democrats.

One noteworthy feature of this period was that for a large part of the time the cabinets were technically minority governments, although they had reasonably assured parliamentary bases by means of agreements, pacts or understandings with support parties. To be sure this was not a new phenomenon: ever since the 1920s, there had been minority governments in all the Scandinavian countries in situations when the centre was unwilling to commit itself to alliances with either the left or the right. What was new, however, was the emergence of a significant force to the left of the Social Democrats. This complicated the rules of the game on three counts: the Socialist People's Party exposed the Social Democrats to electoral competition that imposed constraints on how far they could go in compromises with the centre; it was not accepted as a fully-fledged coalition partner (although it could not be isolated on foreign policy grounds as had been the case with the Communists); and it made the Radicals reluctant to join an oversized coalition with its centre of gravity too far to the left.

What does not become visible if one looks only at the bases of government formation, is the very large extent of consensus that indeed prevailed in many aspects of Danish policy-making. As Damgaard has pointed out, a huge proportion of all 'law-making' in the Danish parliament in the period 1953–73 was either unopposed or supported by all the four 'old' parties. Of the remaining – and perhaps politically more important – share, a very large portion was carried with the support of at least one party outside the government's parliamentary base.[11]

This is, of course, not a characteristic exclusive to Danish parliamentarism. In Norway and Sweden, the Labour and Social Democratic one-party governments often secured the support of at least one of the opposition parties. In the Swedish case, one reason was often that the Social Democrats either could not or did not want to rely on Communist support for their legislative programme. Yet, the deliberate search for the largest possible majority support seems to be a much more significant feature of Danish parliamentary politics. One may conjecture that the Radicals – either as a coalition partner or as a support party – had a special electoral interest in promoting oversized 'law-making' majorities. Whether the Radicals sided with the left or the right, they would always have one flank exposed; but the party could protect its position by involving parties outside the government base in broadly-based compromises. Moreover, the streak of pacifism and foreign-policy neutralism that is part of the Radical left's traditional stand has from time to time set it apart from the other three 'old parties' (for example, on NATO and defence expenditure; the result has sometimes been that legislative decisions have been based on irregular and broad coalitions.

Policy output: how much difference did governments make?

The political balance was not the same within the three countries during the post-war period before the oil crisis in the early 1970s. Sweden was governed by the Social Democrats – alone or as the very senior partner in a coalition – throughout the period. In Norway, the bourgeois parties took over in 1965. In Denmark, the Social Democrats had less parliamentary strength even when they held office in minority or coalition governments, and the country was governed by the non-socialist parties in 1945–7, 1950–3, and 1968–71. How much difference did this make to policy-making and policy output?

In many respects the similarities and parallels in the social and economic developments of the three countries are very prominent indeed. Like most other West European countries, all three enacted an ambitious welfare state programme during the immediate post-war period; and in all of them the ambitions were rather higher than in most other West European countries. Like the rest of Western Europe, the prosperity of the 1960s was accompanied by an expansion of public services; and in all three Scandinavian countries ambitions were again higher than in many other industrially developed countries (but not without exception, namely, the Netherlands).

There were, to be sure, differences in the prevailing social and economic conditions in the three countries. Sweden's economy had been less damaged by the war, and in general the country had larger economic resources at its disposal. A number of circumstances combined to make balance-of-payments deficits the most prominent structural problem for the Danish economy throughout the period: an even higher dependence on foreign trade than Sweden and Norway; a much larger agricultural sector which had to cope with unfavourable terms-of-trade relations in the post-war period; the strains on the economy caused by an – in itself desirable – expansion of the industrial sector from the late 1950s. Structural economic differences created very different preconditions for policy-making in the 1970s: Denmark was particularly hard-hit by rising oil prices; both its agricultural and industrial sectors encountered difficult adjustment problems in the new EC environment. Norway saw its prosperity rise as a result of the new North Sea oil and gas assets, but the repercussions of a rising exchange rate on the manufacturing industry were severe. For Sweden the downturn in the international economy created difficulties both for manufacturing industry and for exports of raw materials.

A set of indicators which summarise these trends in policy-making and economic developments is shown in Table 5.1. The rapid expansion

Table 5.1   Selected indicators of government policy and economic trends 1960–80

		Denmark	Norway	Sweden
Current disbursement by government as % of GDP[a]	1960	21.4	26.4	26.9
	1965	25.7	30.3	30.2
	1970	34.6	36.5	37.2
	1976	42.8	43.8	47.8
	1979	49.4	47.1	56.8
Social security expenditure as % of GDP[b]	1962	10.6	9.7	10.9
	1966	13.4	10.6	13.5
	1968	15.8	13.6	16.3
	1970	17.9	14.7	17.8
	1976	23.7	19.9	26.6
	1979	27.0	21.9	31.0
Consumer prices: Annual average rate of increase in % change from previous year[c]	1961–70	5.9	4.5	4.0
	1971–77	9.5	8.6	8.8
	1978–	10.9	9.4	10.8
Unemployment:[d] May	1972	1.3	1.5	3.3
May	1981	8.6	2.0	1.9
GDP/capita: US$	1973	5,460	4,780	6,140
	1980	12,950	14,020	14,760
Average annual % volume growth of GDP 1975–80[e]		2.6	4.6	1.2

Sources: a) OECD statistics; b) *Yearbook of Nordic Statistics, 1981*. *Note*: the figures for 1976–9 are not quite comparable with those for the preceding years; c) OECD statistics; d) *Yearbook of Nordic Statistics, 1981*. These statistics are not entirely comparable between countries or over time; however, they reflect trends and differences between countries in broad terms; e) OECD statistics.

of the public sector during the 1960s and 1970s is shown in the top section of the table. At the beginning of the 1960s, government expenditures comprised around a quarter of the gross domestic product; by 1970 that share had risen to about a third, and by 1979 to nearly half or more than half in all three countries. What is not shown in the table, however, is that the expansion of government expenditure in Denmark and Sweden in the 1970s was financed to a substantial extent by huge budget deficits.

The trend in social security expenditure is similar, although the figures also indicate that Denmark and Sweden have spent more on social services than Norway in relation to GDP. However, the figures in the time series are not entirely comparable either between countries or over time; the definition of social security expenditure has been widened, and the inclusion of the supplementary pension payments in the last two years makes a considerable difference in the Swedish case. If social security expenditure is calculated instead in terms of the trend in cost per individual, it is found that this cost approximately doubled between 1962 and 1970 and then doubled again from 1970 to 1979 in all three countries.[12] Again, there is also a change in the pattern of government expenditure that is not directly revealed by the figures in the table: the increase in the 1970s includes the impact of greatly increased expenditure on unemployment benefits. We shall return, in the next section, to the figures at the bottom of the table. For the moment it is sufficient to point out that inflation rates up to the early 1970s were rather similar and that the level of unemployment in all three countries remained low throughout the 1960s.

As Nils Elvander has demonstrated in a comparative analysis, there are nevertheless distinctive differences between the three countries if one looks at the timing of policy decisions and at the ways in which 'social engineering' policies as well as economic policies have been pursued. Both in Norway and in Sweden, where the Social Democrats were in firmer and more continuous control, the state has acquired much more effective instruments than in Denmark for the 'steering' of the economy. This applies to state control over investment, capital formation, labour market policies and – especially in the case of Norway – regional policies as well as state industrial enterprises. The different policies adopted by Norway and Denmark to deal with North Sea oil and gas vividly illustrate the difference: Norway established a strategy of firm state control, whereas Denmark effectively handed over all responsibility to one private enterprise.

Equally, the government acquired a much firmer control over housing policy in Norway and Sweden, although the two countries employed different strategies, with a larger public housing sector in Sweden and state control over the financing of housing in Norway.

Denmark had actually embarked upon a policy not dissimilar to the Swedish, but the dismantling of this policy was the price the Social Democrats had to pay for the coalition with the Radicals from 1957. In the social policy field, the impact of the political balance is equally significant: Sweden not only took the lead in introducing a comprehensive system of income-related pensions (supplementary pensions) but also established a system that allowed the state much more influence on the credit market (through the pension funds); pension reforms in Denmark and Norway came later, in periods of bourgeois coalition governments. In the education sector, Sweden also took the lead and pursued the change to a comprehensive school system with determination and consistency; one reason was perhaps that this was one of the policies on which the Social Democrats could count on the Agrarian party's wholehearted support. Norway followed with some delay (actually the final decision came to be taken by a bourgeois coalition government in 1969), whereas Denmark lagged behind and followed a somewhat less radical path. Finally, the change to a pay-as-you-earn tax system could be taken as an example of the impact of coalition politics: the sheer difficulty in coming to an agreement in coalition governments delayed the change in Denmark by more than a decade in comparison with Sweden and Norway.

The differences we have noted here are not easily quantifiable. To some extent they pertain to the timing of policies, which were responses to social and economic development, and sooner or later were adopted by all three countries. To some extent they also pertain to the ways in which policies are implemented: somewhat different approaches to the same problem (for example, mass education) can have very significant social engineering consequences, for example. Moreover, these policy differences are not all attributable to the party complexion of the government. The fact that Sweden in some instances took the lead obviously had to do with its more advanced industrial development and larger resources. Similarly, the fact that Norway pursued a more ambitious regional policy and has applied economic planning more vigorously had much to do with the special needs of the post-war reconstruction period, although it also reflected the ideological orientation of the Norwegian Labour party. Undoubtedly, however, the comparative weakness of the Social Democrats in Denmark goes a long way to explain why Denmark shows a tendency both to lag behind on 'social engineering' legislation and to rely on a more liberal approach to economic policy. The Danish Social Democrats had shorter uninterrupted stretches in office – and when they were in office these were precisely the issues on which compromises with coalition partners or support parties in the centre were necessary.[13]

Social Democratic decline and governmental instability: the 1970s
One year after the return of a Social Democrat government to office
in Sweden – with a socialist majority in the Riksdag as well as in the
electorate – it may seem inappropriate to describe the last decade under
the heading of social democratic decline. Let it be said, therefore, that
we are by no means arguing that the social democratic parties in
Scandinavia are a spent force. But in both Denmark and Norway the
balance has shifted so far that minority governments under Conservative Prime Ministers are holding office. And even in Sweden, politics
can not be the same again since the defeat of the Social Democrats in
1976. The Social Democrats reasserted their basic appeal to the
Swedish electorate in 1982, but the spell of nearly half a century of
social democratic dominance has been broken. The crucial question for
the non-socialist parties of how to form a workable and stable alternative to social democratic governance will force itself upon them again,
although it may well happen later rather than sooner.

In all three countries the early 1970s was a time of political volatility.
The question of membership of the European Communities disrupted
bourgeois unity and caused a deep split in the Labour party in Norway.
The consequences of EC membership and a backlash against steeply
increasing taxation combined to set the scene for a period of turmoil in
the Danish party system. Disenchantment with the cost of the welfare
state no doubt contributed to the Swedish Social Democrats' gradual
decline in the elections of 1970, 1973 and 1976. The effects of the
international recession and the oil-price shocks made life difficult for
governments of all political complexions; but with worrying signs of
increasing unemployment and industrial crisis the impact was particularly damaging for the Social Democrats. Their philosophy of
economic growth as well as their ability to deliver the benefits of the
welfare state – employment and secure living standards – were suddenly in doubt.[14]

Throughout the decade, the problems with the economy seemed to
become increasingly intractable, although the experiences of the three
countries were different in significant respects. The consequences were
probably worst in Denmark: there was a steep increase in unemployment (see Table 5.1), government budget deficits became a major
problem, and foreign debt increased at an alarming rate. In Sweden,
the bourgeois governments were much more successful in keeping
unemployment down but at a high cost. In order to finance a costly
labour market policy as well as rescue operations to prop up failing
industries, the non-socialist parties had to throw overboard the conservative fiscal policy of the previous social democratic era; budget
deficits were mounting. Ironically, during no previous period were so
many private enterprises taken into state ownership: the state took over

a troubled collection of industries such as shipbuilding and textiles. Norway obviously benefitted – as we have mentioned before – from oil and gas in the North Sea. Indeed (see Table 5.1), Norway very nearly caught up with Sweden in respect of wealth (as measured by GDP per capita). But inflationary pressures in the domestic economy and crisis in the country's manufacturing industry created serious problems. In addition, the Labour Government's attempts to harness the impact of the new oil riches through incomes policy caused conflicts of interest among different categories of wage earners which cut right into the party's working-class electoral base.[15]

In broad outline, there was as much similarity in the policy approaches chosen in the three countries during the 1970s as there had been in the 1960s. As noted earlier (see Table 5.1), government expenditure increased its share to comprise about a half of each country's GDP. There was hardly any attempt to dismantle the welfare state – not even in Denmark despite the emergence of a protest party on precisely this issue – and if some plans for expansion of social security measures had to be shelved, the saving was more than outweighed by other factors (for example, the cost of unemployment benefit schemes). Inflation rates were not markedly dissimilar. To the extent that the three countries can be deemed to have weathered the storms of economic recession more or less successfully, the causes are probably as much to be found in external economic circumstances as in their choice of economic policy strategies. Even so, economic policy-making in Denmark continues to be more liberal than in Norway and Sweden (even during periods of non-socialist government in Sweden in 1976–82). In Norway, state control over North Sea oil and gas may again be cited; in addition, the state intervened energetically (though perhaps not very successfully) to sustain manufacturing industry, and a comparatively successful incomes policy was pursued in a comparatively calm labour market. Labour market policies in Sweden maintained a low level of unemployment through extensive programmes for retraining and relief work. In fact, the difference between the unemployment rates in Denmark and Sweden both at the beginning and the end of the period is larger than Table 5.1 suggests; the Swedish statistics record the number of unemployed with the aid of labour market surveys, whilst Denmark uses the number of registered unemployed which always yields a lower figure.

The 1970s was also a decade when political decisions of far-reaching consequence were made. Denmark joined the European Communities, whilst Norway decided to stay outside. Sweden committed itself to a long-term plan to phase out nuclear power production, but rejected a proposal to abandon any further building of nuclear power stations and to close down those in use in the relatively near future. It is noteworthy that all three decisions were made by referenda. But in each case parties and governments were deeply involved and the repercussions on party politics were highly conspicuous. Moreover, as in the preceding decades, there are differences in the timing and devising of policies that are not necessarily captured by the gross macro-economic statistics referred to above. To capture such differences, one needs to look at the ways in which policies are made in governments and at parliamentary politics. It is to the crucial element in that process that we shall now turn: the formation of majorities and governments in the three parliaments.

Alternations in government: three scenarios

The following outline of changes in government will serve to illuminate how changes in the parliamentary balance of power affected the preconditions for decision-making (or non-decision-making) on a wide range of policy issues. In the next section, we shall use these three scenarios to identify some characteristic features of parliamentary politics as well as the setting for decision-making in situations where no party commands a majority on its own. In particular, we shall be concerned with the circumstances under which policy disagreements cause coalitions to fall apart or lead to the formation of minority governments.

The three scenarios are set out in one table each for Denmark (Table 5.2), Norway (Table 5.3), and Sweden (Table 5.4). In the tables the parties are placed in a left-right array in which, however, some of the parties in the centre share the same space. In the latter case there has not seemed to be any certain criterion for further differentiation, and in several instances the party division in the centre reflects the impact of secondary political cleavages. By and large the resulting array may be taken as an ordering on an ideological left-right dimension, ranging from socialism to conservatism. Needless to say, however, there are some ambiguities in the placing of the parties; for example, the proper location of the christian democratic parties, or the relative positioning of the Centre Party and the People's Party (Liberals) in Sweden. Such ambiguities pertain only to the relative positioning of parties in the centre, however. And this problem of positioning only slightly complicates the relationship between the parties participating in coalitions and their placing on a policy scale.[16] In line with coalition theories such as those proposed by Axelrod and De Swaan, we would expect coalitions to be formed by parties that occupy a segment of the scale, so as to include the party or parties that are placed in between those farthest to the left and farthest to the right in the coalition.

The table for *Denmark* (Table 5.2) begins with the period of two-bloc politics that we discussed in the previous section: the Social Democrat

Government (with the Socialist People's Party as a support party) 1966–8; the shift during the years 1968–70 when the Radicals joined the Liberals and the Conservatives in a three-party coalition; and, finally, the return of a Social Democrat Government without any certain support in the centre 1971–3. Perhaps it was dissatisfaction with the performance of both blocs in office as much as anything else that caused the election result in 1973 when all the 'old parties' emerged as losers. After all, in the old Folketing only the Socialist People's Party had opposed Denmark's joining the European Communities, and although a huge majority had endorsed that policy in a referendum, a wave of disappointment set in as the effect on food prices became apparent. Moreover, both the Social Democrats and the bourgeois parties seemed to share responsibility for the steep tax increases of the last few years. With declining trust in the 'old parties', dissatisfaction was articulated through voting for alternatives along the entire left-right spectrum. Most noticeably, the backlash against high taxation was expressed through the emergence of a new populist party on the far right, the Progress Party. Claiming to voice dissatisfaction among old social democratic voters with the party's slide towards the left in recent years, the Centre Democrats emerged as a new party in the centre; as it was opposed in particular to the last government's attempts to increase taxes on owner-occupied houses, it was perhaps also to some extent part of the anti-tax backlash. At the same time, the Justice Party as well as the new Christian People's Party managed to surmount Denmark's low threshold of representation. The combined strength of the far left was also increased, and the Communists won parliamentary representation after some years of absence. The number of parties in the Danish Folketing more than doubled, from 5 to 11.

The proliferation of parties in the centre may have made coalition formation a more intricate matter – because of the sheer number of party leaders involved in such negotiations – but the new parties soon became integrated into the system. What really changed the situation was the Progress Party. It was not only rejected as a coalition party; parties in the centre – especially the Radicals – were distinctly unwilling to join a coalition government that even implicitly counted on the Progress Party as part of its parliamentary base. That meant that no majority coalition could be formed on the centre-right of the party system. On the other side, the socialist parties did not have a majority; and there was in any case little prospect of reviving the close partnership between the Social Democrats and the Socialist People's Party of 1966–8, and no prospect at all that the Social Democrats could rely on support from the far left in a situation where the country's economy urgently required pay restraint as well as a curbing of public expenditure.

Table 5.2   Governments in Denmark 1966–82 (Elections: 1966, 1968, 1971, 1973, 1975, 1977, 1979, 1981)

Years	Seats: Socialist (S) Bourgeois (B)			Party/Parties in Government			
1966–1968	S: 89 B: 86		Socialist People's P (20)	Social Democrats (69) *Jens Otto Krag*	Radicals (13) Liberal Centre (4)	(Agrarian) Liberals (35)	Conservatives (34)	
1968–1971	S: 77 B: 98	Left Socialists (4)	Soc PP (11)	Social Democrats (62)	Radicals (27) *Hilmar Baunsgaard (R)*	(Agrarian) Liberals (34)	Conservatives (37)	
1971–1973	S: 87* B: 88		Soc PP (17)	Social Democrats (70) *J.O. Krag – Anker Jørgensen*	Radicals (27)	(Agrarian) Liberals (30)	Conservatives (31)	
1973–1975	S: 63 B: 84 + 28	Communists (6)	Soc PP (11)	Social Democrats (46)	Radicals (20) Centre Democrats (14) Justice P (5) Christian People's P (7)	(Agrarian) Liberals (22) *Poul Hartling*	Conservatives (16)	Progress Party (28)
1975–1977	S: 73 B: 78 + 24	Communists (7) Left Soc (4)	Soc PP (9)	Social Democrats (53) *A. Jørgensen*	Radicals (13) Centre Democrats (4) Christian People's P (9)	(Agrarian) Liberals (42)	Conservatives (10)	Progress Party (24)

	S: / B:	Communists / Left Soc	Soc PP	Social Democrats	Radicals / Centre Democrats / Justice P / Christian People's P	(Agrarian) Liberals	Conservatives	Progress Party
1977–1978	S: 84 B: 65 + 26	Communists (7) Left Soc (5)	Soc PP (7)	Social Democrats (65) *A. Jørgensen*	Radicals (6) Centre Democrats (11) Justice P (6) Christian People's P (6)	(Agrarian) Liberals (21)	Conservatives (15)	Progress Party (26)
1978–1979	S: 84 B: 65 + 26	Communists (7) Left Soc (5)	Soc PP (7)	Social Democrats (65) *A. Jørgensen*	Radicals (6) Centre Democrats (11) Justice P (6) Christian People's P (6)	(Agrarian) Liberals (21)	Conservatives (15)	Progress Party (26)
1979–1981	S: 85 B: 70 + 20	Left Soc (6)	Soc PP (11)	Social Democrats (68) *A. Jørgensen*	Radicals (10) Centre Democrats (6) Justice P (5) Christian People's P (5)	(Agrarian) Liberals (22)	Conservatives (22)	Progress Party (20)
1981–1982	S: 85 B: 74 + 16	Left Soc (5)	Soc PP (21)	Social Democrats (59) *A. Jørgensen*	Radicals (9) Centre Democrats (15) Christian People's P (4)	(Agrarian) Liberals (20)	Conservatives (26)	Progress Party (16)
1982–	S: 85 B: 74 + 16	Left Soc (5)	Soc PP (21)	Social Democrats (59)	Radicals (9) Centre Democrats (15) Christian People's P (4)	(Agrarian) Liberals (20)	Conservatives (26) *Poul Schlüter (C)*	Progress Party (16)

* In addition to those classified as held by socialist and bourgeois parties, there are 2 representatives each for Greenland and the Faroe Islands. On occasion, some or all of these representatives have weighed the balance in favour of a left-of-centre government; in particular this was the case in 1971 when Krag could count on three of them; a Greenland representative joined the government as Minister for Greenland.

Note: A double line in the table indicates a change in the distribution of seats due to an election.

As the electorate had so clearly shifted towards the right, it was obvious that the burden of governing had, in some form, to fall upon the bourgeois parties. But it had to be a government that did not exclude the possibility of compromise with the Social Democrats; otherwise the non-socialist bloc feared by the centrist parties would actually have been formed. The solution was to allow the Liberals to form a minority government that could count on an understanding both with the Conservatives and with the parties in the middle whilst nevertheless, by its position, indicating a willingness to seek co-operation with the Social Democrats, rather than the Progress Party. The experiment actually worked unexpectedly well, but the basis crumbled after the 1975 election. The Social Democrats regained some of their strength and were unwilling to continue to keep a non-socialist government in office. Perhaps equally important, the Liberals gained considerably at the expense of the Radicals as well as the Centre Democrats and the Conservatives; the Radicals now had good reason to ask themselves whether they would not benefit more from collaboration with the Social Democrats.

As the result of the change in the balance, the Social Democrats took office in a minority government which survived by a sequence of agreements with the parties in the centre, often including the Liberals also. It proved difficult for all these parties to agree upon a coherent economic policy strategy, however, and in 1978 the Social Democratic Prime Minister, Mr Jørgensen, took the unexpected step of forming a coalition government with the Liberals, leaving the Radicals and the other small parties in the centre outside. The best that could be said about this coalition is, perhaps, that it was a bold attempt to create a simpler bargaining situation for the two parties with the greatest weight in the part of the political spectrum where a compromise on economic policy had to be worked out. But it was still a minority government. Furthermore, it was an 'unconnected' coalition that left out precisely the parties that were required to achieve a majority; moreover, it imposed a considerable strain on the relationship between the Social Democrats and the trade unions, who felt that the party had moved too far to the right. After the 1979 election, the base for the Social Democratic government shifted back to its pre-1978 location. The 1981 election, finally, weakened the Social Democrats through a substantial loss to the Socialist People's Party on its left, whilst the Conservatives gained strength at the expense of the other non-socialist parties.[17] For sheer lack of a viable alternative, the Social Democratic minority government stayed on in office until the summer of 1982. When the Social Democrats gave up, it again proved impossible to form a non-socialist majority coalition. Apparently, it was also impossible to find support for a centre-based minority government of the 1973–5 type.

Thus it became the Conservatives' turn to take the lead in the formation of a minority government: a coalition under Conservative premiership with participation by Agrarian Liberals, Centre Democrats and the Christian People's Party. The Radicals stayed outside. This may well mean that the non-socialist parties are more prepared than before to recognise, at least implicitly, the political weight of the Progress Party. With the Conservatives' own strength having increased in the last election, and the Progress Party's weakened (their leader also being given a jail-sentence for tax evasion), it is perhaps now seen as less risky to treat it as a support party than in the period when it still seemed to have a growth potential.

There has been a non-socialist majority in the Folketing since 1973. Yet, the road to a non-socialist majority government has been blocked by two factors. The most obvious one is the existence of the Progress Party. In a more subtle way, however, the left-right array of the non-socialist parties has created tensions that have made collaboration difficult. That is, the Radicals and other small parties in the centre have been reluctant to go along with the kind of economic-liberal austerity programme that would have been the Liberals' and the Conservatives' favoured recipe to overcome the problems with the economy. However, if the Radicals have wished to involve the Social Democrats (and thereby, of course, occupy an influential 'pivotal' position), they have also blocked Social Democratic policy alternatives. For the Social Democrats, both the competition with the parties on their left and their relations with the trade unions have imposed difficult constraints. The party's relationship with the trade unions in terms of overlapping leadership and in other ways is very close indeed. But any policy deals it might have wanted to strike with the unions have ultimately required the consent of the parties in the centre. As a result, the Social Democrats have found themselves unable to deliver on the measures that the trade unions would have wanted in exchange for their support for pay restraint and austerity measures in public expenditure: the economic democracy programme (involving investment funds on which the unions would have representation) fell by the wayside, so did attempts to tackle the housing problem for low-income groups, and so did the plan to bring down unemployment by directing insurance and pension funds to job-creating investments on favourable credit terms. Each of these initiatives may have had its flaws, just as the other parties on the left and centre-left may have been justified in rejecting the Liberal-Conservative approach as socially unacceptable. But the point is that the prevailing balance of strength has often resulted in stalemate rather than in conflict resolution.

There is one mechanism in Danish politics during the 1970s that has frequently been used to break deadlocks in economic policy-making:

comprehensive compromise packages, including the government's economic policy measures as well as incomes policy. They are arrived at in the parliamentary arena, through the government's negotiating an acceptable platform with as many parties as can be persuaded to join in. As Schwerin has pointed out, the result does not fit the corporatist model for incomes policy. Ultimately, it falls upon the political parties to intervene to break deadlocks in the labour market and impose solutions. As Schwerin also stresses, this mode of economic management is difficult to operate when no party commands a parliamentary majority: the dynamics of party competition come to affect labour market relations, just as the parties in their attempts to reach compromise agreements are tied by their respective connections with organised interests. In this diagnosis, the Danish sectoral organisation has not reached a sufficient degree of centralisation to operate in accordance with the much more corporatist Norwegian model.[18] It might be added that, even if it had, the government would in most instances have had difficulty in filling the role prescribed by the corporatist model, given the uncertainty of its parliamentary base. With all their flaws, the broad parliamentary agreements have had an important function to fill in a party system that has found it so difficult to form bases for stable majority governments.

In the 1960s, *Norway* seemed for a time to come very close to a two-bloc system and the prospect of alternation in government by the two blocs. The top section of Table 5.3 shows how the four non-socialist parties in a coalition government held office during a stretch of more than five years. The coalition even survived the 1969 election and was able to continue in office with the barest possible majority. What brought it down was – as mentioned in the earlier section – the question of Norway's membership of the European Communities.

While the bourgeois government was committed to negotiate Norway's joining the EC, the immediate cause of its fall was an incident that cast doubt on the Prime Minister's intentions. But quite clearly the coalition was already in danger because of the growing opposition within the centre parties to the terms for membership that seemed likely. A minority Labour government with a pro-EC posture took over, but it resigned when the proposal to join was turned down in the 1972 referendum, and a small minority government of the parties in the centre held office until 1973. The EC issue itself was divisive, and the referendum campaign widened the splits both among and within parties. In the centre, the Centre Party and the Christian People's Party came out against membership and so did the Liberal Party which, however, formally split on the issue. The Labour Party was badly affected by internal disunity. Opposition to the EC gave new life to the Socialist left. The effects became visible in the 1973 election. The

Labour Party suffered a serious setback, caused by losses to anti-EC left Socialists. In the centre, the old Liberal Party – now divided – was almost extinguished, a fate from which it has not so far recovered. On the far right, a populist anti-tax party gained a few seats, but had far less success than in Denmark. Yet two-bloc politics was able to begin to operate again because of the marginal shift that gave the socialist parties a majority.[19] The internal divisions among the non-socialist parties resulting from the EC controversy meant that there was hardly any effective attempt to challenge the Labour government during the 1974–7 election period, and the Labour Party came back after the election of 1977 with a strengthened position.

As we have already mentioned, the early 1980s saw a major shift towards the right in the electorate, and the 1981 election brought in a non-socialist majority in the Storting. This time, however, it proved impossible to revive the bourgeois coalition of the 1965–71 era. The reason throws an interesting light on the presence of more than one dimension – or cleavage – in the Norwegian party system. The Christian People's Party had made abolition of free abortion a major issue in its campaign, and although it apparently had lost support because of this stance, it refused to join a coalition government that would not commit itself to a change in the abortion law. In this situation the task of forming a minority government went to the party that had been most successful in the election, the Conservatives. It was made clear that the new government would be supported by all the parties in the centre on an agreed economic policy programme; the Conservatives had, as it were, formed a minority government on behalf of the non-socialist majority. Yet, it is noteworthy that the Centre Party also refused to join the government when the Christian People's Party stayed outside (the Liberals were reduced to a tiny minor party). One reason may have been that the Centre Party felt that it would carry too little weight in a coalition government which would have to be dominated by the Conservatives. Indeed it might well have more power to influence policy, if it stood outside together with the Christian Party. Another consideration may have been that the Centre Party did not wish to give the Christian People's Party the tactical advantage of being the only significant party on the non-socialist side that did not share direct responsibility for government policy.

Finally, we turn to the scenario in *Sweden*. In a sense, the first signs of a minority government situation began to show immediately after the first elections to the new unicameral Riksdag. In the Riksdag that began its election period in 1971, the Social Democrats still had a majority together with the Communists, but less strength than the three bourgeois parties taken together. Thus the government had to rely on positive Communist support when it faced a united bourgeois

Table 5.3   Governments in Norway 1965–82 (Elections: 1965, 1969, 1973, 1977, 1981)

Years	Seats: Socialist (S) Bourgeois (B)	Party/Parties in Government
1965–1969	S: 70 B: 80	Socialist Left (2) Labour (68) Liberals (18), Christian People's P (13), Centre Party (18), *Per Borten (CP)* Conservatives (31)
1969–1971	S: 74 B: 76	Labour (74) Liberals (13), Christian People's P (14), Centre Party (20), *Per Borten (CP)* Conservatives (29)
1971–1972	S: 74 B: 76	Labour (74) *Trygve Bratteli* Liberals (13), Christian People's P (14), Centre Party (20) Conservatives (29)

		Socialist Left	Labour	Liberals / Christian People's P / Centre Party	Conservatives	Progress Party
1972–1973	S: 74 B: 76		Labour (74)	Liberals (13) Christian People's P (14) Centre Party (20) *Lars Korvald (CP)*	Conservatives (29)	
1973–1977	S: 78 B: 77	Socialist Left (16)	Labour (62) *Trygve Bratteli* *– Odvar Nordli*	Liberals (2), New Liberals (1) Christian People's P (20) Centre Party (21)	Conservatives (29)	Progress Party (4)
1977–1981	S: 78 B: 77	Socialist Left (2)	Labour (76) *Odvar Nordli* *– Gro Harlem* *Brundtland*	Liberals (2) Christian People's P (22) Centre Party (12)	Conservatives (41)	
1981–	S: 69 B: 86	Socialist Left (4)	Labour (65)	Liberals (2) Christian People's P (15) Centre Party (11)	Conservatives (54) *Kåre Willoch*	Progress Party (4)

Note: A double line in the table indicates a change in the distribution of seats due to an election.

opposition. The change from the 1968 election when the Social Democrats had won an absolute majority in the Riksdag as well as in the
electorate was indeed dramatic. With the introduction of a fully proportional representation system, the Communists now carried a great
deal more weight than before. This could be decisive, as was shown
when the Social Democrats had to drop a planned increase in value-
added tax and instead go for an increase in employers' contributions,
effectively a payroll tax. Ironically, perhaps, the Communists thereby
set a precedent for a subsequent series of changes in the tax system,
some with the support of the bourgeois parties. At a time when all
parties wanted to reduce income tax rates whilst government expenditure continued to rise, increases in employers' contributions (the least
'visible' of all taxes) became for a time a preferred source of government
revenue.

The 1973 election resulted in an even balance, with the socialist
parties holding exactly half of the 350 seats in the Riksdag. On quite a
few occasions a tie had to be broken by the drawing of lots (the Speaker
does not have a casting vote). More importantly, however, the Social
Democrats were forced to adopt the tactics of a minority government by
seeking support on the other side of the boundary between the two
blocs. The issue of overriding importance was to balance the economy
by persuading the trade unions to accept a measure of restraint in their
wage demands. The means to that end was a series of reductions in
income tax rates in order to ensure that more modest wage increases
would yield at least some increase in real income even after tax. The
deals were arranged in a sequence of negotiations: the government first
met the representatives of the interest groups and then presented the
result as a basis for negotiation with the non-socialist parties. The
purpose was to ensure the support of at least one party in the centre.
The tactical goal in the parliamentary arena was to split the bourgeois
opposition and isolate the Conservatives.[20] It worked for a time, but
only for a time. The bourgeois parties won the 1976 election as a united
governmental alternative.

In the 1982 election campaign, the Social Democrats observed wryly
that if the bourgeois parties had kept no other of their promises back in
1976, at least one had been fulfilled: change in power. During the six
years 1976–82 of non-socialist majority in the Riksdag, the country had
seen four cabinets.

When the non-socialist parties won the parliamentary majority in
1976 they had pledged in advance that a three-party coalition government would be formed, and so it was. The end-result was never in
doubt. But there were obstacles. Firstly, the Centre Party and the
People's Party (Liberals), who had established close centrist collaboration while in opposition and had often distanced themselves from the

Conservatives, wanted to give the new government a 'centrist' profile (we are using the term 'centrist' here in the sense of the two parties 'in the middle'). To that end they demanded the post of Prime Minister and also pressed hard for a measure of over-representation in terms of portfolios. The Conservatives conceded the first, but resisted the second. In the end the ministries were allocated on a roughly proportional basis. The office of Prime Minister was taken by the Centre Party, and the centrist profile was further stressed by making the leader of the People's Party Deputy Prime Minister. The Conservatives could not have the Ministry of Finance, but instead the Ministry was divided into a Budget Department and a Ministry of Economic Affairs. The Conservative party leader took the latter; by the sheer political weight of his presence in the government he soon saw to it that the Budget Department was placed in the shadow of his own Ministry.

The second obstacle was much more ominous and consisted of the disagreement between the Centre and the other two parties on the nuclear power issue. The Centre Party – and not least its leader Thorbjörn Fälldin – was deeply committed to a pledge to abolish nuclear energy production and to oppose the construction of any new nuclear power plants. The two other non-socialist parties – like the Social Democrats – wanted to continue to expand nuclear energy production. The disagreement was patched up on this occasion, but a political time-bomb was left ticking.

The third obstacle caused the least difficulty at the time but the outcome was politically significant: the whole range of welfare policies, where there were obvious differences of view between the parties in the centre and the Conservatives, especially in the case of housing policy. By and large, the Conservatives yielded on those issues: the government's declared intent was to preserve the welfare state, and even to expand the social policy programme in some respects. On one issue there was no disagreement: the new government was to achieve a reform of the tax system and a reduction of the tax burden.[21]

A building programme for new nuclear power stations and reactors was already under way when the coalition government took office. The feeling in the Centre Party was that its entire credibility would be at risk if it did not take a stand: the programme had to be discontinued. The moment of truth came in the autumn of 1978 when a decision on a new reactor had to be made: the Centre Party required its coalition partners to consent to a 'no', or at least to refer the matter to a referendum. They accepted neither. The first bourgeois coalition government fell apart. It did so on an issue that had no clear place on the left-right cleavage that defined the boundary in the Swedish two-bloc alignment. Indeed, it was an issue on which firm proponents were found in the trade union movement as well as in industry, among the Social Democrats as well as among the Conservatives.[22]

Table 5.4   Government in Sweden 1971–1982 (Elections: 1970, 1976, 1979, 1982)

Years	Seats: Socialist (S) Bourgeois (B)		Party/Parties in Government			
1971–1973	S: 180 B: 170	Communists (17)	Social Democrats (163) *Olof Palme*	Centre Party (71)	People's P (Liberals) (58)	Moderates (Conservatives) (41)
1974–1976	S: 175 B: 175	Communists (19)	Social Democrats (156) *Olof Palme*	Centre Party (90)	People's P (Liberals) (34)	Moderates (Conservatives) (51)
1976–1978	S: 169 B: 180	Communists (17)	Social Democrats (152)	Centre Party (86) *Thorbjörn Fälldin* (CP)	People's P (Liberals) (39)	Moderates (Conservatives) (55)
1978–1979	S: 169 B: 180	Communists (17)	Social Democrats (152)	Centre Party (86)	People's P (Liberals) (39) *Ola Ullsten*	Moderates (Conservatives) (55)

		Communists	Social Democrats	Centre Party	People's P (Liberals)	Moderates (Conservatives)
1979–1981	S: 174 B: 175	Communists (20)	Social Democrats (154)	Centre Party (64) *Thorbjörn Fälldin* (CP)	People's P (Liberals) (38)	Moderates (Conservatives) (73)
1981–1982	S: 174 B: 175	Communists (20)	Social Democrats (154)	Centre Party (64) *Thorbjörn Fälldin* (CP)	People's P (Liberals) (39)	Moderates (Conservatives) (73)
1982–	S: 186 B: 163	Communists (20)	Social Democrats (166) *Olof Palme*	Centre Party (56)	People's P (Liberals) (21)	Moderates (Conservatives) (86)

Note: Elections are held in September. Under the earlier constitution, the newly elected Parliament did not assemble until January in the following year: with effect from the 1976 election, the election period begins fifteen days after the election. The Social Democratic one-party government had before 1971 been in office since 1957, first with Mr Erlander and from 1969 with Mr Palme as Prime Minister.

Note: A double line in the table indicates a change in the distribution of seats due to an election.

The left-right dimension as well as the boundary between the blocs re-emerged immediately, however, when the new government was to be formed. A majority coalition between the Social Democrats and one of the parties in the centre was not politically feasible: the Centre Party could not and the People's Party would not. A Social Democrat minority government was equally unacceptable to the bourgeois majority. The Conservatives simply wanted their own party and the People's Party to continue in government, counting on the Centre Party's support on all issues, except nuclear power. But the People's Party refused. They had joined the three-party coalition on condition that the Conservatives would be balanced by the combined strength of the parties in the middle; they had insisted that the government's profile should be centrist. They were not willing to join the Conservatives as the junior partner in a two-party coalition. A dissolution of the Riksdag was, of course, technically possible: but it was not an option that looked very promising for the parties in a coalition that had just collapsed. In addition, according to the Swedish Constitution the election period would last only to the next 'ordinary' election at the end of the fixed three-year term, in 1979. The prospect of having two elections within a year was certainly not attractive. It soon became clear that the People's Party was determined to form a minority government, if possible. The Social Democrats then decided that their best strategy was to engineer a split in the bourgeois bloc. They advised the Speaker (whose task it is to nominate a prime minister candidate) that a People's Party minority government was the most viable option available, and pledged to the People's Party leader, Ola Ullsten, that they would abstain on the investiture vote. This outcome was also reluctantly accepted by the Centre Party. As we have seen in the preceding chapter, the constitutional rules for government formation are that the Speaker's nomination is considered accepted, unless a majority of the membership of the Riksdag votes against it. Thus it happened that the People's Party minority government was installed in office with 39 votes in favour (People's Party), 66 against (Conservatives and Communists), and 215 abstentions (Social Democrats and Centre Party).[23]

If the Social Democrats' strategy was to break up the bourgeois bloc, they were soon proved to have miscalculated. The People's Party government functioned, by and large, as a minority cabinet with a bourgeois bloc majority. On the other hand, the two other parties in the bloc had no reason to enhance the status of the People's Party. Most significantly, they denied the government the achievement it had wanted most: the tax reform that the bourgeois parties had jointly promised to carry out. All existing proposals were voted down with majorities of varying composition, and the matter was postponed until after the 1979 election.

Ironically, the Social Democrats helped to restore unity in the bourgeois bloc by changing, at least partly, their stand on the nuclear power issue. Immediately after the Three Mile Island accident, the party leader announced that the risks revealed were such that they necessitated a further study of the security problems before any definite decision could be taken, and that it ought (after the 1979 election) to be referred to a consultative referendum. The Social Democrats still did not endorse the Centre Party's position, but it was a move that went a long way to allay the concerns of a growing anti-nuclear opinion within the party, and it would moreover deprive the Centre Party of an important campaign issue in the 1979 election. It was also a move that the parties in the bourgeois bloc could hardly reject, although their consent was accompanied by harsh words about the tactical devious-ness of Mr Palme's sudden shift of position. With the nuclear power issue removed from the agenda, however, the non-socialist parties also gained an important advantage. They could again present themselves as a united bloc in the 1979 election. They won by a whisker – a majority of one in the Riksdag. This time formation of the government caused little dissension: effectively the old three-party coalition was restored with the Centre Party leader resuming the office of Prime Minister.

Yet, the bourgeois bloc government fell apart again in the spring of 1981. On this occasion the split occurred, quite unexpectedly, on an issue on the left-right dimension: taxation. At first it seemed that the government parties were very nearly in agreement on a plan to carry out a substantial reduction in state income tax and, even more sig-nificantly, to reduce 'marginal taxes' making them less steeply progressive.

The tax reform had an important place in the government's overall economic strategy. It was hoped that by reducing marginal taxes the trade unions could be persuaded to fall in line with the restraint on pay increases that the economic policy programme required. Whilst in broad agreement with the purpose of that strategy, the Social Demo-crats rejected the tax plan as much too unfavourable for people with 'ordinary incomes', industrial workers and lower white-collar em-ployees. The manual workers' central organisation (LO) sided with the Social Democrats. This meant that the economic strategy was in danger. Moreover, when trying to fend off the Social Democratic attacks, the Centre Party – and to some extent the People's Party – began to feel that they had been persuaded to move too far to the right in their efforts to reach an agreement within the government. When the Social Democrats made it clear that they were prepared to compromise, the two parties in the centre grabbed the opportunity. A revised plan, supported by the two centrist parties and the Social Democrats, was agreed upon, almost literally overnight. The Conservatives had been outmanoeuvred, and decided to resign from the government in pro-test.[24]

Again, the bourgeois parties could agree on at least one thing, however. The breaking up of a bourgeois coalition was not the right time to call a fresh election. And even less did the Conservatives want the centrist parties to drift into a closer collaboration with the Social Democrats.

Whilst hurt and angry – and after having demonstrated their feelings by abstaining on the investiture vote – the Conservatives in effect pledged their support for a Centre Party-People's Party government. Thus, the country had again got a bourgeois minority government with a parliamentary bloc majority. On economic policy the three parties even came somewhat closer during the following year, as the Centre Party and the People's Party began to move nearer to the Conservatives' views on the need to cut back public expenditure. Under a new party leader the Conservatives declared again in the 1982 election campaign that they were prepared to join a new three-party coalition. This time it failed. With a socialist majority in the Riksdag, and with the Social Democrats having a larger number of seats than the three bourgeois parties together, it was time for Mr Palme to return to office.

A coalition breaks up: the 1981 Swedish case

Why did the three-party coalition break up in 1981? The precipitating cause was, of course, the centrist parties' compromise with the Social Democrats which the Conservatives genuinely considered an act of betrayal. But there were also contributing factors which have to do with the dynamics of collaboration in government among parties that are approaching an election which they have to fight as competitors. For both the Conservatives and the two parties in the centre there were tactical advantages in increasing the distance between them. Although the Conservative leader could justly claim to have been the architect of the government's economic policy, the Conservatives could hardly have been entirely happy with the way things were going. To put it bluntly, the two centrist parties were too strongly committed to many of the social welfare policies that the government had inherited from the Social Democratic era. Indeed, in many fields the existing social policy schemes had been enacted with their support whilst in opposition. They had not been prepared to go along with the tougher attitude towards government expenditure that the Conservatives would have preferred. Outside the government, the Conservatives could now go into the next election campaign with a much more pronounced right-wing profile.

The two parties in the centre, on the other hand, may well have felt that their role in the government had begun to be dangerously overshadowed by the Conservative party leader in his role as Minister of Economic Affairs. Without the Conservatives in the government, they would be better placed to fight the next election on a 'middle ground' stance where they ran the least risk of losing votes to the Social Democratic opposition. With the benefit of hindsight it is not too difficult to explain why that strategy failed: rather than favouring the centrist parties, it resulted in a polarisation towards the Conservative and Social Democratic alternatives which strengthened the Conservatives' share of the non-socialist vote.

And, finally, why did the Social Democrats again agree to play the role of midwife to a bourgeois minority government? The answer is that they had little choice, if they wanted to exercise any influence on the reform of the tax system. And this they certainly did want. The Social Democrats already had reasonable grounds to hope that they could win the 1982 election, in particular if the bourgeois parties again showed that they were unable to govern together. But the tax issue is always a liability, rather than an asset, for the Social Democrats in an election campaign; somehow they seem to be held responsible for high taxes even in opposition. The prospect of achieving a tax reform well before the election with the support of both the parties in the centre and the trade unions was decidedly welcome.

A record of coalition politics: Sweden 1976–82

What was the record of the non-socialist parties' period in power? First, it should be said that this would not have been an easy time for any government. The shortcomings of the Swedish bourgeois governments were much the same as those of most governments in Western Europe in the aftermath of oil-price shocks and in the midst of an international economic crisis. The inflation rate increased; budget deficits soared and so did the national debt. Unemployment was rising, though the effect was concealed by retraining programmes and job-providing schemes. If there were mistakes in economic fine-tuning, these were perhaps of the kind that any government could have made. Some would take the view, however, that the built-in tension between the centrist parties and the Conservatives in the governing majority contributed to make things worse, especially in respect of the government's fiscal and budget policy. It turned out to be easier to agree upon measures to ease the progressive income tax and to resist increasing the total tax burden than upon reductions in government expenditure. Compromises within the government were achieved at the expense of coherence in economic policy. This may well be true also of one-party majority government, but a coalition government in which the participants are intent upon maintaining their relative positioning on the left-right policy scale appears to be more vulnerable.

In one respect, at least, the government had an easier run than many might have expected; that is, in the case of wage settlements and their consequences for economic policy. Without a statutory incomes policy a Swedish government always has to rely on the highly centralised organisations in the labour market to agree upon wage settlements that are at least reasonably in line with the government's economic strategy.[25] The government is certainly not passive in this respect: it can offer inducements in the form of policy measures that are contingent upon the result of the wage settlements, and it can mop up excessive demand by means of taxation. But its relationship to the interest groups is one of negotiation rather than of law-making; Sweden does not have a command economy. By and large the bourgeois governments were about as successful as the Social Democrats had been. The large manual workers' trade union federation (LO) did not conceal its disapproval of the government's economic policy, and there was, at times, also sharp criticism coming from the white-collar workers' trade union federation (TCO). But this was part of the negotiating relationship, a means of mobilising at least a sector of public opinion to put pressure on the government. There was no attempt, or even inclination, to use industrial disputes as a political weapon: the question of 'who governs' did not arise. It is true, of course, that the famous peace in the Swedish labour market seemed to explode during a few intense weeks in the spring of 1980, with a nationwide strike/lockout in the private sector. But it may well be argued that it was the intransigence of a new leadership of the Employers' Federation rather than the trade unions that was to blame for that short-circuiting. In the end, the bourgeois government came in on the trade unions' side by pressurising the employers to accede to an arbitration award that had already been accepted by the trade unions. With that single exception, the occurrence of industrial disputes remained at a low level, and throughout the period pay increases were held within limits that the government's economic policy could live with. In comparison with other industrialised countries, pay increases were moderate – typically 4–6 per cent in contractual wage increases.

There was no sharp break with the welfare state politics of the previous era. Indeed, there could not be, given that the centrist parties were committed both by their previous support for much of the policies concerned and because they were determined to show that they, rather than the Conservatives, were in charge. Most notably, the bourgeois government continued to pursue an ambitious labour market policy. Yet, there were some changes. Adjustments downwards were made in some social policy programmes: for example, pensions were made somewhat less inflation-proof, and benefits under the health insurance scheme were abolished for the first few days of sickness. It could be argued, however, that the government's fiscal policy and the fact that it had allowed deficit budgeting to go so far, would have necessitated much sharper cutbacks in government expenditure as the next step.

Even less was there any sharp change in respect of legislation that reflected 'social engineering' ambitions or values. The parties in the centre ensured that the aid programme for developing countries – to which they were strongly committed – was continued. A small but interesting example of how long-term trends in cultural change continued to operate is that it was the bourgeois coalition government which enacted legislation that made corporal punishment of children, even in the home, illegal. The ambition to create equal opportunities for women was likewise a strong commitment, although the day-nursery programme partly fell victim to a cutback in government expenditure. In education, no change of direction was made; the school system as well as higher education continued to develop broadly in line with the programme that had been devised – and supported by a fairly broad consensus – during the Social Democratic era.

In sum: policies were adjusted, but the adjustments did not amount to any decisive change of direction. By 1982 the country's economic strategy seemed to have reached an impasse. As the election result showed, many felt it was time for a change towards the right. But a larger portion of the electorate turned to the left.

Parliamentary bases, policy disagreements and coalition politics

Coming together: the forming of coalitions

The dividing line between the socialist and the non-socialist parties has been a recurrent theme, a *leitmotif*, in our discussion of policy-making and government formation in Scandinavia. It is all the more important that the nature of the resulting two-bloc tendency is understood.

Firstly, despite the pragmatic flavour of Scandinavian politics, the dividing line is not merely a matter of political rhetoric. It reflects two different political tendencies, two different ways of thinking about how and why society ought to change; and there is an underlying bedrock of conflicting group interests. The dividing line undoubtedly serves an electoral purpose; it provides the most readily available means by which parties can identify themselves as recognisable tendencies. Yet, the dividing line is not a frontier of confrontation between two hardened ideological belief systems. There is a considerable range of opinions amongst politicians as well as voters on both sides of the divide in the party system. And there is enough consensus on values and beliefs to ensure that politics, most of the time, is a non-zero-sum game, where broad compromises often become preferable to confrontation.

If the positioning of the parties helps to define the situation of choice in an election, it also imposes constraints on the kinds of collaborative arrangements that parties can – or want to – enter into after the election is over. For one thing there is always another election to look forward to: a party that frustrates its own voters' expectations will have to take into account the risk of being punished next time at the polls. Moreover, the image of politicians as mere office-seekers has always relied on a false analogy with the economic theory of the market; there is abundant evidence in Scandinavian politics to show that commitments to policies and concern with the interests represented by their party, in general, carry an overriding weight in politicians' deliberations.

To recognise the political significance of the ideological dividing line is not to say, however, that it need always define boundaries for majority formation which cannot be transgressed. Indeed, the Danish case demonstrates that they can be. It is not even to say that bloc-coalitions are necessarily more stable than coalitions including parties on both sides of the divide. The Social Democrat-Agrarian coalition in Sweden lasted more than five years, the three-party bourgeois coalitions in both countries lasted two years or less.

To a large extent, the two-bloc tendency in coalition formation in the Scandinavian countries is undoubtedly determined by the distribution of strength among the parties, especially the strength of the Social Democrats. When the Social Democrats have a parliamentary majority (either on their own or with a small Communist support party with nowhere else to go), as in Norway and Sweden, the logic of the situation requires the split bourgeois side to present itself as an alternative coalition.

The significance of the size factor is undeniable. A Prime Minister does not include another party in a coalition, if it is not required to achieve a majority. (That is, unless there are constitutional rules – as in Finland – which often create a need for a qualified majority.) The leader of a smaller party will not join a coalition where his party is numerically superfluous, because his party obviously would have very little leverage when it came to deciding government policy.

Denmark, as we have observed before, is a deviant case in respect of the size factor, because the Social Democrats have never reached the same strength as their Scandinavian sister parties, and they have more often than not taken office in coalitions or parliamentary pacts with parties in the centre. With that balance, the centre, especially the Radicals, has also gained a strong bargaining position, and it has, consequently, been able to play an active role as a pivotal party.

How does the game in general look from the bourgeois side of the divide? The important advantage of bloc politics for the non-socialist parties is clearly that it allows them to present a credible government alternative. For the Conservatives, bourgeois coalitions are normally the only access road to a place in the government (note, however, the recent exceptions in Norway and Denmark). They can sometimes gain electorally by staying outside a possible government coalition and allowing the parties in the centre to govern. But this means that the parties in the centre may seek collaboration with the Social Democrats and thus shift the general line of policy-making farther to the left than would be necessary when there is a bourgeois majority.

For the parties in the centre, a bloc coalition government entails costs. They risk being seen drifting too far to the right – losing their separate identity on the left-right scale. Moreover, in terms of policy decisions they cannot exploit fully the fact that they hold the balance of power when there is a non-socialist majority. The first predicament is normally avoided by insisting that a coalition government must have a Prime Minister from the centre, rather than the right. In addition to the obligations flowing from having offered the voters a united coalition as a government alternative, a coalition of this type can disarm the Conservatives by making them share responsibility for government policies.

If the size of the Social Democratic party alone goes some way to account for the two-bloc tendency, it is not the only factor. When the socialist parties jointly have a parliamentary majority, the ideological divide seems to inhibit any coalition between the Social Democrats and the centre. Even in the case of Denmark, it is notable that when a socialist majority emerged in the Folketing, the party system froze in a two-bloc division, 1966–73. The long stretch of Social Democratic minority governments, 1975–82, meant, of course, that two-bloc politics came to an end. But it was also – as we have observed – an anomalous situation, caused by the ostracising of the Progress Party. And without the Progress Party, the bourgeois parties could not form a majority. Bloc politics cannot accommodate extreme parties, unless such parties are reduced to numerical insignificance or virtual political impotence. For the same reason, the strength of the political competition on their left flank makes it difficult for the Danish Social Democrats to practise a two-bloc strategy. Even so, it is noteworthy that they did not entirely give up their inclination to govern on a bloc basis until the pre-requirement had vanished – when the socialist parties had lost their parliamentary majority.

In Norway, the two-bloc division has been taken for granted, even when the bourgeois parties were unable to form a coalition government after the 1981 election. In Sweden the Agrarian-Social Democrat coalition is an obvious exception, and worked well in many respects. As we observed earlier, the coalition was also a special case because the Agrarians, with their distinctive social base, were hardly involved in electoral competition with the Social Democrats. When they changed to become a party with a more general appeal, this was no longer so. For a time the Centre Party became the biggest party in opposition. It had irrevocably established an electoral base in which the voters would have no sympathy for a coalition across the bloc boundary. If a genuine centre party is one that can join alliances both to the right and to the left, the Centre Party ceased to be a centre party at the very moment when it changed its name.[26]

The significance of the left-right divide – over and above the size factor – is that it has become a politically preferred majority base, although more decidedly so in Sweden and Norway than in Denmark.[27] It would be hard to account for the attractiveness of the bloc-basis coalitions unless one recognised that the left-right cleavage is a highly salient feature of election campaigns and of the choice presented to the voters. It is not surprising that parties also prefer coalitions that are congruent with their electoral strategy.[28] In most instances, a coalition that transgresses the bloc boundary will entail a comparatively high cost in terms of concessions on policy – at least for one of the participating parties. This is not all a matter of electoral strategy, however. As we have seen in an earlier section of this chapter, the majority – or bloc majority – position from which the Norwegian and Swedish Social Democrats were operating allowed them to take the lead and impose their own 'social engineering' approach to an extent that the Danish Social Democrats could not. In the latter case it was not for want of trying, but the policy initiatives that created a sharp bloc-divide (for example, housing and 'economic democracy') were precisely those on which the Social Democrats had to yield in order to achieve a collaboration with the centre.

Coalition formation does not necessarily mean the formation of a coalition government. A government can have a broader parliamentary base than the parties that have joined the government. One reason can be that one of the blocs has a majority and is determined to keep the other out of office, but still cannot form a cohesive coalition government. In Denmark, however, the same device has often been used when non-socialist parties have wished to support a Social Democratic government without transgressing the boundary between the blocs through a formal coalition. In a sense, both phenomena are evidence of the political significance of the ideological dividing line – and they have become a prominent feature of Scandinavian parliamentarism.

In this respect the working of the parliamentary system of government has changed since the 1920s, when governments in the centre were frequently formed with the declared intention of balancing the parties to the left and to the right. Such governments did not have a parliamentary base in the form of support parties within one bloc: they were rather sustained by the existence of a *negative majority* (including, of course, the centre itself) against any government formed by parties to the right or to the left of the centre.

The minority governments of the post-war years have in general had a different centre of gravity: either Social Democratic with qualified support from the centre (at times when an all-bourgeois majority formation has proved unworkable), or non-socialist with the entire non-socialist bloc as its parliamentary base. It is a significant feature of the Scandinavian constitutions – and one which explains why minority governments can be formed with such ease – that the boundaries of government bases need not always be sharply defined in investiture or confidence votes.[29] Sweden may serve as one example of how the Constitution facilitates this. Under the 1809 Constitution there was no investiture vote and the constitutional device for a vote of political censure had effectively fallen into disuse. The 1974 Constitution (which came into effect on 1 January 1975) included both investiture votes and votes of censure. (A vote of censure had been introduced already through a constitutional amendment in 1969). However, in both instances it is for the parties which wish to defeat the government (or the Prime Minister designated by the Speaker) to win a majority of the total number of members of the Riksdag; otherwise the nominated Prime Minister or the sitting government is deemed to have survived. This arrangement means that a party wishing to sustain a government – to become effectively part of its parliamentary base – need not cast a positive vote in favour of the government; it is sufficient to abstain. Thus the nuances of within-bloc relations can be expressed, without playing into the hands of the opposite bloc.

Joining or not joining?
In general, formal coalition theory takes it for granted that parties do want to take office – provided that they are not joining a coalition that is oversized or violates some other condition (such as the non-exclusion of parties placed 'in between' the coalition partners). Much less attention has been paid to the situation when parties do *not* want to join a government to which they are nevertheless pledged to give their support. One reason seems to be that existing coalition theories do not fully acknowledge the importance of parties' commitments to specific policies: by staying outside the government, but within its parliamentary base, a party can announce a partial policy disagreement within the bloc, in order to strengthen its bargaining position. Another reason – which sometimes coincides with the first – may be that a party wants to avoid a close collaboration that could become a liability in the next election. Again, formal coalition theory does not really allow such considerations to affect its predictions.

The paramountcy of policy agreements as well as longer-term electoral considerations – rather than mere office-seeking – is indeed striking when one observes Scandinavian coalition politics. Of course, this is particularly true of the situation where a minority government works out parliamentary pacts, because no pay-offs in the form of ministerial posts are involved. But even in the formation of coalition governments, policies seem in general to be a much more important concern than portfolios. A party will naturally wish to take ministries in policy fields where it has a special interest, but by and large the numerical allocation of ministries tends to be roughly proportional to strength.[30] It is true that there was a spectacular row among the bourgeois parties in Sweden, when they formed their first coalition government in 1976. But even then, the number of ministerial posts was hardly at the heart of the matter; the real issue was the policy profile of the government.

Falling apart: the role of policy disagreements

Why do government coalitions break up? Very rarely, it seems, as a result of election outcomes. Coalition governments come to an end not only because they lose their majority in an election, but also because one or more of the participating parties wants to part company. More often than not, this seems to happen before rather than as a consequence of elections. It is this phenomenon that we shall examine in this concluding section. In doing so, we shall concentrate mainly on formal government coalitions because the immediate cause of their dissolution is in general more readily observable. Government coalitions crumble for all to see, whereas the parliamentary bases of minority governments fade away. In a few instances we shall make mention of government formations that failed from the start, because they actually exemplify the same mechanism that leads government coalitions to fall apart.

There appear to be three factors operating when governments fall apart:

i)   the effect of the coalition on parties' prestige or visibility;
ii) the impact of issues that do not have a place on the left-right dimension;
iii) policy decisions that cause tensions among coalition parties because of their positioning on the left-right dimension.

Two of the three factors, it should be noted, bear explicitly on policy disagreements.

i) *The effect of the coalition on parties' prestige or visibility.* This is the least tangible of the three factors, but it is probably an element in most cases of coalition break-up. What we have in mind is the situation that arises when one party emerges as the dominant one, the real locomotive of the coalition. From the other parties' point of view, the risk is that the dominant party will then also get the credit for whatever successes the government may enjoy. In the case of the bourgeois parties, the electoral effect could be significant given that their relative strength continually changes from election to election, with a tendency for the vote to surge towards the party that best catches the current mood in the bourgeois part of the electorate; note, for example, the recent move of electoral support to the Conservative party in all three countries.[31] The party (or parties) which fear that they are becoming overshadowed will begin to feel the need of projecting themselves to the electorate with a higher profile. Breaking up the coalition is one obvious option.

In all likelihood – although we would find it hard to produce conclusive evidence – this factor was salient, though not decisive, when the three-party bourgeois coalition in Sweden broke up in 1981. To take another example of the same mechanism in a very different context, one of the reasons why Poul Hartling found it impossible to reconstruct the parliamentary base for his minority Liberal government in Denmark after the 1975 election may well have been that his government had been too successful in the previous few years. As a result, his own party had won votes and seats at the expense of the remainder of the bourgeois bloc that had formed his parliamentary base. If the same base had been restored the other participants would have been in a weakened bargaining position.

ii) *The impact of a policy disagreement cutting across the left-right cleavage.* Given that Scandinavian government coalitions are determined by the parties' positioning on a left-right spectrum, any major policy disagreement which creates a cross-cutting cleavage is likely to have a disruptive effect. Either one side of the spectrum is divided, and so finds itself unable to maintain a cohesive coalition government, even though the bloc itself has a majority. Or both sides are divided, and it would be possible to form alliances including parties in both blocs, far apart perhaps on the left-right array. But even then, the main axis in the party system would still have an overriding importance and such coalitions would appear 'unnatural' and politically unacceptable.

In general, perhaps, one would expect a policy controversy on a cross-cutting cleavage to be associated with the emergence of a new party. For an established party to move such an issue to the fore can involve the risk of losing as much of its existing support in its preserved area on the left-right axis as it stands to gain. The situation is different, however, when there is already a secondary cleavage present in the system. A party that already owes its voting support to a combination of its place on the left-right axis (normally in the centre) and its position on the second cleavage may well stand to gain from increasing the salience of the second cleavage through a policy controversy. For the Christian People's Party in Norway this was very clearly the case with the abortion issue, although in the end the move seems to have been miscalculated; they lost rather than gained voting support. (It is a measure of the extent of cultural change in Scandinavia that the Conservative Party did not take an anti-abortion stance.) For the smaller and new christian democratic parties in Denmark, Finland and Sweden, on the other hand, the abortion issue had the function of helping them to establish a cross-cutting cleavage.

A prime example of this kind of issue is, of course, the nuclear power controversy in Sweden which led to the downfall of the three-party bourgeois coalition. In this instance, there was at least a recognisable relationship between the Centre Party's stand on nuclear power and its historical connection with a rural-urban secondary dimension in the party system. Gradually in the last decades, that connection had come to be generalised in the form of a wider concern with environmental issues. The dilemma for the bourgeois bloc was, as we have seen, resolved by the formation of a non-socialist minority government. But in the process also the tension between the People's Party and the Conservatives on the left-right scale came into play. The threat to bloc cohesiveness was finally overcome when the Social Democrats suddenly joined the Centre Party's earlier demand that the matter should be transferred to a (consultative) referendum. Interestingly, the way the referendum alternatives were arranged helped to facilitate at least a partial return to the left-right dimension. By including a demand that nuclear power stations must be under public ownership, the Social Democrats ensured that the Conservatives would have to put forward a referendum proposal of their own: thus there were three alternatives to choose from. (Why the People's Party decided to back the Social Democratic proposal remains a somewhat opaque matter. But they, too, had reasons to distance themselves from the Conservatives.)

The European Communities issue in Norway may be taken as another example, inasmuch as the breakdown of the bourgeois coalition reflected an internal division of opinions on the substantive issue at least as much as the specific incident which precipitated the Prime Minister's resignation. In 1972 the same issue necessitated the formation of a bourgeois minority government. The failure of the bourgeois parties in Norway to form a government coalition after the 1981 election because of the abortion issue might be taken as another example. But in that case, an intended coalition was already strangled at birth. Since the Christian People's Party had no friends in the other bloc, the outcome was – as mentioned before – a bloc-based Conservative minority government.

In Denmark, the Radical Liberals' pacifist tradition and their stances on related issues, notably NATO and defence, has had a similar effect, but it hardly amounted to much more than a complicating factor in a situation that was already fraught with difficulties for other reasons.

iii) *Policy disagreements on left-right issues.* These are issues that are associated with the parties' ideological stands (on the socialist side, in the non-socialist centre, or on the right) and their social bases in the middle class or the working class.

The disagreements arise, of course, when one party in a coalition decides that it wants to take a policy initiative which its partners do not want to support because it is seen to be too far to the right or to the left of the agreed coalition platform. The Social Democrat-Agrarian coalition in Sweden, for example, had to come to an end in 1957 when the two parties adopted incompatible positions on the pensions issue.

Given that so much work goes into the preparation of detailed policy programmes when coalitions are formed in Scandinavia, one may wonder why disagreements of this kind should need to arise, at least in the course of an election period. Yet, they occur quite regularly. One reason is that much government policy is reactive: it is a matter of coping with situations created by external events. An example is the fate of the Social Democrat-Liberal coalition in Denmark in 1978–9. It was a coalition across the bloc boundary, and an unconnected coalition to boot. As it was also looked at with disapproval by the trade unions, it was perhaps to be expected that the relations between the two coalition partners would be strained. But added to that was a worsening economic situation requiring more decisive economic policy measures than the parties perhaps expected when the coalition was formed. And when it came to choosing the means of tightening up economic policy, their approaches became increasingly more incompatible.

A rather more subtle cause of strain on a coalition stems from the inescapable fact that the participant parties have to take into account that they will compete in the next election with different stands on the left-right scale. Sooner or later, one of the parties may wish to take a firm, uncompromising position on a policy issue to preserve its identity relative to the others, especially if it is felt that the government's overall policy course is sliding too far to the left or to the right. Thus, for example, the Social Democrat Government in Denmark came to an end in 1981 (although it did, of course, re-emerge after the election), when both the government party and its supporting parties in the centre found it necessary to take a firm stand on how far the government should go in forcing insurance companies and pension funds to make funds for investment available on conditions laid down by the government.

In Sweden and Norway the story of policy disagreements in coalition governments is, for obvious reasons, mainly the story of bourgeois governments. Can they keep together, or are they bound to break up before the end of the election period because of tensions between centre and right? There is, in fact, no certain answer, because there is conflicting evidence. The Norwegian coalition government was in fact quite cohesive on left-right issues.

In the case of Sweden, the same may be said for the first three-party coalition as long as it lasted. But the precariousness of the balance between centre and right came to the surface, when the People's Party insisted on forming a minority government. Yet, as a parliamentary base, the bourgeois bloc remained cohesive on general economic and social policy throughout the period, although its critics argued that cohesiveness was achieved at the expense of coherence. Inasmuch as progressive taxation is a prime example of a policy on the left-right dimension in Swedish politics, that is where the three-party coalition was stranded in 1981. In this case, the policy disagreement was particularly intractable because it had to do with the fair allocation of the tax burden among different income strata. And the income distribution among Centre Party voters is in fact much more similar to that among Social Democrat voters than to the typical income level amongst the Conservatives' electoral supporters. In this case, at least, a policy disagreement became fatal when a difference on the left-right axis was reinforced by an underlying conflict between group interests.

It is difficult to tell, nowadays, whether the range of interests that a large Social Democratic party in Scandinavia is attempting to aggregate is necessarily any narrower than that represented by the non-socialist parties. What is different, however, is that in a bourgeois coalition it is quite likely that conflicts of interest become the grounds on which the participant parties will want to compete with each other in the next election. The parties in the centre will, moreover, wish to optimise their capability of competing for votes with the Social Democrats, a concern that carries less weight for the Conservatives. There will be a centripetal force in relation to the party system as a whole, which will make for consensus politics and compromises across the bloc boundary. But the same force may make for an inherent instability of three-party coalition governments.

Of the two policy-related causes of tension in a coalition, a policy disagreement outside the left-right division is potentially the most difficult to cope with. It cannot be resolved by a shifting of the parliamentary base of the government to a different segment of the left-right scale, even if that were not prevented by the boundary between the two blocs. It can have lasting electoral effects – as the Norwegian case shows – and it could possibly result in a realignment on a new cleavage line. It is no wonder that parties, if possible, remove such issues from the arena of party politics with the aid of a referendum. But that is not so easily done when a major party – like the Swedish Centre Party – stands firmly on one side against most of the others on the issue, and is intent upon using the issue in electoral competition. Yet, it is in the nature of things that such policy controversies are exceptional. If they were not, the ground rules for the game would have changed, since it would mean that the left-right array would have ceased to provide the normal framework for party competition and government formation – and this has not happened.

Disagreements on the left-right dimension vary in intensity. The deterrent to the breaking-up of a coalition is the risk that the other side of the party system may take office, leaving *all* the participants in the current coalition in opposition. That deterrent is clearly weaker in Denmark than in Sweden or Norway. On the other hand, if our analysis is correct, the occurrence of disagreements on the left-right scale is quite probable; they are part of the normal hazards of life for a coalition government.

Consensus politics in a two-bloc context

In addition to government coalitions and what we have labelled the parliamentary base of a government, there is also a third form of coalition: the 'law-making coalitions' that emerge when parties vote on policy measures in parliament. Even at the height of two-bloc politics in government formation, such *ad hoc* coalitions quite frequently transgress the bloc boundaries.

This is not simply because much legislation is passed on a basis of consensus; it is also because the cohesiveness of the blocs pertains primarily to the parliamentary bases for governments. In Denmark, the Liberal minority government 1973–5 (which admittedly had no bloc majority either, if the Progress Party were not to be included) built much of its success on its ability to involve the Social Democrats in *ad hoc* coalitions. The strategy of the Swedish Social Democratic one-party governments throughout the post-war period is an even more illuminating case. Whilst relying on the socialist bloc as the parliamentary base, on a few issues where the division between socialist and bourgeois parties was sharply drawn, the Social Democrats persistently attempted to gain the support of at least one of the parties in the centre in *ad hoc* coalitions; the government sometimes went rather far in its willingness to compromise in order to achieve that result. In some instances, the rationale was, of course, that Communist support was unreliable. But it was also a deliberate strategy to attain broad support for government policies – and, of course, to split the bourgeois opposition. It is, however, a strategy that is more dangerous for a three-party bourgeois coalition to adopt. As the case in 1981 illustrates, if willingness to compromise with the other bloc is pushed too far, it can lead to the breaking-up of the coalition.

The types of coalitions that a Social Democratic government and a bloc-based minority government in the centre, respectively, will be operating with are illustrated in the two figures below.

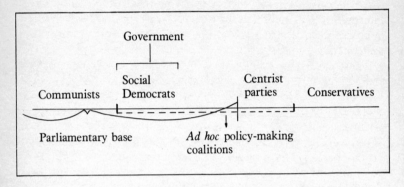

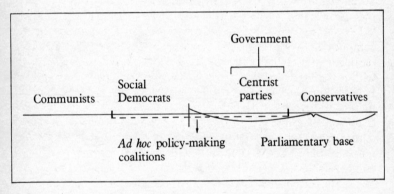

The slow deliberating mode in which policy decisions are prepared in the Scandinavian countries undoubtedly facilitates compromises across bloc boundaries.[32] The institutionalisation of this mode of decision-making has perhaps gone furthest in Sweden, but it is woven into the fabric of the political culture in all three countries. Commissions of inquiry with representatives from both government and opposition parties, as well as interest group participation in commissions, the characteristic Swedish practice of soliciting the views of all concerned interests on commission reports before the drafting of government bills, and the general flavour of the work in the parliament's committees, are all elements in this consensus-seeking process.[33] And so is the involvement of the major interest groups in broad-ranging negotiations on economic policy. Partly because of the links between parties and interest groups, but also because the parties to some extent compete for the votes of members of the same interest organisations, the agreements that a government can achieve with interest groups often become intertwined with the compromises it can agree upon with the parties in opposition: a deal struck in the one arena often lays the ground for an understanding in the other.

These mechanisms help to explain why consensus in policy-making can emerge in the midst of two-bloc politics. But they also explain why the Labour and Social Democratic Governments in Norway and Sweden have transgressed bloc boundaries in agreements on specific policy issues more easily than have the coalitions of bourgeois parties. When a Social Democratic government has struck a compromise with centrist parties in the bourgeois bloc, this may have left a fraction of the party unhappy but party cohesiveness has survived. As long as the Social Democrats have a majority of their own or can treat the party on their left as a marginalised support party, the political effect is minimal. When, on the other hand, a bourgeois coalition government negotiates compromises with the Social Democrats, a rift between the centrist parties and the right can release the forces of internal party competition within the bourgeois bloc; the stability of the coalition is then in – possibly terminal – danger. The inequality between the two blocs in this respect has, of course, depended on the Social Democrats' dominance within their side of the party system. As the Danish case demonstrates, the socialist bloc becomes more vulnerable to internal tensions, when a Social Democratic party encounters a more significant competing force on its left; the break-away of the Centre Democrats in Denmark furthermore shows that the socialist bloc is not immune to the possibility of a splitting off on its right flank.[34]

Although we have characterised Scandinavian politics as consensus-seeking, this should not be interpreted to mean an absence of conflict. The politics of these countries often reflect important conflicts of interest, and from time to time there are intense confrontations between the Social Democrats and the bourgeois parties. Consensus-seeking – in the sense in which we are using the term here – is a mode of conflict resolution in decision-making, rather than a state of nonconflict or avoidance of conflict. The operative characteristic of consensus-seeking in Scandinavian parliamentary politics is the propensity of the parties to anchor policy decisions in the largest possible majority support, rather than in minimal winning coalitions. Indeed, this can be the case even when parliamentary decisions are taken with a bare majority; opposition parties sometimes choose to take a stand against the government, even when they have won concessions that make it unlikely that they will seek to reverse the policy that has been adopted. In terms of policy output, the result is a comparatively high degree of continuity, even when there are changes in party control of government.

We have attempted to show how this style of politics is rooted in the structure of each of the three multi-party systems. As we have also seen, however, no single model could entirely account for the performance of all three party systems. In Norway and Sweden the decisive feature of the party system is its tendency to work as a two-bloc system, albeit with the caveats that one party dominates one of the blocs, and that there can be great difficulties in maintaining the unity of the other. In much the same way as the two competing parties in Downs' model the two blocs are both forced to seek support in the middle ground of electoral opinion.[35]

Critics of Downs have pointed out that his model can be invalidated in the real world of politics, if the more extreme wings of both parties in a two-party system succeed in gaining control over party policy.[36] Citing Britain as a prime example, it has been argued that two-party competition under such circumstances may offer the voters only the choice between two parties that both have evacuated the middle ground of consensus. The result, is 'adversary politics', characterised by sharp changes in the direction of policy when power shifts from one party to the other; presumably there will also be frequent changes, since the parties will merely take turns in frustrating the wishes of a large middle ground sector in the electorate.[37]

Perhaps surprisingly, the preconditions created by a multi-party system and proportional representation in Norway and Sweden seem in fact to have been conducive to two-bloc politics that largely operates in accordance with the predictions of Downs' model for a two-party system. There is little chance of the bourgeois bloc opting for extreme right-wing policies against the wishes of the centrist parties. And in the bloc to the left, the Social Democrats create a strong centripetal force, whilst proportional representation ensures that the extreme left becomes enclosed within a separate party.

Denmark shows more similarity to the alternative model for a multi-party system: the one in which the centre – especially the Radical Liberals in the Danish case – ensures continuity as well as moderation through its position as a 'hinge' party whose participation is normally required for majority formations. But not invariably so. For the reasons given earlier, Danish politics seem to be wavering between a two-bloc tendency and a 'balancing centre' situation. In this context Sartori's analysis of government by a centre that is permanently in office is worth noting.[38] According to Sartori, such a dominance by the centre may well result in continuity in policy, but it is also likely to generate centrifugal tendencies in party competition. The sheer impossibility of a change in power will cause parties on the left as well as on the right to distance themselves from the centre in extreme and irresponsible opposition. Now Denmark does not, of course, match Sartori's dominant centre model. The centre in the party system is too weak and too split to qualify as a dominant centre; it is rather torn between the poles of attraction formed by the Social Democrat and the Agrarian Liberals/ Conservatives. Yet, the small parties in the centre are often in a position to make or break governments as well as to extract concessions from the side they choose to support. The politics of government formation is distinctly more centre-based in Denmark than in the two-bloc systems of Norway and Sweden. It is worth noting, therefore, that there is some evidence of centrifugal drives in the Danish party system: the parties to the left of the Social Democrats and to the right of the Conservatives are indeed stronger in Denmark than in the two other countries.

In conclusion, it may be in order to look at the current British debate on electoral reform in the light of the Scandinavian experience. A change to proportional representation in Britain, it is now argued, would open the way for the formation of an effective political force in the centre. That, in turn, would have a number of consequences, considered to be beneficial: it would make government by coalition the norm and one-party government the exception; it would be conducive to consensus politics, since the support of the centre in general would be required for the making of policies; and it would put an end to the 'adversary politics' that has come to be characteristic of Britain's two-party system.

This may be so. On the other hand, the reality might not turn out quite like that. There are a number of possible variations. Firstly, three-party (or three-bloc) politics does not invariably yield consensus, as the Scandinavian experience of the 1920s illustrates. Secondly, there can be no guarantee that proportional representation produces only one significant party in the centre. Indeed, there are already two. In addition, regional parties may not only gain in strength (as is not unlikely); their presence may well complicate the formation of government majorities. Thirdly, the emergence of a social-liberal balancing centre is not the only outcome that is possible; two-bloc politics, more or less resembling the Scandinavian model, is at least a conceivable alternative. And, finally, it may well be argued that the root cause of the trend towards 'adversary politics' in Britain lies as much in the organisational structure of the existing major parties as in the election system. If so, and if these parties remain unreformed, a party of the centre could find that neither of them would be an easy partner in a consensus-seeking coalition.

These observations are not necessarily to be taken as arguments against proportional representation in Britain. They have served their purpose if they leave the reader with some doubts about the certainty of predictions about changes in party systems.

Notes

1. There is a wealth of literature on the politics of the Nordic countries. Two excellent books on the region as a whole have been published recently: Neil Elder, Alastair H. Thomas and David Arter, *The Consensual Democracies? The Government and Politics of the Scandinavian States* (Oxford, Martin Robertson, 1982); and Barry Turner with Gunilla Nordquist, *The Other European Community. Integration and Co-operation in Nordic Europe* (London, Weidenfeld and Nicolson, 1982).

2. Karl H. Cerny (ed.), *Scandinavia at the Polls. Recent Political Trends in Denmark, Norway and Sweden* (Washington DC, American Enterprise Institute for Policy Research, 1977).

3. This paper is not intended as a contribution to formal coalition theory, but we shall frequently draw upon the concepts of coalition theory and theoretical work that has been done in that field. A comprehensive treatment of coalition theory as applied to government formation is given in Abram de Swaan, *Coalition Theories and Cabinet Formation* (Amsterdam/New York/London, Elsevier, 1973). A collection of studies of government coalitions in several countries (including Denmark and Finland) is presented in Eric C. Browne and John Dreijmanis (eds), *Government Coalitions in Western Democracies* (New York, Longman, 1982).

4. This is a view that has been argued especially strongly by Richard Rose in a recent work: *Do Parties Make a Difference?* (London, Macmillan, 1980).

5. See, for example, Harold L. Wilensky, *The Welfare State and Equality: Structural and Ideological Roots of Public Expenditure* (Berkeley, University of California Press, 1975).

6. Christopher Hewitt, 'The Effect of Political Democracy and Social Democracy on Equality in Industrial Societies: A Cross-National Comparison', *American Sociological Review*, 42, 1977, pp. 451–64. David Cameron, 'The Expansion of Public Economy: A Comparative Analysis', *American Political Science Review*, 72, 1978, pp. 1243–61. John Dryzek, 'Politics, Economics and Inequality: A Cross-National Analysis', *European Journal of Political Research*, 6, 1978, pp. 399–410. Edward R. Tufte, *Political Control of the Economy* (Princeton, Princeton University Press, 1978), esp. Chap. 4. Francis G. Castles and R. D. McKinlay, 'Public Welfare Provision, Scandinavia and the Sheer Futility of the Sociological Approach to Politics', *British Journal of Political Science* 9, 1979, pp. 156–71. Francis Castles and Robert D. McKinlay, 'Does Politics Matter: An Analysis of the Public Welfare Commitment in Advanced Democratic States', *European Journal of Political Research*, 7, 1979, pp. 169–86. Francis G. Castles (ed.), *The Impact of Parties. Politics and Policies in Democratic Capitalist States* (London: Sage Publications, 1982); see esp. chapter by Castles; for a much more qualified view on the importance of party control over government, see the chapter by Manfred G. Schmidt. See also Manfred G. Schmidt, *Wohlfahrtsstaatliche Politik unter bürgerlichen und sozialdemokratischen Regierungen. Ein internationaler Vergleich.* (Frankfurt, Campus, 1982).

7. Seymour M. Lipset and Stein Rokkan (eds), *Party Systems and Voter Alignments: Cross National Perspectives* (New York, Free Press, 1967) Chap. 1; see esp. p. 50. On the concept of the party system 'format', see: Giovanni Sartori, *Parties and Party Systems* (Cambridge, Cambridge University Press, 1976).

8. Walter Korpi, *Den demokratiska klasskampen. Svensk politik i jämförande perspektiv* (Stockholm, Tiden, 1981), pp. 222 ff.

9. A comprehensive description of Swedish parliamentarism during the first post-war era is given in Olof Ruin, *Mellan samlingsregering och tvåpartisystem: Den svenska*

regeringsfrågan 1945–1960 (Stockholm, Bonniers, 1968).

10. Bo Särlvik, 'Party Politics and Electoral Opinion Formation: A Study of Issues in Swedish Politics 1956–1960', *Scandinavian Political Studies*, 2, 1967, pp. 167–202. Bo Särlvik, *Opinionbildningen vid folkomröstningen 1957* (Stockholm, SOU, 1959). Björn Molin, *Tjänstepensionsfrågan, En studie i svensk partipolitik* (Göteborg, Akademiförlaget, 1965).

11. Erik Damgaard, 'Party Coalitions in Danish Law-Making', *European Journal of Political Research*, 1:1, 1973, pp. 35–66. See also Alastair H. Thomas, 'Denmark: Coalitions and Minority Governments' in Browne and Dreijmanis, *op. cit.*

12. *Yearbook of Nordic Statistics, 1981*.

13. Much of the discussion draws on Nils Elvander, *Skandinavisk arbetarrörelse* Stockholm, Publica, 1980). See also Arnold J. Heidenheimer, Hugh Heclo, Carolyn Teich Adams, *Comparative Public Policy: The Politics of Social Choice in Europe and America* (London Macmillan, 1975). For an analysis of the relationships between policy-making and electoral opinions in Denmark and Sweden, see Gösta Esping Andersen, *Social Class, Social Democracy and State Policy* (Copenhagen, New Social Science Monographs, 1980). A long-term analysis of the development of public expenditure is presented in B. Guy Peters and David Klingman, 'Patterns of Expenditure Development in Sweden, Norway and Denmark', *British Journal of Political Science*, 7, 1977, pp. 387–412.

14. The decline of the Social Democrats and the changes in the party systems in the first half of the 1970s in Denmark, Norway and Sweden are treated in chapters by Ole Borre, Henry Valen and Bo Särlvik in Karl H. Cerny *op. cit.* For Denmark, see also Ole Borre *et al.*, *Vaelgere i 70'erna* (Copenhagen, Akademisk Forlag, 1976) and by the same authors, *Folketingsvalget 1977* (Copenhagen, Akademisk Forlag, 1979). See also on the 1973 election Per Bendix *et al.*, *Decembervalget 1973. Hvorfor gik det sådan. Hvorhen førte det.* . (Copenhagen, Schultz, 1974). For the Swedish elections in 1976 and 1979, respectively, see Olof Petersson, *Väljarna och valet 1976* (Stockholm, Liber, 1977) and Sören Holmberg, *Svenska väljare* (Stockholm, Publica, 1981). For electoral trends in Norway, see Henry Valen, *Valg og politikk – et samfunn i endring* (Oslo, NKS-Forlaget, 1981).

15. In addition to Henry Valen's work, *op. cit.*, for a collection of studies concerned with the shift to the right in Norwegian electoral opinion, see Tor Bjørklund and Bernt Hagtvet (eds), *Høyrebølgen – et epokeskifte i norsk politikk?* (Oslo, Ascheschoug, 1981).

16. See the discussion in A. De Swaan, *op. cit.*

17. Ole Borre, 'The Danish Parliamentary Election of 1981', *Electoral Studies*, 1, 1982, pp. 250–54.

18. Don S. Schwerin, 'Norwegian and Danish Incomes Policy and European Monetary Integration', *West European Politics*, 3, 1980, pp. 388–405.

19. Henry Valen, 'Norway: "No" to EEC', *Scandinavian Political Studies*, 8, 1973, pp. 214–26. Henry Valen, 'The Storting Election of 1977: Realignment or Return to Normalcy?', *Scandinavian Political Studies*, New Series: 1, 1978, pp. 83–107. Henry Valen, 'Norway: The 1981 Election Confirms the Trend to the Right', *Electoral Studies*, 1, 1982, pp. 243–50. See also Henry Valen, 'Internal Conflicts and Reactions towards Foreign Politics: A Case Study of the Norwegian Electorate' in Otto Büsch (ed.), *Wählerbewegung in der Europäische Geschichte* (Berlin, Colloquium Verlag, 1980).

20. We are drawing here on Axel Hadenius' study of taxation politics in the 1970s: *Spelet om skatten* (Lund, Norstedts/Studentlitteratur, 1981).

21. For a detailed and informed account of the negotiations that preceded the formation of the government, see Kai Hammerich, *Kompromissernas koalition. Person- och maktspelet kring regeringen Fälldin* (Ystad, Rabén & Sjögren, 1977).

22. The chain of events that led to the downfall of the three-party government is described in Evert Vedung, *Kärnkraften och regeringen Fälldins fall* (Stockholm, Rabén & Sjögren, 1979).

23. For an account of the government formation in 1978, see Olof Petersson, *Regeringsbildningen 1978* (Lund, Rabén & Sjögren, 1979).

24. For an analysis of the party strategies on the tax issue in 1982, see Axel Hadenius, *op. cit.*, esp. pp. 242 ff.

25. For a comparison of the relations between the state and the organisations in the labour market in the Scandinavian countries, see Nils Elvander, 'Collective Bargaining and Incomes Policy in the Nordic Countries: A Comparative Analysis', *British Journal of Industrial Relations*, 12, 1975, pp. 417–37.

26. Cf. David Arter, 'The Finnish Centre Party: Profile of a Hinge Group', *West European Politics*, 2, 1979, pp. 108–26, esp. p. 118.

27. Cf. Olof Ruin, 'Patterns of Government Composition in a Multi-Party System: The Case of Sweden', *Scandinavian Political Studies*, 4, 1969, pp. 71–87; Erik Damgaard, 'The Parliamentary Basis of Danish Governments: The Patterns of Coalition Formation', *Scandinavian Political Studies*, 4, 1969, pp. 31–57.

28. Cf. Ian Budge and Val Herman, 'Coalitions and Government Formation: An Empirically Relevant Theory', *British Journal of Political Science*, 8, 1978, pp. 459–77.

29. For a systematic study of the procedures for government formations, see Henrik Hermerén, *Regeringsbildning i flerpartisystem* (Lund, Studentlitteratur, 1975).

30. However, in Denmark the Radicals have secured over-representation when they have formed coalition governments with the Social Democrats.

31. These tidal movements of the vote among the bourgeois parties occur also when they are in opposition: see Bo Särlvik, 'Political Stability and Change in the Swedish Electorate', *Scandinavian Political Studies*, 1, 1966, pp. 188–224.

32. See, for example, Thomas J. Anton, *Administered Politics: Elite Political Culture in Sweden* (Boston, Martinus Nijhoff Publishing, 1980) and by the same author: 'Policy Making and Political Culture in Sweden', *Scandinavian Political Studies*, vol. 4, 1969, pp. 88–102.

33. On commissions of inquiry, see Hans Meijer, 'Bureaucracy and Policy Formulation in Sweden', *Scandinavian Political Studies*, vol. 4, 1969, pp. 103–16. Not all commissions are of the political interest representation referred to above; as Meijer shows, a large proportion are composed, wholly or partly, of administrative experts. For Denmark, see Erik Damgaard and Kjell A. Eliasen, 'Reduction of Party Conflict through Corporate Participation in Danish Law-Making', *Scandinavian Political Studies*, vol. 3 (New Series), 1980, pp. 105–21.

34. In general, the parties on the extreme left have proved unwilling to join forces with the bourgeois parties to bring down a Social Democratic government. When it did happen in Norway in 1963, the Labour Government came back into office after a few weeks. However, the Social Democrat minority government formed after the 1982 election in Sweden (with a bloc majority together with the Communists) was forced to make concessions to the Communists, even in the parliament's first session, on a proposal to increase VAT. Against expectations, the Communists were prepared to precipitate a government crisis and a dissolution of the Riksdag rather than back down on this issue.

35. Anthony Downs, *An Economic Theory of Democracy* (New York, Harper & Brothers, 1957).

36. Albert O. Hirschman, *Exit Voice and Loyalty* (Cambridge, Mass., Harvard University Press, 1970), esp. pp. 62–75.

37. S.E. Finer (ed.), *Adversary Politics and Electoral Reform* (London, Anthony Wigram, 1975), esp. pp. 3–32. See also: S.E. Finer, 'Adversary Politics and the Eighties', *Electoral Studies*: vol. 1, no. 2, August 1982 and Vernon Bogdanor, *The People and the Party System* (Cambridge, Cambridge University Press, 1981).

38. Giovanni Sartori, 'European Political Parties, The Case of Polarised Pluralism' in Joseph La Palombara and Myron Weiner, *Political Parties and Political Development* (Princeton, Princeton University Press, 1966).
Giovanni Sartori, *Parties and Party Systems: A Framework for Analysis* (Cambridge, Cambridge University Press, 1976), esp. Chap. 6.

6 Coalition Government in a Constitutional Monarchy: The Dutch Experience
Jan Vis

The Kingdom of the Netherlands has more experience than most other democratic societies in running a political system consisting only of minorities. Ever since the introduction of universal suffrage and proportional representation – both in 1917/18 – the system has been dominated by minority parties. Even the largest parties have never commanded more than one-third of the parliamentary seats. Coalition governments consisting of two, three or even more parties, were therefore always unavoidable.

According to most observers the making of coalition governments is by far the weakest link in the Dutch political system. Traditional influences, such as the power of the monarch, are competing with present-day democratic attitudes in a seemingly inscrutable struggle so far as procedures and responsibilities are concerned. But monarchs and politicians have learned to live with it. Codification, however, seems to be impossible; vested interests are still preventing attempts to rationalise the formation process.

Introduction
In the 1920s and 1930s the situation was somewhat mitigated by the existence of three confessional parties which together had a parliamentary majority, but even in that period the formation of coalition governments was complicated. In the early 1930s differences between the three groups, especially the Catholic Party on the one side and the two Protestant parties on the other, increased so much that the system of parliamentary government sometimes came to a standstill. Parliamentary influence on national politics did not, of course, completely disappear, but the composition of the cabinet and day-to-day political business became matters on which parliamentarians seemed to have little influence. Parliamentary government survived but lack of political cohesion in parliament itself made it impossible for the legislature to exercise real influence. For many years similar cabinets were in power, consisting of politicians whose political strength lay more outside Parliament than inside: strong, more or less autocratic men,

sometimes highly esteemed by certain sections of the population but not positively accepted by a parliamentary majority.

In the post-war period the situation improved somewhat through the existence of new political alternatives. The Dutch Labour Party (PvdA), for instance, abandoned its traditional republican and pacifist attitude and became part of the system of governing parties. Until 1958 all the larger parties – larger in the Dutch sense, which means that even a party with 7 or 8 per cent of the vote is large – were in power, not all at the same time but the opposition was never a real opposition. It often happened that in difficult formation processes one of the parties just missed a ministerial office, not by opposing the proposed government programme but simply because other parties refused to set apart a portfolio for the party concerned, sometimes even during the last days or hours of the formation process. On several occasions the number of portfolios was enlarged simply to prevent this situation, but Dutch coalition government at that time never became real proportional government as it exists in Switzerland. One of the tactical rules in the formation process remained that one portfolio is no portfolio at all, and this rule sometimes left smaller parties without power in the coalition. In 1959 the political landscape changed somewhat. Post-war reconstruction coming to an end, parties diverged in their attitudes towards the shaping of the welfare state. Socialists and Liberals (VVD) came into conflict, excluding each other from government responsibility, and as a result the confessional centre forces (the Catholic Peoples' Party (KVP), the Anti-Revolutionary Party (ARP), the Christian Historical Union (CHU), – later, the Christian Democratic Appeal (CDA)) were guaranteed a dominating position. It was this situation that made the formation process a central part of the democratic system. The formation process was no longer decisive for the distribution of portfolios among parties with no fundamental and far-reaching differences, but decisive for the political cause itself – not the voters, but the process after the elections had decided the political colour of the government. Dutch voters never know what kind of government they are going to get after an election – it is just a matter of 'wait and see'. In the formation talks the parliamentary parties decide. There is a well-known expression in Dutch politics – 'one can win the elections and afterwards lose the formation' – and from time to time this does happen: substantial losers remain in office while strong winners go into opposition.

This situation has attracted wide attention because it has something to do with the credibility of the political system, with the essentials of democratic government. The Dutch have learned to live with it but the question of re-shaping the formation process remains one of the most important constitutional issues of the day. Some aspects have been reshaped, of course. The formation process is no longer a matter of give-and-take behind closed doors. Important papers are publicised immediately, politicians give almost daily press conferences during the formation talks. There is some responsibility to the public. But the other side of the coin has become well-known: formation talks are almost endless. The centre-left cabinet of den Uyl (1973–7) was formed in a formation period of five months, the formation of the centre-right first cabinet of van Agt (1977–81) took seven months and the centre-left second cabinet of van Agt (1981–2) took four months.

In September/October 1982 the centre-right Lubbers cabinet was formed in a relatively short period of eight weeks, but this was only the final result of a crisis that started in May with a fatal disagreement in the centre-left van Agt cabinet. A caretaker (or 'interim') government dissolved the Second Chamber (in accordance with majority opinion in the Chamber) and general elections were held on 8 September. The normal relationship between cabinet and parliament was disturbed for more than five and a half months.

Essentially the formation of a coalition government is the construction of an artificial parliamentary majority after the elections. Concerning the question of who is going to run the country, the election results give no answer. They are not without meaning, but they have to be considered as only one of the data. Election results in a minority system produce a change in power relations; they change the minority positions in parliament and they influence the positions in the coalition talks, but they are never the only influence, and sometimes not even the most important one. A losing party can remain the largest one, it can still retain its dominating influence, while a strong winner can be seen as a dangerous enemy which must be removed at all costs to the benches of the opposition.

It is very striking that the Catholic Party has been in power ever since 1918. Electoral results for this party have been of importance only in answering the question of the sharing of power – the number of ministerial portfolios – and yet the Catholic vote has decreased 50 per cent in the last fifteen years. With regard to the Labour Party, in 1977 the outgoing Prime Minister and Socialist leader, Joop den Uyl, received massive support at the ballot box; for the first time in Dutch parliamentary history one party had more than 50 seats out of 150 in the Second Chamber, the Dutch Lower House, and more than one-third of the total number of seats. The socialist Party had really won the election but it lost the formation by pressing several issues too hard, by not accepting ministerial candidates from other parties, by lack of unanimity. It stumbled over its own electoral success.

Constitutional rules: theory and practice

The Dutch Constitution, written in the period of the autocratic monarchy and fundamentally revised in 1848 (ministerial responsibility) and 1917 (universal suffrage) gives no rules whatsoever for the formation process. The only article dealing with the appointment and dismissal of ministers is Art. 86.2: 'the King appoints ministers and dismisses them at will'. The same goes for the basic rule of parliamentary government: the vote of confidence exists only as an unwritten convention. And according to most students this convention exists only in a negative form: any Cabinet is considered to have parliamentary confidence so long as the contrary is not evident. Actually the situation is more complicated. In a political system consisting of minority parties confidence must be constructed by means of negotiations between the parliamentary parties and this constructed confidence exists only for the parliamentary period between one general election and the next. Early elections are never part of the deal made at the beginning of the parliamentary period. They are only held when the coalition fails and political opinion is aiming at a *renversement des alliances*. Changing partners without elections is of course possible but it is generally deprecated since most parties in the election campaigns (especially Liberals and the Labour Party) use the campaign to declare a more or less outspoken preference for partnership with particular parties.

Until the mid 1960s the changing of coalitions without premature elections was normal practice. In the parliamentary period (four years) parliamentary parties were considered fully entitled to change coalitions without any interference from the voters – rather like the Chambre des Deputés in the Fourth French Republic and the German Bundestag. The democratic wave of the 1960s, however, resulted in the widely supported opinion that a forthcoming change of partners had to be legitimised by popular vote.

The result was twofold: (i) coalition governments tended to remain in power longer; (ii) the building of new coalitions became more time-consuming.[1] Most observers now agree that the new 'convention' (no changing of partners without election) is justifiable on democratic grounds but counter-productive as far as the efficiency of government is concerned and from a political view point rather useless since proportional representation never produces clear-cut majorities. In practice, the preference of the ever-ruling Christian Democrats (CDA) remains the decisive factor. For only the Christian Democrats, with no clear preference for partnership with left or right wing parties, are able to change without premature elections, but being the only party with this attitude, they in fact always agree to early elections. Needless to say, the dissolution of parliament is never used in the British way; it simply never happens that all coalition parties are in favour of dissolution. Nor can the electorate decide in the case of a disagreement between the Cabinet and the parliamentary majority. The very issue that splits parliament into a minority (still sustaining the cabinet) and a majority, splits the coalition cabinet itself. The conflict is resolved by the government resigning and making way for an interim cabinet which dissolves parliament. The stick behind the door is useless since the hand which holds it is powerless.

The absence of rules concerning the formation process has two aspects: there are no rules for the process itself nor rules regulating the powers of those involved. The main constitutional data, that the King can do no wrong and that ministers are responsible to parliament, are in a way paradoxical. The search for a new cabinet is the purpose of the cabinet formation; the essential character of the formation is the absence of ministers with really effective responsibility (since no parliament can hold an outgoing minister responsible for the appointment of his successor).

How can the monarch search for ministers and at the same time do no wrong, without responsible ministers? To these difficult questions there are basically two solutions. The first is the old one: nobody knows that the formation process is going on; the Queen and her advisers operate behind closed doors. Only the result is made public and the outcome is the new government itself, appointed by the Queen but responsible to Parliament for its own acceptance of the portfolios. Memories of this old solution are still visible in the closing part of the formation process – the appointment of the succeeding Prime Minister is counter-signed by his predecessor.

Pressure of parliamentary parties, party élites outside Parliament, public opinion, and the media together with the great length of the formation process itself, have made this old solution impossible. Even silent politicians are sometimes news sources; eager newspaper men can reach conclusions simply by observing who is visiting whom. One can talk behind closed doors but politicians never become really invisible, and the knowledge that Mr A after a visit to the Royal Palace has been talking to Mr B and Mr C is always very important, and visible facts lead to conclusions, both true and false, and sometimes politicians fear the latter more than the former.

In the early 1950s political correspondents and the spokesman of the *formateur* reached a kind of gentlemen's agreement – visible facts, mainly visits, should be reported by the spokesman; politicians should no longer be followed by a bunch of curious journalists. The agreement gave some respite to the political news desk and the politicians, and it was really the first step towards more openness in the formation process. Gradually the so-called visible facts were commented on by the spokesman and in the late 1960s a Royal Commission proposed successfully that all relevant formation reports, such as parliamentary advice to the Queen, reports of *formateurs* and *informateurs*, written conclusions, draft and final text of coalition agreements and so on, should be made completely public.

This development gave shape to a new solution of the old question of how the Queen could operate in the formation process without responsible ministers. The new solution was diametrically opposed to the old one: secret negotiations gave way to a kind of open diplomacy. The major part of the process was made public to all Members of Parliament, to political élites outside Parliament, to pressure groups, to the news media and to the public itself. It was a sincere effort to legitimate the process by displaying and presenting the various parts of it. To say it in the German way: 'Legitimation durch Verfahren': legitimation by process or established conduct, and the results were surprising. Almost everyone took part in the formation process, not only the news media but also the trade unions, the employers, public boards and corporations, local government, and almost all backbenchers in the House.

The results were as follows. Firstly, the process became slower: negotiations took more time rather than less. The position of the political leaders was drastically eroded because it is very difficult to negotiate with the whole nation looking over one's shoulder. Yet another unexpected and time-consuming factor arose: the old way of negotiating behind closed doors used to be a multilateral process in which all parties concerned took part at the same time; in a situation of more openness, however, discussions tend to be more bilateral in order to keep the process comprehensible to the outside world (just like multilateral transactions on the stock exchange are more complicated and less comprehensible to outsiders than the essentially bilateral procedure in Parliament or in a courtroom). The role of the Queen became visible and less important; to use her own words; 'I am no more than a letter-box, the advice comes in and the formation mandates come out'.

Of course, there is more to it than that. The Queen voices no political opinions, she does not, she cannot and she will not discriminate between people and parties; but officially she leads the formation process and that means she keeps an eye on the process itself. She has the right to advise, to encourage and to warn, and she uses these rights. When needed, she forces political leaders to come to a conclusion and she does this simply by pointing to her own constitutional position. When all parliamentary advice is made public and the majority of the advice does not reflect majority opinion, she cannot follow her personal judgement without entering the political arena and losing her position as a national symbol above party strife.

The role of the Queen in the formation process is the most discussed topic in the unwritten part of the constitution and probably the main contribution to the great prestige of Queen Juliana (1948–81) and her daughter Beatrix. Both women are said to be well-informed (Juliana by the end of her reign had experienced sixteen formations, Beatrix holds a degree in political science) and very much aware of the political facts of life. Dutch political and public opinion expects the monarch to play an active role rather than being only a figurehead.

Political leaders unwilling to compromise, or not yet willing to compromise – the time factor is always very important – are sometimes more or less openly called to order by the Queen herself. This is a very simple device as was shown in the formation talks of 1977. When the coalition talks between centre and left parties reached deadlock, the Queen received advice from the three parties concerned. Two pieces of advice contradicted the third. At that moment the Queen sent for the three leaders together and some hours later unanimous advice was publicised: 'thanks to the Queen the deadlock was overcome'.

There is another characteristic of the Dutch formation process. It is very long and complicated. The drafting of a proposed coalition programme requires skilled labour. Cabinet makers need professional assistance. Twenty years ago Cabinet makers could afford to draft a few outlines, a selection of the various election platforms. But in the open process of today, even a draft government programme has to be a well-balanced piece of work. The more carefully a Cabinet maker does his homework, the better his chances are. So he needs official assistance and he receives it. For a number of years the office of the Prime Minister has had at its disposal a small but highly specialised team of civil servants well-trained in the sophisticated art of drafting proposals for coalition talks. Constitutionally speaking, their position is a strange one. There is no ministerial responsibility for their activities, at least not for their content. But Dutch politicians welcome their existence and nobody asks constitutional questions. Without public assistance – funds and civil servants – the formation system simply could not operate. It has become part of the official machinery.

Formation process

Although the main subject of this chapter is in a sense the role of the monarch, the process can only be properly understood by dealing with all of its different stages. History teaches us that every government formation is different. For it depends upon the political atmosphere, the current issues, the election results and the degree of co-operation and harmony in the preceding coalition. So any model of the formation process can be only relative. A model cannot be anything more than a formalised description, and its predictive value is small. The very absence of constitutional rules creates the possibility of a number of variations in each case, and often a formation succeeds only because somebody has a bright new idea which can be used once only in that particular situation.

In addition it is important to note that there are in reality two types of cabinet formation. The first is the formation after regular elections; the second is what can be called a 'crisis formation', a formation that is needed whenever the preceding coalition has broken down. Although this second type mostly involves the dissolution of Parliament and new elections also, the political relationships in the two situations are somewhat different.

The maximum life of the Dutch Parliament is four years. Coalition governments are formed at the beginning of a parliamentary period. On election day the ministers become *démissionnaire*, they place their portfolios at the Queen's disposal. Most constitutional specialists agree that this is a convention, and it has been done ever since the introduction of proportional representation in 1918. A new coalition has to be formed based on power relations in the new Parliament. Coalition governments hardly ever lose their majority as a result of elections. They place their portfolios at the Queen's disposal only because a reshuffle of the coalition is sometimes needed, and because the parties want to update the coalition programme. The main characteristic of this situation is the tendency to continue the old coalition – a tendency that is stronger than the tendency to make a new alignment.

Since the portfolios are at the disposal of the Queen, she has to take the first step in the formation process. And for more than fifty years her first step has been to consult separately the Speaker of the Second Chamber, a member of the largest party in Parliament, and the Vice-President of the Council of State (the Queen herself is the formal President of that Council); and together the leaders of all the parliamentary parties in the Second Chamber – even the leaders of the splinter parties are summoned but their visits to the Queen are just a matter of courtesy and lack any real political significance. The leaders of the parliamentary parties are to be seen as the spokesmen of their parties, expressing the opinions of their parliamentary parties, although they may of course voice personal opinions as well. These party opinions are afterwards confirmed in written statements, outlines of which are often handed to the press immediately, while the complete statements are publicised by the *formateur* or *informateur*.

Although most statements give elaborate descriptions of and comments on the political situation, the main question to be answered is: Who is going to be the Cabinet maker or *formateur*? Some indications are already available. There are also certain principles of government formation; for example that the mandate should go to the leader of the largest party in Parliament or to the parliamentary leader of the party which has won the greatest increase in votes in the election. It is noteworthy that the mentioning of names already reflects an opinion on the expected composition of the future coalition, and therefore most advisers also comment on the coalition relations during the pre-election period or on the various stands taken in the election campaign; also comparisons of the election platforms are often made. If the majority in parliament agrees on its advice, or the parties who together have a majority in Parliament agree, the task of the Queen is quite straightforward. She appoints somebody as Cabinet maker or *formateur*. Sometimes the name of the *formateur* has already been mentioned in several advisory statements, sometimes only his party has been mentioned.

But this happy situation hardly ever occurs. The Queen is therefore forced to make her own choice, but her own choice is not really a political one. She puts the ball back into the politicians' court by appointing an *informateur*: somebody with a mandate to explore the chances for a coalition cabinet. *Informateurs* are usually elderly statesmen, such as the Vice-President of the State Council, members of the State Council, or members of the First Chamber. Sometimes even provincial governors have been *informateurs*. An *informateur* needs political experience but, above all, he has to be acceptable to more than one party because he may be the real mediator.

Informateurs can operate in different ways because they are free to interpret their mandates in different ways. Some *informateurs* restrict themselves to inviting party leaders to the negotiating table, starting the talks and advising the Queen to appoint a *formateur* to finish the job. Other *informateurs* act as chairmen during the first part of the negotiations or look after the whole negotiation process. In that case the appointment of a *formateur* who is going to be the Prime Minister is a mere formality.

Formally speaking an *informateur* only explores 'possibilities', which means that the real work is left to the *formateur*. But by inviting only some of the parties to the negotiating table, the *informateur* is discriminating between parties which in his view can take part in a coalition and others which, in his view, cannot. This may seem an arbitrary decision (and sometimes it is), but it has both to be accepted by the parties invited and also to be justified by the outcome of the formation talks. The first round is hardly ever successful. A second round with another *informateur* and with one or more other parties is always needed and sometimes a third round . . . The coalition that is finally constructed is thus more or less legitimised by the failure of the other possibilities.

To understand the practical reality of the process, one must know something about the Dutch political landscape. It is completely dominated by the centre parties, the confessional parties – until 1977 they comprised two Protestant parties (CHU and ARP) and a Catholic party

(KVP), and since 1977 there has been a combination of the three parties called the CDA (Christian Democratic Appeal). The centre bloc, with one-third of the electorate, is open to both sides: the Socialists and D'66 on the left, and the Liberal Party (VVD) on the right; in Dutch politics Liberals and Socialists, that is to say VVD and Labour Party (PvdA), exclude each other. So the real decision is in the centre bloc itself, nine out of ten *informateurs* are affiliated to the confessional party and the selection made by the *informateur* is actually the selection of the powerful centre itself.

In this situation the parties on the two wings (the Labour Party and the Liberals) have to wait and see. They are more or less powerless. But the centre itself is never undivided. Some members prefer a centre-left coalition, others a centre-right, and a large number do not care at all as long as the centre itself remains in power. So the main task of most *informateurs*, belonging to the centre, is to force the centre party to take a decision or to accept the decision already taken.

Most decisions have indeed been taken before the elections. A survey of all post-war Cabinet formations points out that after regular elections the old coalition tends to return, although not without minor changes. A change in partners, sometimes called 'political adultery' or, in a more friendly way, 'changing colour', has hardly ever taken place after regular elections. The only exception was in 1981 when the coalition parties lost their parliamentary majority. All other cases show a basic rule of Dutch coalition politics: whenever the coalition remains undamaged up to election day, the coalition returns. Changes in partners only take place after a severe cabinet crisis; only when relations with the party on one wing are totally disturbed does the centre party go ahead with the party on the other wing.

This changing of partners by the centre never happens without political reason or some justification by political facts. 'So often goes the pitcher to the well that it comes home broken at last'. This probably means that the results of regular elections only seldom influence the outcome of the formation process – at least in Holland. The centre decides in the period between regular elections; parties in opposition can only hope for a cabinet crisis, which is sometimes more useful than a splendid electoral triumph.

Back to the formation process: all *informateurs* keep in touch with the Queen – they are the Queen's advisers (and Queen Juliana was perhaps for the latter part of her reign a wise adviser to her advisers). In his final report (which like his interim reports is published) the *informateur*, if his final report is positive, nominates a *formateur*. The nomination of the *formateur* is generally based on the approval of the party negotiators concerned – often the *formateur* is one of the negotiators. By appointing the *formateur* the Queen simply follows the advice of the *informateur*.

The newly appointed *formateur* starts where the *informateur* ended.

Coalition negotiations comprise a number of separate stages. First there is the coalition programme itself, secondly a kind of political key for the distribution of the various portfolios among the coalition parties, and thirdly a list of proposed ministers and under-ministers. The first and second stages are mostly complete by the time the *formateur* begins; they always need endorsement by the parliamentary parties and when endorsement is given the *informateur* is justified in making a positive report. As far as the personal question is concerned, the leaders of the parliamentary parties present a number of candidates from whom the *formateur* is free to choose. He is not free to ask other people without the consent of the leaders of the parliamentary parties involved. In most Cabinet formations a non-interventionist attitude is taken vis-à-vis candidates of other coalition parties.

The participation of the parliamentary parties in the talks varies considerably from party to party. It is difficult to generalise. Parliamentary leaders with high prestige and closed ranks can operate rather freely. They just inform their parliamentary group and welcome suggestions. But those with less prestige or leading parties with more differences of opinion have to consult with their groups many times. They sometimes have to accept all kinds of amendments to bring to the negotiating table and are sometimes mere messengers commuting between the formation room and their own meeting room. Some parties not only have to deal with their parliamentary party but also with the complete executive of their political party – the Party Council or even the Party Congress.

In these very complex and delicate situations, sometimes heavily over-exposed by the news media, misunderstandings are easily born and blunders easily made. It is like solving a three-dimensional puzzle, and more than once the pieces may not fit. Whenever a deadlock occurs (and they often do), the *informateur* returns his mandate and then everybody waits for the Queen's decision. She invites the leaders of the parliamentary parties for the second time, but not all of them this time – the leaders of the splinter parties who cannot play any role in the Cabinet formation are left out. And then again the opinions of the various parties are confirmed in written statements. To make a long story short, we are back in the first stage. The Queen appoints an *informateur*, sometimes the same person as in the first round, sometimes another – depending upon the situation.

The *informateur* starts talks with the parties who were negotiating in the first round. He suggests various solutions and sooner or later one of his proposals is accepted by all the parties concerned. By this time the *informateur* may consider his job to be finished, whereupon the Queen appoints a *formateur* on the advice of the *informateur*. The *formateur* in this second round can be the same one as in the first round, but it often happens that somebody else receives a mandate. This complicated game of coming and going of *formateurs* and *informateurs* can go on for weeks and months.

Variations and complications

Although in the last ten years the formation process has undoubtedly become more difficult, the main reason is not the existence of a large number of parties – the consequence of a system of proportional representation encouraging small parties. Of the ten parties in parliament only four are generally engaged in formation talks. One reason for this is the position of the centre party, CDA, but according to most observers the main reason is the strong involvement of the major parties: they are very hard to please. Party programmes are very detailed; they are almost draft government programmes. Party leaders lack elbow-room; thanks to press, radio and television, a large number of party members are watching the process.

The formation process has reacted to this heavy pressure by becoming more complicated, more differentiated. In extremely difficult situations the Queen appoints not one *informateur*, but two (one from each side), thus demonstrating that the impartial situation of only one *informateur* no longer exists. One *informateur* can be seen as a mediator; two *informateurs* operate as negotiators. The Queen also appoints two *formateurs* to reduce the mutual distrust. The formation system has also become more differentiated in other ways, concerning the coalition programme or the distribution of portfolios. Some issues are declared to be 'free issues' on which the support of all the coalition parties or of all the members of the coalition parties is not guaranteed, but of course parties have to agree whether a certain issue can be a free one.

If no party coalition can be agreed, there may have to be an extra-parliamentary cabinet. The word 'extra-parliamentary' dates from the period when all members of the Cabinet used to be Members of Parliament. Only in an exceptional situation did the Queen appoint a non-parliamentarian, in a situation where there was no majority in Parliament to support a cabinet. With the cabinet consisting of non-parliamentarians, the majority played a waiting game. Nowadays the parliamentary background is without meaning since ministers, according to the constitution, have to give up their membership of Parliament anyhow. Although most ministers are still recruited from Parliament, a considerable number have no parliamentary experience whatsoever. So the expression 'extra-parliamentary' bears only on the relationship between coalition parties and the Cabinet and not on the origin of the ministers.

This gimmick of 'extra-parliamentary' cabinets can be made more complicated. It can happen that some parties accept the new cabinet as a parliamentary cabinet and in consequence accept strong ties, while other parties accept it only as an extra-parliamentary cabinet. And still another variation is possible: members of the same parliamentary party can take different positions with regard to the new cabinet. The majority of the party may accept the cabinet as a parliamentary one, whereas a minority sit on the fence and call the cabinet extra-parliamentary. This is particularly likely to happen in a period of weak party leadership, a transition period in which a new leader succeeds an old one who, for instance, became a minister or prime minister.

In most cabinet formations the programmatic part is the most difficult: the distribution of portfolios among the coalition parties and the formation of the cabinet itself is, generally speaking, a matter of only days, whereas the drafting and endorsement of the coalition programme takes weeks or months.

For the division of portfolios between the coalition partners the following guide-lines have been developed in the last thirty years. First, portfolios are distributed proportionally according to the parliamentary strength of each coalition partner. Secondly, the Prime Minister is generally a member of the largest coalition party. And thirdly, lack of balance in the distribution of the ministerial portfolios can be corrected by the distribution of the State Secretaries or Under-ministries. Under-ministers or State Secretaries are not members of the cabinet and do not play any role in cabinet decisions. But they are sometimes used by one coalition partner to keep an eye on another; the Minister of Party A is more or less controlled by an Under-minister of Party B. Although Under-ministers officially are only nominated by the Ministers concerned, the distribution of Under-ministries is now an integral part of the cabinet formation itself.

There are other guide-lines: the various aspects of government activity are usually spread among the coalition partners. This means, for instance, that the portfolios of Finance, Economic Affairs and Social Affairs are hardly ever in the same political hands. The same goes for the portfolios of Education and Science on the one side and Welfare on the other, or Interior on the one side and Justice on the other; or Defence and Foreign Affairs. In the distribution of portfolios the premiership counts for only a little more than the other portfolios, say, one-and-a-half to one. The Dutch Prime Minister has a casting vote in the Cabinet whenever the votes are equal, but this advantage is of limited use. A vote in the cabinet is generally the beginning of the end of the cabinet. Nine out of ten decisions are taken unanimously. And the tenth is not taken, awaiting a compromise which is acceptable to all partners.

Conclusion

Coalition government is generally crisis government. In the last thirty
years only two Dutch Cabinets have survived a complete parliamentary
period of four years. All other coalition Cabinets collapsed earlier. This
means that a considerable number of formations took place during
parliamentary periods. Until the late 1960s those formations were done
without dissolution of Parliament. Most of them ended in a reconstruction of the old Cabinet. But in the last ten years public opinion has
become more and more impressed by the thesis that no new coalition
government should be constructed without new parliamentary elections.

New elections, however, cannot be held immediately. Dutch legislation on elections lays down a number of conditions for the dissolution
of Parliament and the nomination of new candidates. Therefore an
interim cabinet is needed, generally a rump cabinet taking responsibility for the dissolution of Parliament. The formation of an interim
cabinet is less complicated than the formation of a fully fledged cabinet,
but in this case also parliamentary support is needed. The Queen
consults with parliamentary leaders as she does for the formation of a
fully fledged cabinet and the dissolution of Parliament is always part of
the agreement on which an interim cabinet is based and operates.

Cabinet formations after a cabinet crisis may be somewhat different
from formations after regular elections. They are no less complicated.
Although the political crisis itself gives an indication of the direction of
the formation, history proves that the creation of a new cabinet of a
different composition can be very time-consuming and painful. The
two longest formations, for instance, in 1972 and 1977 were both crisis
formations.

Adding up all the time devoted to cabinet construction in post-war
Holland shows that this chapter of politics is very time-consuming. Of
the thirty-six years between 1946 and 1982, cabinet formations have
taken three and a half years. Dutch politicians and the Queen spend
about 10 per cent of their time in constructing and reconstructing the
machinery that runs the country. One may ask how the country is run
in the interim periods, when the cabinet is *démissionnaire* after elections.
Especially during the 1977 cabinet formation – the longest one – this
problem was solved in a rather pragmatic way. The official formula is
that the *démissionnaire* cabinet has the duty to do all that is needed in the
interests of the country. That expression can be interpreted, of course,
in various ways, but the outgoing Prime Minister, den Uyl, stated that
he interpreted it as giving him the authority to do all the things that
were urgent and undisputed. In the first weeks of the formation most
subjects were not urgent and were well-disputed, but in end almost
everything became urgent and undisputed. The longer an outgoing

cabinet remains in power, the more powerful it becomes;[2] even though in the last resort the new Parliament draws the line between urgent and non-urgent, disputed and undisputed.

What are the lessons of the Dutch experience?

(i)   The founding fathers of the Constitution never took account of a political system with strongly developed parties. The Constitution therefore still expresses a dualism between Crown and Parliament that in fact does not exist. The real dualism of today is the distinction between the coalition majority and the opposition. But the coalition majority has to be constructed by political leaders since it is not the result of a popular vote.

(ii) In constructing a coalition (or in other words: creating parliamentary confidence) the monarch plays an important role as far as procedures are concerned. Although not entangled in specifically political affairs his position is always delicate and vulnerable. A generally accepted charter on cabinet formation with procedural rules could strengthen his non-partisan position.

(iii) The lack of political responsibility for political acts in the formation

Table 6.1   Dutch governments since 1945

Prime Minister and party	Duration of government	Party composition of coalition
Schermerhorn (PvdA)	24/6/45–3/7/46	PvdA, KVP, CHU, non-party
Beel (KVP)	3/7/46–7/8/48	PvdA, KVP, non-party
Drees (PvdA)	7/8/48–15/3/51	PvdA, KVP, VVD, CHU, non-party
Drees (PvdA)	15/3/51–2/9/52	PvdA, KVP, VVD, CHU, non-party
Drees (PvdA)	2/9/52–13/10/56	PvdA, KVP, ARP, CHU, non-party
	(this party lost parliamentary confidence in May 1955 but was restored in two weeks)	
Drees (PvdA)	13/10/56–22/12/58	PvdA, KVP, ARP, CHU
Beel (KVP)	22/12/58–19/5/59	KVP, ARP, CHU
	(interim – caretaker – government)	
De Quay (KVP)	19/5/59–24/7/63	KVP, ARP, CHU, VVD
	(lost parliamentary confidence in December 1960 but was restored in ten days)	
Marijnen (KVP)	24/7/63–14/4/65	KVP, ARP, CHU, VVD
Cals (KVP)	14/4/65–22/11/66	KVP, PvdA, ARP
Zijlstra (ARP)	22/11/66–5/4/67	KVP, ARP
	(interim or caretaker government)	
De Jong (KVP)	5/4/67–6/7/71	KVP, ARP, CHU, VVD
Biesheuvel (ARP)	6/7/71–20/7/72	KVP, ARP, CHU, VVD, DS'70
Biesheuvel (ARP)	20/7/72–11/5/73	KVP, ARP, CHU, VVD
	(interim or caretaker government)	
Den Uyl (PvdA)	11/5/73–19/12/77	PvdA, KVP, ARP, PPR, D'66
Van Agt (CDA)	19/12/77–11/9/81	CDA, VVD
Van Agt (CDA)	11/9/81–29/5/82	PvdA, CDA, D'66
	(internal crisis in October 81, restoration after 17 days)	
Van Agt (CDA)	29/5/82–4/11/82	CDA, D'66
	(interim or caretaker government)	
Lubbers (CDA)	4/11/82–	CDA, VVD

process makes the Dutch way of forming governments highly questionable, since the primary rule of parliamentary government (ministerial
responsibility) cannot be observed for a considerable period of time.

(iv) Coalition replacement during a parliamentary period without early elections is possible only in theory; according to current parliamentary
opinion, however, replacement is possible only after dissolution of Parliament.

(v) Dissolution of parliament always needs full parliamentary endorsement
and is mostly carried out by an interim (or caretaker) cabinet.

(vi) Outgoing (*démissionnaire*) cabinets become more powerful the longer they
last.

(vii) Coalition cabinets tend to succumb to internal disagreement, more than to
loss of parliamentary confidence. Current parliamentary opinion, that
replacement is possible only after the dissolution of Parliament, mostly
prevents the MPs of the government parties from joining forces with the
opposition.

(viii) General elections never confirm a coalition cabinet in office, since coalition
parties tend to stress their own political identity instead of the identity of
the coalition. All coalition cabinets resign on election day.

(ix) Prime ministerial government is more difficult in coalition cabinets than in
one-party cabinets. Reshuffles are almost impossible since they affect the
position of all coalition partners; they can only take place with the agreement of the parliamentary parties of the coalition.

(x) Individual loss of confidence is very unusual since it affects the cohesion
and the very existence of the coalition cabinet; an impending loss of
confidence in individual cases tends to develop into a cabinet question.

Notes

1. During the first twenty years after 1946 the number of interim crises was 6, in the
   period 1967–82, 3. The average formation period in 1946–66 was 48 days, in 1967–82
   79 days.
2. More than once the budget of the new fiscal year has been introduced during cabinet
   formation (1956, 1977, 1981 and 1982).

7 Coalition Government and Policy Outputs in the Netherlands
Ken Gladdish

The Netherlands presents in an acute form the difficulty of scrutinising and appraising policy outcomes under conditions of coalition government. All the familiar factors which make it so difficult to assess performance of party administrations are present: the legacies of previous governments, the unravelling of the precise aetiology of ideas and proposals, the extent of contributions from expert bodies, pressure groups and the bureaucracy, and the national and international circumstances confronting each successive cabinet. On top of these generic problems, Dutch coalition governments exhibit a special dilemma for the analyst in that they involve only a partial turnover of component parties. There is therefore a continuity of party membership of successive coalitions which makes the ascription of policy even more elusive than usual. There are also fewer clear watersheds between administrations in terms of major policy innovation.

But there are still further complications. There is first the fact that all coalition governments in Holland contain parties whose rationale is religious or confessional rather than ideological. This means that underlying positions on many issues, especially in the realm of socio-economic affairs, cannot readily be inferred from party labels. Secondly, classifications of the political complexion of governments in terms of party composition may be substantially affected by the actual balance of parties within each cabinet and the distribution of the more important portfolios. And thirdly the behaviour of parties in the cabinet may be very much influenced by the size and stability of their support in parliament.

Dutch multi-party cabinets exhibit perennial tensions between party identity and collective responsibility. Parties in government have a continual eye both to electoral advantage and to the need to retain the endorsement of their parliamentary groups. At the same time, issues which could be contentious from the standpoint of inter-party relations within cabinets tend to be played down for the sake of cabinet survival. Election campaigns are usually conducted on the basis of individual party platforms rather than potential coalition alliances. The formation of cabinets therefore requires post-election programmes to be devised

which it is hoped will hold the parties together for a four-year parliamentary term.[1] For cabinets under these conditions both to emerge
and to cohere, there has to be less emphasis upon policy innovation than
upon consensus and accommodation. So that in general there is a
disposition towards less dramatic shifts of policy from one government
to the next than is associated (not always accurately) with alternating
single-party government.

There are further inhibitions upon the free flow of policy initiatives
in the Dutch context. The relatively modest position of the Netherlands in international terms and the nature of its economy endows all
governments with rather less leverage upon events than larger and more
influential states are assumed to possess. Foreign and defence policies
are in consequence consistently moderate and unspectacular. Similar
constraints apply to all aspects of economic and fiscal policy which
either rely upon or need to respond to the behaviour of external
agencies. So the scope for autarchic responses to the international
climate is distinctly limited whatever the party composition of successive governments.

The perpetual circumstance of only partial turnover among the
parties participating in government argues a high degree of policy
continuity. How true this is will be examined in the course of this
chapter. There are in addition institutions developed since the war
which would appear to reinforce assumptions of continuity. The Social
and Economic Council (SER) and the Central Planning Bureau were
both established to promote consistent long-term approaches towards
social and economic management; the first to harvest the accords of the
main 'social partners' (employer organisations and labour federations),
the second to supply governments with projections derived from a
model of the economy geared to an evolving set of agreements about
social and economic objectives.

The more these structural, institutional and environmental features
of the Dutch scene are paraded, as they are insistently in the literature,[2]
the greater the uncertainty whether any significant variations in overall
policy outputs are possible from one coalition to another. If this is so, a
review of governmental performance over time would merely record
the impact of changing events upon a basic uniformity of response, a
verdict with conceivably trenchant implications for competitive politics
in a state where the provisions for representation are meticulously
democratic.

The methodological problems of testing out this kind of hypothesis
are unusually daunting. Even without the peculiarities of the Dutch
case, the complexities of social and economic management in advanced
industrial democracies are such that the partisan element of what
parties seek to achieve can become almost instantly lost in a Byzantine

maze of technical intricacy. Thus the task of attempting to disentangle political inputs from mere situational reflexes may appear quite impossible.

This chapter concentrates on the record of Dutch coalitions since the beginning of the 1970s, though with some reference to the earlier context where appropriate. A list of the successive coalitions during this period showing their composition in party terms is set out in Table 7.1.

Four coalitions were in office during the ten years between 1971 and 1981 but effectively they can be translated into three distinct administrations:

(i)   A centre-right government from July 1971 until May 1973,
(ii) A left-centre government from May 1973 until December 1977,
(iii) A centre-right government from December 1977 until September 1981.

This must be slightly qualified by the fact that each government operated as a caretaker administration in its final months of office pending the formation of the new cabinet. But essentially the decade can be reduced to a pattern of five and a half years of centre-right and four and a half years of left-centre government. During the first of the three administrations, under the Minister-presidency of Biesheuvel, the three confessional parties held eleven to thirteen ministerial portfolios out of sixteen. The Cabinet was therefore clearly dominated by the confessionals. In the second administration, presided over by den Uyl, the confessionals held only six portfolios; the secular parties were thus dominant within the Cabinet, although the Labour Party, with seven out of sixteen ministries, was not in a position of overwhelming strength. The third coalition, under van Agt, saw confessional portfolios (the three parties having now unified as the Christian Democratic Appeal) rise to ten out of sixteen posts, effectively restoring a confessional majority.

In terms of cabinet composition the second administration, from 1973 to 1977, is clearly distinctive, and this is so not merely in respect of the decade under review but of the entire period since 1948. For the cabinet of 1946–8 was the only occasion when the Labour party held half the portfolios within a coalition. Between 1948 and 1973, however, the complexion of the Dutch party system experienced a significant shift of orientation. The fulcrum position of the major confessional parties makes for standard descriptions of the system as one which is operationally centre-based.[3] And this appears to be a valid characterisation since the confessionals have been willing to form coalitions with secular parties on both the right and the left. For groupings to be ambidextrous, however, is not necessarily to be even-handed, and coalitions to the right have predominated over the quarter century since 1958.[4]

Table 7.1   Dutch governments since 1967

Date installed	Parliamentary seats	Minister-president & party composition of cabinet	Distribution of portfolios	
			Ministers	*State Secretaries*
5.4.1967		*de Jong (KVP)*		
	42	KVP	6	4
	15	ARP	3	2
	12	CHU	2	3
	17	VVD	3	2
			14	11
6.7.1971		*Biesheuvel I (ARP)*		
	35	KVP	6	5
	13	ARP	3	2
	10	CHU	2	2
	16	VVD	3	2
	8	DS'70	2	2
			16	13
20.7.1972		*Biesheuvel II (ARP)*		
	35	KVP	6	5
	13	ARP	3	2
	10	CHU	4	2
	16	VVD	3	2
			16	11
11.5.1973		*den Uyl (PvdA)*		
	43	PvdA	7	5
	27	KVP	4	6
	14	ARP	2	2
	7	PPR	2	1
	6	D'66	1	3
			16	17
19.12.1977		*van Agt I (CDA)*		
	49	CDA	10	10
	28	VVD	6	6
			16	16
11.9.1981		*van Agt II (CDA)*		
	48	CDA	6	6
	44	PvdA	6	7
	17	D'66	3	3
			15	16
29.5.1982		*van Agt III (CDA)*		
	48	CDA	9	5
	17	D'66	5	3
			14	8

Date installed	Parliamentary seats	Minister-president & party composition of cabinet	Distribution of portfolios	
4.11.1982		*Lubbers (CDA)*		
	45	CDA	8	8
	36	VVD	6	8
			――	――
			14	16

Information for the period 1967–77 is derived from the chapter on 'Government Formation' (Andeweg, van der Tak and Dittrich) in R.T. Griffiths *op. cit.*, (Table 9.1, p. 229).

Legend:
- KVP Catholic Peoples' Party
- ARP Anti-Revolutionary Party
- CHU Christian Historical Party
- VVD Liberal Party
- DS'70 Democratic Socialists 1970
- PvdA Labour Party
- PPR Radical Party
- D'66 Democrats 1966
- CDA Christian Democratic Appeal

What might be regarded as simply the exigencies of parliamentary arithmetic have, since the latter 1960s, been overtaken by evidence of an increasing polemical gap between Labour and the confessionals. The breakdown of the established mechanisms of consensus and the development of 'new left' concerns within the Labour party sharpened the focus of political debate. The major confessional groups, most notably the Catholics who had seemed closest to Labour interests since the war, were thus subjected to the pressures of a more polarised setting. In terms of party positions on apparently basic socio-economic convictions, the confessionals remained somewhat closer to the left than to the right, according to an authoritative survey of 1972.[5] But in terms of ideological commitment, Labour sought to distance itself, in alliance with support parties, from the traditional centre grouping in its desire to break the confessional dominance of cabinet formation and perennial policy-formulation.

The dynamics of government formation and operation during the 1970s therefore came rather closer to a pattern of binary alternatives than the traditional model of Dutch politics implied. There still remained a considerable area of overlap, cross-thread and nuance; and the mathematics of party representation still dictated flexibility and accommodation. Thus in 1981 the CDA under van Agt found itself once more in a coalition with Labour, although the outcome was distinctly unpropitious. Yet something nearer to a left-right dichotomy was discernible in Holland in the 1970s than had previously been acknowledged, albeit within a system which could not be comprehensively polarised, and, ironically, under circumstances where policy options were far more restricted than they might have seemed in the 1960s.

One associated feature of this development was the emergence of a more personal style of leadership. It was signified by the approach of den Uyl who took the Labour party into the election of November 1972 at the head of a 'progressive alliance' which included the Radical Party (PPR) and D'66. This was a further step in a process begun the previous year, which broke with three previous conventions of party behaviour. One was the traditional divorce between party leadership in Parliament and participation in government. Another was the reluctance, post 1918, to form pre-election alliances: and the third was an equal reluctance to rule out possible coalition partners in advance of elections.

The new strategy could scarcely be accounted a success. For after an unusually long and turbulent period of negotiations over the formation of a cabinet, den Uyl was compelled to accept ministers from both the Catholic Peoples' Party and the Anti-Revolutionary (Protestant) Party in order to ensure majority support in Parliament. Nevertheless a change of style in Dutch governmental politics had been signalled which would have repercussions on party behaviour in future coalitions, though not necessarily upon policy outcomes. The sphere in which precise data about policy outcomes is most readily available is that of economic management. Its consideration in relation to broad social objectives is therefore a useful way of seeing how far performance appears to have differed between the two types of coalition, centre-right and left-centre.

Any discussion of economic and social policies in the 1970s must be set in the context of two dominating factors. The first is the pattern of public commitment and popular expectation built up since the early 1960s in Holland as in Western Europe generally. The second is the economic environment from 1973 onwards, in which all advanced industrial nations were trapped in a surge of price increases for raw materials, notably oil, which led by stages to deep recession and levels of unemployment unprecedently high for the post-war period.

The first factor is one which would militate against efforts by governments of the right to rephrase social priorities. But it also served to impose upon governments of the left the task of maintaining objectives which they endorsed ideologically in the teeth of economic disarray. The second factor reversed the relationship between social aims and economic management. The economy had somehow to be shored up, if necessary at the expense of social benefits. The question by the mid-1970s had thus become: How much of the commitment to comprehensively high living standards could be maintained, and at what economic cost? And would the verdicts of governments of differing ideological hue vary significantly on this central issue?

The build-up of public commitment in Holland can be summarised in various terms. Tables 7.2 and 7.3 highlight different aspects of this progression.

Table 7.2   Development of the volume of certain state expenditures

	1955	1960	1965	1970	1975	Share in the 1977 budget (%)
General administration	100	100	130	130	150	8.4
Defence	100	85	90	95	85	11.2
Foreign relations (incl. foreign aid)	100	120	105	230	520	3.4
Commerce and trade	100	75	195	210	370	2.6
Education, science, culture and recreation	100	195	280	380	465	26.8
Social provisions, health and environmental protection	100	65	80	105	235	22.8
Housing and physical planning	100	310	390	395	555	7.9
Total	100	107	134	174	230	
Net national income in real terms	100	120	155	205	224	

Source: R.T. Griffiths, *op. cit*, p. 28.

Table 7.3   Share of the collective sector in the net national income

	1953	1963	1973	1974	1975	1976	1977
Social security premiums	5.2	10.9	18.3	19.4	20.3	19.9	19.7
Taxes	26.3	25.2	29.8	30.4	30.6	31.1	31.6
Total	31.5	36.1	48.1	49.8	50.9	51.0	51.3

Source: *ibid*, p. 31.

These developments took place within a distinctive style of government and public management which was to some extent fashioned by wartime experience and the need for national unity in the period of reconstruction. Accounts of the rebuilding of the economy post 1945 and of the institutions set up to serve that task demonstrate the espousal by all parties of a corporatist system of setting goals and settling strategies.[6] Some of the consequences of this approach are interesting, *inter alia* in terms of the relationship between political forces and constituencies. For the first time in Dutch politics, the democratic left, in the shape of the newly consolidated Labour party, became a major co-partner in government. Between 1948 and 1958, four successive cabinets were led by W. Drees of the Labour party, as Minister-president. Government strategy in this period, however, was highly consensual and indeed traditional in terms of the economic structure and its operation. Corporate devices for reaching agreement on major questions of economic distribution drew upon the deferential co-operation of the trade union federations vis-à-vis both employers and government. The result was that, with Labour in government, wage levels in the Netherlands remained surprisingly low by comparative international standards,[7] thus creating a very strong competitive position for Dutch products and manufactures.

Breaches in the unified edifice of national corporatism and co-operation between the 'social partners' began to appear by the end of the 1950s and were clearly signalled by the breakdown of central agreements on incomes in 1963. This rupture of the consensual pattern took place under a centre-right government composed of the major confessional parties plus the Liberals. Labour had not held office since 1958 and over the ensuing fifteen years would participate in government for a mere 18 months, from 1965–6. Paradoxically, however, the acceleration of public commitment to welfare services, social security, education and health care was concentrated in the decade and a half prior to 1973 when Labour was out of power at national level.

If this circumstance invites enquiry, explanations are available at many different levels. One is in terms of unique prosperity which was particularly dramatic in the Dutch case. The strong competitive position of the economy generated relatively sudden affluence which made resources available to a society impatient with historically low living standards for the majority. Another is the emergence of greater militancy by industrial unions and their members (as distinct from the national federations) which may well have benefitted from the absence of Labour in government as a restraining influence. And a third realm of explanation is the continuingly accommodative style of Dutch political bargaining.

By the 1970s the complexion of the Dutch polity in the form of its social and economic imperatives and observances approximated more closely to the Scandinavian democracies than to other West European states, as Table 7.4 indicates. But unlike Sweden and Denmark this did not reflect the long-term dominance of a powerful Social Democratic

Table 7.4 Public expenditure (including social security) as a percentage of net national income

	1967/68	1972	1977
Netherlands	45.0	50.7	60.5
Germany	40.4	41.7	49.4
France	40.6	40.9	48.4
United Kingdom	40.2	41.3	47.7
Sweden	42.2	50.1	66.6
United States	33.5	35.0	37.0

Source: OECD, *Economic Survey, Netherlands*, March 1979, p. 7.

party over other political formations. Instead it signified the response of a consensual system to pressures for and convictions about the distribution of resources within a now affluent society and the recognition of economic and social needs throughout the population. The generalised nature of this consensus presents a further difficulty for the analysis of policy outcomes in partisan terms or in relation to the party composition of government coalitions.

To refer back to an earlier point, it is not that party programmes, either in the 1960s or thereafter, became identical or even expressed similar priorities. The manifestos of the major parties in the election of 1981 continued to show significant differences of approach and concern. But the dynamics of a centre-based system, certainly in the Dutch case, disclose a propensity for the centre to absorb and accommodate the contentions of the time, apparently without either ideological brakes or the need for ideological accelerators. That this is the Dutch experience requires emphasis, because the character of the confessional parties is undoubtedly a potent factor in this process. The point has, of course, to be qualified so as to exclude certain ethical issues, such as abortion, on which the confessionals take a stance which might be thought out of tune with the times.

The fondness for corporatist strategies in policy formulation also owes something to the internal characteristics of the confessional grouping. For until the 1970s both Protestant and Catholic formations covered separate trade union federations as well as employer organisations and professional and producer interest groups.[8] The scrutiny of public policy in the 1970s in relation to the composition of coalition governments must therefore be set against a background of relatively high consensus among national elites in their long-term acceptance of social and economic commitments, of a dedication to corporatist institutions and strategies since 1945 (and indeed originating much earlier[9]), and of the vulnerability of a small open economy to the ravages of world recession.

The Biesheuvel Cabinet took office in June 1971, after, by Dutch standards, a relatively short period of formation negotiations (69 days) following the election of April. The main feature of the election results, apart from a rise in voter volatility to 13 per cent,[10] was a substantial loss of seats by the major confessional parties, whose parliamentary strength declined from a total of 69 seats to 58. Labour had gained 2 seats but were scarcely *papabile*, having campaigned as a rival formation to the confessionals and Liberals of the outgoing government. A continued confessional-Liberal coalition could not, however, command a majority in the Second Chamber without additional support, which was recruited from the newly-formed Democratic Socialists 1970, whose 8 seats ostensibly provided a secure base for a new five-party administration.

In terms of party policies there were, of course, distinctions of both approach and emphasis between the coalition partners. The Catholic People's Party, which had the largest stake in cabinet (6 ministries), had campaigned on a programme, drafted in 1970, whose principal socio-economic tenets were of a leftward inclination. They included: more equitable incomes and a better distribution of wealth, pension rates equalling 70 per cent of income at retirement, and acceptance of increased taxation (to rise from 29 per cent to 31 per cent of national income). The Anti-Revolutionary Party (3 ministries, including the Minister-president) had stressed in its programme the importance of private ownership and a freer wages policy, though it also supported co-partnership in industry, higher succession and wealth taxes, and, if necessary, higher taxation on capital gains.

The Christian Historicals, although less specific in their platform, concurred broadly with the Anti-Revolutionaries. But the Liberals were opposed to further tax increases alongside their general philosophy of urging a freer market economy and the primacy of private enterprise. DS'70, which turned out to be the joker in the pack, had based its breakaway from the Labour party upon unease at the escalation of public revenue and commitments. Yet it was to defect from the cabinet in 1972 in protest against proposed economies in social welfare programmes.

The economic situation confronting the Biesheuvel Cabinet was complex and difficult to interpret.[11] In the period 1966–70, the output of the business sector had increased at a higher annual rate than in the period 1961–5; and since productivity had also improved on the preceding five years, unit wage costs had decreased slightly. But wages were rising at a rate which was causing consternation, and in 1970–71 the increase of money wages for the year reached 12–14 per cent. Consumer prices were also rising at a higher annual rate than in the first half of the 1960s. More solemn signals of alarm were, however, being sounded by the figures for accelerating government expenditure and for the growing share of national income taken up by wages and salaries, on the one hand, and transfers and social security payments, on the other. These and other indicators are summarised in Table 7.5.

Table 7.5   Medium-term prospects: selected indicators

	1961	1966	1972
			(Projections)
	Average annual rate of change in per cent		
Output	5.2	5.8	5.3
Employment	1.3	0.8	1.3
Output per man	3.8	5.0	4.0
Wage bill per man	10.0	10.4	10.0
Unit wage costs	6.0	5.1	5.8
Disposable real worker income	4.7	3.7	4.0
Consumer prices	3.8	4.2	4.0

	1961	1971	1975
			(Projections)
	Per cent of net national product at market prices		
Net tax revenue	25.7	28.5	29.6
Social Security contributions	9.1	17	10.2
Government non-tax revenue		3.5	3.3
	Per cent of national income at market prices		
Wages and salaries	53.1	61.8	63.7
Transfers and social security payments	12.7	18.4	19.9
Other income	26.6	17.5	16.6
Government authorities	20.4	22.6	23.0

Source: OECD, *Economic Survey, Netherlands*, November 1971, p. 35.

In 1970 the established system of central wage settlement had stalled and the labour federations had withdrawn from national consultations in protest against a new Wages Act giving government powers to intervene in wage agreements. Unofficial strikes in Rotterdam had resulted in substantial wage increases, prompting the de Jong Cabinet to introduce a six-month wage freeze from January 1971. At the same time VAT was raised from 12 to 14 per cent, and a surcharge was imposed on direct and indirect taxes, with the aim of reducing demand and curbing inflationary pressures.

The Biesheuvel Cabinet took office, therefore, at a point where economic stop-gap measures by its predecessor would need either to be extended or relinquished. It took the latter course, though with some uncertainty. The conclusion of the OECD *Economic Survey* of November 1971 was that 'the international environment and domestic social and political considerations have complicated the task of policy formulation'.[12] Such verdicts were to become a refrain of OECD analysts throughout the 1970s.

By 1972 the economic tapestry facing the five-party coalition was disclosing a number of disturbing features.[13] Unemployment, though still less than 3 per cent of the work force, was higher than at any point since the early 1950s. It was accompanied by mounting inflation (7.8 per cent), and indexation clauses now covered virtually all wage-earners as against only 10 per cent in 1970. Business investment had slackened, there was a net capital outflow, and a continuing expansion of public spending. Conflict between the 'social partners' over income distribution was becoming exacerbated.

Proposals for the 1973 budget were based upon a 10.5 per cent rise in public revenue and a 12.5 per cent rise in public expenditure. This represented a 50 per cent increase over the original estimate for 1972, and a 20 per cent increase over the actual outcome for that year. Then in December 1972 there was a breakthrough in the form of a tripartite agreement between employers, trade unions and the government on a social contract. The package was an elaborate one embodying limited wage (up to 3.5 per cent) and price (up to 5.5 per cent) increases, a gradual introduction of a 40-hour week, a freeze on business profits (already announced in November) and vigorous efforts to combat unemployment.

After a prolonged period of dissensus, the new agreement seemed a triumph of accord; but the Biesheuvel coalition was not to reap the benefit. The defection of DS'70 from the government, in September, had precipitated fresh elections held in November 1972. The results registered a further dramatic decline in confessional party support, from 58 seats overall to 48; and although the Liberals had gained seats, no centre-right majority was possible. Instead six months of caretaker government followed the elections, until a new left-centre cabinet took office in May 1973.

The record of the comparatively brief administration of the confessionals and Liberals under Biesheuvel could be regarded as one of moderate success in economic management, though the coalition was fortunate enough to come to an end *avant le déluge*. Its overall ideological profile, assessed with regard to its economic and social policy stances, was equally moderate, and concerned to try to restore a deteriorating consensus rather than to innovate. It was a government very much of the confessional centre and the last, given the subsequent rise of Liberal support, which would be able to treat the secular right as a minor partner.

Its successor was of a decidedly different stripe. The negotiations which eventually produced the five-party cabinet under den Uyl in May 1973 were of unprecedented length (163 days). Labour had conducted its election campaign in November 1972 at the head of a three-party alliance which was originally committed to not forming a coalition on the basis of a programme devised after the elections. This proved impossible to fulfil since the 'progressive alliance' held only 56 seats out of 150. The negotiations were long and acrimonious and resulted in a cabinet whose parliamentary status was ambiguous. It included both Catholic and Anti-Revolutionary ministers though their parliamentary groups provided only conditional support for membership of a cabinet under a Labour premier.[14]

The uncertainty of the status of the den Uyl coalition was accompanied by confusion over the government's programme, since it comprised two distinct texts: one the platform of the progressive alliance and the other the joint election document of the confessionals. The confessional platform was broadly the same as before. Labour's programme embodied both the new left-wing concerns within the party and an emphasis on popular participation which reflected the outlook of the two minor parties in the alliance, D'66 and the PPR. Economic growth was considered subordinate to greater equality, protection of the lower income groups, and more democratic involvement in social, economic and political institutions. Objectives included more public control over private investment and finance, co-determination in industry, and the direct election of mayors and provincial officers.[15]

In the economic sphere party intentions were quickly overtaken by international events. The ministries responsible for dealing directly with the impact of the crisis of autumn 1973, when the world oil price trebled, and of the rise of 46 per cent in the cost of imported raw materials during 1974, were distributed among three of the parties in the coalition. Finance was in the hands of Labour, Economic Affairs was held by a minister from the Catholic People's Party, whilst Social Affairs was under an Anti-Revolutionary minister.

The new cabinet began, in the short space before the crisis, with a campaign against unemployment. A job creation and retraining scheme was introduced together with a wage-cost subsidy to relieve long-term unemployment. An elaborate package was assembled to steer wage increases and to safeguard the low-paid, the results of which, by the end of 1974, seemed to have been positive in that the dramatic rises in wage costs had been moderated.[16] Then in January 1974, a Special Powers Act was passed giving the government authority, for a period of 12 months without specific parliamentary assent, to regulate prices, wages, dividends, redundancies, working hours and foreign labour contracts. This was followed in March by an announced increase in public expenditure (3–3.5 per cent) and public investment (3.5–4 per cent) to offset unemployment and the downturn in demand. In the event, however, public expenditure rose by only 0.5 per cent and public investment fell during the year by 5.5 per cent.[17] As had happened before, the management of the economy and especially the public sector was shown to depend upon more than cabinet decisions.

Some of the difficulties confronting the hybrid coalition during the critical year of 1974 can be illustrated in the realm of monetary policy. By restricting credit and maintaining high interest rates, it was hoped to reduce liquidity and thereby combat inflation. But these aims ran counter to public expenditure policies (albeit unfulfilled) designed to offset reduced demand and thereby combat unemployment. The relative successes of the government's wage policies in 1973 and 1974 were threatened at the end of 1975 when attempts to achieve a central agreement once again foundered. In response, the cabinet decided to order limited wage increases and to re-enforce price controls. It also decided, despite its general commitment to protect wage-earners, not to permit full indexation of pay in relation to prices in the second half of 1976.

The dominant impression of the efforts of the den Uyl coalition, from 1974 to 1976, is that of a government composed of disparate elements struggling with a complex and demanding economic situation. Its priorities could be summarised as:

(i) to tackle unemployment by increasing demand through public measures, subsidising new jobs and moderating wage increases;
(ii) to pursue greater equalisation of income for the low-paid, women and the unemployed;
(iii) to pursue a better geographical distribution of enterprise by some concerted regional policy.

But its policies were pitted against world recession and inflation. Increasing demand meant possibly stimulating inflation. Moderating wage rises meant conflict with the trade unions, as reflected in successive failures to achieve central wage agreements. Expert advice from the SER was that rising labour costs had been excessive, had depressed business and discouraged investment. But the further expansion of public expenditure had resulted in raising labour costs because of the need for increased taxes and social insurance contributions; whilst financing greater public spending through borrowing fuelled interest rates and fed back into higher business costs.

All in all, the administration under den Uyl could be regarded as exemplifying the typical dilemmas of a mild left concern to maintain social objectives in the face of economic adversity. These dilemmas were compounded by the diversity of a coalition of five parties, two of which could not be entirely confident of the whole-hearted support of their parliamentary groups.

Despite these difficulties, the den Uyl Cabinet, unlike its predecessor, managed to survive until very nearly the end of its parliamentary term, finally breaking up just before the next elections were due in March 1977. The two most significant features of the election were firstly that the three major confessional parties were now united as a single formation, the Christian Democratic Appeal; and secondly that Labour made a dramatic gain of ten seats. The negotiations which followed lasted until December and constitute the longest delay ever in the formation of a Dutch cabinet. At several points in the sequence of negotiation, Labour, Democrats '66 and the CDA seemed on the verge of agreement; but each occasion was frustrated over the details of cabinet composition. Eventually the proposed formation collapsed, and a CDA-Liberal coalition was put together in November/December, with remarkable speed but dissent on the part of some members of the CDA parliamentary group.

The new cabinet's programme bore a strong resemblance to that which had emerged in the abortive discussions between the CDA and Labour. Its central objectives were the reduction of unemployment and inflation, a tight control of public expenditure, and a limitation of the budget deficit. Its detailed agenda included two items which had been part of Labour's election manifesto: a levy on excess profits to supply a special investment fund, and extended worker participation in the management of firms. So although in party terms the cabinet would be construed as centre-right, its programme was not readily distinguishable from that of its centre-left alternative. And this could not simply be attributed to continuity of personnel, since only 2 of the 16 ministers had held office in the previous coalition.

In the field of economic policy it is difficult to see the change of government in 1977 as representing any significant shift of emphasis. The prime issues of economic direction appeared once again to be viewed managerially rather than in partisan terms. So that, paradoxically, four years of a left-centre coalition had in fact restored a large measure of consensus on basic policy imperatives among elites.

The van Agt Cabinet produced in 1978 a statement of priorities (Blueprint 1981) which was based upon a macro-economic forecast by the Central Planning Bureau. It illustrated how consensual these priorities had become in the face of economic pressures. There was a settled conviction that unit labour cost increases must be reduced, and

that pay rises were therefore to be minimised. Nevertheless, redistributive concerns continued to be observed; small wage increases for
those on low incomes were to be balanced by small decreases for the
higher incomes. Even the second priority, though seemingly more
centre-right in emphasis, had acquired consensual status by 1978. The
consensus was that the rate of growth of public spending needed to be
curbed by economies in social security benefits and public sector
wages.[18]

By 1979 the overall economic situation was showing signs of im-
provement. Real GDP rose during the year by 3 per cent, mainly
through a recovery in exports. Unemployment, however, remained
relatively high, and the share of national income taken up by collective
claims continued to grow. Government expenditure was again accelerating, and employment in the public sector was 14 per cent higher than
in 1973.[19] It seemed evident that whatever the complexion of successive
coalitions, the leviathan of the public sector continued to be enlarged.

The government's major policy aims for 1979 and 1980 continued to
be virtually identical with those of the den Uyl administration post-
1974; the moderation of unemployment and inflation, and the protection of the purchasing power of the average wage-earner. In the
sphere of social policy the commitment to extensive social security and
welfare was maintained; a commitment which could seem extravagant
to external economic analysts, as the OECD survey for March 1980
(p.58) made plain:

It would appear that the simultaneous pursuit of a large number of economic
and social goals has given rise to inconsistencies or self-defeating elements in
policy programmes. Social security improvements have reduced the productive
potential of the private sector through their effects on labour supply. The
almost unavoidable simplification of a fairly centralised income determination
process, and a shift in emphasis towards redistribution in favour of low income
groups, have not permitted a sufficient increase in income differentials in favour
of industrial employment to offset apparently increasing preferences among the
labour force for non-industrial jobs. The rising financial burden of the social
security programme has come into increasing conflict with the goals of income
restraint and has brought additional charges to employers which discourage
employment and reduce profitability in the enterprise sector.

1980 saw the government pursuing the now familiar course of a wage
freeze which was elaborated into a statutory wage policy to apply until
the end of the year. In August the rise of social security costs, estimated
to reach 35 per cent of general government outlay by 1981, led to a set of
measures designed to pare down total expenditure without radically
changing existing programmes[20] – a mix of policies which had become
standardised regardless of the party composition of the government.

The van Agt Cabinet endured until the early months of 1981. Its record in the economic field paralleled closely that of its predecessor. This would imply that the model of the operation of coalition government in the Netherlands approximating most nearly to reality was, in the 1970s, that of a basic similarity of response to circumstance within the frame work of a high consensus about commitments and priorities. This finding conforms to the accepted liturgy of the politics of accommodation, originally propounded back in the 1960s, notably in the first edition of Lijphart's book, *The Politics of Accommodation* but subsequently modified in the light of the breakdown of the 'three-pillar' system and resultant changes in the pattern of political mobilisation.[21]

This brief summary of the record of three coalitions does not, of course, extend beyond the tactics of economic management. A study of other policy areas might reveal significant differences in approach between administrations; and a comprehensive appraisal of government performance over the decade would doubtless disclose greater variation in the behaviour of cabinets, and of individual ministers within cabinets, than emerges from this account. It does nevertheless seem that policy outcomes in the socio-economic realm during the 1970s reflected a similarity of response to major issues on the part of governments of differing composition and apparently differing complexion. How far this might be construed as a sign of the virtues of the Dutch system of governmental politics remains an open question.

Notes

1. On the issues relating to cabinet formation see Andeweg, van der Tak and Dittrich in R.T. Griffiths (ed.), *The Economy and Politics of the Netherlands since 1945* (The Hague, Martinus Nijhoff, 1980); Jan Vis, Chapter 6 of this volume; K.R. Gladdish, 'Two-party versus Multi-party, Britain and the Netherlands', *Acta Politica* VII, No. 3, 1972.
2. For example, D. Coombes and S. Walkland (eds), *Parliaments and Economic Affairs*, Part V, 'Parliament and Economic Policy in the Netherlands' (London, Heinemann for Policy Studies Institute, 1980); E. den Dunnen in A. Courakis (ed.), *Inflation, Depression and Economic Policy in the West* (London, Mansell Information Publishing, 1981); R.T. Griffiths (ed.), *Government, Business and Labour in European Capitalism* (London, Europotentials Press, 1977), Chap. 8.
3. An early authoritative statement of this aspect was made in H. Daalder, 'Cabinets and Party Systems in Ten Smaller European Democracies', *Acta Politica* VI, 1971.
4. H. Daudt, 'Political Parties and Government Coalitions in the Netherlands since 1945', *Netherlands Journal of Sociology* 18, 1982, offers a more generic view of the admission of Labour to coalitions.
5. A Leiden University Survey of Dutch MPs, variously reported, most accessibly by H. Daalder, 'The Netherlands' in S. Henig (ed.), *Political Parties in the European Community* (London, Allen & Unwin for Policy Studies Institute, 1979).
6. See A. Lijphart, *The Politics of Accommodation, Pluralism and Democracy in the Netherlands*, (Los Angeles, University of California Press, 2nd. edn, 1975), Chaps VI and VIII.
7. *ibid.* and J. Windmuller, *Labour Relations in the Netherlands* (Ithaca NY, Cornell University Press, 1969).
8. See J. de Beus and H. van den Doel, 'Interest Groups in Dutch Domestic Politics' in Griffiths, *op. cit.*

9. *ibid*; also Lijphart, *op. cit*, pp. 114–15.
10. Voter volatility in the three previous elections had been: 1959 – 5%, 1963 – 6%, 1967 – 10%. Clearly the Dutch voter was increasingly varying his and her options. For a recent detailed analysis see R. Andeweg, *Dutch Voters Adrift, On Explanations of Electoral Change 1963–1977* (Leyden University, 1982).
11. OECD, *Economic Survey, Netherlands*, November 1971.
12. *ibid.*, pp. 45–6.
13. OECD, *Economic Survey, Netherlands*, May 1973.
14. Daalder, *op. cit*.
15. S. Wolinetz, 'The Dutch Labour Party' in W. Paterson and A. Thomas (eds), *Social Democratic Parties in Western Europe*, (London, Croom Helm, 1977).
16. P. de Wolff and W. Driehuis, 'Economic Developments and Economic Policy' in Griffiths, *op. cit.*, p. 46.
17. OECD, *Economic Survey, Netherlands*, March 1976.
18. OECD, *Economic Survey, Netherlands*, March 1979.
19. OECD, *Economic Survey, Netherlands*, March 1980.
20. OECD, *Economic Survey, Netherlands*, April 1981.
21. Lijphart, *op. cit*. The first edition appeared in 1968.

8   Coalition Government in Belgium
Jan de Meyer

In so far as government formation is concerned, one can distinguish three periods in Belgium, since the creation of the state in 1830: a brief period of 'unionist' government up to 1847, a period of 'homogeneous' government from 1847 until the First World War and, from then until the present, a period of coalition government.[1]

During the first period governments were not specifically party governments, even if they contained only representatives of one particular political tendency. Rather, they appeared as governments of union, which were also, to a large extent, governments of the king. Leopold I intervened actively in their formation and in their activities. Indeed, during that period, there were not really political parties in the modern sense: there were, of course, Liberals, on the one side, and Catholics or conservatives on the other, but they did not oppose each other as such very strongly. Majorities in parliament were nearly always very disparate and on most votes Liberals and Catholics were to be found voting on each side. The supporters of each tendency could not even be delimited with much precision, but we know that two of the governments of this period contained only Liberals and that the other eight governments, including the provisional government of 1830–31 contained both Liberals and Catholics.

It was only after 1847 that Liberals and Catholics began to oppose each other clearly and there began a long period of party government, although the government of De Decker from 1855 to 1857 attempted a brief return to unionism. Each time, except from 1854 to 1856 and for a few weeks in 1870, one or other of the two parties enjoyed an absolute majority in parliament, allowing it to govern on its own. The role of the king was therefore considerably reduced, but nevertheless Leopold II in 1871 provoked the dismissal of the Anethan government and in 1884, at least indirectly, that of the Malou government. Thus, there were from August 1847 to January 1916, with the exception of the De Decker government, sixteen homogeneous governments: five Liberal governments, governing for a total of a little more than 26 years, and eleven Catholic governments, ruling for a total of around 39 and a half years. During this second period Belgium offered a perfect example of the classic parliamentary regime.

The entry into parliament from 1894 of a third party, the Socialist

Party, as well as of a small Christian Democrat Party, led by the Abbé Daens, did nothing at first to change this state of affairs. Universal suffrage with plural voting, in force from 1893[2] to 1919, allowed the Catholics in effect to preserve their absolute majority, even after the introduction in 1899 of proportional representation, until the introduction of full universal suffrage in 1919.[3]

The second period lasted until the First World War. Parliament did not sit from August 1914 to November 1918; no election took place between May 1914 and November 1919. In January 1916, the de Broqueville government, in power since June 1911, and installed in Normandy from October 1914, transformed itself into a government of national union, two Liberals and a Socialist joining the eleven Catholics who were already members of it; from June 1918 to December 1921, there were four other governments of national union.

After the 1914–18 war, the political situation was profoundly altered. Since the elections of 1919, no party has ever succeeded in obtaining an absolute majority in parliament, except, from 1950 to 1954, the Social Christian Party (the name given to the former Catholic Party in 1945). The principal competitors of the Catholics or Social Christians are at present the Socialists, the Liberals having been relegated to the third position. The evolution towards a multi-party system has been accentuated. The Daensists disappeared but new parties have entered parliament. The Communists have won seats at every election since 1925, the Flemish Nationalists at every election since 1919, except those of 1946, 1949 and 1950, and candidates of Francophone or Walloon Parties have won seats at every election since 1965. The Rexists gained seats in 1936 and 1939. A *Union démocratique pour le respect du travail* has been represented in parliament since 1978, and the ecologists have sat there since 1981.

The situation has become even more complicated, moreover, because, for some years, the three traditional parties have each split into a Flemish and a Francophone party. Catholics were already so divided in 1936, remaining however associated with each other within the *Bloc des Catholiques de Belgique*. In 1945, they reunited into one party, the Social Christian Party, comprising a Flemish wing and a Walloon wing. Since 1969 the two wings have again become two different parties. The Liberals and the Socialists split some time later; there have thus been since 1973 two Liberal parties and since 1978 two Socialist parties. There was even, for a certain time, a Liberal Party of Brussels, just as there has already been in Brussels in each election since 1968 one list of Flemish Socialist candidates, distinct from that of the Brussels Federation of the Socialist Party.

The linguistic cleavages which have split each of the three traditional political 'families' have not yet affected the composition of the coalition governments. There has not yet been a situation in which one party of a particular family was in government while the other party of the same family was in opposition. But each party plays its own role in so far as the formation and defeat of governments is concerned.

Another complicating factor results from the existence of different political tendencies within parties.

On the Socialist side, for example, there have often been tensions and conflicts between a moderate and pragmatic tendency on the one side, and a rather more radical and doctrinaire tendency on the other, the first generally prevailing over the second at least since the First World War. Since the Socialist Party has been divided into a Flemish and a Francophone party, the Francophone party has appeared to adopt attitudes more radical than the Flemish party as far as economic and social questions are concerned; but, on the other hand, on questions of foreign policy and defence, and specifically disarmament, the Flemish party holds a rather more pacifist view than the Francophone party.

The Catholics or Social Christians have really been united only on the defence of the ideas and interests of Belgian Catholicism. From this point of view the situation has not changed much since the 'deconfessionalisation' of the party in 1945. On other issues they have always been deeply divided amongst themselves, not only as regards relations between the linguistic communities, which have come to a head on two occasions, resulting in a split into two different parties; but also on other political questions, notably in the economic and social sphere. The 'estates', which have constituted since 1921 the basic organisation of the Catholic Party and which since 1945 the Social Christian Party has pretended to ignore, have never in fact ceased to exist. There are continued differences between Conservatives and Christian Democrats: when it comes to coalition formation, the former lean towards the Liberals, the latter towards the Socialists. There are, it seems, fewer internal disagreements amongst the Liberals.

Since the First World War there have been only coalition governments in Belgium, with the exception of three homogeneous Social Christian governments which followed each other from 1950 to 1954 and three minority single-party governments, formed in May 1925 by the Catholics, in March 1946 by the Socialists, and in June 1958 by the Social Christians. These three minority governments enjoyed only an ephemeral existence. The first two were overthrown immediately: they failed to obtain a vote of confidence in their investiture speech. The third gained a vote of confidence thanks to a favourable vote from three deputies of other parties, but stayed in power only a little more than four months until the formation of a coalition government of Social Christians and Liberals. The other 45 governments since January 1916 have been coalition governments.

These have all been majority governments with two exceptions, also ephemeral: the Tindemans Governments of May 1974 and March 1977. The first of these was a minority government, composed of Social Christians and Liberals which gained the confidence of parliament thanks to the abstention of the 'communal' parties and which transformed itself from June 1974 to a majority government when the representatives of the Rassemblement Wallon came to join them. It again became a minority government in March 1977 through the dismissal of the ministers belonging to the Rassemblement Wallon, but it immediately dissolved parliament, thus anticipating its parliamentary defeat.

The coalitions have always comprised at least two of the three traditional political families; they have often comprised all three. Since the Second World War they have sometimes also contained 'non-traditional' parties. Since January 1916 there have been fourteen 'tripartite' governments, that is, governments comprising Catholics or Social Christians, Socialists and Liberals; and two other governments which, as well as Catholics, Socialists and Liberals, also contained Communists. These sixteen governments have been in power for a total of nineteen years.

There have also been during this period 24 'bipartite' governments, that is, governments comprising representatives of only two of the three traditional political families; and six other governments which contained, as well as the representatives of two of these families, representatives of non-traditional parties. These thirty governments have exercised power for a total of nearly 43 years. There have been thirteen coalitions of Catholics or Social Christians and Liberals, exercising power for a total of around 20 and a half years, thirteen coalitions of Catholics or Social Christians and Socialists exercising power for a total of a little more than 17 years, and four coalitions of Socialists and Liberals exercising power for in total nearly six years; each of these figures includes coalitions in which non-traditional parties participated.

The governments comprising all three traditional political families have occurred in periods of war or crisis. There were, as we have seen, governments of this type during and immediately after the First World War, from January 1916 to December 1921. There were also such governments from September 1939 to July 1945; the situation was then very similar to that of 1914 to 1918 in that the parliament elected in April 1939 did not meet from May 1940 to September 1944 and remained in existence until February 1946. There have also been tripartite governments from May 1926 to November 1927, from March 1935 to February 1939, from January 1973 to May 1974, and from May to October 1980, all periods of domestic crisis. But this formula has only been applied in peacetime for a total of around two years since May 1945, although it was used for around eight and a half years between November 1918 and August 1939.

Before September 1939 the Socialists were in power, with two exceptions, only in tripartite governments: they participated very briefly in bipartite governments from 1925 to 1926 and at the beginning of 1939, each time with the Catholics, for a total of about a year. By contrast, until September 1939 there were six bipartite coalitions between Catholics and Liberals, governments lasting in total slightly more than eleven years: this was the main type of government in the inter-war period.

Since the end of the Second World War bipartite coalitions have become more diversified. There have been eleven coalitions of Social Christians and Socialists governing for a total of around 16 and a half years, seven coalitions of Social Christians and Liberals, governing in total for around nine and a half years, and four coalitions of Socialists and Liberals, governing for a total of nearly six years. These figures include coalitions in which the non-traditional parties participated. We may say that the dominant coalitions since 1945 have been those comprising the Social Christians and Socialists.

The Communists participated in five governments for a total of a little over two years between 1944 and 1947. The Rassemblement Wallon participated in one government for nearly three years from 1974 to 1977, the Volksunie in two successive governments for nearly two years from 1977 to 1979, and the Front démocratique des francophones in three successive governments during a period of nearly three years from 1977 to 1980. Another party, L'Union démocratique belge (UDB), which existed for some time after the Second World War, was part of the government for some months in 1945–6. It is, broadly speaking, only during the last seven years that parties other than the traditional ones have been associated with government: this represents around a fifth of the period between September 1944 and the present.

In each of these cases there were special circumstances. The participation of the Communists can be explained by the situation which existed immediately after the Liberation; they remained in government after the election of 1946 for as long as the Socialists and Liberals had need of them to form a majority against the Social Christians. The participation of the UDB, which was a party created by some Christian Democrats, followed the move into opposition by the Catholic Party over the 'royal question' in July 1945; it ended after the election of 1946, which reduced the representation of the UDB to only one member in the Chamber of Representatives. The participation of the Rassemblement Wallon, the Volksunie and the Front démocratique des francophones occurred within the context of the communal difficulties of the last few years, but it is explained also by the importance which the parliamentary representation of these parties had acquired: following the elections of 1974, the Social Christians and the Liberals had need of some support to be able to govern without the Socialists, and following the elections of 1977 and 1978, the Social Christians and the Socialists, governing without the Liberals, would have found it difficult to secure the two-thirds majority which they needed to be able to vote the institutional reforms they wished to achieve.

The role of the king has not fundamentally altered since the First World War but it has become more difficult. When no party or political family enjoys an absolute majority in parliament, the political colour of the government is not self-evident: the king must then try to find a coalition which can command an absolute majority in parliament. Only if such a coalition cannot be formed does the king resign himself to letting a minority government be formed.

After the resignation of a government, the king consults first the resigning Prime Minister, the presidents of the Chamber of Representatives and of the Senate, the leaders of the traditional parties, and also, more and more, the leaders of the other parties.[4] He often consults also with other politicians and nearly always, for over the last fifty years, with economic and social interlocutors.[5] These consultations are normally held on an individual basis; but it can sometimes happen that the king convokes the leaders of several parties in a collective audience.[6] One of the main objects of these consultations is, of course, to find a coalitional basis for the new government.

On the basis of these consultations, the king names a *formateur* who, if he succeeds in his task, normally, but not necessarily, becomes the prime minister of the new government.[7] Several *formateurs* can be employed in succession.[8] The designation of a *formateur* is, very often but not necessarily, preceded by that of an *informateur*,[9] or of several successive *informateurs*. Sometimes an *informateur* is nominated after the failure of a *formateur*. In a particularly difficult case the king recently nominated two 'mediators', charged with acting together.[10]

When this process has resulted in the formation of a government, the government appears before parliament. The prime minister puts forward his policies: there follows a debate which is terminated by a vote on a motion of confidence, allowing one to see if the new government enjoys a parliamentary majority. This has been the customary procedure since November 1918.

The purpose of this procedure is clearly not that of allowing the king to decide personally what should happen. These consultations and the designation of *formateurs*, *informateurs* and, on occasion, mediators, have as their aim the bringing about of an agreement on the formation of a viable coalition government whose existence can be confirmed by a vote of confidence in parliament. It is in essence the parties who decide the formation and maintenance of the coalition.

But the role of the king is not purely passive. In this matter, as in others, he cannot impose his own personal point of view, but he can in his confidential conversations with politicians ask their views, give them advice, and perhaps encourage or warn them.[11] He is thus not prevented from exercising influence over the parties, and this can be beneficial in the political life of the country.[12] The king can try to prevent the dislocation of the governmental coalition if it appears to him that this dislocation would occur for no good reason, that it would be harmful to the general interest.[13] When a new government is needed, the king can try to make his preferences clear as regards the formula for a new coalition; he can for example try to secure the participation of particular parties or political families, when this appears to him desirable in the public interest.[14]

It appears that Belgian kings have generally exercised their role in a constitutional manner, and that they preside without involving themselves too deeply in the negotiations leading to the formation of coalition governments.[15] Though the procedure formally takes place around the king, in reality it is the parties which dominate the process. But in this connection there are differences between the practice followed in the inter-war period and that followed more recently.

Before 1940, negotiations prepared by the *informateur*, if there was one, and effectively conducted by the *formateur*, took place as much between persons and to some extent parliamentary groups as amongst parties; they led to the rapid formation of a governmental team rather than to the precise definition of a programme. It was then only on the Socialist side that each time the party organisation as such took part in the negotiations; and it was also the Socialist negotiators who sought on each occasion to discuss a programme.[16]

Since the end of the Second World War, the role of the parties has become more and more preponderant and the preliminary negotiation of a programme also prevailed more and more; the practice of the Socialists has been adopted by the other parties also. At the same time, the participation of the parliamentary groups has been progressively reduced, almost to vanishing point.

At present, a coalition is normally constituted by a formal governmental agreement,[17] defining in a detailed manner the programme which the coalition proposes to adopt: it is in reality a treaty concluded by the representatives of the parties constituting the coalition and submitted then for the approval of the congress or conferences of each of these parties. It is only when this approval has been obtained that the formation of the government can proceed. The parties composing the coalition consider this agreement as the very basis of the government's existence and they mutually undertake that 'their' ministers and 'their' parliamentarians will apply it faithfully.[18] The parties do not content themselves with agreeing a coalition programme. They also come to an understanding on the structure of the government and the distribution of the ministerial portfolios. In fact each of them appoints 'its' ministers.

This process can take a good deal of time. Since the custom of the governmental agreement has become formalised, governmental crises have often lasted a long time: they were settled quite quickly during the inter-war period, but during the last few years they have frequently been prolonged over several months. This did not necessarily result in greater clarity or coherence in governmental agreements.

In reality, it is the leaders of the parties, rather than the *formateurs*, who determine the programme and the composition of the government; they are the real *formateurs*. It depends, moreover, on them how long the government lasts: the prime minister is, like all the other ministers, at their mercy at all times.[19] The interpretation and execution of the governmental agreement gives rise, furthermore, by reason of its very nature to frequent difficulties, which place the existence of the government in jeopardy. Thus it is the parties which form and dissolve successive coalitions, and which make and unmake governments.

The period of coalition government has been one of governmental instability. There have been, since January 1916 – nearly 67 years – 52 governments, of which the average length has been little more than fifteen months, although during the period of homogeneous government, which covered a little over 68 years, there were only seventeen governments, with an average duration of a little more than 48 months. If one excludes from this calculation the periods of foreign occupation, the average duration of governments since 1916 has been only just a little over fourteen months.

The period of coalition government has also been one of parliamentary and constitutional instability. Legislatures from November 1918 to May 1940 and since September 1944 have lasted on average a little less than 36 months, although their normal term would be 48 months; those from 1847 to 1914 whose normal term was 24 months had an average duration of a little more than 22 months. There were only two amendments of the Constitution up to 1919; since 1919 there have already been six.[20]

One has to ask however – what degree of democratic legitimacy does such a regime of coalition government possess?

The combined application of universal suffrage and proportional representation has certainly had the consequence that, since 1919, the diverse political tendencies have been more faithfully represented in parliament than before. But it has also without any doubt contributed

Table 8.1   Representation of parties in the Belgian House of Representatives

	Communists	Socialists	Catholics or Christian Democrats	Liberals	Flemish Nationalists	FDF	RW	Other parties	Total membership
1939–1946	9	64	73	33	17			6	202
1946–1949	23	69	92	17				1	202
1949–1950	12	66	105	29					212
1950–1954	7	77	108	20					212
1954–1958	4	86	95 + 1	25	1				212
1958–1961	2	84	104	21	1				212
1961–1965	5	84	96	20	5				212
1965–1968	6	64	77	48	12	3	2	2	212
1968–1971	5	59	69	47	20	5	7		212
1971–1974	5	61	47 + 20	34	21	10	14		212
1974–1977	4	59	50 + 22	21 + 9 + 3	22	9	13		212
1977–1978	2	62	56 + 24	17 + 14 + 2	20	10	5		212
1978–1981	4	26 + 32	57 + 25	22 + 14 + 1	14 + 1	11	4	1	212
1981–	2	25 + 34	43 + 18	28 + 24	20 + 1	6	3	7	212

Table 8.2   Participation of parties in Belgian Governments

	Communists	Socialists	Catholics or Christian Democrats	Liberals	Flemish Nationalists	FDF	RW	Other parties	Prime Minister
1944–1944	x	x	x	x					Pierlot
1944–1945		x	x	x					Pierlot
1945–1945	x	x	x	x					Van Acker
1945–1946	x	x		x				x	Van Acker
1946–1946		x							Spaak
1946–1946	x	x		x					Van Acker
1946–1947	x	x		x					Huysmans
1947–1949		x	x						Spaak
1949–1950			x	x					G. Eyskens
1950–1950			x						Duvieusart
1950–1952			x						Pholien
1952–1954			x						Van Houtte
1954–1958		x		x					Van Acker
1958			x						G. Eyskens
1958–1961			x	x					G. Eyskens

Lefèvre
Harmel
Vanden Boeynants
G. Eyskens
G. Eyskens
Leburton
Tindemans
Tindemans
Tindemans
Tindemans
Vanden Boeynants
Martens
Martens
Martens
Martens
M. Eyskens
Martens

Period					
1961–1965			x		x
1965–1966			x		x
1966–1968		x	x		x
1968–1971			x		x
1971–1972			x		x
1972–1974			x	x	x
1974–1974			x	x	x
1974–1977	x			x	x
1977–1977			x		x
1977–1978		x		x	x
1978–1979		x		x	x
1979–1980	x			x	x
1980–1980				x	x
1980–1980			x		x
1980–1981				x	x
1981–1981				x	x
1981–			x		x

to creating a situation in which the electorate finds itself almost totally deprived of influence on the determination of policy and on the choice of government. From this point of view, the regime has become less democratic than when there was a property suffrage and majoritarian voting: it is, without question, formally democratic, but not democratic in reality.

It is true that in 1831 there were less than 40,000 electors out of a population of over four million, and that in 1892 there were less than 140,000 for over six million inhabitants. It is also true that in the system of majority voting of that epoch, these electors did not enjoy a great deal of choice in so far as the composition of parliament was concerned. But they really could choose between a Liberal policy and a Catholic policy, between a Liberal government and a Catholic government.

It is true that today all Belgian adults, nearly seven million out of ten million inhabitants, are electors. At the same time it is true that they can, thanks to proportional representation, determine to their hearts' content the division of parliamentary seats between the numerous parties who solicit their votes. But they are practically powerless to decide upon policy or government: it is the parties which decide on these matters without feeling bound by the results of the elections, except to the extent that they can see that there is not a parliamentary majority for this or that coalition.[21]

Another fact merits consideration. The Catholics or Social Christians have been in government during nearly the whole of the period of coalition government:[22] only for two brief intervals, one of a little more than one and a half years, the other of a little more than four years, have they found themselves in opposition.[23] With the exception of these two intervals they have been in power without interruption since 1884; they have governed Belgium alone or with others for nearly a century.

Notes

1. During each of these three periods there have also been in some governments one or, very rarely, a few ministers with no definite political allegiance. Their role has been primarily a technical one; their presence has not altered the political colouring of the government.
2. Until 1893 Belgium had a property-owners' franchise. It is only since 1893 that the vote has been compulsory.
3. In fact only universal male suffrage was introduced in 1919. Women were not given the right to vote in parliamentary elections until 1948.
4. King Leopold III in 1936 was the first to call into consultation the leaders of parties other than the traditional ones. Such consultations remained exceptional until about ten years ago; but they have now become customary.
5. Leopold III was also in 1935 the first to call into consultation these social and economic interlocutors. Those consulted in this way normally include the Governor of the National Bank and representatives of the Belgian industrialists, trade unions, and of the Socialists, Christians and Liberals.
6. Thus, in June 1936 and again in November 1937, Leopold III received together two

leaders of each of the traditional parties. Similarly, in the course of the negotiations which followed the elections of December 1978, King Baudouin in March 1979 received together the presidents of the two Social Christian Parties, the two Socialist Parties, the Volksunie and the Front démocratique des francophones and then, again, the presidents of the Flemish Social Christian Party and of the Francophone Socialist Party.

7. It can happen that the *formateur* helps to bring into existence a government led by someone other than himself. Thus, Van Zeeland was the *formateur* in 1950 for a government the prime minister of which was Pholien. Similarly, in 1979, Vanden Boeynants was the *formateur* for a government headed by Martens as prime minister.

8. In 1937 eight *formateurs* in succession were nominated before the Janson government could be formed.

9. It was also Leopold III who first nominated an *informateur* in 1935.

10. In February 1979. They were a Flemish Socialist and a Walloon Social Christian.

11. Compare Bagehot in *The English Constitution*.

12. See on this subject André Molitor, *La fonction royale en Belgique* (Brussels, 1979), pp. 26–45, and Raymond Fusilier, *Les monarchies parlementaires* (Paris, 1960), p. 198.

13. See Molitor, *op. cit.*, p. 28.

14. *ibid.*, p. 32.

15. *ibid.*, p. 27.

16. See on this subject, Carl Henrik Hoejer, *Le régime parlementaire belge de 1918 à 1940* (Uppsala, 1946), pp. 318–33.

17. See on this subject Leo Neels, *Regeringsverklaringen en regeerakkoorden Rechskunding Weekblad*, 1974–75, no. 38, pp. 2369–2410.

18. In 1977, when the construction of the fourth Tindemans government was taking place, they even claimed to make commitments beyond the duration of the legislature.

19. Since January 1940 no president of a party has been at the same time a member of the government.

20. The instability seems to have been aggravated in the course of the last few years. Since early spring 1968 there have already been six elections, fourteen governments and three amendments of the Constitution.

21. In general, the parties tend not to bind themselves in advance as to what coalitions they will participate in. Moreover, a change of partners can take place without it being necessary to have fresh elections.

22. This results of course from the fact that, since the end of the nineteenth century, the cleavages on social and economic questions have tended to be more important than the cleavage between the Church and its opponents.

23. In 1945, the Catholics left the government on account of the royal question, which put against them the Socialists, the Communists, the Liberals and the UDB, but even before that issue was resolved they came again into the government with the Socialists from March 1947. The antagonism between clericals and anti-clericals was revived on account of the education question during the legislatures from 1950 to 1954, in the course of which the Social Christians, enjoying an absolute majority in parliament, governed alone, and from 1954 to 1958, in the course of which, having lost their majority, they were replaced by a coalition of Socialists and Liberals. The Social Christians came back to power after the elections of 1958 which gave them an absolute majority in the Senate; the education question was then solved by a pact concluded between the three traditional parties.

9 Party Politics and Coalition Government in Italy
Geoffrey Pridham

Understanding Italian coalitions

It is a commonplace to say that Italy 'has no government', or that it is perpetually, even unashamedly, 'ineffective'. Coalition politics is seen to be at the centre of this problem. It is time, however, for this conventional judgement to be accorded more critical attention than it is usually given.

The picture of ineffectiveness is certainly the message carried by the media. One British newspaper has featured leading articles about the state of Italian government stretching back over a decade with such stark headings as: 'Italy's permanent crisis'; 'Italy's recurrent *crisi di governo*'; 'Italy's political crisis'; 'How unstable is Italy?' and 'Sad lessons from Italy'.[1] The same paper recently pointed to another image of Italian government, its complexity: 'Italian governmental politics are a bizarre and Byzantine game whose details are followed only by the immediate players, while the rest of the world finds it difficult even to pretend to take an interest'.[2] Italian journalists tend to report on the manoeuvrings of politicians in amazing detail, even using the over-subtle phraseology which accompanies their coalition behaviour. The impression is strongly conveyed that competent policy-making is distinctly secondary to office-holding.

This is also the conclusion usually drawn by academic observers of the Italian scene. Giuseppe Di Palma has written: '. . . politics thus becomes a pure game of power, mostly concerned with *sottogoverno*, log-rolling, minute compromises, reciprocal non-interference. It is more difficult and not necessary to govern; it is easier and sufficient to sit in government'.[3] The tendency of academic work, certainly through the 1970s and beyond, has also been to emphasise that Italy is 'without government' (Allum), that it suffers from a 'non-working' multi-party system because of the inability of political élites to bridge fragmentation (Lijphart), and that it remains the least stable of West European governments. It is now fashionable in political, academic and journalistic circles to speak of 'the Italian crisis', but what is significant is that this is seen as being social, economic and political as well as institutional.[4]

The above summary of views about Italy's governmental predicament provokes many questions. But any discussion of Italy's governmental problem has to look well beyond the institutional dimension.
This could, of course, be said of any country, but it is particularly true
of Italy in the 1970s and 1980s. Italian coalitions cannot be fully
understood if attention is confined to the institutions. In Italy, serious
consideration must also be given to party activity outside the parliamentary arena, the importance of historical conditioning (political
culture and values, prior coalitional experiences, enduring mistrust
towards the Communist Party), the need for social consensus, public
attitudes towards coalitional behaviour and the influence of foreign
governments.

Moreover, how does one go about evaluating governmental effectiveness, and by what criteria? Conventionally, the criteria used
measure policy performance against policy requirements and expectations, and here Italy must clearly be regarded as highly deficient.
Yet there remains an element of one-dimensionality about repeated
accusations of Italy's 'ungovernability', for 'governmental ineffectiveness' is a term open to different interpretations. Historical parallels
have been drawn between the Italian political system and that of the
Weimar Republic – deep economic crisis, chronic cabinet instability,
and coalitional politics of a seemingly destructive kind – but the
essential difference so far as Italy is concerned is the existence of a
steady and ubiquitous party system (on the political parties see Table
9.1), where the main parties have performed a centripetal function and
especially so during the crisis of the 1970s and 1980s, when the
Communist Party (PCI) adopted a protective attitude towards the
political system. The problem of Italy's 'governability' may well
revolve around 'stagnation' as much as 'instability', for if there is going
to be 'movement' in Italian politics it is almost certain to be transmitted
through the channels of the party system.

This leads us to the question of coalitions, since if parties 'move' it is
in response either to each other or to social and/or economic change, or
more probably both. Italy is commonly and justifiably described as a
partitocrazia ('party-ocracy' or 'party state'), where the parties individually and together permeate public life and provide such will and
effectiveness as exist. Given that Italy's state institutions are weak, the
parties' role must be seen as all the more crucial, and hence coalition
politics is indeed central to how the country is governed. Clearly,
therefore, coalitional behaviour provides the clue both to the 'complexity' of Italian government which so puzzles outside observers and
also its 'ineffectiveness', but how exactly does the Italian form of
coalitional behaviour operate, what motivates and determines it and
what are its consequences?

Table 9.1   Political parties in Italy (parliamentary seats – Chamber of Deputies
– and % of vote)

	Christian Democratic Party (DC)	Communist Party (PCI)	Socialist Party (PSI)	Social Democratic Party (PDSI)	Republican Party (PRI)	Liberal Party (PLI)
ELECTION (Chamber of Deputies) (Total Seats)						
1948	305	183	(with PSI)	33	9	19
(574)	(48.5)	(31.0)		(7.1)	(2.5)	(3.8)
1953	263	143	75	19	5	13
(590)	(40.1)	(22.6)	(12.8)	(4.5)	(1.6)	(3.0)
1958	273	140	84	22	6	17
(596)	(42.4)	(22.7)	(14.2)	(4.5)	(1.4)	(3.5)
1963	250	166	87	33	6	39
(630)	(38.3)	(25.3)	(13.8)	(6.1)	(1.4)	(7.0)
1968	266	177	91 (with PSDI)		9	31
(630)	(39.1)	(26.9)	(14.5)		(2.0)	(5.8)
1972	267	179	61	29	15	20
(630)	(38.8)	(27.2)	(9.6)	(5.1)	(2.9)	(3.9)
1976	263	227	57	15	14	5
(630)	(38.7)	(34.4)	(9.6)	(3.4)	(3.1)	(1.3)
1979	262	201	62	20	16	9
(629)	(38.3)	(30.4)	(9.8)	(3.8)	(3.0)	(1.9)
1983	225	198	73	23	29	16
(630)	(32.9)	(29.9)	(11.4)	(4.1)	(5.1)	(2.9)

The above list includes only those parties that have acted as coalition partners; other parties include the neo-Fascist MSI and the Radical Party).

Despite the 'centrality' of coalitional behaviour to Italy's politics, there has been surprisingly little real investigation of the subject. Covered intensively in the press, which for its own reasons of short-term reporting emphasises the tactical side of élite behaviour, the problem of Italian coalition politics has lacked in-depth analysis which takes a longer perspective. That is precisely why explanations of this subject have been coloured by vague impressions rather than characterised by perception.

The scant academic literature on Italian coalitions has usually been segmental, concentrating on this feature or that. In an essay noting the very absence of systematic work on the subject, Pasquino focused on the role of elections in influencing government formations in Italy's multi-party system, with special reference to the 1976 election, which saw a sharp rise in Communist support.[5] He noted that in multi-party systems electorates are rarely asked to pronounce clearly on coalition formulas and came to the conclusion that in Italy's case the emphasis has been placed on forming a large consensus around governments rather than on promoting innovative leadership.

The absence of alternation in Italian government – essentially because of the PCI's limited legitimacy – has tended to stimulate other particular approaches. The 'consociational' theorists have obviously been drawn to the Italian case with the rapprochement between Christian Democrats (DC) and Communists in the 1970s as an interesting example of possible accommodation among élites in a fragmented society. Pappalardo has developed these ideas but argued sceptically that particular attention should be given to leader-follower relationships and élite control in determining the extent and stability of consensus-building.[6] Similarly, Putnam has applied spatial models of party competition, and through extensive survey work among regional politicians has reached the conclusion that the 1970s witnessed depolarisation between party élites but simultaneously a widening of the gap separating élites from their constituents – thus offering a negative proof of Pappalardo's hypothesis.[7] Di Palma had already begun in his book on the Italian Parliament[8] to look at trends of legislative concurrence between government and opposition, identifying a certain conflict between accommodational practices and party ideology and identity. There is little other empirical work, save for Zuckerman's examination of the key influence of the DC's organised factions in controlling cabinet positions and favouring different inter-party alliances in the 1960s and early 1970s.[9] Studies of a more all-embracing and yet systematic kind have not so far been attempted. Marradi's chapter on government coalitions in Italy is historical and descriptive, but it neglects the important period of the 1970s, dwells on the institutional and not enough on the party-political dimension, and fails to offer any new interpretative insights.[10]

Conventional theories about coalitional behaviour unfortunately do not help much in working out a comprehensive approach. Theories based on the size of coalitions do not really apply, since 'unnecessary' actors have been the rule rather than the exception. Theories based on policy range do have some relevance as a test of coalitional cohesion, but once again oversized coalitions in Italy (and the multiplicity of motives on the part of different actors) give these theories a limited applicability.[11] There is another basic problem in trying to obtain a theoretical angle to this subject: Italian coalition politics, as we shall see, features a strong informal element, whereas coalition theories so far have invariably confined themselves to looking at formal coalitions. Beyond this problem, the party dimension of coalitional behaviour (seen as crucial in the Italian case) has rarely been brought into play by coalition theories, which more often than not have been too one-dimensional in their approach. Only Sven Groennings[12] provides something of a multi-dimensional framework, including a useful check-list of party-political and other variables as a guide to further research, and these are indeed applicable to Italy.

What follows is the outline of an approach to the study of Italian coalitions.[13] Coalition theories presented so far have a limited use, not only because they are insufficiently comprehensive, but also because they are predicated too much on the risky assumption that prospective or actual coalition actors can or wish to calculate rationally. The value of an empirical study is not so much due to the fact that Italian coalition politics has its several unique characteristics, but is rather to emphasise and illustrate that coalitional behaviour is intrinsically a complicated and sometimes 'messy' business in Italy, and no doubt elsewhere. A multiplicity of factors – some visible, others covert – affect coalitional behaviour. What this chapter seeks to do is to try and identify the motivations, procedures and consequences of coalitional behaviour in Italy. In doing so, it is worth noting that one of the reasons for the inscrutable impression created by the subject is the lack of hard evidence from practitioners to complement the one-sided coverage in the press. Party élites in Italy have been noticeably reticent about publishing their version of activity at the top (perhaps understandably so because of the corrupt under-belly of the Italian political world), although the important period of 'National Solidarity' with Communist involvement in government decisions (1976–9) has produced various accounts by leading politicians.[14]

The institutional framework: the importance of being sceptical
Italian political institutions are weak. More specifically, they are characterised by a dispersal of executive power, a heterogeneous and sluggish administrative system and generally a substantial gap between formal structures and 'real' government.[15] The formal structures in Republican Italy's parliamentary democracy, as provided for in the Constitution of 1948, consist of a head of state (President), the executive in the Council of Ministers (cabinet) under the direction of the President of the Council of Ministers (Prime Minister), and the legislature in the form of two houses, the Chamber of Deputies and the Senate, elected for five years by proportional representation.

In looking at the legislature, Di Palma has commented that Italy's political system lacks 'institutional persuasion';[16] that is, it does not possess a certain momentum of its own which can regulate the flows and pressures of political life. It is not built strongly enough to promote effectiveness in decision-making, nor is it readily responsive to new demands. The more critical situation facing Italy in the 1970s has highlighted these institutional weaknesses more vividly than ever before, so that the question of institutional reform focusing on improving the mechanisms for leadership (for example, strengthening the

Prime Minister's powers, considering changes in the PR method of the electoral system, discussing the possibility of introducing some form of presidential government) came to the forefront of Italian political argument by the late 1970s.[17] Despite some regional devolution in the 1970s (a late implementation of one provision in the 1948 Constitution), Italy has by and large a centralised system so that a considerable onus is placed on decision-makers in Rome. As many Italian commentators have said, their country is a 'difficult democracy'.

This institutional weakness is bound to condition profoundly the nature of Italian coalition politics. For example, coalition studies, whether theoretical or empirical, have usually concentrated on the institution of the cabinet, its composition and its performance being the main criteria for estimating the dividends acquired by individual coalition partners. In Italy, this yardstick certainly has some relevance but it is one among several, even though cabinet participation, as elsewhere, enjoys a visibility at least in the eyes of the media, not to mention foreign opinion.

Making the distinction between formal structures and 'real' government, the cabinet would obviously be counted among the former, but how much does it also feature within the latter? As an institution, the Italian cabinet is unwieldy (it includes all ministers and usually comprises around 27 members), it is the victim of regular crises leading to its political collapse (on average at least once a year), it is procedurally inefficient lacking adequate co-ordination, there is an absence of collegiality or collective responsibility (ministers' first and foremost loyalty is to their individual parties) and it is not necessarily the focal point of decision-making.[18] This is not to say that the cabinet has never had its periods of activism – one may cite the examples of De Gasperi's premiership in the later 1940s and the early centre-Left alliance when the Socialists (PSI) first joined the DC in government in the 1960s – but its importance as a policy-making body has fluctuated because this has depended on political factors and not on any innate institutional vitality. Any such political momentum must come from the parties involved in government; namely, through the medium of coalition politics.

But before turning to this issue it is first of all necessary to establish how far the institutions constrain coalition behaviour or, alternatively, provide opportunities for it in terms of governing the country. The problem here is that it is difficult to locate neatly the executive process, compared with more 'efficient' European political systems like those in France and West Germany. Executive power is dispersed, increasingly so in recent years, with such agencies as the president of the Bank of Italy, the heads of the public corporations and, not least, certain key ministries acting very autonomously as both policy-making centres and channels for extensive patronage.

So far as the more visible institutions are concerned, coalition politics has played an important, though at times ambiguous, role. The cabinet is seen as the focal point of institutional instability but, as several studies of Italian government have pointed out, there has been considerable stability of ministerial personnel either holding the same post continuously or being re-shuffled. They have above all owed their career stability to their long-serving leadership of a small coalition partner (for example, Ugo La Malfa of the Republican Party [PRI]), or, in the case of DC ministers, to their enduring control of individual factions (*correnti*). It might also be pointed out that, while cabinets have fallen, alliance formations have quite often persisted; there were, for example, six centre-Left governments during the period 1963–72, interrupted only by two brief DC minority administrations. Taking this same period, according to Zuckerman, cabinet dissolutions and re-formations were often caused by competition among factions, either within or between parties, for a better distribution of posts.[19] Patronage and prestige and not just access to policymaking (so far as cabinet membership allows this) have motivated this behaviour.

A similar point may be made about the role of Prime Minister. Institutionally, this position is relatively weak in that it has provided mediative rather than innovative leadership,[20] not least because of the demands arising from having to settle conflicts between partners in Italy's multi-party coalitions as well as between factions, especially in the DC. But there have been some exceptional cases of stronger leadership: De Gasperi, Fanfani and Moro. More often than not, heads of government (always from the DC, except for Spadolini, 1981–2) have owed their appointment to their positions as faction chiefs rather than authoritative leaders of their party, so that their survival in office has depended on their continuing alliance with other DC *correnti* but also, significantly, on other coalition parties.[21]

These points throw some interesting light on prime-ministerial incumbency. The continuous occupation of this position by the DC since 1945 (only broken for a year-and-a-half in 1981–2) would confirm the practice in most countries of this post's going to the leader of the largest coalition partner. Such conventions may, however, be open to change and this certainly seems possible in Italy. Even before the appointment of Spadolini (Republican) in 1981, there were in 1979 the first two attempts since 1945 to break with the precedent when President Pertini invited La Malfa (also of the PRI) in February/March and later Craxi (PSI leader) in July of that year to form a government. As it was, both were unsuccessful, primarily because of the DC's refusal to coalesce and hence lose the top position in government. They also failed because in 1979 the PCI was demanding formal participation in the cabinet; whereas in 1981, when Spadolini attempted it, this unrealisable demand was no longer PCI policy and the DC, on the defensive because of the unprecedented P2 scandal,[22] felt obliged to concede the premiership. The DC regarded this at the time as a temporary aberration for otherwise, as DC circles explained, 'our people would start thinking that having 38 per cent of the vote would not count for anything'.[23] The return of the DC to the Palazzo Chigi (seat of the Prime Minister's office) in the ebullient form of Fanfani at the end of 1982 may not necessarily presage a new and long string of DC premiers, for the Spadolini 'experiment' may indeed be used as a precedent. It is the declared ambition of Craxi as part of the PSI's more aggressive strategy as a third force to claim the Palazzo Chigi for himself, depending both on his party's making electoral gains and whether the DC wishes to exclude the PCI from national office at any cost (the PCI, on the other hand, has not demanded the premiership as a price for its co-operation). Finally, it should be pointed out that the Prime Minister's role has increased in authority over the past decade owing to administrative upgrading of this office and greater recognition of the need for 'an institutional centre to give the system a degree of coherence'.[24] The post has accordingly become much more attractive to party competitors; and it is no surprise that some of the more far-reaching proposals for strengthening the Prime Minister's powers have issued from the Socialists.

There is one further party-political aspect of the institution of the cabinet worth noting. This is that the party actors with the greatest individual weight and influence, the parties' general secretaries, are invariably not members of the cabinet. The reason is that their control of party affairs and promotion of party interests would be more difficult if constrained by ministerial responsibility. Yet they are the most powerful architects of party and ultimately government strategy, as distinct from everyday ministerial decisions over policy matters. The supreme example in recent times must be Aldo Moro who, although no longer party secretary (officially he was president of the DC, working in harmony with Zaccagnini as party secretary), guided the DC through the difficult and tortuous relationship of 'convergence' with the PCI from the mid-1970s. Andreotti, Prime Minister at the time, recorded this revealing comment in his diary on 6 March 1978 during the formation of the historic government which brought the PCI 'into the majority', though not into the cabinet, for the first time since 1947:[25]

I extended the invitation once more to Moro that he should preside over the government, disposed as I was to stay outside or within it as he saw fit. He rejects this firmly. He thinks he can help from outside perhaps in an irreplaceable way, given that in the DC's parliamentary group he has woven a relationship with persons that places a premium on manoeuvres and factions. Also with the other parties he thinks he can be useful without a direct personal responsibility.

Recognition of the importance of party secretaries in the policy process had come from involving them in various plans to buttress governmental leadership. The previous year (1977) Moro had floated the idea of a 'directory' – it was understood this would include the party secretaries concerned, as well as chairmen of parliamentary groups – to overcome a stage of malaise affecting the 'National Solidarity' government. This proposal, aimed at stabilising control over government business, was soon deflated by different party interests failing to combine, coupled with suspicion within the DC from those factions unenthusiastic about any closer arrangement with the Communists. The idea was not in fact new. It had, for instance, been proposed in 1972 by La Malfa as a solution for more disciplined support of the government by the parliamentary majority; and in the same year Fanfani came up with this same proposal during his forlorn attempt to form a government, but his reputed authoritarian sympathies alienated its possible supporters both within the DC and in the other parties. Cossiga (Prime Minister, 1979–80) did succeed for the first time in setting up such a 'directory' of the secretaries of the three parties in his government (DC, PSI, PRI) meeting with himself to 'establish direction and take the most relevant decisions in the working of the government'.[26] These meetings were not formalised and in any case lapsed once Cossiga fell. As one political observer commented at the time: 'It is the first time that an organism of this kind has been constituted, even though in an informal manner . . . previously meetings of party secretaries, all brought together round the same table, were called "summits" and were considered exceptional events'.[27]

The lesson of these various examples confirmed the clear preference of party secretaries for maintaining their power positions outside the cabinet as external string-pullers. Proof of this came with the fall of Spadolini in 1982. As non-DC Prime Minister and head of a small party (the PRI had only 3 per cent of the vote) he had based his position on a close alliance with President Pertini and on his own personal popularity, unusual for an Italian leader, as well as his recognised arbitrative skills and his perceived honesty. But this political base was insecure, for Spadolini's popularity began to sink once his brave attempt at controlling the economy – with persistent balance-of-payments problems, inflation already well into double figures, still rising, and a chronic public sector deficit – came unstuck. Spadolini's last months in office were marked by vicious quarrelling among his coalition partners, dubbed as 'Spadolini's Babylon', which became public in a prolonged row between two ministers from different parties – Andreatta (DC) at the Treasury and Formica (PSI) at Finance – over financial measures. Behind this quarrel lay considerations of party tactics and strategy, for the DC wanted to regain the premiership and the PSI aimed at early elections, so that once the secretaries of these two major parties in the coalition together closed in on Spadolini the red carpet of national office was swiftly pulled from under him.

This recent example of Spadolini and the general role of party secretaries illustrated a number of interesting features of Italian government, whereby the key factor was the ability or will of the parties to co-operate or not. In the final crisis of his government Spadolini had sought to reassert his authority by demanding the resignations of the two quarrelling ministers, although constitutionally he only had the right to nominate them, but the parties were not prepared to allow him this; while this very quarrel highlighted the inefficient division of ministerial control over the economy (there were also Ministers for the Budget and Industry as well as the Treasury and Finance). Concerning the latter, it is relevant to note that these four ministries – whose firm co-operation is essential in dealing with Italy's economic crisis – are usually shared out between different parties, not to mention different DC factions, and are therefore very vulnerable to coalition tensions. On policy matters, the Spadolini example illustrated the recurrent problems facing effective decision-making; Spadolini himself once described the role of Prime Minister as 'a permanent obstacle race'. In fact, his government had performed with some success in its policy with regard to terrorism, in taking foreign policy decisions (for example, over the Middle East) and in promoting some investigation into what was called 'the moral question' of P2; but, when it came to the crucial problem of the economy and Spadolini's personal determination to impose necessary and harsh measures, his government collapsed. The role of party secretaries provided a crucial lesson on the character and functioning of Italian institutions: there was a strong informal side to governmental activity, for much could influence this from outside the executive structures and, when institutional innovation did occur or was attempted (as in bringing the party secretaries more directly into the decision-making process), this was improvised and *ad hoc*.

This general point may be further examined by looking at the process of government formation and, in particular, at the role of the Italian President. The head of state has normally played an intermediary rather than merely advisory role – the practice of coalition politics tends to require that – and at first sight it would seem that the instability of cabinets (i.e. the regular need for government formations) would enhance the role of the President politically. In a sense, this is what has happened for it has been rightly said that the President's power is in inverse proportion to that of the cabinet.[28] The Constitution does not specify any particular political role, but offers him opportunities of being more than an observer in the political game. He can, for example, veto legislation and dissolve Parliament. In fact, he possesses much discretionary power, or rather the logjams that often occur in coalition politics, together with the frequent absence of a clear leader of the DC, give that power more salience and require him to be an active midwife in the process of government formation. One should add that Italian presidents have themselves acquired much experience from long political careers and used that experience to considerable effect: Saragat (1964–71), former leader of the Social Democratic party (PSDI) and Foreign Minister, was instrumental in helping to keep the centre-Left coalition partners in agreement; Leone (1971–8), a former DC Prime Minister and hardened in the ways of his party's factional politics, similarly proved a useful conciliator in governmental crises. But this role as active intermediary, according the President a political role of some significance, may fluctuate depending on the state of coalition behaviour. As one constitutional lawyer has written: 'His role has appeared stronger for a very simple reason: when government coalitions are easily achieved, the role of the president is reduced; when, on the other hand, it is difficult to resolve a crisis, the powers of intervention of the head of state become active'.[29]

It is ultimately impossible to avoid the party dimension when looking at the possibilities of presidential power as a solution to Italy's governmental ineffectiveness. The presidential incumbent is himself a creation of coalition politics, being elected by both houses of Parliament meeting in plenary session. Intra- and inter-party manoeuvres lead to an extensive number of ballots (21 in 1964, 23 in 1971, and 16 in 1978). The President's seven-year term of office does, of course, permit him, once elected, a certain independence, but in so far as he seeks to exercise political muscle he eventually runs up against the party factor. The recent case of Pertini (elected in 1978) illustrates this problem. Pertini has gained a reputation for a more dynamic interpretation of his role compared with any of his predecessors, as witnessed by his constructive impatience in dealing with coalition partners in dispute, his forthright public manner (as in severely reprimanding government incompetence over the earthquake disaster of 1980) and generally for his distaste for 'corrupt' political élites. His popularity – he is a former Resistance hero – is certainly crucial to understanding his personal determination to try and check executive instability, notably in refusing to grant early elections on several occasions. His role came particularly to the fore during Spadolini's term of office, when both worked in tandem and Pertini's support allowed the Prime Minister to overcome several threats to his position. Pertini's influence has also been due to the fact that coalition formation and maintenance became more difficult during the course of the 1970s, but a concern among the parties that this trend might lead to 'creeping presidentialism' ignores the fact that its base is a shifting one and possibly ephemeral. In fact, the appointment of Fanfani as Prime Minister in December 1982 against Pertini's own wishes was explained by the DC's presenting a united front with only the one nominee, who also had the backing of the Socialists.

Italian government is clearly characterised by powerful informal procedures alongside and sometimes conflicting with the formal ones. The basic reason for this is the weakness of the country's political institutions, having limited constitutional powers and not regularly operating as effective policy-making organs, combined with the predominance of the party dimension. 'Real' government, therefore, revolves around the political parties acting individually or, more often, together whether through informal procedures or formal structures, aside from certain public agencies which are really independent of the parties (for example, the Bank of Italy and the security forces). Any attempt to break with or challenge this dominance of coalition politics is likely to be at best temporary. As already seen, the Prime Minister's limited constitutional position does not allow him to act (literally) 'above party' – or, for that matter, 'above faction' – as, for instance, has been the case with the West German Chancellor. De Gasperi (Prime Minister, 1945–53) must be regarded as the major exception because of unrepeatable historical circumstances (notably identification with the founding of the post-war Republic at the time of the Cold War), and also because it was only later in his premiership that the DC's factions began to develop, and hence weaken its internal solidarity. In short, the formal institutional structure hardly constrains the operation of coalition politics; rather, it is the very weakness of the structure which places it at the mercy of the latter.

The party dimension

Seeing that political parties and their inter-relationships are so crucial to the way in which Italian government operates, it is necessary to turn to the main patterns of coalitional behaviour in Italy and to identify and illustrate exactly how political parties have conducted their coalition relationships. Sven Groennings drew attention in his *The Study of Coalitional Behavior*[30] to the need for a more comprehensive approach in assessing party-political variables, including those which are located or stretch outside the institutional framework, such as ideology, social base, structure and prior party relationships. In Italy there are five broad patterns which will be discussed.

Patterns in coalition formulas

Historically, it is possible to identify patterns in the application of different coalition formulas (see the list of governments in Table 9.3 below). Following the end of the War, the DC led a series of cross-party

Table 9.2   Coalition formations in Italy, 1945–83

1945–47	Cross-party governments, including DC, PCI and PSI
1947–57	Centre-right governments, including DC, PSDI, PLI and PRI
1957–63	Mainly DC minority governments
1963–72	Centre-left governments, including DC, PSI, PRI, and PSDI
1972–73	Centre-right government
1973–74	Centre-left governments
1974–76	Minority governments led by DC
1976–79	'National Solidarity' governments under the DC, with wide party support including the PCI
1979–80	Centre-right government
1980–83	Centre-left governments

cabinets, including the PCI, from 1945 to 1947; the expulsion of the PCI at the height of the Cold War led to a period of centre-Right coalitions (usually called 'Centrism') from 1947 to the mid-1950s, under DC dominance with the participation of such other parties as the Republican (PRI), the right-wing Liberals (PLI) and the Social Democrats (PSDI), who had broken away from the Socialists remaining in opposition with the PCI; a transition period then occurred leading eventually to the centre-Left coalitions from 1963 to 1972, with the inclusion of the PSI and the exclusion of the Liberals; while the decade since 1972 has been characterised by unstable and rapid experimentation with different formulas, including a brief centre-Right Government under Andreotti, a transient return of the centre-Left, minority government, the period of 'National Solidarity' under Andreotti (1976–9) with the informal involvement of the PCI, and since 1980 another period of (unsteady) centre-Left government.

Undoubtedly, the last stage of alliance instability has reflected the 'Italian crisis' transmitted through the behaviour of the parties. In fact, the word 'emergency' entered Italian political vocabulary in 1973, linked to the outbreak of the energy crisis which profoundly affected the country's economy.[31] The term 'emergency' also came to refer to the possible inclusion of the PCI in government. As will be noticed in the list, there have been interludes of DC minority administrations for these have characterised transition periods (see Table 9.3.).

Two general points may be drawn from looking at these historical patterns. Coalitions are very much the rule in Italian politics, not least because of the country's multi-party system, reinforced by proportional representation as the voting method, for no party – except for the DC in 1948 – has acquired an absolute majority, and then in 1948 the DC still chose to form a coalition with three other smaller parties. It is therefore no surprise that alliance thinking features prominently in political debate and manoeuvres in Italy. A typical speech by a politician almost certainly gives generous attention to relationships with other 'political forces', whether this be in the form of specific proposals or – more commonly – couched in the subtle and vague statements preferred by Italian political elites. Furthermore, Italian coalitions have usually been heterogeneous, not merely because they are numerically multi-party, but also because the parties tend to reflect social fragmentation. Accordingly, while prior alliance relationships may affect individual party preferences (habitual affinity makes coalition formations, though not necessarily coalition maintenance, that much easier), there is an instability or fluidity about actual coalitional behaviour.

The absence of alternation

One very salient aspect of Italian coalition formation has been the absence of alternation; namely, the replacement of the one major party in power by the other. This has derived from the lack of legitimacy of the PCI as a prospective governing party. Until the 1970s, what is now fashionably known as 'the Communist question' (i.e. whether the PCI enters government or not) was not seriously considered. A PCI role in government was regarded as an absolute impossibility in the sense that the leadership of the DC, as the dominant governing party, based its position on excluding the PCI as its nearest rival from power; while, at the mass level, anti-Communist arguments carried much weight (outside Communist circles) and the DC was thereby able to gain electoral success from this appeal. It was not in any case the PCI's strategy to demand governmental participation as such. In the 1970s this situation changed to the extent that a PCI role in government entered the alliance thinking of the other political parties; the PCI has, to use one of the delicate phrases of Italian coalition politics, entered 'the area of government'. There are several reasons for this: the collapse of alternative coalition possibilities (notably the 'organic' centre-Left) and the emergence of a more fluid coalitional situation; the PCI's strategy of the 'historic compromise', demanding more explicitly than before a role in government; and, behind this, the decline of anti-Communist attitudes at the mass level (a PCI role in government has become more 'culturally' acceptable) together with the argument that the 'Italian crisis' demands PCI co-operation for reasons of system stability. Andreotti, Prime Minister during the crucial period of 'National Solidarity', wrote in his diary then:[32]

The DC is not by itself in a position to support a government for the extreme seriousness of problems demands the greatest concentration of energies precisely because it is a matter of extraordinary difficulties.

Full integration of the PCI in government has, however, not so far

Table 9.3   Composition of Italian cabinets, 1945–84

Period of office (Number of months)	Prime Minister	Parties in the cabinet
1. 6–11/45 (5)	Parri	Action Party, DC, PCI, PLI, PSI, PDL (Democratic Labour)
2. 12/45–7/46 (6)	De Gasperi	DC, PCI, PSI, Action Party, PDL, PLI
3. 7/46–2/47 (6)	De Gasperi	DC, PCI, PSI, PLI, PRI
4. 2–4/47 (3)	De Gasperi	DC, PCI, PSI
5. 5/47–5/48 (11)	De Gasperi	DC, PSDI, PLI, PRI
6. 5/48–1/50 (20)	De Gasperi	DC, PSDI, PRI, PLI
7. 1/50–7/51 (17)	De Gasperi	DC, PSDI, PRI
8. 7/51–6/53 (23)	De Gasperi	DC, PRI
9. 7/53 ($\frac{1}{2}$)	De Gasperi	DC (external support of PRI)
10. 8/53–1/54 (5)	Pella	DC (external support of PRI, PLI and Monarchists)
11. 1/54 ($\frac{1}{2}$)	Fanfani	DC
12. 2/54–6/55 (16)	Scelba	DC, PSDI, PLI (external support of PRI)
13. 7/55–5/57 (22)	Segni	DC, PSDI, PLI (external support of PRI)
14. 5/57–6/58 (13)	Zoli	DC (external support of Monarchists and MSI)
15. 7/58–1/59 (7)	Fanfani	DC, PSDI (external support of PRI)
16. 2/59–2/60 (12)	Segni	DC
17. 3–7/60 (4)	Tambroni	DC
18. 7/60–2/62 (18)	Fanfani	DC (external support from PSDI, PRI, PLI)
19. 2/62–6/63 (16)	Fanfani	DC, PSDI, PRI (external support of PSI)
20. 6–11/63 (16)	Leone	DC
21. 12/63–6/64 (7)	Moro	DC, PSI, PSDI, PRI
22. 7/64–1/66 (18)	Moro	DC, PSI, PSDI, PRI
23. 2/66–6/68 (27)	Moro	DC, PSI, PSDI, PRI
24. 6–11/68 (5)	Leone	DC
25. 12/68–7/69 (6)	Rumor	DC, PSI, PRI
26. 8/69–2/70 (6)	Rumor	DC (external support from PSI and PSDI)
27. 3–7/70 (3)	Rumor	DC, PSI, PSDI, PRI
28. 8/70–1/72 (17)	Colombo	DC, PSI, PSDI, PRI
29. 2–6/72 (4)	Andreotti	DC (external support from PRI, PSDI and PLI)

Period of office (Number of months)	Prime Minister	Parties in the cabinet
30. 6/72–6/73 (12)	Andreotti	DC, PSDI, PLI (external support from PRI)
31. 7/73–3/74 (8)	Rumor	DC, PSI, PSDI, PRI
32. 3–10/74 (7)	Rumor	DC, PSI, PSDI
33. 11/74–2/76 (15)	Moro	DC, PRI (external support from PSI and PSDI)
34. 2–7/76 (5)	Moro	DC (external support from PSDI)
35. 8/76–3/78 (19)	Andreotti	DC (abstention from PCI, PSI, PSDI, PRI, PLI)
36. 3/78–3/79 (12)	Andreotti	DC (external support from PCI, PSI, PSDI, PRI)
37. 3–8/79 (4)	Andreotti	DC, PSDI, PRI
38. 8/79–4/80 (8)	Cossiga	DC, PSDI, PLI (abstention of PSI and PRI)
39. 4–10/80 (6)	Cossiga	DC, PSI, PRI
40. 10/80–6/81 (8)	Forlani	DC, PSI, PSDI, PRI
41. 6/81–8/82 (13)	Spadolini	PRI, DC, PSI, PSDI, PLI
42. 8–11/82 (3)	Spadolini	PRI, DC, PSI, PSDI, PLI
43. 12/82–	Fanfani	DC, PSI, PSDI, PLI

(The party of the Prime Minister is given first among the list of Cabinet participants).

taken place, for what occurred during the 1970s was its partial and temporary involvement in government – during 1976–9 the PCI gradually joined a legislative but not an executive coalition. This fell in line with a characteristic of coalitional change in Italy up to that time. A distinction is made in Italian political vocabulary between *alternanza* (partial change of coalition partners though limited by the perpetuation of the DC in power) and *alternativa* (total change in dominant coalition partner, or what in 'Anglo-Saxon' vocabulary is known as 'alternation'). In terms of alliance relationships, the PCI's 'historic compromise' was itself proposing the former with its rejection of the '51 per cent formula' (a possible majority of the Left) and desire for an alliance with the DC as well as other parties. Following the collapse of the 'National Solidarity' alliance the PCI only then came round to considering the second proposition of an *alternativa*, though its implementation naturally depends on other parties of the Left, most of all the PSI. Meanwhile, continuing depolarisation among party élites – surveys on the DC indicate a greater readiness to consider a firm alliance with the PCI, after the experience of 'National Solidarity'[33] – and decline of anti-Communist attitudes in general could lead in the future to *alternanza* involving direct participation of the PCI in government, with the worsening of the 'Italian crisis' as the probable key determinant. The main general point from looking at this second pattern of Italian coalitional behaviour is the importance of the pro-/anti-system positions of individual parties. Pro-system parties are conventionally known as belonging to the 'constitutional arc', and the PCI is now generally accepted as belonging to this. Only the neo-Fascist MSI and the new parties of the extreme Left (for example PdUP, DP) are seen as remaining outside it. Putting it crudely, the PCI has joined the 'power game' although so far this has not led to its participation in the formal executive structures.

The variety and informality of alliance relationships

Coalitional or alliance behaviour in Italy is distinguished by much variety in the form of alliance relationships, including a strong informal element. This pattern allows for a flexibility in the application of alliances (parties may co-operate loosely when ideological considerations prevent them from entering a formal coalition), makes for ambiguity in the meaning of alliances (parties are more free to interpret them differently for their own ends), and tends more than anything else to sow confusion among outside observers of the Italian political scene.

It is no joke to say that intending students of Italian coalitions have to settle down and learn a specialised and subtle vocabulary, that adopted by politicians and their friends – or enemies – in the media. For example, the process of government formation following a cabinet collapse is known as 'being in crisis' (*crisi di governo*), when, if there are serious problems awaiting attention, the country is said to 'be in a delicate phase'. During this time prime-ministerial nominees accept their charge 'with reservations' (official language), which are 'dropped' if they succeed. It is quite common for Prime Ministers to return to office (this is called *autosuccessione*), though sometimes at the head of a different coalition (a 're-mixing of the cards'). It is necessary to re-member, if one is trying to assess cabinet instability, that some governments are deliberately short-term either because they are formed to administer the country as 'electoral governments' during a campaign for Parliament, to tide over the dead summer season (*governi balneari*, 'seaside' or 'sunbathing governments') or, more urgently, when they are formed in a transition period before a new coalition, in which case they are known as 'governments for [literally] current affairs'. (Anglo-Saxon terminology prefers for all of these the one term, 'caretaker government'). During its rapprochement in the 1970s with the PCI, the DC was seen as 'throwing bridges towards the PCI', following 'a strategy of attention' towards it or, in the paradoxical but pregnant phrase of Aldo Moro, the two parties were following 'converging parallels'. As to the possibility of the PCI's entering government, then a formal coalition would have entailed an 'emergency' or 'national unity government', as distinct from a half-way formula of 'national solidarity' where the PCI supported the cabinet from outside in a 'legislative majority'; although another solution was to include as ministers experts or 'technicians' sympathetic to the PCI but not from its leadership. This whole process was described at the time of 'National Solidarity' as a 'crawling historic compromise' (mainly a journalistic term), but since the withdrawal of PCI support in 1979 there has been a series of 'cooling-off governments' (*governi di raffreddamento*) when the main parties have embarked on a *chiusura* or 'closing-up' towards each other (a much used term in Italian politics with ideological undertones).

Such terminological diversity in Italian coalition politics illustrates a basic paradox. Party élites on the one hand engage in ideological rhetoric and, on the other, accept a high degree of cross-party working arrangements in parliamentary life. Di Palma in his study of the Parliament identified tension between the practical acceptance of compromise out of necessity and abstract reservations about this, for deputies are 'strongly partisan in their relation to their parties and followers'.[34] His work was conducted in the early 1970s, since when the rapprochement between the DC and PCI in particular went through stages beyond the 'legislative concurrence' which he had observed. Until the 1970s the informal element in Italian coalitional behaviour had consisted chiefly of the fact that 'legislative coalitions' were not necessarily co-terminous with 'executive coalitions', i.e. parties would give external or 'parliamentary' support to minority cabinets. The greater articulation of alliance vocabulary is, one might say, indicative of the more fluid and complex state of coalition politics that emerged in the 1970s, not least because the PCI came to be seen as a participant in this activity, with the added ideological problems this entailed. For instance, the 'National Solidarity' governments of 1976–9 under Andreotti progressed from a state of *non-sfiducia*, or 'no non-confidence' in 1976–7 (the PCI and other parties agreed to abstain from voting in Parliament), through the 'programmatic agreement' of 1977–8 based on a joint policy document between the DC minority government and the PCI, PSI, PSDI, PRI and PLI to the 1978–9 situation, when the DC accepted the PCI as part of the formal parliamentary majority (*nella maggioranza*) and there was a re-negotiated government programme.

In assessing the variety and informality of Italian coalitional behaviour, there is an important distinction to be made between its arithmetical and political dimensions. What may be arithmetically possible is not necessarily politically feasible; equally, what may be politically desirable – on the part of intending coalition partners – may not be arithmetically possible. What is, of course, interesting in political practice is the actual relationship or interaction between the two dimensions, for the distinction is rarely a clear-cut one. For instance, election results create arithmetical possibilities in the game of coalition possibilities, but they may also be said to pronounce on the credibility of coalitional alternatives, depending on the extent to which party leaders have made some prior commitments, and these are 'debated' in the election campaign. In other words, the political can influence the arithmetical, or be assumed to have done so; just as the arithmetical might also create its own political pressures, forcing reluctant politicians into alliances or allowing them to rationalise their new coalition positions. This distinction between the arithmetical and political dimensions may be usefully applied to any parliamentary democracy where coalition politics is the norm, with the structure of the party system and expectations as to whether coalitions should be formal or not being the key variables in determining the relationship between the two dimensions. In the case of Italy, the existence of a multi-party system and considerable scope for informal coalitional solutions – assisted by the convoluted political language that accompanies alliance relationships – makes for greater flexibility than in other countries, where conflicts or contradictions might emerge more flagrantly between the two dimensions. This pattern of coalitional behaviour has eased the incorporation of the PCI in the game of coalition politics without upsetting the system. Andreotti, a genius at weaving political alliances, had this to say in 1976 about his new government, which was dependent on informal Communist support:[35]

The abstentions range from the Communists to the Liberals. It seems to me that this sense of collective responsibility cannot be misinterpreted as the historic compromise, as some would have it. In the Christian Democratic party, there are few voices of nostalgia for predetermined majorities as before, but everybody knows that today these majorities just don't exist. In politics there is a saying that is always valid: *rebus sic stantibus* [circumstances being what they are] . . . I don't believe, objectively, that the present governing structure makes the road toward participation in the government either any easier or any more difficult for the Communists. The Christian Democrats, for instance, determined that the future would be less compromised by this formula than by a super 'emergency government'. Politics is also a creative art, and works of art are not programmed.

At least, it is with such subtlety of interpretation that Italian party élites tend to view what is in fact a significant event in Italian coalitional history; foreign opinion, however, usually views such matters differently, in more black-and-white terms.

International constraints

It is no surprise that international constraints enter into Italy's coalition politics. The main pressure has traditionally come from the United States since the onset of the Cold War, which had a strong polarising effect in Italy. American interest has been motivated by considerations of ideology (anti-Communism) and strategy (Italy's position on Europe's Southern flank in the Mediterranean, and US bases on its territory), and has led to considerable involvement in Italian domestic politics, including a strong CIA presence and the covert financing of selected political parties. The DC, the most notable of these cases, consistently based its electoral appeals and its claim to government on the argument that Italy's international responsibilities ostracised the PCI from government. Changes in coalition formulas involving the political Left moving into the 'area of government' – first the PSI in the 1960s, then the PCI in the 1970s – were accompanied by the party in question modifying its stand on the key foreign issues (namely, membership of the European Communities and of NATO) and some nodding approval from Washington. For example, the gradual process of introducing the centre-Left (the PSI moving into government) was only consummated once President Kennedy withdrew earlier American objections. The second time round, the involvement of the PCI in supporting the Andreotti governments proved – perhaps understandably – more complicated in this respect, not least because foreign governments (West European as well as American) expressed deeper and cruder ideological objections. Kissinger, then US Secretary of State, warned during the 1976 Italian election – when the question of the PCI entry to government was the foremost issue – about 'serious consequences' if this should happen. Almost certainly such intervention had some influence – the kind of floating voters now attracted to the PCI had stronger pro-Western loyalties than hardcore party supporters – for, as one PCI leader commented at the time: 'Many Italians wanted to vote for us for clean government and for social reform, but feared the Soviet Union and were concerned about Italy's ties to the West'.[36]

Foreign intervention over Italian governmental participation has been starkly one-dimensional in that it has dwelt exclusively on the formality of whether the PCI actually enters the cabinet. It has, so to speak, applied 'Anglo-Saxon' concepts of coalitional behaviour to the Byzantine world of Italian politics. This difference of mentality did, of course, allow Italian party élites a flexibility of solution through their practice of informal alliances. It is interesting to note that Italian politicians were a good deal more cynical about this question out of reach of the public eye. Andreotti wrote in his diary in July 1976 after Schmidt's blunt statement that Italy would become isolated if the PCI came to power:[37]

> I believe that we must not show ourselves hysterical or touchy. We will have time to explain to the Chancellor the situation and ask his advice. He represents the country to which we have had to pledge gold from the monetary reserve to guarantee the latest loans. We cannot feel offended because he busies himself with what happens with us . . . us debtors. I firmly oppose any public polemics with Bonn on this matter . . . I find myself between the hammer and the anvil: I cannot deny that to a large degree the protest is right [the public controversy over Schmidt's statement], but it would be serious for Italian interests to engage in controversy with the Chancellor of Federal Germany. The agreement between the political parties is essential, but so too must we be in agreement with partner and allied countries. I continue the complicated action of fireman. . . .

In fact, maladroit statements from abroad were privately regarded as unhelpful by party élites in Rome, including DC leaders (in Andreotti's words, one American official warning was 'useless and inopportune'), during what was regarded as the delicate exercise of working out an arrangement with the PCI, required both by the outcome of the elections in 1976 (which saw a substantial rise in PCI support) and the PSI's demand that the PCI be involved in government.

Various general points arise from looking at the international dimension of Italian coalitional behaviour. There is a long record of the influence of foreign governments, but it none the less remains one among several determinants or constraints. Some countervailing influence is provided by changes in party positions on foreign affairs. In 1974 the PCI abandoned its absolute opposition to Italy's membership of NATO, while more recently Berlinguer's progressive distancing of his party from Moscow, as over Poland, has strengthened one precondition for an eventual participation of the PCI in any Italian government. For example, late in 1977 La Malfa, the PRI leader, publicly advocated a closer governmental role for the PCI following Berlinguer's independent stance in his speech at the 60th anniversary of the October Revolution in Moscow. Another possible countervailing influence may be related to public opinion, for there has been some evidence of a decline in pro-American sympathies among Italians during and beyond the 1970s.[38] In addition, this survey of the international factor has called attention to a general feature of coalition politics, its public and private faces. Politicians in Italy may be cynical – and are rarely fundamentalist – behind closed doors about their arrangements, but they are not all the same free agents. Public constraints *are* important, not least because leaders cannot ignore their bases in their parties which continue as electoral rivals to engage in ideological rhetoric to win votes. This leads us to the fifth and final pattern of Italian coalitional behaviour.

Political parties and their social bases

There are various basic and less visible determinants of coalition behaviour which may be conveniently categorised together under the rubric of 'political culture'. These would include the societal, as distinct from the institutional, role of political parties, looking at their vertical and not just their horizontal activity; the need for social consensus as a factor conditioning coalition politics; the influence of public attitudes and electoral pressures; and, drawing on all these various factors, for they inter-relate strongly, the problems of bridging social fragmentation. It is such broader considerations, which the media do not see so readily, that throw much light on and provide a necessary context to the tactical manoeuvres of party élites, for they do much to explain their different motives. In other words, coalition behaviour has to be viewed in the wider context of the party system as a whole, above all because Italy's political system is, as noted before, a *partitocrazia*. This is a variation on the theme, therefore, of political parties acting in a very real sense as 'gatekeepers'.

One crucial aspect of this study is how party strategy in broad terms (the 'theory') is translated into actual coalitional behaviour (the 'practice'). The relationship between the two can hardly be described as either linear or automatic; indeed, it is subject to different intervening variables. These must include institutional factors (the possibilities for exercising power) as well as, obviously, the strategies of other parties and how far these may concur or converge. However, very basic to understanding the relationship between party strategy and coalitional behaviour are the respective parties' roles as channels for expressing interests, as representatives of constituencies, and as carriers of ideologies. One Communist member of parliament explained this lucidly:[39]

> You keep talking about parliamentarians and the electorate as if they were some sort of undifferentiated and disembodied entities floating in mid-air. But behind them is a definite reality, which is made up of parties, organisations, ideologies, historical commitments, and divisions, which is the Italian reality. I don't know any such thing as the electorate in general. I know there are electorates of each party, each with its own . . . demands and aspirations, and this is the reality which we recognise . . . You ask each member of Parliament about his ideas, what he does . . . but these questions don't have any sense if you ignore the parties and the social classes to which we belong . . . It's understood that each member of Parliament feels that he has particular responsibilities toward his base and his party, because after all we are a country with strong party organisations.

It would be expected that a Communist leader would speak more emphatically in such terms than either a Socialist or a Christian Democrat, and particularly more so than a leader of one of the small parties which lack the mass base and organisational articulation of the major parties. Undoubtedly, the nature of the party in question is one variable in examining this problem, but taking account of such variation the general approach of looking at parties societally and vertically is indispensable to studying Italian coalitions.

Central to the parties as mass organisations in this respect is the question of élite control or, alternatively, of vertical constraints on leaders. A serious coalition-watcher in Italy could do well by following closely such events as party congresses, which provide clues about the internal positions of the leaders and the moods and currents of party life which usually help to determine what emerges externally as alliance behaviour. Party congresses have quite often been the occasion on which new directions in party strategy have been resolved, but their actual implementation depends more continuously on the way in which party structures operate.

This may be illustrated by looking briefly at the two main parties. The DC internally is dominated by its factions (*correnti*), which both determine élite behaviour horizontally as at the national level and control party life vertically. By and large, the DC is a party character-ised by low participation among its membership, so that leaders are not too constrained from below. They are, however, strongly constrained by electoral considerations, as will be shown below. The key factor in determining DC coalitional behaviour is therefore the balance of the *correnti*, or rather the alliances between them within the party. It is well known that, for example, speaking of the early 1980s some *correnti* have favoured a coalition with the PSI and others preferred an arrangement with the PCI, with the former (maybe temporarily) in the ascendant. The PCI is a different kind of party, mass-structured, highly bureau-cratic and based on the principle of democratic centralism. It is a very disciplined party, so that, while internal differences over strategy have existed among its leaders, these are not articulated by means of organ-ised factions. This discipline, coupled with Berlinguer's public credi-bility and suppleness as a tactician in guiding the PCI, has explained his maintenance of the party secretaryship despite setbacks to the 'historic compromise' since the late 1970s. Nevertheless, internal pressures did seriously modify the PCI's change of course in refusing further co-operation with the DC and returning to parliamentary opposition in 1979. These would include: growing restlessness among party activists, especially the more critical younger generation of them, at the lack of expected policy results from the 'National Solidarity' governments, trade union militancy over economic sacrifices and, not least, electoral setbacks for the PCI, beginning with local elections in 1978 and con-firmed by its loss of votes in the 1979 parliamentary elections. It is interesting to note here that Italian parties have generally suffered in their internal discipline from coalitional experience – most notably, in promoting factionalism within the DC and also within the PSI once it joined the centre-Left governments. There were also signs that the practice of democratic centralism suffered at least marginally from the PCI's experience of supporting the Andreotti Government and the above-mentioned pressures, although this could also be attributed to a more independent outlook among younger party cadres.

The question of party ideology in coalition politics must be treated with some care in Italy. It is undoubtedly basic in understanding why parties divided by a significant ideological gulf – most notably the DC and PCI – have found it impossible, at least so far, to move from informal arrangements into a full coalition. Conventionally, parties of the Left are more conscious of their ideological *raison d'être* in alliance behaviour, and this is also true of the PCI, despite its flexibility as the archetypal 'Eurocommunist' party. But it does depend on the very salience of 'ideology' and how it is transmitted. In the case of the PCI, this has been expressed in the importance of policy results indicating progress towards its desired 'social transformation' and enduring hostility within the party base towards the DC after a long tradition of antagonistic rivalry. The DC is more difficult to categorise ideologic-ally, especially because its placement along the political spectrum is complicated by the importance of the factions so far as these reflect different ideological currents within the party. Ideologically-motivated reservations or preferences over alliances tend to be expressed in terms of 'party identity', and on these grounds the DC appears as a party of the *status quo*. Some DC leaders have been more explicit about this problem. Fanfani, one of those less enthusiastic about 'convergence' with the PCI, once commented:[40]

The parties, all the parties, operate in order to realise, at least in part, a certain model of society, they all have their ultimate objectives. Only recently, Berlinguer has repeated in the clearest possible way that the final objective of the PCI's role in Italy is to promote the evolution of Italian society towards a model that is not separate from the Communist model.

It should be added that anti-Communism has traditionally been dom-inant among the ranks of the DC membership, and hence any strategic innovations by DC leaders towards closer co-operation with the PCI cannot ignore this constraint.

The need for social consensus as a factor in coalitional behaviour follows from the preceding discussion of the societal role of parties. In Italy this usually refers specifically to what are called 'social forces'; namely, interest groups. It has been a cardinal feature of the country's *partitocrazia* that interest groups are traditionally allied with the political parties, especially with the PCI and DC. The control of the parties over such groups is therefore crucial in creating a social consensus behind coalition formations. With the DC, interest articulation has been transmitted *via* the factions, and this explains their struggle for particular posts in government which provide more patronage than others. The DC has rightly been called a 'mass-clientilism party' by Mario Caciagli, although he was writing with particular reference to its role in the South.[41] It is well known, for instance, that the national bureaucracy in Rome is strongly populated by Southerners, as a result among other things of the DC's acting as a channel for employment in what is an economically backward area of the country. Party control over interest groups is not, however, absolute, notably in the case of the trade unions which, since the late 1960s, have acquired more autonomy and between themselves co-operated regularly across what was formerly a party divide. This trade union co-operation has created an important basis for social consensus, though one now somewhat divorced from the alliance behaviour of the parties. The trade unions have therefore begun in the 1970s to act on governments as a direct pressure group in their own right. A significant example of this new relationship occurred in December 1977, when a massive strike and demonstration by the metal-workers' union demanding more decisive governmental action to deal with the economic crisis forced the PCI into demanding full participation in the cabinet in place of its benevolent abstention (the result was eventually a compromise with the PCI's being included 'in the majority').

In general, the onset of the recession and growing social tension has created a situation where the parties' ability to maintain a social consensus has lessened, where the odds against government success have lengthened and accordingly party leaders find they have less room for manoeuvre in their coalitional arrangements. This is particularly true of the parties of the Left, above all the PCI, for they have had to accommodate themselves to coalition politics at a later stage than the DC, settled in power since the 1940s. The PSI became disillusioned with the centre-Left governments because of the failure to implement social reforms (not least because of DC obstruction), followed by its own loss of electoral support. One might say that the same occurred with the PCI a decade later, but this leads to the question of electoral pressures on coalitional behaviour.

It is a truism to say that electoral pressures affect coalitional behaviour, for clearly they must do so in a parliamentary democracy. This may vary according to the political space between individual parties (or rather: the Left-to-Right images of the parties among the voters) as well as the degree of polarisation. Conceivably, coalitional relationships may affect parties' electoral chances; there may be a freer exchange of voters between parties closely in alliance or the loss of support by parties moving into new alliances. Until the late 1960s Italy evidenced a marked degree of electoral stability, so that this problem was contained. It became something of a joke, though not untrue, to say that party leaders would seek the extra percentage point to strengthen their muscle in coalition negotiations; a joke which could incidentally be extended to leaders of rival *correnti* within the DC. The 1970s saw the beginning of greater electoral movement than ever before with the predictable consequences of greater uncertainty and fluidity for coalition formation. Andreotti's formation of a centre-Right coalition in 1972–3 (with the inclusion of the right-wing PLI and the exclusion of the PSI) was a direct attempt to check the alarming electoral rise in the early 1970s of the neo-Fascist MSI, threatening, as this did, the electoral base of the DC. More significantly, the dramatic increase in PCI support in the mid-1970s was crucial in forcing the DC to reach an accommodation with this party from 1976. Apart from the problems of new majority-building in the legislature, DC leaders were able to rationalise their alliance with the PCI on the grounds of the latter's greater legitimacy.

Electoral pressures or movements are bound to promote or constrain coalitional options; but there is another allied facet, namely, how party élites actually interpret or, indeed, instrumentalise election trends. Important to Craxi's strategy as PSI leader in furthering his party's role in government and becoming Prime Minister is a significant advance beyond the roughly 10 per cent acquired in recent elections. All it requires in coalition politics is evidence of electoral movement, seeing that other (political) factors will determine such a possible outcome; the DC remains on the defensive, while the PCI still suffers from the lack of full legitimacy, something which Craxi has aggressively exploited as one of the polemical weapons of his strategy.

Nonetheless, party leaders with their electoral calculations and alliance manoeuvres can run the risk of public alienation. It is a fair assumption that the prevalence of coalition politics since the War has habituated the public to this and its consequences, such as the need for compromise between different party élites, and the Italians have always adopted a healthy cynicism towards their political leaders. On the other hand, the picture of Byzantine intrigue conveyed by the media would reinforce a distinct impression of opportunism. The very complexity of Italian coalition politics – its multi-dimensional character, as expounded in this chapter – is something virtually impossible to explain to what is a fairly unsophisticated public, and hence the one-dimensional interpretation of the media is hard to break. During the formation of his government with Communist support in early 1978, Andreotti mused: 'We have the duty to explain this to public opinion and it would be a mistake to present this remarkable event in Italian history as a matter of political or downright ideological confusion'.[42] All the same, the public in its wisdom acts as a constraint on the antics of politicians, or at least the politicians choose to see it thus. It has long been a common assumption among party élites in Rome that the public does not take kindly to a party which is seen to initiate the collapse of a coalition, and this has restrained some leaders, particularly if an early election is one possible outcome of a government crisis (which it often is). In the light of current trends, this constraint is likely to remain powerful because of a growth of mass-level consciousness of issues and electoral volatility as well as signs of a decline in public esteem for the main parties.

Finally, we come to the basic question of social fragmentation and whether party élites succeed in bridging this or are fundamentally circumscribed by it. Is coalition politics in Italy functionally centri-petal, or is it culturally centrifugal? Lawrence Dodd has emphasised the problems of coalitional compromise against a background of cleav-age-related policy stands in his theory of coalitions.[43] Italy is a country with a high level of fragmentation, witnessed by the North/South socio-economic divide, the disruptive effects of rapid postwar indus-trialisation and, of course, the existence of the Marxist and Catholic sub-cultures, of which the PCI and DC have respectively been the principal political spokesmen. This deep background problem to Italian coalition politics has led, as noted in the introduction to this chapter, to Italy's becoming a focus of interest among consociational theorists, primarily because of 'convergence' between the parties during the 1970s. Despite the collapse of co-operation between the DC and PCI, are there nevertheless longer-term trends or changes that are likely to promote a repetition, perhaps longer lasting, of such grand coalition politics in the future?

Speaking as of 1983, there are both positive and negative signs, though these are not necessarily contradictory. The very practice of the 'National Solidarity' governments in 1976–9 established a quasi-coalitional precedent for any further rapprochement between the DC and PCI. This is a general point, for looking specifically at the two main parties concerned the experience was varied. The DC was able to adjust to this arrangement, outmatching the PCI in tactical skill (the DC leaders had had ample experience of this in their long years in govern-ment), and there is some evidence that DC élites have lost some of their earlier inhibitions about compromise with the PCI.[44] By and large it was not a happy experience for the PCI for, while some of its policy aims were achieved (for example, modernisation of rent control, some devolution of powers to local authorities, an abortion law), these did not meet the high expectations that accompanied its 1976 election success and were in any case a far cry from the social changes advocated by the party. In the short term, the PCI found that it could not carry its social base. Nevertheless, there has been a distinct growth of élite-level consensus (without this necessarily being transmitted always into governmental co-operation) through the 1970s into the 1980s. Arguments about the 'Italian crisis' do cut ice with many political leaders (Moro was an important example of this outlook), though these can run up against party interest. But party interests may change. The DC's loss of credibility makes it more ready to make greater concessions for the sake of staying in power; the PCI, having learnt some painful lessons from 1976–9, is, however, likely to make firmer policy demands and probably full participation in government as the preconditions for its co-operation. Nevertheless, as shown in this chapter, party élites are less able than before to control their supporters, whether activist or electoral, and one might add to this the broader change with the weakening of the two sub-cultures as a result of secularisation, generational change and the corrosive effects of economic recession. In conclusion, it might therefore be said that horizontally the prospects for bridging the political divide have improved, but that vertically, while there has been some loosening of traditional social fragmentation, party élites have nevertheless remained very constrained by their political bases and are indeed now operating in a much more unpredictable situation.

Conclusion

Altogether, the preceding examination of the main patterns of Italian coalitional behaviour has identified many points of comparison with other countries (the heterogeneous nature of coalitions, electoral pressures, even problems of alternation) and others which are more specific to the Italian case (the strong informal element in coalitional behaviour, the role of foreign influences and problems of social fragmentation). In general, they have emphasised the importance of viewing this subject multi-dimensionally – an approach that could well be developed in examining other countries' coalition politics – and in particular of looking well beyond the institutional dimension. The latter point is more applicable to Italy than to most other countries in Western Europe, not only because of the weaknesses of its political institutions but also because it presents a virtually classic example of a *partitocrazia* or 'party-ocracy'. This means that any comprehensive explanation of coalition politics has to take account of party-political determinants at deeper and broader levels than those which focus on national parliamentary life in the Palazzo Montecitorio, on the dealings of the Prime Minister in the Palazzo Chigi, or even on the strategists in Botteghe Oscure, the Piazza Gesù or the other national party headquarters. If viewed only in the light of what goes on in Rome, Italian coalition politics is very likely to present a picture which is often bizarre, sometimes comical and also irresponsible considering the state of the 'Italian crisis'.

This multi-dimensional approach, furthermore, allows for a greater appreciation of the dynamics of coalitional behaviour in Italy. 'Movement' in Italian politics will almost certainly occur through the channels of the political parties acting individually and in reaction to each other, apart from the impact of major environmental influences, such as the energy crisis with its profound effects on the Italian economy. In order to understand why parties 'move' or not, it is necessary to give consideration to the variety of factors which motivate them, in addition to the obvious and visible ones of acquiring power and of policy demands – historical conditioning, the imprint of social structure, public pressures and, not least, the need of party leaders to carry their followers in their strategic courses. Party élites are far from being free agents in their coalitional behaviour, though the actual influence of different factors may well vary according to a given situation. Some coalition theories have sought to emphasise the importance of the limited political information possessed by the actors engaging in coalition politics. At first sight, this seems a plausible explanation for the Italian case, particularly if one recalls the German aphorist, Georg Christoph Lichtenberg, who said: 'Man becomes a sophist and super-subtle in fields where he has no adequate store of solid information'. A more realistic assessment is to see political élites as subject to a multiplicity of pressures, often contradictory, some more visible to outsiders than others, and of which political operators may not always be fully aware.

The final and most searching question is whether Italian coalitional behaviour viewed in its dynamic framework promotes instability or stagnation. The answer must lie ultimately in the profound nature of the 'Italian crisis', which is beyond the capability of any government to solve in the foreseeable future. But then, what West European government has been able to provide a secure answer to the economic recession? In so far as Italian coalition politics helps to determine the outcome of what is undoubtedly a gloomy situation, then this study provides the following conclusion: while focusing on the institutional dimension suggests a pronounced picture of instability, a wider and multi-dimensional examination of the subject indicates rather one of stagnation.

Notes

1. *The Times*, leading articles published in 1980, 1974, 1972, 1970 and 1969, in that order.
2. *The Times*, 7 May 1982.
3. Giuseppe Di Palma, *Surviving without Governing: the Italian parties in Parliament* (Berkeley, University of California Press, 1977), p. 252.

4. See Luigi Graziano and Sidney Tarrow, *La Crisi Italiana* (Turin, Einaudi, 1979).
5. Gianfranco Pasquino, 'Per un' analisi delle coalizioni di governo in Italia' in A. Parisi and G. Pasquino, *Continuità e Mutamento Elettorale in Italia* (Bologna, Il Mulino, 1977), pp. 251–79.
6. Adriano Pappalardo, 'The Conditions for Consociational Democracy: a logical and empirical critique', *European Journal of Political Research*, 1981, pp. 365–90; also section on Italy in his book, *Partiti e Governi di Coalizione in Europa* (Milan, Franco Angeli Editore, 1978).
7. Some of the results of this work are available in R. Putnam, R. Leonardi, R. Nanetti, 'Polarisation and Depolarisation in Italian Politics, 1968–1981', paper presented at the 1981 annual meeting of the American Political Science Association.
8. Di Palma, *op. cit.*
9. Alan Zuckerman, *Political Clienteles in Power: Party factions and cabinet coalitions in Italy* (Beverly Hills, Sage Publications, 1975), and his *The Politics of Faction: Christian Democratic rule in Italy* (New Haven, Yale University Press, 1979).
10. Alberto Marradi, 'Italy: from "Centrism" to Crisis of the Centre-Left Coalitions' in Eric Browne and John Dreijmanis, (eds) *Government Coalitions in Western Democracies* (New York/London, Longman, 1982), pp. 33–70.
11. The applicability or not of different coalition theories to the Italian case is discussed by Marradi, *ibid.*, pp. 48–56.
12. See Sven Groennings, 'Notes toward theories of coalition behaviour in multiparty systems: formation and maintenance', in Sven Groennings, E.W. Kelly and Michael Leiserson (eds), *The Study of Coalition Behaviour* (New York, Holt, Rinehart and Winston, 1970), Chapter 23.
13. This approach will be developed in the present author's forthcoming book, *Political Parties and Coalitional Behaviour in Italy*, to be published in 1985.
14. These include Guilio Andreotti, *Diari, 1976–1979; gli anni della solidarità* (Milan, Rizzoli, 1981); Andrea Manzella, *Il Tentativo La Malfa: tra febbraio e marzo 1979, nove giorni per un governo* (Bologna, Il Mulino, 1980); Giovanni Spadolini, *Da Moro a La Malfa: marzo 1978-marzo 1979, diario della crisi italiana* (Florence, Vallechi, 1979); Fernando Di Giulio/Emmanuele Rocco, *Il Ministro-Ombra si confessa* (Milan, Rizzoli, 1979). Evidently this unprecedented experience of the 'National Solidarity' governments inspired various leading politicians to provide their own accounts of it. Although not equivalent to memoirs, these publications provide some insights into Italian coalition politics. In general, apart from the lack of political memoirs there is also an absence of substantial biographies of leading Italian politicans.
15. See, for instance, Sabino Cassese, 'Is there a government in Italy? Politics and Administration at the Top' in Richard Rose and Ezra Suleiman (eds), *Presidents and Prime Ministers* (Washington, American Enterprise Institute 1980), pp. 171–202.
16. Di Palma, *op. cit.*, pp. 35–6.
17. Stefano Bartolini, 'The Politics of Institutional Reform in Italy', *West European Politics*, July 1982, pp. 203–21.
18. Cassese, *op. cit.*, pp. 173–7.
19. Alan Zuckerman, *Political Clienteles in Power*, *op. cit.* pp. 38–42.
20. Cassese, *op. cit.*, pp. 201–2.
21. See Antonio Lombardo, 'Sistema di correnti e deperimento dei partiti in Italia', *Rivista Italiana di Scienza Politica*, April 1976, pp. 139–61.
22. This scandal broke in 1981 and involved corruption in a vast freemasonry network extending through most elites in Italian public life. 'P2' was the name of the masonic lodge in question and was short for 'Propaganda Two, Oriental Rite'.
23. Quoted in *Panorama*, 6 December 1982, p. 61.
24. Cassese, *op. cit.*, pp. 180–1.
25. Andreotti, *op. cit.*, p. 189, entry for 6 March 1978.
26. See report in *Panorama*, 1 September 1982, p. 40.
27. *ibid.*
28. P.A. Allum, *Italy – Republic without Government?* (London, Weidenfeld and Nicolson, 1973), p. 117.

29. Francesco D'Onofrio, quoted in *Panorama*, 20 August 1979, pp. 30–31.
30. Sven Groennings, E.W. Kelly and Michael Leiserson (eds), *The Study of Coalition Behaviour*, (New York, Holt, Rinehart and Winston, 1970).
31. Spadolini, *Da Moro a La Malfa*, *op. cit.* pp. 104–5.
32. Andreotti, *op. cit.* p. 186, entry for 27 February 1978.
33. See Putnam *et al.*, *op cit*.
34. Di Palma, *op. cit.*, p. 219.
35. Interview with *Time Magazine*, 13 December 1976.
36. Quoted in Howard Penniman (ed.), *Italy at the Polls; the parliamentary elections of 1976* (Washington, American Enterprise Institute, 1977), p. 313.
37. Andreotti, *op. cit.* pp. 20–21, 23, entries for 13 July and 17 July 1976.
38. Penniman, *op. cit.*, pp. 314–15.
39. Quoted in Di Palma, *op. cit.*, pp. 160–61.
40. Interview in *Panorama*, 17 December 1979, pp. 53–4.
41. Mario Caciagli, 'The Mass Clientilism Party and Conservative Politics: Christian Democracy in Southern Italy' in Zig Layton-Henry (ed.), *Conservative Politics in Western Europe* (London, Macmillan, 1982), pp. 264–91.
42. Andreotti, *op. cit.*, p. 186, entry for 27 February 1978.
43. Lawrence Dodd, *Coalitions in Parliamentary Government* (Princeton, Princeton University Press, 1976).
44. See Putnam *et al.*, *op. cit.*

Coalition Strategies: The Case of
British Local Government
Colin Mellors

Studies of political coalitions rarely include material about Britain.
Although bargaining and the pooling of resources to achieve political
victories feature at every political level in all countries, governing
coalitions, continuous groupings formed in order to obtain government
office, are not common features of Britain's political tradition. As a
consequence, it is to the experiences of mainland Europe that we most
frequently turn in order to learn about the formation, membership,
operation, durability and, so far to a lesser degree, the policy consequences of such coalitions. This is not to deny that there have been
isolated twentieth century Westminster coalitions. Lloyd George's
wartime coalition, the National Government of the 1930s and the less
extensive Lib-Lab Pact from early 1977 to autumn 1978 are three
examples of inter-party co-operation. None of these three, however,
would be readily seen as great political successes for those involved and,
in a country where one-party rule remains the norm, most political
leaders remain hostile to the notion of coalition government. Indeed,
the tendency to produce a decisive result is one of the alleged virtues of
Britain's simple-majority electoral system.

Recently, however, interest has grown in the operation of non-
majority political systems. In part, this is due to renewed interest in
electoral reform,[1] since most other systems would, given present voting
behaviour, deny an overall parliamentary majority to any one party.
Alternating one-party rule would, therefore, be replaced by coalition
government. Even without a change of our electoral system, it is
possible to overstate the tendency of present arrangements to produce
winning majorities. Of the twelve post-war elections, four (1950, 1964,
February 1974 and October 1974) failed to produce a majority sufficient to last for a full-term parliament.[2] Finally, the formation of the
Liberal-SDP Alliance further increases the likelihood of a balance of
power situation emerging from a general election. A rather more
modest share of the poll at a general election than the Alliance achieved
at early by-elections could still be sufficient to prevent any one party
emerging as a clear winner.

In fact, there is one level of British politics where balance of power situations are far from unusual. Although the word coalition is studiously avoided and agreements tend to be more limited and temporary in nature, local government is rich with examples of shared rule and minority government. There are, of course, important differences between national and local political settings in terms of activities, traditions, degree of partisanship and, most importantly, their legal and organisational bases. As with any political system, appreciation of the cultural context is an important prerequisite to the accumulation of more general knowledge. Nevertheless, local government in Britain does present a fruitful, though surprisingly neglected, arena for the study of coalition behaviour.

Party politics in local government

Although the size and finances of British local authorities are unusually large by European standards, they do differ in many important respects from the national governments which are studied elsewhere in this book. Some of these characteristics have relevance for the study of coalition behaviour. The most important is the absence of any formal cabinet system. Whereas in most political systems, cabinet formation and the allocation of office is a major preoccupation of both students of, and participants in, coalitions, British local authorities have no legally distinct executive. It is instead the full council which is the formal governing body. Local government officers, in contrast to their Whitehall equivalents who are servants of the Crown and not Parliament, serve the council as a whole and not simply the majority political group. Governing and opposition parties do not, strictly speaking, exist in local political systems. Thus, for example, when the Bains Committee recommended the introduction of Policy and Resources Committees (the nearest equivalent in local authorities to a cabinet), it saw no difficulty in suggesting that membership of this central policy committee should include representatives from all political groups on the council.[3]

The formal absence of a cabinet in local government does not, of course, preclude the *de facto* existence in many authorities of a governing party which, through its majority on the full council and in various committees, has effective policy control of the local authority. In the majority of local authorities there is one-party rule and in such authorities the focus of decision-making has become the committee or sub-committee. Indeed, there are provisions for the delegation of powers from the full council to such bodies.

One consequence of there being no local government cabinet system is that specific offices (i.e. committee chairmanships) are much less often the subject of a negotiated deal at the local level. Committee chairmanships are not akin to ministerial office and, as will be seen later, there can be dangers in accepting such places. Measuring the pay-offs involved in political arrangements in local government is not simply, as is frequently the case at central level, measuring and identifying the attainment of government office.

The organisation of elections is another distinctive characteristic. These take place at fixed intervals and are held annually in metropolitan districts (one-third of the council retiring each time), every four years in counties (full council retiring) and with other districts given a choice between these two patterns. Clearly, there is a greater temptation to fashion a durable solution in a hung council where there are four years before the next election than in one where there are just twelve months to wait in anticipation of a more decisive result.

Added to these legal and organisational features is the extensive level of central control over local government. Enforced budget cuts by the present Government clearly inhibit the involvement of non-Conservative groups in power-sharing exercises since there are few political advantages to be gained in inflicting unpopular cutbacks.

Despite these differences, party battles in local government can be just as lively as at Westminster. The fierceness of the party struggle in municipal politics existed well before the rise of the Labour Party in the early twentieth century. Political conflict had been a feature of local government since the 1835 Municipal Corporations Act. What the Labour Party in the town halls did achieve was the development of a more programmatic style of local politics. In Leeds, for example, they brought about a new standard of election manifestos and were early practitioners of a nationally linked municipal policy.[4] Group discipline, moreover, owes much to Labour's rise. Although, as Bulpitt has shown,[5] group practices varied widely throughout the country, the creation of Model Standing Orders for Labour Groups was an important departure in the conduct of municipal politics. Although the formal organisation of local authorities excludes an executive, tight discipline and one-party control created 'governing' parties. Other parties necessarily followed this example.

Partisanship further increased following reorganisation in 1974 (1975 in Scotland). Fewer and larger authorities meant fewer Independents. Greater competition for council places meant that fewer would be returned unopposed. Larger wards had the dual impact of increasing the costs of an election and, perhaps, reducing the repute of local candidates. The effect was to link even more councils with national party labels and force many previous Independents to express an explicit party identity, which was for the most part a Conservative commitment. Although a variety of factors sustain distinctly local patterns of conflict, especially in expanding areas and coastal towns, and this helps ensure the survival of some Independents,[6] the 1972

Local Government Act generally made prospects bleak for non-party candidates. In 1973, Conservative or Labour parties were the largest group on 53 per cent of English and Welsh local authorities. By 1979, this figure had increased to 79 per cent.

Local balances of power

The term balance of power can cover a wide variety of situations. It may mean that one party is just short of an overall winning position but has a clear lead over the remaining parties, who may themselves be reasonably balanced in size or clearly ranked in terms of their numerical strengths. Alternatively, two leading parties of roughly equal strength may be competing for the support of one or more smaller groups. Finally, there may be three or more parties all approximately equal in strength. The possible permutations are considerable. Equally, the arrangements which are made to cope with the situation can vary greatly in both nature and degree of formality.

The simplest is to take no action. Since there is no need to form a cabinet, one party (usually, though not necessarily, the largest) can simply assume all the committee chairmanships and govern from a minority position without any other parties being involved. This approach is dependent upon getting such appointments through the Annual Meeting (Statutory Meeting in Scotland). This minority one-party control could, of course, also operate with the tacit support of one or more other groups, in return for which they may seek some institutional pay-off (representation on committees or the creation of specific organisational units) or policy commitment.

The next, more explicit, form of co-operation is two-party power-sharing (or more than two parties if this is necessary to achieve an overall council majority). Again, the formality and extent of this form of agreement can vary. Where such an arrangement does exist it generally contains an understanding that the pact is subject to periodic review (usually annually) and each participating group retains freedom of action. Such an arrangement, therefore, by no means guarantees consistently parallel voting. Finally, there is all-party power sharing – the least likely arrangement outside the rural, traditionally non-partisan, areas.

Between May 1981 and May 1982 some 83 English, Scottish and Welsh local authorities found themselves without one party in overall control.[7] It is a short comparative study of the ensuing twelve months in the 61 English authorities (plus the experiences of Bradford Metropolitan District Council and Lothian Regional Council since May 1982) which forms the basis of the account which follows.

Party attitudes

Inevitably, party attitudes to the question of inter-party co-operation

Table 10.1   *Non-majority local authorities May 1981–May 1982*

	England			Wales		Scotland		Total
	London[a]	Counties	Districts	Counties	Districts	Regions & Islands	Districts	
Non-majority	1	8	60	1	5	1	7	83
Independent majority[b]	—	1	34	3	13	5	16	72
Normal majority	32	36	238	4	19	6	30	365
Total	33	45	332	8	37	12	53	520

a Includes Greater London Council.

b Independent majority is widely defined here as meaning any local authority with an overall majority of members who are not from one of the main political parties contesting parliamentary seats throughout Britain (i.e. other than Conservative, Labour, Liberal, Social Democratic Parties).

are influenced by local conditions and all four Westminster-based major parties avoid adopting too firm a position on the issue. None, of course, openly refer to the word 'coalition'. This, however, does not mean that they rule out any kind of coalition, but simply pre-election pacts and continuous, governing, coalitions. Even this statement needs qualification. Pre-election pacts are acceptable to Liberals and Social Democrats and, somewhat earlier, clear electoral pacts between Liberals and Conservatives operated in Rochdale in the 1950s and 1960s.[8] Although the parties would be most reluctant to recognise them as such, local agreements are therefore really episodic coalitions which retain separate identities and keep an awareness of future situations.[9] Nevertheless, there are distinctive party lines.

Not surprisingly, the Liberal Party (the most likely candidate for coalition partnership) has the most developed views on this subject.[10] A campaign booklet issued by the Association of Liberal Councillors, *Life in the Balance*, sets out the political pitfalls very clearly:[11]

Balance of power in reality is the toughest position in which any group of Liberal councillors can find themselves, and taxes their individual and collective skills to the limit. It can make or break them, leading on to further electoral success or to extinction . . . [It] involves difficult decisions and compromises.

Mixed experiences of local power-sharing have led to a dominant view in the party that opportunities should always be explored but treated with some caution. After such a long exclusion from national power, there is an obvious temptation to grab at any possibilities. Such achievements may well turn out to be very short-lived and, especially given the nature of local government, playing the balance of power may give a higher and longer-term yield than striking any formal deals. As the *Scotsman* newspaper noted when the Liberal-SDP Alliance opted to support a Conservative Administration in Lothian Region in May 1982:[12]

The agreement . . . holds more [political] risks for the Alliance than the Tories. In Scotland, Lothian has now become their test bed in local politics. Their movements will be watched closely.

At the other extreme, the Labour Party takes the most severe view of coalitions and, whilst not formally prohibiting local groups from involving themselves in inter-party agreements, clearly discourages such moves. Clause 6 of the Model Standing Orders for Labour Groups stresses that when in opposition Labour groups should avoid taking on any committee chairmanships or vice-chairmanships. The Labour Party does have particular difficulties in entering any inter-party agreements. There is a natural reluctance to modify party programmes and the nature of all but the firmest coalitions tends towards a fragmented rather than a corporate policy process. Party priorities will vary from committee to committee rather than be on the council-wide basis which would be more in accord with Labour strategy. As a consequence, most groups prefer to sit out the balance if this allows a retention of their ideological purity. This is, of course, especially true at a time of enforced spending cuts in local government when there are apparent long-term advantages in not having to be associated with some of the harsher spending decisions which local authorities are having to make.

There is, however, in some local Labour groups a sign of a more pragmatic approach to the question of hung councils. At a conference held in Leicester in October 1982 to share Labour groups' experiences in hung councils, at least one Labour leader welcomed the 'more considered view now being taken by Labour groups who do not have overall control'.[13] The counties which had been traditional Conservative strongholds afforded particularly tempting political bait. In one, Cheshire, Labour had assumed control with Liberal support, in return for which, among other things, a chairmanship and several vice-chairmanships were taken by the junior coalition partner. As the Labour leader acknowledged, the deal had not been easy to sell to his own party:[14]

Where any form of agreed or arranged package between the Labour and Liberal groups is even contemplated . . . any arrangements so reached will inevitably mean a reduced trust by the group in those involved in negotiations . . . The issues and problems that arise for the politicians are not for the fainthearted, nor is it an easy task for those who aren't prepared to compromise nor for those who aren't prepared to accept criticism for those compromises.

Though other Labour group leaders have been less adventurous in their approach, there is evidence of a greater willingness to explore the possibilities opened up by hung authorities, especially where some political power can be obtained whilst ideological purity is retained.

The attitudes of the Conservative and Social Democrat parties fall midway between those of Liberals and Labour. Naturally, the Social Democrats, being a new party, have relatively little direct experience of local coalitions (although there is the well-publicised case of their involvement with the Conservatives in Lambeth between May and November 1982)[15] and they work closely with Liberal councillors. Again, like all the other parties, their central organisation recognises the importance of responding to local circumstances and gives relatively limited consideration to the question at their annual local government training conferences. By way of help, local SDP councillors are also put in touch with a local MP who can offer guidance in these matters. Pragmatism is the hallmark of the Conservative Party, and their Central Office affords limited advice to local Conservative groups in balance of power situations. In contrast to Labour's corporate view of local government which logically precludes loose coalition, the more federalist Conservative conception of local government is more amenable to power-sharing. Agreement on a prudent budget is a crucial test and if this can be agreed then co-operation in other policy areas does not seem to present insurmountable difficulties.

Two other factors can influence the attitude of political parties – past experience and the ideological distance of potential coalition partners. It is an important theme of coalition theory that coalitions are easier to build and more durable in nature when partners are ideologically close.[16] The concept of ideological range is obviously important in inter-party agreements, although in Britain, as in most political systems, it is not possible to plot a place for political parties on a left-right policy scale which applies to all areas. Liberals, for example, do not neatly sit midway between Conservatives and Labour on all policy issues. Moreover, the concern in local government is not so much with selecting partners for a long-term governing coalition as with a series of voting coalitions which may, if necessary, continuously regroup so as to minimise ideological distance over any given issue. All permutations are therefore possible and no one combination of parties is likely, because of ideological proximity, to predominate in inter-party deals.

Past experience also clearly influences party attitudes. It is a feature of coalition behaviour that the largest non-majority party frequently displays a reluctance to enter into bargaining with smaller parties if this means sharing rewards in a way which distorts the relative initial strengths of these partners. Any experience of alternative deals being struck between this smaller party and one of the other parties, with the result that any initial advantage of the non-participating party is lost, will soon break down the reluctance of that latter group.[17] Faced with a continuous exclusion from office, strategies easily become modified, as subtle changes in some Labour groups have suggested.

Other variables
Further factors affect the likelihood of coalition formation. Some are general; others are peculiar to the setting of local government. Three general forces against inter-party co-operation can be applied to the case of British local government. These are: a tradition of closed bargaining groups, distrust in one potential partner, and self-exclusion.[18]

In many local authorities there is a tradition which exists between Conservative and Labour groups that, in the event of an indecisive election, the larger of these two parties takes control without resorting to co-operation with a smaller party. It is the maintenance of a pattern of alternating single-party rule despite the failure to achieve an overall majority. Distrust of a potential partner also militates against inter-party agreements. In Berkshire, for example, the Labour group held that 'no formal agreement should be reached with the Liberals on the grounds that they cannot be trusted'.[19] Finally, deliberate self-exclusion, in order to protect ideological purity or maximise longer-term benefits, is a most frequent force against political agreements. All parties are concerned with avoiding too close an identification with the policies of another party. This is especially true when political and economic conditions dictate contraction rather than expansion of local authority services.

There are in addition a number of factors which are specific to local government. They include:

i)   The traditions of the area. The nature of local politics is much influenced by traditions of local conflict or, alternatively, co-operation.
ii) How long the balance of power is likely to exist.
iii) The precise nature of the power balance (see earlier).
iv) The attitudes of local party leaders and relations between them.
v)   The attitudes of chief officers, who may treat the situation as a temporary phenomenon and therefore be less inclined to encourage formal arrangements.
iv) The previous political composition of the local authority.

A taste of power after long exclusion is an enticing goal. There is great temptation for Labour groups to wrest power from Conservatives in their county strongholds and Conservatives to sample the delights of control in the urban-based districts long held by the Labour Party. Above all, coalitions essentially operate against the previous winning party (anti-Labour in the towns and anti-Conservative in the countries). This is almost as important as the ideological proximity of the partners, especially as this compatibility is only really crucial at the time of the annual budget.

Arranging control of the local authority

The initiative for political agreements most frequently comes from the smaller, balancing, parties which attempt to exploit the uncertain political situation. In so doing, they are careful to appear even-handed and attempt negotiation with all potential power-sharing partners.[20] There are essentially three institutional pay-offs available when entering into negotiations: chairmanships (and vice chairmanships), committee representation, and the creation of specific units (committees or departments) which are themselves reflections of policy orientation. In addition, there are, of course, a range of policy pay-offs.

Since local authorities lack a separate executive, obtaining committee chairmanships is not, by contrast with Cabinet office, a key goal for those involved in the local balance of power. The sharing of chairmanships in some local authorities (hung and majority-controlled) owes much more to traditions of low partisanship and party co-operation in the running of a council than to any exertion of political resources and coalition-building. Thus among the eight counties without one-party overall control since 1981, Cheshire is a notable exception in sharing the chairmanships between parties. In most authorities, smaller parties, whose co-operation may well be necessary during the year, are usually content to let one party take these offices and seek rewards in other areas. The general pattern is then that a minority administration is formed. Occasionally, these arrangements can be far from stable. In Berkshire, for example, Conservatives at first took all the chairmanships. Early in 1982 they resigned all of them in reaction to the spending plans of the combined forces of Labour and Liberal councillors and for a few months the council essentially operated without an administration. Management panels kept the authority ticking over and each committee meeting took a fresh vote to elect a chairman for the session. In June 1982, following a by-election success, the Conservatives again resumed all the chairmanships.

Proportional representation is a more sought-after goal for small parties involved in coalition arrangements. It means, of course, that the balance of power situation is carried through to the committees. It may, as an incidental effect, result in rather fewer reversals of committee decisions at full council because of the similarity in party balances. More importantly, it is a way for the smaller parties to achieve a structure conducive to policy pay-offs, and the allocation of committee places on a proportional basis emerged in many hung councils between 1981 and 1982. Equal access to officers' briefing sessions is a related part of many negotiated bargains and it is notable how far chief officers in many authorities have scrupulously operated a policy of briefing all groups. In Cheshire, for example, officers on their own initiative produced a 'convention regarding relations between the political parties represented on the council'. Though never formally adopted,[21] it heralded an approach carried out, according to the Labour group leader, 'with total integrity, total impartiality and total confidentiality'.[22] Thus, for example, before the 1982–3 budget was prepared, officers provided each party group with a separate, and confidential, budget strategy. In a sense, this is a reversion to the traditional role of officers as servants of the full council and away from the more Whitehall-based version which has emerged in strong one-party authorities with officers sometimes appearing more as servants of the governing party.

Limited structural change can also emerge from these political deals. This can simply mean a streamlining of the committee system, sometimes an easing of the burden on the manpower resources of small political groups. More innovatory is the creation of performance review units in several hung authorities, almost always as a result of Liberal-SDP pressure. An efficiency audit was, for example, an early achievement of the Liberal group in Cheshire. When the three Liberal-SDP councillors, holding the balance on Lothian Regional Council since May 1982, reached an agreement with the minority controlling Conservative group, one of the items in the six-point agreement with the Tories was that 'A Performance Review Committee will be set up with an agreed remit composed of 15 councillors from all parties with an Alliance chairman and two other Alliance members'.[23] Similarly Blackburn, which has never experienced one party in overall control since reorganisation, now has a Finance and Performance Working Group chaired by a member of the Ratepayers' Group. A concern with efficiency and effectiveness in the use of public resources is one area where the ideological distance between local Conservative and Liberal groups can frequently be bridged.

Policy agreements

Although shared policy packages rarely emerge, and are rarely sought, from local coalitions, it is in the area of policy rather than the allocation of committee chairmanships that the pay-offs of local inter-party cooperation are most visible. In a political system which does not require the formation of a 'governing' coalition, parties feel a natural reluctance to commit themselves to a common programme. All parties have a marked interest in keeping the policy consequences of their agreement as imprecise as possible, in order both to retain as much freedom of action as possible and to conceal policy concessions which result from the deal. The nature of coalitions in local government, which are at best usually a series of sequential agreements rather than a formal alliance lasting over a period of time and a coherent range of issues, is more amenable to this looser approach.

In most agreements, therefore, even a formal and written understanding between parties usually avoids precise policy statements. Only in the area of finance is there any likelihood of common aims. Thus, the six-point Conservative-Alliance agreement in the Lothian Region includes an undertaking that:[23]

The Alliance will vote for a proposal that any monies deducted from the Rate Support Grant by the Secretary of State shall be returned to the rate-payers, though the Alliance reserve their right to oppose any Conservative proposals on this subject up to that point.

The document also includes the hope that 'where possible, an agreed approach to (other) major issues should be worked out'.

Budget strategy is one of the major tests for hung local authorities. In the last financial year many such authorities endorsed what were essentially Liberal spending strategies. In the counties, the Liberals most frequently found partnership with Labour in restoring some Conservative cut-backs from the previous year, whilst in the cities it was the Conservatives who benefitted from Liberal support in trimming the more ambitious Labour spending approach of earlier years. The 1982/83 budget exercise was, of course, set against the possibility of financial penalties being imposed by central government for excessive spending. This threat acted as a powerful determinant of group behaviour and had the effect in many areas of closing the ideological gap between Conservative and Liberal groups. In Lothian, for example, the Alliance leader argued that 'while they [Alliance groups] differed about the figure for cuts, they supported the Conservatives' tactics for avoiding a threatened Government spending penalty'.[24] Whilst the Alliance preferred a £13.8m. cut-back, they therefore allowed the passage, by abstaining, of a £31m. package of cuts on the casting vote of the Conservative convener. In Bradford, a £5m. cuts exercise, replacing Labour's previous £7m. growth programme, enjoyed Liberal support. Despite some difficulties about which departmental programmes would be sacrificed, only a £217,000 measure to help the unemployed escaped from the original plans. In neighbouring Calderdale the Conservative budget was lost and the Tory group resigned all their committee chairmanships.

The political situation in Calderdale is a good example of the consequences of constantly regrouping coalitions. With several years' experience of a balance of power, there are many examples of shifting policy. Calderdale Liberals seem especially adroit at using this voting strength to achieve maximum policy pay-offs. Thus, when Conservatives held the chairmanships, they were denied Liberal support over low rates and secondary education. When Labour took control, they were unable to win Liberal support for a council house building programme and their policy on council house sales.

The agreement in Bradford in May 1982 which led to Conservative acceptance of what amounted to a Liberal mini-manifesto is, therefore, unusual. Soon after the local election results were announced, the Conservative leader expressed a willingness to see if a common programme could be formed with the Liberals. As a result a seven-point Liberal programme was accepted. It called for:

stop to growth budget; review of council services; external audit; study of unused land; reversing policy of rating empty property; approval of area management idea; survey of council house stock and tenants' needs; ending of county highway agreement and more money for snow clearance.

Within six months five of these seven points had been acted upon.

Bradford's policy package is, however, an exception to the rule. Beyond broad common approaches to financial strategy and, perhaps, an implicit support for a particular area of minority party interest (housing policy or schemes for individual wards), shared policy programmes are avoided. Even in Bradford, Liberal members have not regarded the pact as binding and have used their voting power to defeat their Conservative partners on a number of occasions. Since these are not, by contrast with national politics, taken as votes of confidence, lost votes and reversals of committee decisions simply become one of the hazards of life in hung councils.

Constantly regrouping voting coalitions may well benefit smaller parties in hung authorities, enabling them to secure more policy pay-offs (they are an example of the 'relative weakness effect' of coalitions in local government), but they increase the difficulties of achieving a coherent programme rather than isolated policy outputs. As one leader has noted:[25]

For the sake of political expediency . . . we are more likely to get a series of *ad hoc* service improvements year after year and this therefore increases the difficulties in achieving in a corporate sense the development of programme-orientated services.

Elsewhere in this book, Manfred Schmidt has considered the circumstances in which shared control tends towards *policy-immobilisme* (policy underproduction) or *policy overproduction*. His argument that the former is more likely in times of economic crisis and the latter in expansionist times, when ideological disharmony can be overcome, cannot be tested here since the time-span is limited to a single year in which the political and economic climate was distinctly hostile. There can, however, be little dispute that recent hung authorities are characterised by policy underproduction.

Stability and internal mode of operation

At the most basic level, local authorities can and do operate without single-party control. The administrative arrangements which are made at the Annual Meeting may not survive the whole twelve-month period (Calderdale experienced two wholesale resignations of chairmanships in 1980–81) but the initial threats of non-controlling parties to make the authority ungovernable rarely materialise. This should not be taken to imply that local coalitions operate smoothly. Six months of non-majority rule in Bradford were described by a local newspaper as 'the most alarmingly chaotic period in its history . . . a tied up in knots local authority'.[26]

The balance of power situation has consequences for the internal location of power. In single-party-controlled local authorities, the full council is frequently relegated to acting as a debating chamber, a 'rubber stamp' or a final court of appeal. Group discipline ensures that committee decisions go through without too much difficulty. Without single-party majorities, reversals of committee decisions at full council are much more likely. Even Policy and Resources Committees can prove 'impotent and irrelevant'.[27] The route from sub-committee through committee to full council can be a very long one.

Minds are changed, voting coalitions regroup and even attendance levels can be a decisive factor. Mid-meeting adjournments of the full council to form a winning coalition are not infrequent. Almost inevitably it means more time, at formal meetings (a 20-hour marathon council meeting in the case of Berkshire and a 6 a.m. finish to one in Basildon), at briefing sessions, and in selling coalition packages to respective party groups.

The real difficulty, however, is not organisational but one of policy direction. Policy focus, as already noted, becomes short-term (according to one Chief Executive 'days and weeks rather than years') and coherence across committee areas is often lost. 'Administration without strategy' is one way of describing this situation.[28] Planning is an obvious area which suffers, both because of the shorter time focus and the less integrated approach. There are a number of instances of policy clashes between local authority planning and housing committees. Difficulties are compounded when party leaders themselves are reluctant to make early decisions, or to be too specific in their proposals, for fear of excluding potential voting partners. One Chief Officer referred to the near-impossibility of persuading the leader of a three-party coalition to announce his budget intentions and review of capital projects.

Uncertain and unstable local coalitions create a new environment for local government officers. The change is that much more distinct when it follows a sustained period of one-party rule or the controlling group includes many newly elected councillors. Almost invariably the input of chief officers in local authority decision-making increases. Without a clear-cut strategy they are faced with the choice of either passively sitting out the period of uncertainty or actively taking the initiative. In some previously single-party-controlled authorities, a passive approach is enforced by a retention of the idea of a more 'limited' role for officers despite the new political situation. In most authorities, however, officers adopt a more active role. Cheshire's experiences offer a valuable guide to the difficulties.[29]

For the officers, the operation of a hung council provides the opportunity for a new and challenging dimension to their jobs, requiring greater skills in tact, discretion and 'political awareness'.

The Chief Executive, in particular, assumes a crucial role and when local authorities have displayed a degree of governmental effectiveness and policy coherence during a period of non-majority control they owe much to the political agility of their principal local government officer.

Coalition behaviour in British local government

Local government affords an unusual opportunity to study coalition behaviour in Britain in a formal political setting. Such studies are less possible at the national level where single-party governments predominate and the tightness of party discipline restricts the possibility of 'roll-call' research on the lines of that undertaken on the US Congress. The tightness of the British party system now spills over into most local authorities, but at this level indecisive election results are much more common. Non-majority local councils therefore provide easy access to material on inter-party coalitions.

Gamson defines coalitions as 'temporary, means oriented, alliances among . . . groups which differ in goals. There is generally little value consensus . . . [which] . . . makes the pursuit of power itself . . . an ideal basis for coalition formation since it is an instrument for the achievement of widely ranging and even incompatible goals'.[30] Political studies of coalitions most frequently focus on the formation of governing coalitions and, in particular, the quantitative and qualitative awarding of Cabinet posts.[31] As we have seen, this is not an appropriate approach in the case of local authorities largely because a separate executive does not feature in the British local government system. Where coalitions do occur, therefore, they take the form of a series of single-issue-based agreements. These have been referred to as repetitive[32] or, possibly, episodic[33] coalitions. It is inappropriate, even where two or more parties coalesce on a wide range of issues throughout the twelve-month period, to refer to them as continuous, governing coalitions, except in very few authorities. Formal power-sharing is much more likely in non-partisan rural authorities, with or without one party in an overall majority position, than it is generally in hung councils.

Faced with a balance of power situation, smaller parties entering into an understanding with one of the larger parties (either by supporting or, more usually, not opposing their taking control) only infrequently seek a sharing of committee chairmanships or vice-chairmanships as the price of that co-operation. They look instead for institutional pay-offs such as ensuring that the power balance is reflected throughout the structure of the authority (proportional committee places), equal (i.e. disproportionate to size) briefing facilities and, sometimes, modification of the committee structure (creation of performance review units etc.). Which party will be allowed to take control depends on such factors as previous political composition, ideological proximity (especially concerning budget strategy), who will make the best offers concerning the institutional pay-offs which are sought, and any past experiences of co-operation. The nature of personal relationships between leading figures can also be crucial.[34]

Whichever party assumes control, there is no guarantee of continuing support or, more accurately, non-opposition. The taking of chairmanships at an Annual Meeting does not amount to a governing coalition and, therefore, ideological proximity here is a less important factor than in more continuous associations. There can be subsequent regroupings over individual policy areas so as to minimise the ideological gap between groups and, for the smaller parties, maximise policy successes. The annual budget is the most important test and, therefore, the most appropriate occasion to discover who votes with whom. The desire to retain separate identities, in view of future electoral considerations, will itself tend to encourage regrouping even when it is unnecessary to maximise policy successes.

Time and space are important variables in coalition behaviour. Unlike many experimental coalitions, there is here no one winning occasion. Past and future considerations are important.[35] The assumption of much coalition behaviour that power is sought at any price is not appropriate. Some groups on some occasions will benefit from their involvement in a coalition; others benefit (or perceive benefit) in non-involvement. What most frequently happens in hung local authorities is that minority control is assumed through the willingness of another party to lend support, or not oppose, that control without at the same time accepting formal responsibility for their policies or controlling position.[36] Time is an important factor here since without past and future considerations (past relationships, the consequences after the next election, keeping separate identities etc.) majority winning coalitions would probably be more likely. Considerations of space include, besides the external political and economic environment, local traditions, relationships between party leaders and between politicians and officials, and levels of trust between groups.

Whatever form of arrangement is made, and between whom, the experience of hung councils during 1981–2 suggests some common patterns of operation. Power shifts from the committees to the full council, the decision-making process slows down, officers assume an enhanced role, short-term priorities override longer-term considerations and there can be inter-committee conflicts. Not only officers find their work changed, more opportunities are given to individual councillors to exert their influence and their roles may become more 'trustee' than 'delegate' in nature. Accountability can be as blurred as policy direction.

Non-majority local authorities do then offer a neglected opportunity for the study of coalitions in the British setting. The constitutions of local authorities deny research into the most frequent area of coalition inquiry, cabinet formation, and the shift in focus to the operation of coalitions and consequences for policy is marked. An emphasis on the aspect of past and future considerations, inevitable in 'repetitive' coalition activity, is also distinctive. For those who are frustrated by the lack of research opportunities caused at national level by the single governing party Westminster model, local government in Britain is an area worthy of greater consideration than it has in the past received.

Notes

1. See, for example, S.E. Finer (ed.), *Adversary Politics and Electoral Reform* (London, Anthony Wigram, 1975).
2. Note, also, the decline in the two-party pattern of voting behaviour. I. Crewe *et al.*, 'Partisan Dealignment in Britain', *British Journal of Political Science*, 1977.
3. *The New Local Authorities: Management and Structure*, HMSO, 1972.
4. See M. Meadowcroft, *Transition in Leeds City Government 1903–28* (unpublished M. Phil. thesis, University of Bradford, 1979).
5. J.G. Bulpitt, *Party Politics in English Local Government* (London, Longman, 1967).
6. W.P. Grant, 'Local Parties in British Local Politics: A Framework for Empirical Analysis', *Political Studies*, 1971.
7. Remaining Independent or 'Local' party controlled authorities should not be overlooked since these councils display many of the characteristics of non-majority councils.
8. Bulpitt, *op. cit.*, pp. 78–9.
9. See B. Hinckley (ed.), *Coalitions and Time* (London, Sage, 1976).
10. M. Clay, *Life in the Balance*, Association of Liberal Councillors' Campaign Book No. 7, undated.
11. *ibid*, p. 2.
12. *Scotsman*, 17 May 1982. See also R. Liddle, 'How I lost sleep propping up an unpopular Tory minority council – or the perils of holding the balance in Lambeth', *The Social Democrat*, 3 December 1982 (the title says it all).

13. *Labour Weekly*, 12 November 1982.
14. B. Jeuda, 'Managing a Hung Authority', *Local Government Policy Making*, 9: No. 1, 1982.
15. See Liddle, *op. cit.*
16. E.C. Browne and J. Dreijmanis (eds.), *Government Coalitions in Western Europe* (New York/London, Longman, 1982), pp. 344–5 and p. 352.
17. Hinckley, *op. cit.*, p. 16.
18. Brown and Dreijmanis, *op. cit.*, pp. 346–7.
19. *Guardian*, 13 March 1982.
20. Bradford and Lothian experiences are good examples of tactics. See *Yorkshire Post*, 7 May 1982, *Telegraph and Argus*, 7 May 1982 (for Bradford) and *Scotsman*, 10 May 1982 (for Lothian). See also M. Clay, *op. cit.*, pp. 15 and 17.
21. A new version is expected to be adopted early in 1983.
22. Jeuda, *op. cit.*, p. 11.
23. *Scotsman*, 14 May 1982.
24. *Glasgow Herald*, 26 May 1982.
25. Jeuda, *op. cit.*, p. 14.
26. *Keighley News*, 24 September 1982.
27. A. Blowers, 'Checks and Balances: The Politics of Minority Government', *Public Administration*, 1977.
28. M. Dyer, *Independent Politics in Kincardineshire* (Ph. D. thesis, University of Aberdeen, 1973).
29. Jeuda, *op. cit.*, p. 12.
30. W. A. Gamson, 'A Theory of Coalition Formation', *American Sociological Review*, 26, 1961, p. 374.
31. See, in particular, E. Browne, 'Aspects of Coalition Payoffs in European Parliamentary Democracies', *American Political Science Review*, 67, 1973 and, more generally, A. De Swaan, *Coalition Theories and Cabinet Formation* (Amsterdam/London/New York, Elsevier, 1973), and S. Groennings, E.W. Kelly and M. Leiserson (eds), *The Study of Coalition Behavior*, (New York, Holt, Rinehart and Winston, 1970).
32. B. Hinckley, *Coalitions and Politics* (New York, Harcourt, Brace Jovanovich, 1981), pp. 69–79.
33. T. Caplow refers briefly to 'continuous', 'episodic' and 'terminal' coalitions in 'Future Development of a Theory of Coalitions in the Triad', *American Journal of Sociology*, 64, 1959, p. 489.
34. See Hinckley, *Coalitions and Politics*, *op. cit.*, Chap. 4.
35. See Hinckley, *Coalitions and Time*, *op. cit.*
36. Browne and Dreijmanis, *op. cit.*, pp. 348–9.

11 Coalitions and Political Institutions: The Irish Experience
Brian Farrell

In the literature of comparative politics Ireland often appears as a deviant case. Almost uniquely among the newly evolved nation-states of the twentieth century it has maintained a stable political system that exhibits the major institutional characteristics of the liberal-democratic model: free elections, parliamentary responsibility, party competition and alternation in government.[1] The origins of the system might have suggested a less stable and orderly future.

Within a crowded five-year period between 1917 and 1922 the course of Irish political development accelerated from anticipated Home Rule (to be granted by Britain to the leaders of the Irish Parliamentary Party) to the assertion of independent sovereignty by the newly-forged 'national front' party, Sinn Fein. In a spectacular victory in the 1918 general election Sinn Fein routed the Parliamentary Party, established a separate Irish assembly (Dail Eireann) and created a new state system.[2] To some extent the exigencies of military necessity combined with political convenience to maintain that initial phase of one-party parliament and government through to 1922; it might well have solidified into some variation of the typical post-colonial, one-party state. Instead, following the major 'treaty debate' on the settlement of the long-standing issue of Anglo-Irish relations, the 'national front' of Sinn Fein split into two large sections which forged out of the crucible of civil war the basic party groupings that have dominated the Irish system ever since.[3]

A simple bi-polar cleavage might have created a conventional two party system. But other factors contributed to a different outcome. The dominance of Sinn Fein had thrust aside other Irish political interests: the already established Labour Party, the rump of Southern Unionism, the remnants of the Irish Parliamentary Party and the inchoate sectional interests of farmers and rate-payers. The division of Sinn Fein provided these forces with an opportunity; although the Treaty was the central issue of the 1922 general election, these other groupings secured 40 per cent of the first-preference vote and 34 of the 128 seats in the Dail. That fragmentation of opinion appeared likely to be a persistent feature of the emerging system with the adoption of the single-transferable vote (STV) method of proportional representation. The acting chairman of the committee established by the Provisional Government in 1922 to draw up a constitution for the new state recorded a typical comment:[4]

It is certain that in Ireland many parties will be present in the Chamber. It will be impossible according to the English method to form a Government without coalition in which there will be inevitable 'jockeying' for ministerial power.

The deputy prime minister Kevin O'Higgins, predicted in 1922 that 'we will have groups here – small groups of seven or eight. We will not have parties on definite lines of political cleavage'.[5]

In fact, in the twenty-one general elections held since that date, despite the operation of STV, the typical outcome has been single-party government. The norm of partisan, adversary-style parliamentary politics was soon established. It was not seriously challenged in either of the first two decades of the state's existence, as each of the two offshoots of Sinn Fein, in turn, monopolised executive power. In the first ten years the executive was controlled by Cumann na nGael, the precursor of the contemporary Fine Gael party. Since 1932 Fianna Fail, led until 1959 by Eamon de Valera, has usually formed the government. On only five occasions, spanning to date just a dozen years (1948–51; 1954–7; 1973–7; 1981–2(i); 1982(ii)–), has Ireland experienced coalition governments.

By the early 1940s a national political consensus on the central issue of neutrality, fears of the possible destabilising effects of an electoral contest in war-time, and the known organisational weakness of their party encouraged some Fine Gael spokesmen to raise the prospect of a national government. This was rejected by Fianna Fail, and de Valera used the opportunity to castigate the concept of coalition government as inherently unstable, undesirable and unnecessary in Irish circumstances. That ended debate on the matter, but when the 1948 general election created a stalemate, the five parties in the Dail other than Fianna Fail came together without any public discussion and formed an alternative coalition administration under John Costello, of Fine Gael. The combination of Fine Gael, the two separate parliamentary Labour parties, Clann na Talmhan (mainly representing small farmers in the West) and the newly founded republican Clann na Poblachta could muster only 67 seats; they required the support of Independent deputies to surpass Fianna Fail's 69 seats. Moreover, it is a measure of Fianna Fail success in denouncing the concept of coalition that the combination chose to describe itself as 'the Inter-Party Government'.

The creation of the first Inter-Party government offered a credible alternative to Fianna Fail. Although the parties in that alliance campaigned separately, the following three general elections were perceived as offering the national electorate a choice between two governmental teams. In essence the second Inter-Party government, 1954–7, also under Costello – although encompassing a smaller spread of parties – was a direct descendant of its predecessor.[6] Each was a pragmatic response to the question: how to provide an effective challenge to the electoral hegemony of Fianna Fail.

The 1960s saw a significant re-assessment. In 1959 the leaders of both Fianna Fail and Fine Gael – De Valera and General Mulcahy – stepped down; that seemed to signal a softening of the historic cleavage that had dominated Irish politics since 1922. In 1960 the new leader of the Labour Party, influenced by an analysis that suggested that Fine Gael rather than Labour had gained electoral strength from coalition, committed his party to an independent, socialist policy. But Fianna Fail victories in a series of four general elections (1957, 1961, 1965, 1969), prompted a reappraisal. Labour leaders backed away from their rejection of coalition; Fine Gael leaders recognised the reality that they could not defeat Fianna Fail without an alliance. Negotiations to agree an electoral pact were eased by the growth of the social-democratic wing within Fine Gael.

Even under the pressure of an unexpectedly early election in February 1973 the two parties were able to offer themselves as a 'National Coalition' with a 14-point policy 'Statement of Intent' agreed between senior members and published the day after dissolution.[7] This National Coalition, under the premiership of Liam Cosgrave of Fine Gael, served until 1977 when it offered itself, unsuccessfully, for re-election. In the aftermath of defeat there was in each party a change of leader and some discontent at the negative impact of coalition on party identity and support. The problem was more pronounced for Labour than for Fine Gael and was not fully resolved prior to the 1981 election; the annual conference of the party bound the leader to report any post-electoral negotiation on coalition to a special delegate conference for ratification.

All parties fought independent election campaigns and while Fine Gael urged its supporters to give later preferences to Labour there was no certainty that the parties would co-operate in government. Nevertheless, following negotiations between the two party leaders and a special delegate conference of Labour to confirm the agreement, the two parties managed to form a second Coalition, under the Fine Gael leader, Garret FitzGerald, dependent on the support of Independent deputies mainly identified as being on the left of the Irish political spectrum.[8] Unable to retain that support for a harsh and rigid budget after defeat on an excise measure, this second National Coalition dissolved the Dail in January 1982.[9] Following an indecisive general election, Charles Haughey, the Fianna Fail leader, formed a minority government of Fianna Fail with the support of the left-of-centre Workers' Party and other Independent deputies.

Initially an effort was made to strengthen this fragile parliamentary base. A Fine Gael backbencher was offered nomination to the European Commission, but Fianna Fail did not gain the anticipated extra seat in the subsequent by-election. Its minority position was weakened by a challenge to the leader's position by dissidents in the parliamentary party. Immediately after the summer recess of 1982 that challenge was renewed. The polls showed a consistent decline in support.[10] In parliament the death of one Government backbencher and the severe illness of another eroded its position. At the same time, Fianna Fail remained the largest party and Fine Gael claims that it could break through to majority support were not credible. Whether the electorate would be offered a coalition alternative to single-party Fianna Fail government remained an open question. The full range of arguments was deployed at the Annual Conference of the Labour Party in October 1982. Three composite motions proposed three basic strategies. All posited an independent Labour programme and election campaign; one then favoured Labour rejecting both coalition and support for a minority government; another recommended post-electoral support for a minority government; the third, strongly urged by the Labour leader, Michael O'Leary, proposed to empower 'the Administrative Council and the Parliamentary Labour Party to jointly decide an electoral strategy and the formation of government'. In the event, constituency delegates and union bloc votes rejected all three proposals and accepted the strategy of 1981: a special post-election delegate conference to hear the report of the Party Leader and 'to decide whether or not the Labour Party shall enter into government, support a minority government or enter into opposition'. Shortly afterwards the Labour Party leader resigned from both the leadership and the party, the government failed to carry a parliamentary motion of confidence and, after a round of negotiations between the leaders of Fine Gael and Labour and another Labour delegate conference to ratify the agreement reached, the two parties formed another coalition government which took office in December 1982.

What has been the effect of these coalition experiences on Irish political institutions? The first was the product of pragmatic political necessity rather than of coherent political theory. It was formed to keep Fianna Fail out of office and to provide an alternative administration. Similarly, its institutional deviations from the established norms of single-party Cabinet government were responses to these circumstances rather than the products of some general coalition model. They were designed to hold the government together. However, some of these arrangements have become institutionalised aspects of coalition government in Ireland. Thus in all five coalitions to date the (largely honorary) office of Tanaiste, or deputy prime minister, has been held by the leader of the second largest party.[11] Equally the powerful post of Finance has always been retained by the largest party.[12] Some other innovations have remained peculiar to the 1948–51 Inter-Party Government. In particular, the exclusion of the Secretary to the Government from attendance at Cabinet meetings was at the behest of an individual minister; it has not been repeated.[13] But, overall, neither the two Inter-Party Governments nor the three subsequent coalitions have significantly deviated from the norms of cabinet government maintained by single-party administrations.

Initially the formation of the first Inter-Party Government suggested a major shift in the relationship between Taoiseach (prime minister) and Cabinet. Typically the constitutional and legal authority of this office has been buttressed by the political power and influence of party leadership. The majority party in the Dail has been able to nominate its head as Taoiseach; he in turn has chosen and nominated his government ministers from among its senior members. The right to 'hire and fire' has been circumscribed by the constraints created by the interaction of STV, the nature of authority and personal relations, and the need to maintain party strength and unity. But, at the very least, the Taoiseach has been *primus inter pares*, the most influential political actor in government and parliament. In 1948 that position was very considerably weakened.

The leader of Fine Gael, a veteran of the Treaty split and subsequent civil war, General Richard Mulcahy, took the initiative in forming the first Inter-Party government in 1948.[14] His party had reached its nadir, he was determined to force de Valera from office and was prepared to forego any claim to be Taoiseach. Besides, he was unacceptable to some of the other parties in the proposed coalition. The allocation of Cabinet posts was determined by the parliamentary arithmetic of party strengths; choice of personnel was left to the individual parties. Only after all other offices had been arranged was John Costello, a former Attorney General and Fine Gael frontbencher, invited to become Taoiseach. Reluctantly he accepted.[15]

His emergence marked a major change in the customary relationship of Taoiseach and Cabinet. He did not have the authority attached to party leadership, and had had no choice in the selection of ministers. He was deprived of the customary patronage available to a Taoiseach, including the constitutional right to nominate eleven members of the Senate; these were disposed of by the party leaders in accordance with their strengths in the Dail. Costello did choose his own Attorney General and also recruited his son-in-law as an informal economic adviser.[16] Subsequently the reduced authority of the Taoiseach over his ministers was marked in a number of ways. It was the Parliamentary Labour Party which nominated both a minister and a parliamentary secretary when vacancies arose in posts allocated to the party. Similarly towards the end of the government's period of office, when a controversy over a proposed Mother-and-Child medical scheme led to a political crisis, the decision to ask for the resignation of the Minister for Health was made by his party leader not by the Taoiseach.[17]

Following his re-appointment after the general election of 1954 Costello's influence was greater. He was a former Taoiseach and the acknowledged leader of the more compact second Inter-party grouping. But, while this gave him more weight in the allocation of ministerial office within his own party, the distribution of seats was arranged between the parties and Labour once more filled its quota through election within the parliamentary party.

In the three subsequent coalitions the same problems did not arise. Detailed arrangements for the conclusion of a Fine Gael–Labour coalition were conducted over a period of months in 1972 between a small group of senior frontbench deputies. There was an internal challenge to Cosgrave's leadership within Fine Gael but this disappeared with the dissolution of the Dail. The parties fought on an agreed platform with Cosgrave clearly designated as the challenger to the incumbent Taoiseach. Successful in the election, he was strong enough both to cement an alliance by offering Labour more than its share of government seats and to make his own choice of nominees within his own party. He was careful to include known internal opponents as well as loyal supporters. The choice of men and allocation of portfolios was undoubtedly his own. During the life of this National Coalition government his leadership was not challenged, and there was no occasion to test the issue afterwards since he resigned immediately following the 1977 defeat.

In 1981 the Fine Gael party leader, Garret FitzGerald, was clearly identified and markedly preferred in the polls as alternative Taoiseach to the Fianna Fail leader, Charles Haughey.[18] It was he (with a small group of personal confidantes) who formulated the party programme, conducted the negotiations with Labour leader Michael O'Leary on the formation of a new coalition, and presented the joint programme for government to his party.[19] Dr FitzGerald exercised the same decisive authority in selecting his governmental team and weighting it deliberately in favour of his own supporters within the party: three former Fine Gael ministers were not offered posts; a newly elected young deputy was appointed to the major portfolio of Agriculture; the Minister for Foreign Affairs was personally nominated, without election, to the Senate; another close associate was appointed to the unprecedented post of adviser to the Government with the right to attend Cabinet meetings.[20]

In the second election of 1982, despite the clear reservations expressed at Labour's Annual Conference, the two party leaders were again to conduct negotiations for an agreed policy. There was considerable speculation that the newly elected Labour leader, Dick Spring, would be in a position to strike a better bargain on the substance of policy, but the outcome did not appear significantly different. The agreement was again accepted by a special delegate conference. Dr FitzGerald once more appeared determined to stamp his authority on his own Fine Gael party: there was a complete reshuffle in the allocation of Cabinet portfolios, involving some evident demotions, and four former junior ministers were not reappointed.[21] Overall it could be said that FitzGerald exerted at least as much personal influence in the selection of government personnel as any head of an Irish single-party government. His position in this respect was far removed from that of Costello over thirty years earlier.

Other problems of control and unity have persisted. The concept of collective responsibility is enshrined in the Irish constitution and was for long vigorously maintained.[22] Combined with an almost slavish attachment to executive secrecy, it has typically led to a disciplined blanket of silence over internal Cabinet disagreements. Particularly under de Valera successive Fianna Fail Governments presented themselves as impregnable monoliths.[23] Ministers spoke only on their own departmental responsibilities. Broader policy statements were left to the Taoiseach or his nominee. There were no public disputes between ministers; nor were there resignations or sackings arising from policy disagreements.

That changed with the advent of the first Inter-Party government. In speeches outside the Dail some ministers trespassed on the responsibilities of others and indicated significant policy disagreements. Within the House, similar divergencies were noted in debates. There seemed to be a major re-interpretation of the conventions of collective responsibility in the rhetorical questions of the Minister for Finance:[24]

> Have we got to the stage when, on a matter which may be an important point of policy when it is decided, we cannot have freedom of speech? Have we got to the stage when men, just because they join the Government circle, must all, as one Deputy said, when they go out of the council chambers speak the same language.

In fact it appears that two factors were responsible for ministerial indiscipline in this first coalition. One was the inexperience of ministers, reflected in some other gaffes.[25] The other was the determination of a minor party leader to exert influence over the whole range of government policies. This included efforts to secure the resignation of the Secretary to the Department of Finance and to block the re-appointment of the Governor of the Central Bank.[26]

There was less indiscipline in later coalitions. Ministers tended to limit their public remarks to their own areas of responsibility. They were more supportive of each other in Dail debates and, while person-ality differences were known and publicised, they exhibited a group loyalty comparable (sometimes perhaps even superior) to that shown by single-party governments. There was a notable example in 1976. In an intemperate speech the Minister for Defence attacked President Cearbhall O Dalaigh for exercising his prerogative right to refer a bill to the Supreme Court.[27] The President resigned, occasioning a consti-tutional and political crisis. The Taoiseach did not seek and would not accept the minister's resignation. No member of the government expressed public disagreement. Coalitions had discovered that collec-tive responsibility was a protection worth paying for. The demands of harsh economic policies in a period of extended recession appear to be placing strains on the latest coalition; in a much-publicised statement Taoiseach and Tanaiste joined in rebuking the new Minister for Finance for proposing a budget deficit target publicly in advance of any Cabinet discussion of decision.[28] However, while this proposal may have been an injudicious attempt to commit governmental colleagues, it is scarcely an infringement of the doctrine of collective responsibility.

Another element of strain has been noted by Basil Chubb. He has suggested that 'the propensity of the inter-party governments to use cabinet committees is perhaps further evidence of their need for devices to deal with lack of accord, actual or potential'.[29] There is evidence that Costello was prone to divert controversial issues to such committees. But this was less an innovation than Professor Chubb suggests in a comment made before any Cabinet archives were available. Three points might be made here, although a definitive judgement must await full access to the archives. First, that Cabinet committees were less rare than suggested and a regular system of standing committees had already been established under de Valera's administration. Second, that Costello's technique was not totally effective since some of the committees never even met. Third, that in the small scale of the Irish system, irrespective of whether the government is formed by a single party or a coalition, a determined minister cannot be prevented from raising an issue directly with the Taoiseach by referring it to a Cabinet committee.

At the parliamentary level parties in coalition have found it difficult to match the disciplined solidity of Fianna Fail. On occasion, when disagreements could not be either resolved or avoided, the issue has been left to a free vote in the Dail. This marks a distinct departure from the regimented adversary system of Irish parliamentary politics. In the most dramatic example in July 1974 the Taoiseach and another minister joined some other party colleagues in voting against a family planning bill which had been discussed in Cabinet and was presented in government time by the responsible minister.[30] However, such examples are rare and typically coalition frontbenchers have been able to impose solid parliamentary discipline and preserve collective responsibility in the division lobbies.

For backbenchers other problems arise. In the Irish system they are expected to be loyal to their leaders in government. Typically they fulfil that expectation. They vote with their ministers, virtually never oppose them in parliamentary debate and rarely even address parliamentary questions to them. Clearly that presents additional strains under coalition government. Backbenchers are expected not only to acquiesce in the collective leadership of members of their own party but to give the same support to ministers of other parties. Added to this, there can be an element of resentment among some government backbenchers at ministers who are occupying positions to which they may feel entitled. This resentment, evident in some critical constituency responses to FitzGerald's appointments in 1981, was again provoked by the dropping of junior ministers from the 1982 administration. A further factor is the element of competition at constituency level: a backbencher may gain support from a local ministerial colleague of the same party; he may lose important early preference votes to a minister from another party. Despite all such considerations, the record shows a remarkable degree of loyalty and discipline among coalition backbench deputies. Like their ministerial colleagues the majority seem to accept that the advantages of being associated with the government of the day and sharing, however slightly, its power, influence and patronage outweigh the disadvantages of any loss of identity or support.

The obverse of this solidarity is reflected in the fact that coalition governments have been as unyielding as single-party governments in making concessions of any kind, whether in terms of procedure, information, still less 'power-sharing' to the Opposition of the day. Irrespective of composition, governments have maintained an adversary style in parliament. Oppositions have seen their main function as presenting themselves as alternatives to, rather than partners of, the government. Both sides have remained committed to a traditional, and largely artificial, parliamentary mock-battle in which the real prize is less the issues of politics than the opportunity to either retain or gain governmental power. They have been aided in this by the conservative consensus of Irish politics.

Superficially coalitions have brought together almost the whole spectrum of parliamentary representation. But ideological differences have rarely been acute in Irish politics and never very wide. The system has been described as 'politics without social bases'.[31] Nevertheless, in a model in which a predominant centrist party has confronted a fragmented opposition, it has required a combination spanning the narrow Irish spectrum from right to left to achieve alternation in government.

The spread was at its widest in the first Inter-Party Government. On the 'right', Fine Gael and some Independent deputies were still identified as representing business, large-farmer and Protestant 'Commonwealth' interests. Strung along from centre-left to 'left' were the small-farm Clann na Talmhan, the two Labour parties and the new republican-socialist Clann na Poblachta. No subsequent coalition was so diverse. Generally the effective combination of Fine Gael and Labour has been sufficient. In 1981 they needed the support of Independent socialist deputies to secure a parliamentary majority. Although these alliances have created some internal party dissension, this has been largely contained.

The question of the attitude of the electorate towards coalition government and the effect of coalitions on party support has remained controversial. Fianna Fail has consistently opposed the idea of coalition in principle and, although it has formed minority governments dependent on other parties and independent deputies for survival, it has never conceded a share in government to these parliamentary allies. Given the scale of Fianna Fail electoral support and its durability in government this has helped to maintain a widespread acceptance of single-party government as the norm, with coalition regarded as a deviance. That view is largely shared by the other parties. From time to time they have made a virtue of necessity and argued (notably in the course of the 1973 election) that the attachment to single-party government is a British convention and that Ireland might follow its European Community partners and recognise the positive advantages of coalition government. The emphasis on a power-sharing executive as a solution to the internal governmental problem of Northern Ireland has been a further strand in the argument. But, in the main, Fine Gael and Labour have at best accepted coalition as a necessary evil, the essential price for replacing Fianna Fail in government. Within each party at the level of the party activists there has been resistance and argument that coalition has weakened party identity, policy and support.

Within Fine Gael, resistance to coalition has mainly been articulated by deputies from rural areas and from urban constituencies where the two parties are competing for seats. During the last decade and particularly since the accession of Dr FitzGerald to the leadership in 1977 a deliberate effort has been made to promote the image of Fine Gael as a social democratic party. But this has been accompanied by an apparently successful campaign to win back traditional support among larger farmers and businessmen which might be regarded as more suitable for a party which is affiliated to the Christian-Democratic group in the European Parliament. As Fine Gael comes close to effectively challenging the hegemony of Fianna Fail as the national 'catch-all' party, the costs of coalition in terms of electoral support may be calculated more nicely. In some measure just such considerations lie behind some recent calls for a grand alliance of Fianna Fail-Fine Gael. However, the current party leadership remains pragmatically inclined to coalition with Labour as the effective means of securing governmental power. There is also the possibility that the parliamentary presence of socialist Independent and Workers' Party deputies has reduced the sense of Labour as an alien political group for the more traditional Fine Gael voter. Although the danger of Fine Gael being 'contaminated' by Labour has been articulated and although the party's 'relative indeterminacy' has been noted, as of now Labour is the likely and willing partner in future coalitions.[32]

As the smallest established party in the Irish system, Labour has always been more concerned about both identity and ideology. Because of its structure and tradition it is less prone than Fine Gael to accept control either by the party leader or the parliamentary party. Committed to a socialist rhetoric and programme, presented with varying degrees of passion over time, it is caught on the horns of a dilemma: on its own it cannot secure government, in coalition it can only secure (at best) a partial implementation of socialist policies. The tension between ideological, left-wing activists (mainly concentrated in urban areas) and pragmatic parliamentarians (overwhelmingly representing rural constituencies) has increasingly focused on the issue of coalition.

The 'pro-coalitionists' have noted that the first Inter-Party government enabled the party to solidify its support, restore unity and gain acceptability. They have shown that the party needs voting transfers from Fine Gael to maintain and increase its parliamentary representation and have suggested that traditional Labour voters need representation in government to secure their interests. They have argued that it is better to implement some Labour policies in coalition than to be left powerless in an indefinite period of opposition and that fluctuations in popular support have been caused less by the prospect of coalition than by confusion about whether or not Labour would participate in government.

'Anti-coalitionists' have pointed to the increase in Labour's share of the first preference vote in the 1960s when the party committed itself to a go-it-alone policy advocating a workers republic and proclaiming that 'the seventies will be socialist'. They have argued that coalition has purchased governmental power at the expense of socialist principle, has weakened the party's identity and made Labour a 'Fine Gael Mark II'.

They note the challenge to the party posed by other socialist groups, the erosion of its urban support and the failure to make significant inroads into the rapidly growing younger electorate.

Whatever the views of professional politicians and party activists across the political spectrum, there is ample evidence that an increasing proportion of the Irish electorate contemplate coalition with equanimity and no longer regard single-party government as necessary to the effective operation of the system. The analysis of transfer patterns in the Irish STV system of proportional representation is notoriously difficult, being subject to a high degree of individual and local factors. However, overall it is evident that a substantial majority of party supporters in both Fine Gael and Labour are prepared to follow their leaders in giving later preferences to agreed coalition partners, and since 1973 the solidity of these transfer patterns has compared favourably with the disciplined continuance of preferences within Fianna Fail.[33]

Results of public opinion polls confirm these findings. There was no polling of significance in Ireland before the 1970s. Over the last decade there has been a very considerable growth in the number both of published polls commissioned by the media and private polls conducted on behalf of parties and candidates. These have not yet been subjected to comprehensive academic analysis, and it is clear that the data must be interpreted in the particular political contexts in which the polls were conducted and allowance must be made for the influence of the large bloc of Fianna Fail supporters with a strong anti-coalition bias. But a comparison of polls shows considerably less resistance to the concept of coalition and a decline in the assumed superior efficacy of single-party government. It suggests a greater willingness to accept that coalition is a standard and workable solution to government formation for an electorate firmly wedded to proportional representation.

Overall, then, it appears that coalition has had only a marginal effect on Irish political institutions. The conservative canons of collective Cabinet responsibility have been maintained and the dominant relationship of government to parliament continued. Partisan affiliation does not appear to have changed significantly, although Fine Gael and Labour supporters have tended to extend their later voting preferences to accommodate to coalition. In a system so long dominated by a single majority-bent party, coalition has provided the only possibility of alternation of parties in government and has given Fianna Fail the opportunity in opposition to review its policies and its organisation. The Irish experience indicates that in a stable parliamentary system the difference between single-party and coalition governments imposes no unmanageable burden.

Notes

1. For a recent discussion and summary of literature see R.K. Carty, *Party and Parish Pump: electoral politics in Ireland* (Wilfrid Laurier University Press, 1981).
2. Cf. B. Farrell, *The Founding of Dail Eireann: parliament and nation building* (Dublin, Gill and Macmillan, 1971).
3. On the origins of the parties see M. Manning, *Irish Political Parties* (Dublin, Gill and Macmillan, 1972). F.S.L. Lyons has a full discussion of the Treaty debate in three essays in B. Farrell (ed.), *The Irish Parliamentary Tradition* (Dublin, Gill and Macmillan, 1973). On the 1922 election see M. Gallagher, 'The Pact General Election of 1922, *Irish Historical Studies*, XXI, 84, September 1979.
4. Darrell Figgis, memorandum 'Proposal for the Creation of an Executive' quoted in B. Farrell, 'The Drafting of the Irish Free State Constitution', *Irish Jurist*, vol. V, n.s., Part I, Summer 1970, p. 132.
5. K. O'Higgins quoted in B. Chubb, *Cabinet Government in Ireland* (Dublin, Institute of Public Administration, 1974), p. 23. Chap. 5, pp. 40–52, is one of the few published accounts of cabinet government in Ireland. Another is A.S. Cohan, 'The Open Coalition in the Closed Society: the strange pattern of government formation in Ireland', *Comparative Politics*, II, 3, April 1979, pp. 319–38. Cf. his 'Ireland: coalitions making a virtue of necessity' in Eric C. Browne and John Dreijmanis (eds), *Government Coalitions in Western Democracies* (London/New York, Longman 1982), pp. 260–82 and C. O'Leary, *Irish Elections, 1918–1977: parties, voters and proportional representation* (Dublin, Gill and Macmillan, 1979), pp. 38–45.
6. Costello formed a government of Fine Gael, Labour (re-unified) and Clann na Talmhan. It was supported by the three Clann na Poblachta deputies but MacBride did not participate in the government and in 1957 withdrew parliamentary support.
7. The addition of the adjective 'national' was inspired by T.F. O'Higgins of Fine Gael. For the text of the 'Statement of Intent' see T. Nealon (ed.), *Ireland: a parliamentary directory, 1973–74* (Dublin Institute of Public Administration, 1974), pp. 68–9. For an account of the 1973–7 period see H. Penniman (ed), *Ireland at the Polls* (Washington DC, American Enterprise Institute for Public Policy Research, 1978).
8. On the 1981 election see B. Arnold, 'The Campaign' in T. Nealon (ed.), *Nealon's Guide 22nd Dail and Seanad Election '81* (Dublin, Platform Press, 1982), pp. 136–41. Cf. V. Browne (ed.), *The Magill Book of Irish Politics* (Dublin, Magill 1981).
9. On the first 1982 election see B. Farrell, 'The 1982 General Election: campaign and analysis' in T. Nealon (ed.), *Nealon's Guide 23rd Dail and Seanad Election '82* (Dublin, Platform Press, 1982), pp. 136–41. Cf. V. Browne (ed.), *Magill Guide to Election '82*, (Dublin, Magill, 1982).
10. For a useful summary of the polls see the Nealon and Magill *Guides* above and the useful series of *IMS Polls*, vol. I, nos. 1 and 2 published by Irish Marketing Surveys Dublin.
11. In all cases to date the leader of the Labour Party. Although this ancient title suggests some right of succession, the position is essentially honorary. To date, only one Tanaiste, Sean Lemass, has succeeded to the office of Taoiseach. It may be noted that the former Tanaiste, George Colley, declined to accept ministerial office in the Fianna Fail Government formed in 1982 when he was refused re-appointment at Tanaiste.
12. In all cases to date the Finance portfolio has been retained by Fine Gael. Although constitutionally the Tanaiste acts when the Taoiseach is unavailable, in practice the Minister for Finance is recognised as number two. Curiously three of the five ministers appointed were young men joining the Cabinet for the first time. In 1948 P. McGilligan, who had been a minister under Cumann na nGael, was appointed. He was unwilling to resume this onerous office in 1954 (becoming Attorney-General) and G. Sweetman was appointed. In 1973 R. Ryan was nominated. In 1981 Fitz-Gerald ignored Ryan and two other former ministers and appointed J. Bruton, whose only previous governmental experience was as parliamentary secretary to the Minister for Education (1973–5) and to the Minister for Industry and Commerce

(1975–7). In 1982 FitzGerald chose another young Minister in forming his second administration and nominated A. Dukes, first elected in 1981 and appointed to the senior post of Minister for Agriculture in the first FitzGerald Cabinet.

13. On this point and on Costello's performance in office see B. Farrell, *Chairman or Chief? the role of the Taoiseach in Irish politics* (Dublin, Gill and Macmillan, 1971), chap. 4. The objecting minister was S. MacBride on whom see below note 26.

14. On Mulcahy's attitude to de Valera see M. Valiulis, ' "The Man They Could Never Forgive" – the view of the opposition: Eamon de Valera and the Civil War' in J.P. O'Carroll and J.A. Murphy (eds), *De Valera and his times: political development in the Republic of Ireland* (Cork University Press (forthcoming)).

15. On Costello's reluctance see Farrell, *Chairman or Chief? op. cit.*, p. 43. Cf. R. Mulcahy on Costello 'asked to make up his mind inside 24 hours whether he would leave all that his life meant to him by way of profession and the ordinary course of the life he had been used to', *Parliamentary Debates Dail Eireann*, vol. 146, col. 19, 2 June 1954. On the allocation of offices see Chubb, *op. cit*, pp. 41–2. Cf. Ms. P 35/208, *McGilligan Papers* (University College, Dublin, Archives Department).

16. Costello sought advice from Cecil Lavery, SC about taking on the responsibility of Taoiseach and was told he had an obligation to accept office. He then turned the tables and demanded that Lavery become Attorney-General.

17. On this controversy see J. Whyte, *Church and State in Modern Ireland 1923–1979*, (Dublin, Gill and Macmillan 1980), chap. VII. The official files for this period, lodged in the State Paper Office in December 1982 indicate that the Taoiseach had drafted a demand for the resignation.

18. These polls are reported in Farrell, *Nealon '82*, *op. cit.*, p. 137. For comparable data May-September 1982 see J. Meagher (ed), *The IMS Poll*, I, Irish Marketing Surveys Dublin 1982.

19. See *Magill '81*, p. 185.

20. The adviser appointed, Alexis Fitzgerald, was son-in-law of the former Taoiseach J. Costello and had served informally in the two Inter-Party Governments. Under the Irish Constitution two members of the government may be chosen from the Senate and the Taoiseach is entitled to nominate 11 senators; FitzGerald used both powers to make Professor James Dooge Minister for Foreign Affairs. This power had only once before been exercised – by de Valera when a member of his government had failed to retain his seat. Alan Dukes was the newly-elected deputy nominated to Agriculture; to date only three other deputies have been so elevated on their first day in the Dail.

21. There was also a major change in the Labour participation in government both in terms of personnel and allocation of portfolios. For a fuller discussion see B. Farrell, 'Government Formation and Ministerial Selection' in H. Penniman, (ed.) *Ireland at the Polls 1981–82* (forthcoming).

22. Constitution Article 28.4.2 'The Government shall meet and act as a collective authority and shall be collectively responsible for the Department of State administered by members of the Government.' Cf. B. Chubb, *Cabinet Government in Ireland*, *op. cit.*

23. 23. On de Valera's relationships see B. Farrell, *Chairman or Chief? op. cit.*, Chap. 3 and 'De Valera: unique dictator or charismatic chairman' in O'Carroll and Murphy, *op. cit.*

24. P. McGilligan, 23 March 1950, quoted in Chubb, *op. cit.*, p. 44. Cf. the same minister's earlier version 'I have always understood that party politics did work on compromises, and that men having differing views came together and hammered out a policy. We will probably have to do so openly here in the Dail. I do not think that is an unwise procedure'. *Parl. Debates Dail Eireann*, vol. 110, cols. 2052–3, 25 May 1948.

25. See the discussion in B. Farrell, *Sean Lemass: a political biography* (Dublin, Gill and Macmillan (forthcoming)).

26. Cf. R. Fanning, *The Irish Department of Finance 1922–58* (Dublin, Institute of Public Administration, 1978), pp. 407 ff.

27. See M. Gallagher, 'The Presidency of Ireland: implications of the "Donegan affair" ', *Parliamentary Affairs*, vol. 30, no. 4, Autumn 1977.

28. See *Irish Times*, 13 January 1983.

29. B. Chubb, *Cabinet Government*, *op. cit.* p. 45.

30. For a discussion of the political implications of the Taoiseach's vote see Mary Robinson, *Irish Times*, 24 July 1974. Subsequently a Fianna Fail Minister abstained on a similar measure put forward by his Government.

31. J. Whyte, 'Ireland: politics without social bases' in R. Rose (ed), *Electoral Behaviour* (New York/London, Macmillan, 1974).

32. The 'contamination' phrase was used by John Kelly, a former Fine Gael Attorney-General and Minister who declined to join the Opposition Frontbench in 1982 and was not subsequently appointed to office in the second FitzGerald Government. On the party's 'relative indeterminacy' see the discussion in R. Sinnott, 'The Electorate' in H. Penniman, (ed.) *Ireland at the Polls 1977*, *op. cit.*

33. For transfer patterns see M. Gallagher, 'Party Solidarity, Exclusivity and Inter-Party Relationships in Ireland, 1922–1977: the evidence of transfers', *Economic and Social Review*, vol. 10, no. 1, October 1978, pp. 1–22; A.S. Cohan, R.D. McKinlay and A. Mughan, 'The Used Vote and Electoral Outcomes: the Irish general election of 1973', *British Journal of Political Sciences*, 5, pp. 363–83; Brendan J. Whelan and Richard Sinnott, 'Labour Transfers to Fine Gael Fell Slightly', *Irish Times*, 1 July 1977, discussed in R. Sinnott, 'The Electorate' in Penniman *op. cit.*

12 Conclusion
Vernon Bogdanor

Coalition government, as should be clear from the essays in *Coalition Government in Western Europe*, is a particular mode of executive rule, separate both from presidential government and from the classical model of Cabinet government as adumbrated by authorities such as Bagehot and Morley. 'The practical choice of first-rate nations', declared Bagehot in the concluding paragraph of his introduction to the 1872 edition of *The English Constitution*, 'is between the presidential government and the parliamentary; no state can be first-rate which has not a government by discussion, and those are the only two existing species of that government. It is between them that a nation which has to choose its government must choose'. The essence of Cabinet government as exemplified in the English Constitution was, for Bagehot, that it was 'framed on the principle of choosing a single sovereign authority, and making it good', while the American system was based 'upon the principle of having many sovereign authorities, and hoping that their multitude may atone for their inferiority'.[1]

The unity of the Cabinet was derived from its containing members drawn from a single party; and indeed, John Morley's chapter on the Cabinet in his biography of Walpole, a *locus classicus* on the nature of Cabinet government said to have the imprimatur of Gladstone, explicitly stated that one of the four principles of Cabinet government was that the Cabinet must be chosen from members of the same party. When that fundamental condition is removed, not only is the operation of the Cabinet affected, but so also are the relationships between Cabinet and the legislature, and the roles of the Prime Minister and of the head of state. Moreover, the very significance of elections can alter when, instead of producing a single-party government, they serve only to offer a signal to political leaders indicating which combination of parties might be able to join together to form an acceptable coalition.

Coalition government is more than a modification of parliamentary government. It cannot be understood unless it is recognised as a specific type of government with its own conventions and rules, all flowing from the fundamental principle of power-sharing. The effects of coalition government will indeed be apparent throughout the whole of the political system, so that the working of institutions such as the Cabinet and the legislature will prove very different from that of their counterparts in systems dominated by the Westminster Model.

This reality has been obscured from political scientists for many reasons, the chief of which has been that the constitutions of the countries discussed in this book say nothing about coalition, even though some of them contain provisions which in fact facilitate the formation of coalition governments. This is because the constitutions of Western European states were drawn up with very different problems in mind. The constitutions of Norway, the Netherlands and Belgium were promulgated in the nineteenth century – in 1814, 1815 and 1831 respectively. Their framers were primarily concerned with establishing the principle of parliamentarism, that the government should depend upon the confidence of the legislature rather than upon the approval of the king. These constitutions did not seek to regulate the relationships between the parties, which for most of the nineteenth century were loosely organised and individualistic. The framers of these constitutions could not be expected to envisage the rise of organised and tightly disciplined political parties, let alone the evolution of a multi-party system which would make coalition government inevitable.

Twentieth-century constitutions, with the exception of the 1974 Swedish Instrument of Government, have also failed to lay down procedures regulating the process of formation and dissolution of coalition governments. The 1919 Constitution of Finland and the 1937 Irish Constitution were concerned with emphasising their countries' independence from Russia and Britain respectively. The Italian Constitution of 1948 and the German Basic Law of 1949 reflected the need to establish democratic government on a firm enough foundation to withstand challenge from anti-democratic parties. In Italy, this was to be done by a constitution which emphasised the rights of minorities, and gave parliament a good deal of influence over the executive, thus frustrating strong government which was equated with Fascism. In West Germany, the Basic Law aimed to entrench democracy in a quite different way. It sought to strengthen democratic government through provisions in the electoral law which would make it difficult for small parties to secure representation in the Bundestag, and through provisions in the Basic Law, make it impossible for irresponsible parliamentarians to overthrow a government without being ready to support an alternative. Neither the Italian nor the German constitutions offer any guidance on the procedures necessary to make coalition government work successfully.

Sweden's 1974 Instrument of Government seems exceptional in that it attempts to describe the government formation process in some detail. The Instrument removes from the monarch any part in the formation of government, Article 1 declaring that 'All public power in Sweden emanates from the people'. Instead the Speaker is designated as responsible for initiating the government-formation process, and Chapter 5, Articles 2 and 3 of the Instrument describe the process which is to be followed when a new government is to be formed. The Speaker is to 'convene representatives of each party group within the Riksdag for consultation'. He is to 'confer with the Vice Speakers and shall then submit a proposal to the Riksdag'. The Riksdag then votes on the proposal, and the Speaker's nominee is confirmed unless an absolute majority of the Riksdag votes against him. If the Riksdag rejects four such proposals from the Speaker, then new elections are held. Yet the Instrument does not – and perhaps cannot – describe the principles which the Speaker should follow in nominating a Prime Minister. Elections in multi-party political systems will frequently produce a situation in which a number of different governmental combinations are possible. How is the Speaker to use the discretion which the Instrument of Government gives to him? On this, the Instrument is silent.

In each of the countries studied in this book, therefore, the written constitution plays a purely formal role. Nowhere does it attempt to lay down any general principles to regulate the governmental formation process. It is, from this point of view, of purely emblematic significance. The problems which constitutions were promulgated to resolve – ensuring that the head of state acts on advice, ensuring that the government retains the confidence of parliament, creating conditions within which democratic government has the strength and self-confidence to resist threats from anti-democratic elements – are on the whole, fortunately, the problems of the past, except perhaps in Italy, where the foundations of democracy are by no means invulnerable to extremists. Constitutions have nothing to say on the formation of coalitions whose necessity derives from the existence of multi-party politics; and it is this silence which has obscured the fact that coalition government operates in a very different fashion from systems of government in countries dominated by the Westminster Model.

The head of state
The first of the significant differences from the Westminster Model lies in the altered role of the head of state. For in a coalitional system the head of state is always liable to find himself playing a more active role in the government formation process than is customary in Britain or in other countries where single-party majority government is the rule. Wherever the possibility can arise of more than one government being formed after a general election, the exercise of discretion on the part of the head of state cannot be excluded. But expectations about the role of the head of state differ in different countries. In Belgium and the Netherlands the active role of the monarch seems to be generally

accepted. For many Belgians the king has become a vital symbol of national unity in a state deeply divided by linguistic conflict. King Baudouin, it is sometimes said, is the only real Belgian; everyone else is either a Fleming or a Walloon.

In the Scandinavian monarchies, however, and especially in Norway, the monarch is expected to adopt a more passive role after the British model. In Sweden, the main purpose of the reform delegating the powers of the monarch to the Speaker was to assuage the concern of the left wing of the Social Democrats that the monarch would be biased against them. In Norway, the existence of a party system in which the parties are clearly divided into two blocs has made the monarch's task a much easier one than in Belgium or the Netherlands. There will in general be a clear majority for one or the other of the two blocs, and parties will rarely seek coalition with a partner from the opposite bloc. Difficulties have arisen in Norway only in 1971 and 1972 when the two-bloc system broke down because the EEC issue cut across the division between the socialist Left and the anti-socialist Right. The issue divided the Right, excluding the Conservatives who were pro-EEC from any anti-EEC government, and excluding the centre and the Christian People's Party who were anti-EEC from any pro-EEC government.

Denmark, together with Finland, enjoys the most complex multi-party system of all the countries studied in *Coalition Government in Western Europe*. Yet since 1920 the monarch has been able to escape direct political involvement as a result of certain conventional 'rules of the game' which have been developed. These rules of the game have been accepted by the political parties precisely to avoid embarrassing the monarch, and on occasion candidates for the premiership have avoided pressing their claims so as not to place the monarch in a difficult position. Thus the comparative ease with which the process of government formation takes place in Denmark owes more to the co-operative style of Danish political culture than to the rules themselves.

In constitutional monarchies, the monarch and those advising him have generally sought to preserve two principles which are perhaps incompatible. The first is that the monarch should be politically neutral, remaining above the party battle; that indeed is the essence of constitutional monarchy and a precondition of its survival. But the second principle valued by monarchs and their advisers is that the monarch should retain his prerogative powers intact. This is deemed essential in order that the monarchy should retain the respect of the populace; for a mere automaton, a monarch who retains no significant discretion at all invites, so it is believed, disrespect because he seems to have no function in the country's system of government.

In the constitutional monarchies of North-Western Europe, the logical incompatibility between these two principles – if incompatibility there is – has been mitigated by the exercise of tact on the part of monarchs. In multi-party situations where coalition government is a necessity, preservation of the institution of monarchy depends both upon the tact of the monarch and the willingness of the political parties to do everything possible to avoid the monarch's involvement in the processes of party politics.

A republican constitution, as the examples of Finland and Ireland demonstrate, does not necessarily make for smoother relations between the head of state and the government. Ireland is unusual amongst democracies in directly electing the head of state and, in the debates on the 1937 Constitution, de Valera declared that 'nobody would propose getting the whole people to elect a person unless it was proposed to give him substantial powers'.[2] Yet the Irish President has in practice found it difficult to exercise the very modest powers which the Constitution in fact gives him. In 1976, President Cearbhall O'Dálaigh found himself accused by the Minister for Defence of being a 'thundering disgrace' for exercising his constitutional right to refer a government bill to the Supreme Court. Yet, as Brian Farrell shows, it was the President and not the minister who resigned. The President has also been given the constitutional right 'in absolute discretion' to refuse a dissolution advised by a Taoiseach (Prime Minister) 'who has ceased to retain the support of a majority' in the Dáil. (Art. 13.2.2). Yet this power has never been used, even though in October 1982 some constitutional authorities believed that the President should, after the minority Haughey Government was defeated in the Dáil, have refused a dissolution rather than permit a third election to be held within a period of eighteen months. The President dissolved the Dáil, and it may well be that the use of his power to refuse a dissolution has now fallen into desuetude, to be used only in pathological circumstances. The fact of popular election, therefore, does not provide the Irish President with democratic legitimacy, and in practice he must be as circumspect as the British sovereign in his actions in the process of government formation and dissolution. Fortunately, the Irish President has not yet had to face problems of the kind which have troubled Belgian and Dutch monarchs.

The Finnish President, elected indirectly by means of an electoral college, enjoys a good deal more influence than the Irish, not only in the formation and dissolution of government but also in the political life of the country in general, and especially in foreign affairs. Indeed, Finland is from one point of view an anomaly amongst the countries studied in this book; for it is less a parliamentary regime than a country with a bicephalous executive and in this respect, as Pesonen and Thomas point out, more like the French Fifth Republic than its Nordic neighbours. Yet the role of the Finnish President owes as much to the country's peculiarly exposed diplomatic position, to the necessity of having a respected political leader to deal with the Soviet Union, and to the personal prestige of Presidents Paasikivi, Kekkonen and Koivisto as it does to the provisions of the constitution. Under President Kekkonen, indeed, the personal likes and dislikes of the president played almost as important a role as genuinely political factors in determining the choice of Prime Minister and the political composition of cabinets.

The first constitutional consequence of coalition government, then, will be a changed role for the head of state. His role in nominating a Prime Minister and in dissolving Parliament may no longer be a merely formal one. Belgium and the Netherlands have been in the forefront of those countries which have sought to deflect criticism of the monarch in this process through the institution of the *informateur*. Yet there can be no institutional method which guarantees that the head of state will not have to make a decision which is regarded by one of the political parties as being unfair. If, as in Sweden, the monarch is deprived entirely of his role in the government formation process, the problem is not resolved but merely transferred into the hands of the Speaker, a figure more likely perhaps than a constitutional monarch to find himself subject to the temptations of partisanship.

Coalitions and cabinet government

Although the countries studied in this book are all governed by means of a cabinet system, coalition can exert a profound effect on the working of Cabinet government. The essence of Cabinet government as under-stood in Britain was defined by Morley in terms of four principles. The first was that the Cabinet was to be subject to the convention of collective responsibility. 'The first mark of the Cabinet, as that insti-tution is now understood, is united and indivisible responsibility'. 'The Cabinet', Morley continued, 'is a unit – a unit as regards the Sovereign, and a unit as regards the legislature'. Secondly, the Cabinet was answerable to the majority of the House of Commons, and so indirectly to the electorate which created that majority. Thirdly the Cabinet was 'except under uncommon, peculiar, and transitory circumstances', selected exclusively from one party. 'There have', declared Morley, 'been coalitions of men of opposite parties, but in most cases, down to the present time [i.e. 1889], coalition has been only the preliminary of fusion'. Finally, Cabinet government provided for the special role of the chairman of the Cabinet, the Prime Minister, 'the keystone of the Cabinet arch', and indeed the working and success of the Cabinet must depend in large measure upon his leadership.[3]

Coalition government directly contradicts Morley's third principle, since by definition the coalition Cabinet is no longer selected exclusively from the members of one party. To what extent will this affect the other principles laid down by Morley? Will a coalition Cabinet work after the same manner as a single-party Cabinet; or will it retain merely the forms of Cabinet government while conceding the essence?

It is impossible to give a dogmatic answer to these questions. Collective responsibility can be preserved under a coalition government, and the Prime Minister might well remain 'the keystone of the Cabinet arch', but these ideals are far harder to achieve in a coalition than in a single-party government. The working of a coalition cabinet will be profoundly affected by the need to secure inter-party consensus. In addition to the normal disagreements between Cabinet ministers on political and departmental matters, there will be an additional source of dispute resulting from the conjuncture of two (or more) different parties. There is thus bound to be an extra degree of tension in the deliberative and decision-making processes of the Cabinet. The parties which form the coalition will be torn between a desire to preserve the unity of the government against attacks from their opponents, and an unwillingness to merge their separate identities with those of their coalition partners especially if they are likely to find themselves opposing each other on the hustings at the next general election.

It will, therefore, be more difficult for the Cabinet to hold together as a unity when the government is a coalition. Collective responsibility may have to be suspended on subordinate issues as it was in Norway during the period of the Borten coalition between 1965 and 1971, and in Britain under the National Government in 1932 when the expedient of 'the agreement to differ' was adopted. An alternative method of resolving inter-party differences is the referendum – used in Sweden in 1980 as a means of preventing the issue of nuclear power from breaking up the three-party, anti-socialist coalition for a second time.

These expedients, however, will not be sufficient to preserve Cabinet unity. For, as well as a willingness to avoid pressing contentious issues which might break up the coalition, there must also be, amongst the coalition partners, a positive striving for agreement. There will have to be co-operation between the parties comprising the government, and sometimes, for example in West Germany, as Klaus von Beyme demonstrates, special institutional machinery will be devised for this purpose. The introduction of such machinery is not of course essential to secure the resolution of inter-party disputes, and indeed machinery can never be sufficient to ensure agreement if the will to agree is not present. But, whether there is special institutional machinery or not, it is evident that the negotiations between party leaders are bound to play a special role in coalitions, and agreement between the leaders can easily replace the Cabinet as the forum within which authoritative

governmental decisions are made. The Cabinet can easily become a rati-
fying rather than a decision-making body, and its role would then be
very different from that of a Cabinet under a single-party government.

Coalition government is bound to affect the role of the Prime
Minister as chairman of the Cabinet. He will have less authority over a
coalition Cabinet than he would in a single-party government because
he will have to share his authority with the leader of the other party (or
parties) in the Cabinet. Indeed, in most coalitions the Prime Minister is
unable to choose those members of his Cabinet who do not belong to his
own party, although he may have the power of veto. Instead these
ministers will be chosen by their respective party leaders. They will be
representatives of their parties as well as ministers in the Cabinet. The
Prime Minister will in general be unable to dismiss them without
incurring the wrath of their party, and this is bound to limit the extent
to which the Cabinet can be, in Morley's words, 'a unit'. The Prime
Minister will often find himself unable to follow the normal practice of
the British Cabinet by summing up the opinion of the Cabinet as
revealed in discussions around the Cabinet table. Instead he will have to
take account of the position of the various parties comprising the
coalition. He will have to act as a mediator between the parties as well as
leader of the Cabinet, and this role as a mediator will be shared with
other party leaders. Thus, while the forms of Cabinet government may
well be preserved, the pressures which make for Cabinet unity in a
single-party government may be subtly undermined in a coalition.

Coalitions and parliament

It is frequently argued, especially by British advocates of proportional
representation that coalition government, which would result from
proportional representation, would lead to a strengthening of the role of
Parliament vis-à-vis the executive. Stuart Walkland has referred to the
common experience of many West European states, where multi-party
legislatures, supporting coalition governments elected on proportional
systems, are able, by virtue of the complex political linkages between
government and assembly, to impose fairly consistent discipline on
their respective executives.[4] For Nevil Johnson, the very acceptance of
the principle of power-sharing entailed by coalition would have to be
reflected in the relationships between Parliament and the executive.
'But since coalition would express recognition of the necessity of
sharing power,' he argues, 'there would be less hostility to the idea that
the House of Commons might from time to time insist on its preferences being heeded in the decisions of government'.[5]

Continental experience, however, should instil a sense of caution
when confronting such predictions. For although it is true that the
legislatures of West Germany and Scandinavia play a more effective

role in the scrutiny of legislation than the House of Commons, there is not, in these legislatures, the high degree of cross-voting and intra-party dissent which, as the painstaking researches of Philip Norton show, have become characteristic of the House of Commons since 1972.[6]

Indeed a coalition government is likely to be *less* able to afford breaches of party discipline than a single-party government. This is because coalitions are usually set up as a result of an inter-party agreement on policy. This agreement or pact which may or may not be published is, in effect, the constitution of the coalition, and the parties comprising it bind themselves to accept its terms. The agreement must be honoured in good faith if the coalition partners are to retain confidence in each other. Dissenting votes on the part of the backbenchers of one of the parties in the coalition, therefore, may not only threaten the government's majority as they would in a single-party government; they also threaten the very basis upon which the coalition has been set up. There is therefore a greater need for party leaders to exert discipline than in a single-party government.

On the Continent, coalitions are facilitated by list systems of proportional representation which can have the effect of making the individual MP a delegate of his party. The presupposition of a list system is that parties are the basic unit of representation and that the legislature should represent parties in proportion to their popular support. The party, therefore, claims for itself the right to decide which of its supporters shall sit in the legislature to put forward the party's point of view. A corollary must be that if the party decides to enter a coalition, this decision must be loyally supported by all of the party's representatives in the legislature. If it is not, action can be taken against the dissenting MP by putting him in a lower position on the party list, and so making it unlikely if not impossible for him to be elected. Party leaders, therefore, have the assurance that, if they enter into a coalition agreement, it will be honoured. It is this assurance which makes coalition governments easier to construct on the Continent than in political systems where the first-past-the-post electoral system is used.

In Ireland, use of the single transferable vote should in theory encourage the Dáil to exert its influence upon government. For under STV party leaders cannot ensure that party loyalists are returned by the electors nor party dissidents defeated. There are no safe seats for individual candidates and no assurance of election through a high place on a party's list. In fact, however, STV in the Irish Republic has been superimposed upon a profoundly localist political culture in which an MP's duty is seen as being primarily towards his constituents rather than as a scrutiniser of legislation. For this reason the Dáil is one of the weakest legislatures in Western Europe, and a coalition government need not in general fear defeat from backbenchers of its component parties (although a minority coalition can be defeated from outside its ranks as occurred with Garrett FitzGerald's Government in January 1982, and Charles Haughey's Government in October 1982). But there is no necessary reason to believe that STV would work in a similar way in a society whose preconceptions were different from those of the Irish Republic.

It is difficult, then, to make satisfactory generalisations about the relationships between government and parliament under a coalition. The more effective legislative role enjoyed by Continental legislatures may well be a function of norms of parliamentary behaviour rather than a product of coalition government or a particular electoral system. This conclusion of course leaves open the issue of whether the power-sharing arrangements characteristic of coalitions can themselves serve to alter relationships indirectly by altering the norms and expectations of legislators. But the evidence available does not allow of any conclusive answer to this complex question being given.

Coalitions and elections
Where no single party can be expected to win an overall majority, elections will perform a different function from that which they play in countries where single-party government is the norm. As Jan Vis writes describing the Netherlands (p. 155), 'Election results in a minority system produce a change in the power relations; they change the minority positions in parliament and they influence the positions in the coalition talks, but they are never the only influence, and sometimes not even the most important one.' This generalisation can be applied to all coalitional systems. Elections do not choose governments, they alter the power relations between the parties. On occasion indeed an increase in electoral support for a party can decrease its chances of being in government, since its competitors become frightened that the successful party is eroding their own position. That is what happened to the Labour Party (Pvd A) in the Netherlands in 1977. After gaining massive support in the election, it found itself removed from government because it placed its demands too high and frightened its potential coalition partner. Thus, in Vis's words, 'one can win the election and afterwards lose the formation' (p. 154). The formation of a government, then, is the process of artificially constructing a majority which the electorate itself has been unwilling to create by giving one party sufficient support to enable it to form a government on its own.

In such coalitional systems, pivot parties – parties which can form coalitions with parties of either Left or Right – will have a crucial role to play. In West Germany, the FDP has been in government since the founding of the Federal Republic in 1949 except for the years 1956–61 and 1966–9. In the Netherlands, the Catholic party – the KVP – has been in power since 1918 either in its own right or as part of the Christian Democratic Appeal (CDA). The KVP is in fact the only party in the world to have been continuously in government since 1918 except for the Communist Party of the Soviet Union! In Belgium, the Catholic or Social Christian Party has been in power since 1884 except for two brief intervals after the second World War. In Denmark the Radikale Venstre party – which has been called the party of the resounding maybe – has also attempted to play a pivotal role, although it has taken part in an anti–socialist government only between 1968 and 1971; while in Ireland, the Labour Party has been willing to enter a coalition only with Fine Gael, although it supported a Fianna Fáil minority government from 1932 to 1933.

It is easier for the confessional parties in Belgium and the Netherlands to act as pivot parties than it is for the FDP in West Germany or Radikale Venstre in Denmark. For the pattern of mobilisation and recruitment of the confessional parties places them operationally in the centre, and they contain within themselves a wide spectrum of opinion allowing them to move to the left or right without ideological strain. The FDP, on the other hand, has to combine its role as a pivot party with a liberal ideology, and the two can sit uneasily together. For the FDP does not seek merely to be a corrective to the excesses of Social Democrat or Christian Democrat governments in West Germany, but also to make positive progress towards the construction of a liberal society.

The position of the FDP is different in another respect from that of the confessional parties in Belgium and the Netherlands. For, unlike them, it declares before the general election who it will support as a coalition partner in government. This occurs both in federal and in *Land* elections. The Belgian and Dutch confessional parties, by contrast, make no such declaration, just as the Liberals in Britain have been unwilling to declare whom they will support if a general election results in a hung parliament – the Liberal/SDP Alliance will, presumably, adopt the same strategy.

In West Germany, it is the provision made by the electoral system for two votes – one for a constituency candidate, and the other for the *Land* list – which encourages the FDP as a minor party to declare its allegiances before the election. For if it is to increase its votes, it needs to offer a positive incentive to the supporters of one of the major parties to help it pass the 5 per cent threshold; although it can also appeal to supporters of the opposition party, as in the 1980 federal election when some CDU/CSU voters used their constituency vote to aid their CDU/CSU candidate, but their list vote for the FDP because they were hostile to the pretensions of the CDU/CSU candidate for the

Chancellorship, Franz Josef Strauss.

The problem for the Irish Labour Party is different both from that of the confessional parties in Belgium and the Netherlands and from the FDP. For it has to decide not which party to support in a coalition, but whether to put itself forward in a general election as an independent socialist alternative or as a coalition partner with Fine Gael. The first alternative, that supported by the party activists, resulted in 1969 in Labour securing a higher percentage of first preference votes than it has been able to achieve since. The consequence, however, is that a Labour presence in government comes to be postponed to the indefinite future. The coalition alternative, although it has yielded Labour only a continuous decline in first preference votes, has at least allowed the party to participate in government – between 1973 and 1977, June 1981 and January 1982, and again from November 1982. The first alternative offers only impotence; but the second must make many voters wonder why they should vote Labour rather than Fine Gael; while on the Left of the Labour Party, a new independent socialist party, Sinn Fein the Workers Party, threatens its original constituency. The Irish Labour Party, then, has not yet succeeded in constructing a firm enough identity enabling it to withstand the erosion of its vote from Fine Gael to its Right and Sinn Fein the Workers Party to its Left.

Table 12.1   Irish Labour Party: first preference votes since 1969

1969	17.02%	1981	9.89%
1973	13.67%	1982, February	9.12%
1977	11.64%	1982, November	9.40%

Changing coalition partners

Elections play a lesser role in the choice of government under a coalitional system than under the Westminster Model. A change of government in a coalition often results from a Cabinet crisis causing a split between the coalition partners, rather than defeat in a general election. Indeed, since, except in West Germany and the Irish Republic, it is difficult for coalition partners to appeal to the electorate as a coalition, a coalition will generally find itself unable to seek endorsement at the polls. In many of the countries studied in this book, however, – with Belgium, Denmark, Finland and Italy being the exceptions – a change of coalition partner is regarded as illegitimate without fresh elections. A *fliegende Wechsel* – change of partner without elections – is thought to be contrary to democratic norms. In the conflict between the principle of parliamentarism – that the government should have the support of parliament – and the principle of democracy – that the government should enjoy the support of the electorate – it is the principle of democracy which is emerging victorious.

The outcome of this conflict can be seen at its clearest in West Germany. Article 67 of the Basic Law provides that a proposal of no confidence in the Chancellor can be expressed only by the Bundestag electing a successor to the Chancellor. The purpose of this constructive vote of no confidence was, of course, to avoid the Weimar experience of irresponsible opposition and frequent dissolutions of parliament. But it makes possible the removal of a Chancellor in whom the *electorate* still has confidence. In April 1972, the CDU/CSU moved a constructive vote of no-confidence – which failed by only two votes – to unseat the SPD Chancellor, Willy Brandt, and replace him by the leader of the CDU/CSU Rainer Barzel. The leader of the FDP which was in coalition with the SPD was then Walter Scheel, and he told the Bundestag that 'Today we are faced with an attempt to alter the political majority without allowing the electorate to participate. Whether or not this is technically legitimate, it is an act which strikes at the nerve of our democracy'.

These words were quoted with glee by the FDP's enemies in September 1982 when the party deserted its SPD coalition partners and joined the CDU/CSU in proposing a motion of constructive no-confidence against the Chancellor, Helmut Schmidt. The motion succeeded and led to the installation of Helmut Kohl as Chancellor. But it occurred just one week after the *Land* elections in Hesse which, against many expectations, confirmed the SPD in power despite a strong challenge from the CDU, while the FDP, having failed to surmount the 5 per cent threshold, secured no representation in the *Land* parliament at all.

The constructive vote of no-confidence, therefore, could easily appear as an attempt by two parties which had lost favour with the electorate to oust a party which still retained the voters' confidence. For this reason, it was important for the new Chancellor to go to the country as soon as possible. The Basic Law, however, makes no provision for a Chancellor with a majority dissolving the Bundestag. Kohl, therefore, was reduced to the expedient of calling under Article 68 for a vote of confidence which he deliberately lost so that elections could be held in March 1983: Willy Brandt had adopted a similar expedient in 1972.

The Basic Law not only makes it difficult for a coalition partner to cross the floor – and this, no doubt, is one reason why the coalition between the SPD and the FDP lasted until 1982 when, in the view of many, it had lost its way some time before; it also denies a Chancellor the means of testing whether a coalition newly formed between parliamentary elections enjoys the support of the electorate. The Chancellor's only resource is to misuse a provision of the Basic Law intended to secure a quite different purpose. It is hardly surprising that constitutional reformers in the Federal Republic are now arguing that, with the Weimar trauma having been finally overcome, the time has arrived for the Basic Law to be amended so as to make dissolution easier.

Coalitions and policy outcomes

The final issue raised by the essays in *Coalition Government in Western Europe* is the most complex and yet perhaps also the most important of all those dealt with in the book – the question of the effects of coalition upon policy outcomes. The stereotype of coalition which most British commentators accepted unquestioningly until recent years was that of the French Fourth Republic or the Italian Republic – a weak government of squabbling cabals forever at the mercy of temporary deals and blackmailing extremists. This stereotype has now been replaced for many British political scientists by an alternative – the West German or Scandinavian model, which is one of strong, stable and moderate government made possible by a system of proportional representation. To achieve a government of this type is indeed a principal aim of those who seek to reform the British electoral system.

Manfred Schmidt offers a penetrating critique of this latter model. Its success is due, in his view, less to the existence of coalition government than to the framework of economic growth within which it has so far operated. Stability in West German politics was a product of this particular framework, of an era of history which is now passing away. For, during a period of economic growth, political leaders have been able to set the agenda of government and so ensure that it embraces their own particular aspirations for the future; in a recession, on the other hand, the agenda is set for politicians by economic reality, and political leaders are left without increments with which to bargain.

It is no reflection on Manfred Schmidt's essay to say that, in the editor's view, this case is not finally proven. The recession, after all, has so far been too short-term a phenomenon to enable confident generalisations to be made about its political effects. Political science, it is true, has been too prone to establish as generalisations what may be truths relative only to a specific and perhaps untypical period of economic affluence. We lack – fortunately – sufficient experience of the politics of recession to be able to sketch its outlines adequately. Yet, even so, there are grounds for arguing that those countries which have been best able to withstand the effects of recession are those such as Austria and Norway which have retained strong mechanisms of social consensus sustained by proportional representation.

The disciplines of coalition can help to bring about national unity in divided societies. In Belgium and the Netherlands, the government formation process – a complex one of constructing a consensual basis for government between sharply opposing ideological and, in Belgium, linguistic, groups – has played a crucial role in containing conflicts which might otherwise have torn the country apart. In Israel, also – a country which belongs conceptually if not geographically with the countries studied in this book – the process of coalition-building has been one of accommodation. Italy, on the other hand, as Geoffrey Pridham demonstrates, is a prime example of a country where coalition government is accompanied not so much by instability as by stagnation. One of the pressing tasks of political science, surely, is to attempt to discover the conditions under which coalition government is likely to lead to consensus and progress and those under which it will result in *immobilisme*.

The Westminster Model works best in homogeneous political societies. In Canada, it has come under serious strain, while in Northern Ireland it has proved entirely inappropriate. Yet, as the history of Northern Ireland since 1973 has shown, coalition cannot impose a consensus where none exists. What it can achieve, as the experience of many Continental countries demonstrates, is not only to reflect, but even to help create, a consensus where the preconditions for it are present. Those who favour coalition government in Britain do so because they believe that a basic consensus in British society is frustrated by the adversary process at Westminster. A coalition, on this view, will be better placed to mobilise consensus in the interests of social and economic modernisation. Others would counter with the claim that parliamentary conflict in Britain is but a reflection of social conflict, and that a healthy polity must be founded upon the clear articulation of sharply opposed conceptions of the political world. The essays in *Coalition Government in Western Europe* will not serve to resolve these complex issues, but they may do something to clarify them.

References

1. Walter Bagehot, *The English Constitution* in *Collected Works* (London, Economist, 1974) Vol. 5, pp. 202, 349.
2. Michael Gallagher, 'The Presidency of the Republic of Ireland: Implications of the "Donegan Affair" ', *Parliamentary Affairs*, Vol. 30, 1977, p. 375.
3. John Morley, *Walpole* (London, Macmillan, 1928 edn), pp. 154–6. The biography was first published in 1889.
4. S.A. Walkland, 'Whither the Commons?' in S.A. Walkland and Michael Ryle (eds), *The Commons in the 70's* (London, Fontana, 1977), p. 254.
5. Nevil Johnson, 'Adversary Politics and Electoral Reform: Need We Be Afraid?' in S.E. Finer (ed.), *Adversary Politics and Electoral Reform* (London, Anthony Wigram, 1975), p. 88.
6. Philip Norton, *Dissension in the House of Commons 1974–1979* (Oxford, Clarendon Press, 1980).

Index

Lemass, Sean 5
Leone, President Giovanni 210
Lijphart, Arend 13, 185, 200
Lloyd George, David 8, 10, 11–12, 231
Lothian 234, 236, 240, 241
Lowell, A.L. 13, 33
Lubbers, Raad 155
Lyng, John 79

MacDonald, Ramsay J. 7, 8, 10
Mellors, Colin 3, 5, 231–47, 278
Meyer, Jan de 14, 187–99, 278
Morley, John 263, 268, 269, 270
Moro, Aldo 206, 207, 208, 217, 227
Mulcahy, General Richard 250, 252
Müller, Hermann 10, 23

NATO 49, 69, 71, 110, 143, 219, 220
Netherlands 3, 5, 14, 25, 26, 85, 110,
    153–86, 264, 268, 272, 273
  Central Planning Bureau 170, 183
  confessional parties 153, 154, 161, 169,
      171–3, 176, 177, 178, 180, 181,
      183, 273; ARP 154, 161, 174, 178,
      181; CDA 154, 156, 162, 164, 171,
      174, 183, 273; CHU 154, 161, 178;
      KVP 153, 154, 155, 162, 173, 174,
      178, 181, 273
  Constitution 156–9, 167, 264
  D'66 162, 174, 181, 183
  DS' 70 178, 180
  Labour Party (PvdA) 154, 155, 156,
      162, 171, 173, 174, 176, 178, 181,
      183, 272
  Liberals (VVD) 154, 156, 162, 176,
      178, 180, 183
  monarch, role of 156, 157–64, 166, 167,
      265, 276
  Radicals (PPR) 174, 181
  Social and Economic Council 170, 182
von Neumann, John 13
Norway 7, 53, 59, 61, 63, 64–5, 67, 70,
    78–81, 88–9, 94, 101, 107, 110–11,
    115, 122–5, 137, 142, 144, 145, 148,
    264, 266, 269, 276
  and EC 61, 79, 80, 97, 107, 114, 115,
      122–3, 142, 266
  Agrarian Centre Party 65, 78–9, 80,
      101, 107, 122, 123
  Christian People's Party 60, 65, 78, 79,
      80, 122, 123, 142, 266
  Communists 60
  Conservatives 65, 78–9, 80, 123, 142,
      266
  Constitution 88–9, 264
  Labour Party 64–5, 78–9, 80, 101, 105,

107, 114, 122–3, 147
  Liberals 78–9, 80, 122, 123
  monarch, role of 59, 88–9, 266, 268
  New People's Party 79, 80
  Progress Party 81
  Socialist People's Party 64, 80; –
      Electoral Alliance 80

O'Dalaigh, President Cearbhall 255, 267
OECD 53, 54; *Economic Survey* 180, 184
oil, North Sea 111, 112, 115
O'Leary, Michael 251, 253

Paasikivi, J.K. 74, 76, 77, 268
di Palma, Guiseppe 200, 203, 204, 217
Palme, Olof 70, 91, 94, 131, 132
parliament, role of 1, 6, 12, 13, 14, 31, 70,
    83–94, 100–02, 135–50, 153, 155–7,
    167, 168, 203, 208, 259, 263, 264,
    268, 270–72, 274–5; term 7, 61, 70,
    130, 160, 196; *see also* dissolution
parliamentary base/support 5, 6, 31, 60,
    62–4, 69, 71, 72, 75–8 *passim*, 80, 84,
    85, 91–4 *passim*, 99, 101–6, 108–10,
    114, 116, 121–3 *passim*, 126, 132,
    135–50, 153, 155, 160–62, 169, 178,
    180, 181, 187–8, 192, 198, 208, 217,
    225, 249, 251, 252, 256–7, 259, 268,
    271, 274
parliamentary groups 27–9, 32, 33, 35, 82,
    86, 89, 93, 163, 169, 181, 183, 192,
    193, 208
pay-offs *see* coalition formation,
    bargaining
Pekkala, Mauno 77, 86
Pesonen, Pertti 5, 14, 59–96, 267, 279
Pertini, President Sandro 206, 208,
    210–11
policy 1, 14, 34, chapter 3 *passim*, 82, 86,
    chapters 5 and 7 *passim*, 201, 239,
    243, 276–7; agreements 12, 32–3, 35,
    45–6, 52, 82, 86, 88, 92, 99, 122, 131,
    133, 140, 146, 147, 165, 169–70, 176,
    180, 193–4, 217, 235–45 *passim*, 254,
    269, 271
  disagreements 26, 39, 45, 48, 49–51, 98,
      99, 116, 122–3, 127, 131, 139–45,
      254
  immobilisme 1, 14, 39, 51–2, 54, 55,
      242–3, 277
  overproduction 39, 52–5 *passim*, 242
political parties
  élites 17, 27, 86, 157, 158, 177, 200,
      202–4 *passim*, 210, 213, 215,
      217–22, 225–8
  secretaries 207–9